A Greater Look at Greater Buffalo

Late afternoon puts Buffalo in sil-houette. Photo by Dennis R. Floss

A Greater Look at Greater Buffalo

BY JIM BISCO

"PARTNERS IN PROGRESS" BY
DEAN RICHMOND AND MITCH FLYNN

PICTURE RESEARCH BY KIM A. RUIZ

Produced in cooperation with the Greater Buffalo Chamber of Commerce

Windsor Publications, Inc.

Northridge, California

Windsor Publications, Inc. — History Books Division
Publisher: John M. Phillips
Editorial Director: Teri Davis Greenberg
Design Director: Alexander D'Anca

Staff for *A Greater Look at Greater Buffalo*
Senior Editor: Julie Jaskol
Director, Corporate Profiles: Karen Story
Assistant Director, Corporate Profiles: Phyllis Gray
Editor, Corporate Profiles: Judith Hunter
Production Editor, Corporate Profiles: Una FitzSimmons
Sales Representative, Corporate Profiles: Glenn Edwards
Editorial Assistants: Kathy M. Brown, Laura Cordova, Marcie Goldstein,
Marilyn Horn, Pat Pittman
Proofreader: Susan J. Muhler
Designer: Marvin R. Warshaw
Layout Artist: Ellen Ifrah
Layout Artists, Business Profiles: Susan Wells, Mari Catherine Preimesberger

Library of Congress Cataloging-in-Publication Data

Bisco, Jim, 1949-
    Buffalo: a greater look at greater Buffalo.

"Produced in cooperation with the Greater Buffalo Chamber of Commerce."
    Bibliography: p. 486
    Includes index.
    1. Buffalo (N.Y.)—History. 2. Buffalo (N.Y.)— Description. 3. Buffalo (N.Y.)—
Industries. I. Title.
F129.B857B57   1986   974.7'97   86-26717
ISBN 0-89781-198-4

Opposite: Buffalo's revitalized waterfront is one of the city's major attractions. Photo by Lester J. Kuhn

Pages six and seven: Buffalo's skyline hugs the shore of Lake Erie in the glow of late afternoon. Photo by Dennis R. Floss

Page nine: Buffalo City Hall is a backdrop for the American flag. Photo by Robert McElroy

Contents

In Gratitude

For researching and developing such an economic overview, many thanks are in order to the wide variety of people who assisted me in this project. Naturally, in a broad perspective such as this, there are industries, companies, organizations, and individuals not discussed in depth, or not mentioned. No short-shrifting should be perceived in those cases. I've earnestly tried to address the areas that are playing major roles in Western New York's economic rebirth. That's not to imply that the individual is not contributing something to the whole. But we are talking about the *whole*. Therefore, I hope I've maintained a balance of highlights and growth factors throughout.

I couldn't have accomplished this book without the encouragement of Pat Donlon, who first recommended me for the task. I couldn't have accomplished it without the insight and spark provided by my editor, Julie Jaskol. I couldn't have accomplished it without the time and thought that the various movers and shakers of Buffalo business generously granted me. I couldn't have accomplished it without the piles and piles of books, magazines, newspapers, brochures, etc., that provided me with much of the background.

Above all, a special thanks to my wife Lorraine and my children, Nathan and Allison, for their patience and support throughout the fifteen months that they were forced to live with me and those two words that inhabited our home everyday: ''the book. . . .''

JIM BISCO
Buffalo, New York

Preface

"Make it while you can." That's what my father would always tell my mother whenever he had consented to work a double shift or an extra day at the steel mill. It became his pat buffer when it seemed to her that he lived in the coke ovens.

That response provided my first economic perspective of the area. Of course, I didn't realize it at the time. This child's-eye view simply saw a hardworking father who tried to make the most of both his job and his family life.

I remember the smell of eggs frying at nine in the evening, just before he would leave for the night shift. He'd fill his lunch box with a fried egg sandwich, a sweet roll, and a banana, and then take off in the dead of a winter's night or the swelter of a summer dusk. He'd work hard for his money. The unmistakable aroma of steel mill sweat and soot permeated his work clothes.

Although it seemed as though over half his life was spent swing-shifting, he always made time for us. Unlike a lot of his fellow steelworkers who'd bend an elbow at the local bar after their shifts, Dad would always head right home. He built a good place for us and saw to it that we lived comfortably.

My father's work ethic characterized the backbone of Greater Buffalo's economy. It is an area built on the sweat and toil of the laborer, whether in a steel mill, grain mill, factory, or harbor. Although it was the forethought and action of the executive who put these laborers to work, ultimate survival depended on the sweat of the brow—at least for most of the area's economic history.

The steel industry prospered throughout Dad's forty-year career, but he knew that foreign competition was gaining. As the 1980s rolled around, his predictions came true. The smokestacks of the area's major steel plants no longer pumped man-made clouds into the horizon. The wheeze, grind, and clang of the steel-making machinery no longer echoed into the night.

My father never lived to see the roar of the giant ovens snuffed out as unceremoniously as a cigarette butt. Four decades of inhaling steelyard air collapsed his lungs and rusted his heart. In retrospect, I guess it was better that he didn't have to suffer the inevitable fate of his co-workers, many of whom still live within the sprawling shadow of the deserted plants.

Dad died just a month and a half before Nathan, his first grandchild, was born. Nate, five years old at the time of this writing, will be attuned to—and may eventually be part of—many different sights and sounds of the area work force: the click of computers,

the figuring of research assistants, and the clatter of the subway train.

The most prominent workday roar may very likely be that of construction, the continued shaping and reshaping of a city. A city that was built by the sweat of the brow. A city that is being rebuilt by the thought behind the brow.

It is to my father, George, and my son, Nathan—who represent both the roots and hopes of Greater Buffalo—that this book is dedicated.

CHAPTER ONE

Buffalo 2000

Picture this. The twenty-first century has just arrived. The whole country is celebrating in a big way. It's the highest of high-tech eras, much more sophisticated in appearance than those futuristic projections from science fiction films of forty or fifty years ago.

As an employee and delegate of Amalgamated Whozits, you're heading for the site of this year's national convention of United Whozits and Whatzits of America.

Buffalo, New York. Hmmm. You've heard a lot about how the city pulled itself up by the bootstraps in the 1980s and really moved ahead in the 1990s. But could Buffalo possibly rival the excitement of a Las Vegas or Miami convention?

You remember what the convention chairman reported when Buffalo was chosen as the site four years ago. He said he was impressed with how sophisticated and advanced the city had become. And how much activity there was. And what fun he had during that brief two-day visit.

It occurs to you that Johnny Carson—who just celebrated his seventy-fifth birthday behind the Tonight Show desk—hasn't uttered a Buffalo joke in years. So, how about Buffalo? Well, the plane is landing at Greater Buffalo International Airport. You'll soon find out.

Popular and Populated

The first thing that impresses you about the area is the activity. The projections of the mid-1980s have come true. The census bureau found at the time that Erie County's three-decade decline in population had ended. The bureau predicted a 4.4 percent cumulative population increase in the Buffalo area, and a 17 percent growth in employment by the year 2000.

This so-called "Mid-America" study, which linked Buffalo to the

Opposite: The Goldome Center reflects a bright future for downtown Buffalo. Photo by Robert McElroy

ELIA
G.A.Elia Construction Corp
BUFFALO NY
716 854-1006

Construction along Buffalo's Pearl Street tells the story of downtown renewal. The Norstar Bank building towers in the center of the photograph. The building at right is the old Genesee building, now renovated and functioning as a Hyatt hotel. Photo by Robert McElroy

great industrial belt that extends from Pittsburgh to Chicago, said that Erie County's population would increase by about 44,000 and that 73,000 new jobs would be created. Per capita personal income in Erie County was expected to grow about 30.8 percent by 2000, compared with a projected increase of 31.7 percent for all metro areas of the country.

Indeed, such economic projections began to gain impetus as early as January 1986 when the Purchasing Management Association of Buffalo reported that general business conditions rebounded to the highest level in nearly eight years.

The landscape of the city on the cab ride downtown provides evidence that Buffalo has been riding the crest of this economic wave. As you exit off the sleekly refurbished Kensington Expressway downtown, you see a high-tech-oriented industrial park along the Elm-Oak corridor. You see the sweeping skyline of the Goldome and Norstar buildings to the north. You catch a glimpse of the rapid transit cars shuffling back and forth along Main Street. And you see crowds of strollers enjoying the many outdoor events and merchandise stands along the pedestrian mall. When you arrive at your designated hotel—one of a variety of lodgings from the elegant to the more budget-oriented—you unpack and decide to see for yourself just what all the hubbub about Buffalo is all about.

The Mall and All

The first thing that wows you is the pedestrian and transit mall, a $42.5-million project that turned downtown Main Street into a bright, contemporary, dynamic, strollers' paradise. It is graced with nearly 300 shade trees, light towers and standards, tiled walkways, attractive benches, and a series of three-by-nine-foot banners that graphically capture the seasons, holidays, or the work of local artists.

Walk toward Lafayette Square in the heart of downtown and you encounter Buffalo Place, a magnificent retail complex patterned after Toronto's Eaton Centre. The exciting atmosphere of Buffalo Place with its fountains, banners, sculpture, lights, and atriums, in addition to its unique array of shops, has really reversed downtown Buffalo's decline as a retailing center over the past decade. In fact, a number of "skywalks" make for a completely walkway-linked downtown retail area, returning the city to its former glory as the area's shopping hub.

By the year 2000, not only have Buffalo sports teams captured the Super Bowl and the Stanley Cup, but the expanded baseball stadium downtown is bustling with the National League Bisons, a

Opposite: Buffalo's light-rail rapid transit makes its way along the transit mall with the Goldome Center in the background. Photo by Peter R. Barber

remarkably strong expansion club that finished second in the eastern division last year and is now caught up in pennant hopes.

Waterfront Views

A short walk to the Buffalo waterfront reveals a rebirth that is an ocean away from the industrial activity that once characterized the harbor area. The waterfront is a colorful mix of parklands, office and residential development, some industry, and recreational projects, the most magnificent of which is Canal Street.

You've never seen a tourist attraction like this before. Through creative reopening of some of the old city canals, Canal Street recreates an 1860s rough-and-tumble waterfront neighborhood when Buffalo was a major commercial and shipping center during the golden age of the Erie Canal.

The faithful recreation of the period is built into the architecture and the flavor of the various street vendors and citizens of the era who stroll about the area. Replicas of nineteenth-century canal boats take visitors from the end of the city's rapid transit system at the foot of Main Street to Canal Street's attractions.

All of these attractions are "uniquely Buffalo," according to the catalyst of this so-called megaproject, D. Ward Fuller, president of American Steamship Company. They include:

Above, left: City Hall rises behind waterfront apartments. Photo by Peter R. Barber

Above: The sun sets on the River Mist housing project, Buffalo's new waterfront housing development. Photo by Joe Traver

a major theme ride similar to Disney World's "Pirates of the Caribbean," showing visitors the original waterfront rowdiness of Canal Street. With holograms providing a three-dimensional effect, you board a small canal boat and see all the saloons, dance halls, and minstrel shows that characterize that era; another ride that takes you through a history of Buffalo, from the silversmith who traded with the Indians and started the city to the modern era of the Erie Barge Canal, the Pan-American Exposition, the beginning of the Pierce-Arrow and American Express companies, and the present rebirth of the city; then, for edge-of-the-seat excitement, you view a three-dimensional film beginning with a helicopter ride from the shores of Lake Ontario up the Niagara River, relating the history of Niagara Falls. Similar to the one shown at Toronto's Ontario Place, this film takes you over the huge hydropower stations before passing the Niagara Gorge, past the whirlpools to the American and Canadian Falls. The helicopter then lands you, the viewer, on Goat Island where a floating capsule awaits you—the last of the Niagara Falls daredevils! Through the magic of 3-D cinematography and

Opposite: The observation tower at Erie Basin Marina dominates this waterfront scene. Photo by Robert McElroy

Above: Erie Basin Marina in downtown Buffalo provides dock space for recreational boaters. Photo by Robert McElroy

Dolby sound, you plunge over the falls in your capsule, rescued thereafter by the Maid of the Mist below.

Canal Street also includes a variety of other related theme ideas, including a maritime museum centering on the restored *Canadiana*—the fondly recalled Crystal Beach excursion boat—and other ships.

A walk to the Marina Marketplace next to Crawdaddy's Restaurant and you're inside a festive retail complex designed to capture some of the flavor of Boston's Quincy Market or Baltimore's Harbor Place. The two-level complex features a variety of specialty shops that, combined with those in Buffalo Center, give the city a unique retail variety.

Across the river from the Marina Marketplace and the Erie Basin Marina—the original waterfront development—is the restored magnificence of the Buffalo Lighthouse. This is the oldest building in the city still on its original site. It was erected in 1833, a year after Buffalo was incorporated. Thanks to the Buffalo Lighthouse Association and the Coast Guard, public access to the landmark has been provided, a park-like setting surrounds its historic charm,

and the tower once again beams its light as it did nearly 167 years ago.

A view from the lighthouse tower offers a breathtaking spectrum of waterfront development: the rows of fashionable townhouses and condominiums from the Erie Basin up to LaSalle Park, the Gateway Bridge roadway span that links the foot of downtown Buffalo to Fuhrmann Boulevard and all of the surrounding activity it has spurred, the four-mile-long artificial reef that lures fishermen from all over the eastern seaboard and Canada, and the expanded small boat harbor that lures just as many boaters.

As you head back toward downtown, you smile and nod. Buffalo has really taken advantage of its natural resource, you think. This rivals the most fabled of waterfront cities.

A Transit Ride

You've enjoyed subways ever since your father introduced you to the underground ride when you visited New York City during the 1964 World's Fair. So, you're back downtown and buying your token for a ride on Buffalo's Light Rail Rapid Transit.

When the $530-million project was begun by the Niagara Frontier

Left: Buffalo's light-rail rapid transit system provides efficient, economical transportation for commuters. Photo by Joe Traver

"A Taste of Buffalo" gives residents and tourists alike the chance to sample delicacies from a variety of restaurants in a festival setting downtown. Photo by Robert McElroy

Transportation Authority (NFTA) in April 1979, it was the largest construction project in the city of Buffalo since the building of the Erie Canal in 1825. The subway system is an important part of the revitalization of Buffalo; it's a proven fact that all cities perceived as being progessive and inviting have rapid transit.

This kind of sophisticated commuting is the main means of transportation in the year 2000. Originally designed as only a 6.4-mile span, the system now links Amherst, Hamburg, and the Tonawandas, and a line directly to Niagara Falls is being planned.

As you pass station after station along the route, you can easily see why it has become an underground tourist attraction. The variety of station art is unmatched by any other transit system you've seen. The twenty-three pieces of art merge spectacularly with the architecture, which is composed of brick, natural stone,

Left: Niagara Falls sported this laser image of an apple during a 1985 sesquicentennial celebration. The American Falls are shown at left. Photo by Robert McElroy

Above: Patrons throng a popular Buffalo nightclub called 2001. Photo by Robert McElroy

cast-in-place concrete, glass, and stainless steel. The art, which ranges from neon lighting to mosaic tile, is the work of some of the best artists both nationally and locally. This is riding in style, you think as you breeze along. What a way to commute every day!

Downtown at Night

Not too long ago downtown Buffalo went dark after quitting time. Now, theater and films light up the Theater District nightly. Dozens of events like gourmet food festivals and world premieres bring thousands of visitors downtown on weekends and even week-nights. Clubs like the Tralfamadore Cafe bring in top names in jazz, pop, and comedy. Crowds flock nightly to the baseball games at

The sun sets spectacularly beyond the Peace Bridge, spanning the Niagara River between Buffalo and Canada. Built in 1927, it was named in honor of a century of peace between the two countries. Photo by Dennis R. Floss

the downtown stadium. And nowhere—absolutely nowhere—is that don't-step-downtown-after-dark stigma apparent any longer.

Giving downtown Buffalo a very distinctive world-class "signature piece" is the largest permanent laser installation ever. Installed along the downtown mall by the NFTA, this so-called sky chronometer sends pillars of laser-beamed light into the nighttime heavens to mark the passage of the hours. At the same time, the light is deflected into a horizontal laser show that stretches along the entire length of the mall. Remarkably, the chronometer is visible thirty miles from Buffalo at ground level!

Secondary laser installations augment the show, creating a variety of balletic light sculptures in the sky and on the ground, designed to complement the NFTA's light towers and standards and a light show funded by a Junior League/*Buffalo News* "Show House" project.

This cybernetic show, similar to those seen at the Disney parks, uses sensors and computers to change the landscape lighting in tune to sounds and movement in the square. It's been described as a "people form of art."

Together, these light shows really bring Buffalo's image full circle from the turn of the last century when the city was known as a pioneer in urban electric lighting.

As you move through this very twenty-first-century metropolis, you smile. This is truly the City of Light once again, in more ways than one. Buffalo is a city that struggled in the dark for a long time, against many odds. Now, as the subway comes up from underground and heads into the bright and bustling Theater District, the light at the end of the tunnel illuminates as far as the eye can see.

Back to the Future

The preceding scenario is, of course, a projection. But that's not to imply that the probability of such a scene is remote. Most of it is possible and, indeed, some of it has already happened. The rapid transit line is in motion and already seriously considering expansion. . .the pedestrian mall has become a reality. . .the downtown baseball stadium is underway.

Of course, plans and projects progress past the blue-sky stage only through unified efforts. Funding is critical. A clear perception of the possible results is needed on the part of everyone involved. The mayor's team, the Common Council, and the state chambers of commerce all have a strong overall perception of the work that still needs to be done in order to make the Buffalo renaissance complete.

Greater Buffalo Chamber of Commerce

The Greater Buffalo Chamber of Commerce, one of the largest and most prestigious chambers in the nation, traces its roots back to a meeting held January 16, 1844, when a merchant named Russell H. Heywood suggested the formation of a group he called the Buffalo Board of Trade. The purpose of the board was "to cultivate friendship among the businesses of Buffalo, to unite them in one general policy for the general benefit of trade and commerce of Buffalo, and to make a market for western produce." Heywood became the first president of the organization upon its formation on March 11, 1844.

The Buffalo Board of Trade was the pioneer organization of its kind in the Great Lakes region. The organization was renamed the Buffalo Chamber of Commerce on February 21, 1912, and later renamed once again on June 7, 1962, as the Buffalo Area Chamber of Commerce. It underwent another name change on July 1, 1986. The present Greater Buffalo Chamber of Commerce, as with its predecessors, has had as its principal thrust to encourage companies to locate in the area, to create job opportunities in the private sector, and to encourage businesses to remain in the city and grow.

Today the Greater Buffalo Chamber of Commerce has more than 8,500 members, principally in Erie and Niagara counties and the metropolitan area. Its membership roster also includes companies in Canada, Japan, Taiwan, and Hong Kong. Its largest foreign membership is in Canada, with about 400 Canadian businesses having representatives in Western New York.

The chamber has seven groups: Administration and Finance, to

The Greater Buffalo Chamber of Commerce has helped to build Buffalo into one of the top cities in the nation for overall business improvement.

create a more effective, higher productivity service center for chamber priorities; Affiliates, created to organize and manage the chamber's specialized organizations and enhance membership in them; Business Development, devoted to attracting businesses to greater Buffalo and to establishing the area as an international trade center; Convention and Tourism, to increase the number of convention delegates from outside the area and establish greater Buffalo as a major convention and tourism center; Governmental and Community Affairs, to increase awareness of the private-sector impact on political and legislative activities; Marketing and Communications, to make greater Buffalonians and nonresidents more aware of the products and services available in the area; and Public Affairs, created to develop meetings and activities to improve the chamber's capacity to influence public decisions by improving information flow throughout greater Buffalo's leaders.

The chamber of commerce, with its predecessor organizations,

was the father of many business and civic groups over the years. About 1908 the Buffalo Real Estate Association and the Retail Merchants Board were part of the chamber. The Manufacturers Club merged with the chamber two years later, and in 1921 the organization formed the Buffalo Foreign Trade Association.

The chamber's Bureau of Charities and Surveys, as well as other groups, was in many respects a forerunner of today's Buffalo Better Business Bureau, which the chamber organized in 1912. It became a separate organization in 1927.

Late in 1985 a national magazine rated Buffalo 13th out of 74 cities in terms of overall business improvement for that year. Its unemployment rate was below the national average, and the average factory income of $25,930 was the second highest in the nation. The Buffalo metropolitan area is indeed moving forward on a broad front, thanks in no small measure to the continuing zealous efforts of the Greater Buffalo Chamber of Commerce.

Buffalo celebrated the Fourth of July in style at Riverside Park. Photo by Joseph M. Cascio

A unified spirit, quiet diligence, and imaginative thinking are the keys to continued progress here. As you'll discover throughout this book, a wide variety of forward-thinking, industrious individuals are working on ways to build Buffalo's capabilities and image.

For example, consider the program currently in progress that links the People's Republic of China with University at Buffalo's School of Management. UB professors are traveling to China to establish a management training program there, and China's best and brightest will come here as students, learning to be good managers. At the program's end, American executives from across the country will come to Buffalo to attend the first graduation of these Chinese management students.

The contacts made by UB in the People's Republic not only help reach a market of millions of people, but also set up Greater Buffalo as a center for international trade, returning the city to its former prominence as a world port.

In an article written by Charles Anzalone for *Buffalo*, the *Buffalo News* magazine, he speaks of UB professors trying to "spawn a new order of Marco Polos" by teaching executives of national and local companies the nuances of trading with the Chinese. For the local firms, it makes the university a real catalyst of the local economy.

As Anzalone so poignantly observes, "All kinds of possibilities come to mind. Scores of Chinese youngsters spooning Rich's Fresh 'n Frosty Mellocream dairy products into their mouths, writing on cards designed by New Buffalo Graphics while their parents break the seal on Bison Brand chip dip may sound farfetched, but the foundation is starting to form. [Two UB professors] speak of being in Beijing and watching young Chinese walk around with Buffalo Bills shirts. In areas where UB has become an economic ambassador, Buffalo is a symbol of international status. Buffalo is big."

Is there a better example of the promise of Western New York economy and image-building? Hopefully, there will be many examples forthcoming, as not only the university but all local sectors continue to work toward such lofty economic goals.

The perception of the area by outsiders is quite another thing. Many have misconceptions about Buffalo. About the snow. About industry. About progress. The movers and shakers around the city continually put their heads together attempting to create a marketing campaign for Western New York.

How does one spread the word that Buffalo is rebuilding, is modernizing, is one of the most attractive and pleasant places in which to live? Many employers recall how difficult it often is to recruit new employees here. Once they arrive, however, and sample all the pleasures and conveniences of this area, they don't want to leave.

One hears this time and time again. How do we bottle this and market it to the outside world? Consider it a work in progress, perhaps the most challenging project of Buffalo's future.

This book should shed some light on the wonders of Greater Buffalo. It is called "A Greater Look at Greater Buffalo" for good reasons. First, the look these days is definitely a *greater* one, as compared to a decade or two ago. Second, in 1986, the Chamber decided to re-name itself the Greater Buffalo Chamber of Commerce. And, indeed, it *is* a greater area today, as you'll see on the following pages.

It is in that spirit that this perspective is written.

CHAPTER TWO

From Birth to Boom

Trailblazing a City

The population of the Buffalo area 200 years ago consisted of the Seneca Indians and one white man, Cornelius Winne, a Dutchman from Hudson River country who established a small trading post for transactions with the Senecas. A few years later, British captain William Johnston also arrived and built a sawmill that furnished the Indians with boards and planks. By 1797 silversmith Asa Ransom set up a business in which he fashioned earrings and trinkets for the Senecas, thus bringing the first simple refinements of civilized life to the region.

At the time the area was known as Buffaloe's Creek. Legend has it that a half-breed Indian from the Far West named Buffaloe journeyed here in the mid-1700s and settled on the banks of a creek. Early travelers who encountered his campsite began to refer to it as Buffaloe's Creek. When a village began to emerge beyond the creek, the name stuck, minus the "e."

As the eighteenth century came to a close, the native Senecas—led by their chief, Red Jacket—surrendered most of their Western New York land to the white man, not in battle but in negotiations around their council fires. After twenty days of fireside talks in the late summer of 1797, Dutch speculators with the Holland Land Company purchased 1.3 million acres of the Indians' land for $100,000.

Afterward, Joseph Ellicott, principal surveyor of the Holland Land Company, organized a corps of 150 engineers and took with him about $8,000 worth of rations and supplies for a six-month survey of the newly acquired land.

Opposite: The Burning of Buffalo, painted by Raymond Massey, depicts the events of December 1813, when the village of Buffalo was burned by the British and the citizens prepared for a short-lived defense. Courtesy, Buffalo and Erie County Historical Society

Based on the experience of working with his brother, who helped design the topography of Washington, D.C., Ellicott plotted a similar grid system of streets for this area, with some east-west avenues striking off in spoke-like fashion from the hub of a public square (Niagara). Except for a few concessions to urban renewal, today's Buffalo street plan retains that basic design.

To please his Dutch employers, Ellicott decided to name the hamlet New Amsterdam. What would later be known as Main and Niagara streets were called Vanstaphorst and Schimmelpennich avenues. Neither those names, nor New Amsterdam, stuck, but Ellicott's other street names did: Mohawk, Huron, Chippewa, Delaware, Swan, Seneca, Eagle, and Terrace.

Canandaigua and Batavia were the principal settlements in Western New York at the time. Rochester was unknown. Soon, an inclination to migrate west was developed among the early New England settlers and a tide of emigration spread across New York State and into this region.

During the first decade of the nineteenth century, between 400 and 500 citizens settled in the area, with brick plants and sawmills among the earliest businesses.

Very shortly, the potential of the huge adjoining waterway would be discovered and change the course of industrial development, moving the local economy with the force of a swift current over the next 150 years.

The Industrial Flow Begins

There was a time when Buffalo was a muscle-flexing Goliath of industry in this country, with a population that more than doubled Chicago's. It was the 1840s and the beginning of the boom times for the Queen City, so named because of its strategic position along the waterway.

Because of its ideal Great Lakes location, Buffalo quickly rose to prominence as one of the most important shipping capitals of the young nation. During the 1840s, Buffalo controlled more shipping on the Great Lakes than any other community.

Although its harbor facilities were primitive at the time, Buffalo's

Right: Walk-in-the-Water, *shown here in about 1800, was the first steam-powered vessel to sail on Lake Erie. Courtesy, Buffalo and Erie County Historical Society*

Opposite: This drawing portrays Buffalo, already an active port on Lake Erie, in about 1815. Courtesy, Buffalo and Erie County Historical Society

shipping industry began in 1805 when the then-village became a congressionally designated port of entry, shipping wheat westward to the outposts in return for corn, fish, fur, and lumber.

Soon the War of 1812 reduced the growing frontier village into a smoldering pile of rubble. After the marauding British troops finished torching Buffalo, only one house, a blacksmith shop, and a jail were left standing.

The families that survived the bloody war determinedly rebuilt their homes while the Harbor Association, believed to have been the first instance of an organized commercial union in the area, took to the formidable task of rebuilding the local economy.

Headed by businessmen Charles Townsend, Oliver Forward, and

This imposing home, built in 1824, was the residence of Judge Samuel Wilkeson, an early Buffalo mayor who is considered the father of Buffalo Harbor. The home stood for eighty-nine years at the south half of the present City Hall site. Courtesy, Buffalo Area Chamber of Commerce

Judge Samuel Wilkeson, the association secured a loan of $12,000 from the State of New York in the spring of 1820 to improve the harbor facilities, the water of which never rose higher than a man's waist. They realized that if improvements were not made, the projected Erie Canal would never reach Buffalo.

The construction of two piers and a dam across the original mouth of Buffalo Creek proved costly. The $12,000 loan was soon exhausted and an appeal was made to citizens for further aid. They responded by raising approximately $1,000 in cash and goods. Beyond monetary assistance, though, many citizens contributed their services to the project, as well as vessel owners and captains, who offered the services of themselves and their crews to speed the progress.

The typical working day in that era was sunrise to sunset, six days a week. The project was completed in a grueling 221 days, during which Judge Wilkeson reported that "the men hired for the job stayed on it to the finish, almost without exception; there was practically no absenteeism, and only one case of intoxication on the job. Furthermore, there were no fights among the workers."

By 1821 the harbor improvements had been completed, and the effect upon the economy was felt soon afterward. To illustrate, only 120 vessels arrived and departed during the 1820 shipping season. By 1825, the year that the Erie Canal opened, the figure had tripled. And in just two years of the canal opening, shipping traffic rose to 972.

The Birth of a City and Industry

The canal initiated the beginning of the local grain industry as agricultural products moved through Buffalo eastward from the Midwest, and on to foreign customers as well. Manufactured products from the East and settlers seeking wide open spaces ventured west through Buffalo. Most of the local business was tied closely with Great Lakes and canal shipping.

As the canal continued to pump up the local economy, the first significant event of the 1830s was the incorporation of Buffalo as a city on April 20, 1832. Future U.S. President Millard Fillmore was among the citizens organized behind the effort.

The first half of the decade saw the economy also boosted by the prolific industrial and mercantile development of Benjamin Rathbun. Within several years, he had put up more than 100 buildings, including stores, hotels, brick plants, machine shops, a bank, and a jail.

However, his banking practices didn't quite match his Monopoly-

The George H. Notter boat yard was located at the foot of Virginia Street adjacent to the Erie Canal. Notter built "vessels, tugs, steamers, and canal boats" for early waterborne commerce. Courtesy, Buffalo and Erie County Historical Society

This circa-1840 lithograph of early Buffalo portrays the First Presbyterian Church (left,) and St. Paul's Church (right). Courtesy, Buffalo and Erie County Historical Society

board strategies. In 1836 over-borrowing and check forging led to his confinement in the very jail he built. His losses created a local depression that preceded the country-wide Panic of 1837.

Nevertheless, progress continued in the new city. During the same year that many Buffalonians dependent upon the Rathbun empire were devastated by the turn of events, the area's first railroad was built. The power of the locomotive opened up the possibilities of year-round commerce.

Previously, local business had come to a halt from late fall until early spring when deep snow and ice closed roads and lake traffic. The coming of the train signaled an end to Buffalo's hibernation as an isolated, remote country village each winter. By the end of the nineteenth century, the area would become a railroad hub in the East with twenty-nine railroad companies running a total of 250 passenger trains daily. At the time, the old *New York Sun* reported that Buffalo led the nation in trackage with 600 miles of rails,

Terrace Market and the Liberty Pole are shown in this lithograph of about 1840. Courtesy, Buffalo and Erie County Historical Society

compared to Chicago's 593, New York City's 464, and Philadelphia's 400.

As the decade of the 1840s rolled around, Buffalo's population rose by 80 percent. By 1843 lake traffic increased to 5,884 vessels during shipping season. A year later, the Buffalo Board of Trade—the forerunner of the current Greater Buffalo Chamber of Commerce—was organized. It was the first of its kind in the Great Lakes region and the sixth oldest in the country.

In that same year, Joseph Dart's first steam-driven grain elevator stood on Buffalo Creek. His ingenious method of transferring grain from lake boats into storage holds through a series of buckets moving perpendicularly along a steam-driven belt provided the biggest boom ever to the local economy. No longer did throngs of grain handlers have to lift the cargoes onto their backs. In less than a decade, local grain shipments jumped from 112,000 bushels to two million.

By 1854 ten grain elevators used Dart's device, unloading 22,400 bushels an hour with a total storage capacity of 1,550,000 bushels. Buffalo had replaced Rochester as America's grain-milling center. For well over a century, Buffalo flourished as one of the most prominent grain ports in the country, topping 100 million bushels annually by 1880 and 200 million by 1896.

The city's population continued to grow, from 42,000 in 1850 to

Above: The Buffalo lighthouse and harbor are featured in this 1840s scene. Courtesy, Buffalo and Erie County Historical Society

Opposite: The Niagara Suspension Bridge was opened on August 1, 1848. The bridge, which spanned the Niagara River, stood 230 feet above the river and was 759 feet long. Niagara Falls can be seen in the background of this lithograph. Courtesy, Buffalo Area Chamber of Commerce

This artist's rendering depicts the town of Black Rock in 1825. Black Rock rivalled Buffalo for port city status, but Buffalo assumed this role after building a breakwall. Black Rock, which stood about where Ferry Street is now, was eventually absorbed by Buffalo. Courtesy, Buffalo Area Chamber of Commerce

81,000 by 1860 to 118,000 by 1870. A significant portion of these increases were attributable to the variety of European immigrants who, in efforts to make easier transitions to a new culture, clustered in ethnic neighborhoods across the city.

As more and more harbor and canal improvements boosted the shipping industry, the expansion of rail traffic beginning in the 1850s with the introductions of the Erie and New York Central railroads spurred other industries.

This was apparent in the early 1860s when Buffalo had 502 manufacturing enterprises which employed a total of 6,000 people. Just thirty years earlier when the city was incorporated, there had been only forty manufacturers, all small in scale and relatively primitive.

Opposite: The Erie Canal bustled with barge activity in the 1870s. Courtesy, Buffalo and Erie County Historical Society

A Growing Industrial Force

After the development of the grain industry, the lumber trade was next to prosper. White, Norway, and yellow pine, hemlock, hardwoods, shingles, and lath were brought to the joint markets of Buffalo and Tonawanda by lake and rail from Minnesota, Michigan, Wisconsin, and Ontario.

At the turn of the century, both markets handled an average of 900 million board feet of lumber annually, a quantity second only

Below: This 1853 drawing by artist J.W. Hill shows Buffalo's emergence as a vital Eastern port. The waterways played a major role during the Civil War years. Courtesy, Buffalo Area Chamber of Commerce

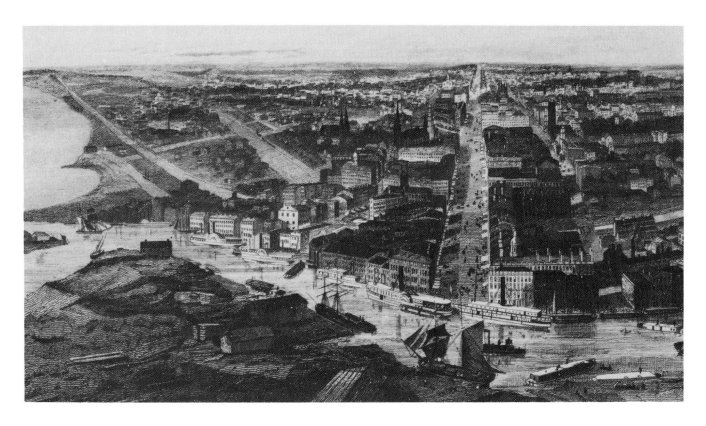

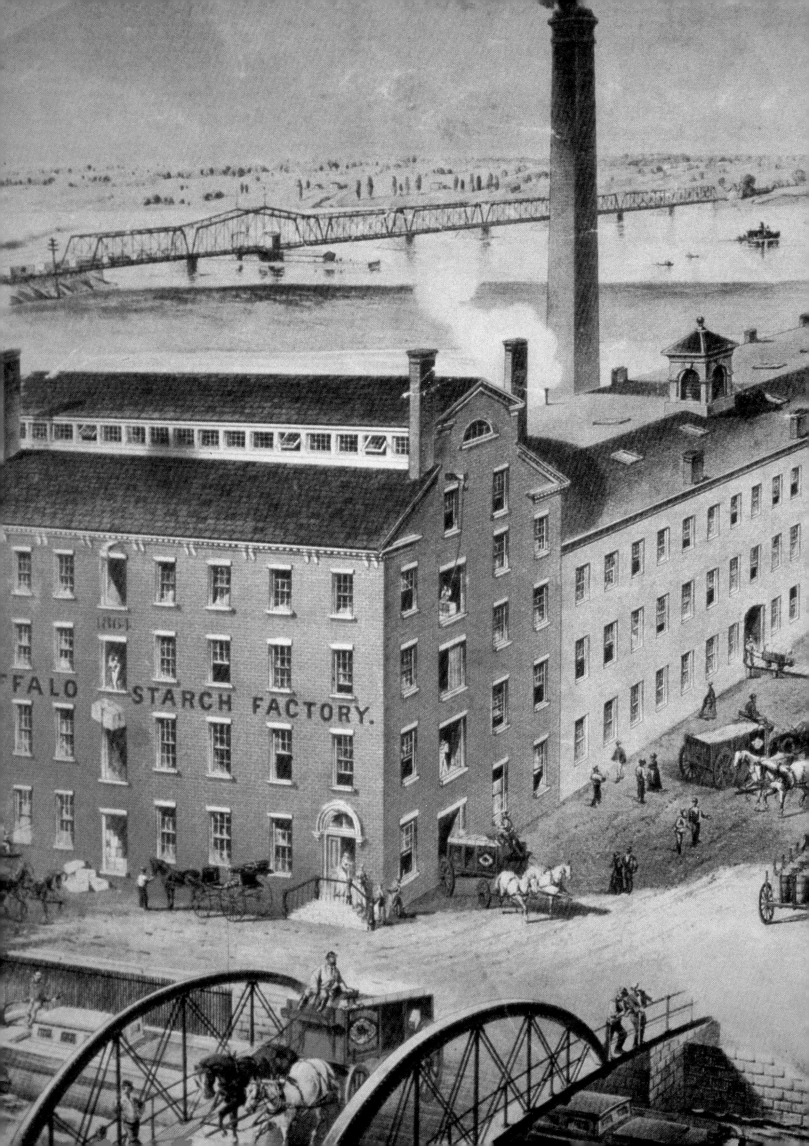

to Chicago. During that period, the world's largest producers and jobbers of hardwoods and hemlock were headquartered in Buffalo.

As the grain and lumber industries grew, so did banking. Before the mid-1840s, there was very little banking stability. Almost anyone could start a bank. Deposit insurance was unheard of. The chaotic state of the currency caused further complications.

Eldridge G. Spaulding, who brought the Farmers & Mechanics Bank to Buffalo in the early 1850s, became a congressman during the Civil War. During his term, he devised the greenback currency that didn't require gold backing, thus allowing the federal government to use it as needed.

Along with Spaulding's bank, Marine, Manufacturers & Traders, Buffalo Savings, and Western New York Savings were among the other banks that were established during this period, helping to stabilize the area's growing prosperity.

Buffalo Gets the Power

By the time Buffalo celebrated its fiftieth year as a city in 1882, the population had grown to 170,000 with 1,137 manufacturing enterprises. Among the new industries emerging during the latter part of the nineteenth century were leather tanning, iron making,

Opposite: The Buffalo Starch Factory is representative of the many manufacturing firms that prospered in mid-nineteenth-century Buffalo. The factory ranked third in world production in 1877. Pure water was a requisite for the production of starch, and the factory was located on the banks of the Niagara River. Courtesy, Buffalo and Erie County Historical Society

Right: The railroad was largely responsible for the growth and prosperity of nineteenth-century Buffalo. By 1887, Buffalo was the terminus of eleven trunk-line railroads that radiated north, east, and south. Courtesy, Buffalo and Erie County Historical Society

Left: The old Buffalo Cotton Factory is pictured here in about 1870. Courtesy, Buffalo and Erie County Historical Society

Below: The gold-domed structure of the Buffalo Savings Bank (now the Goldome Bank) can be seen at right in this 1924 scene looking north from Genesee Street. Courtesy, Greater Buffalo Chamber of Commerce

Established in 1878, Buffalo Forge Company specialized in the manufacture of portable forges and blowers. By 1883, the firm dominated the market, distributing their products to every state in the union. Courtesy, Buffalo and Erie County Historical Society

shipbuilding, flour milling, brewing, and the manufacturing of furniture, wallpaper, soap, bicycles, and railroad cars. Retail stores selling clothes and specialty merchandise created a shopping hub along Main Street.

Many Polish and Italian immigrants built up the population and the work force during these decades, residing where the earlier immigrants—the Irish and Germans—had settled.

As the so-called Gay '90s were made even happier by Buffalo's continued growth, former Buffalonian Grover Cleveland had entered his second term as U.S. president. In the waning months of his presidency, the electric age dawned in Buffalo with an overpowering influence on industry and life in general.

At midnight, November 15, 1896, electricity was transmitted from Niagara Falls to Buffalo for the first time. At last, the power of the Cataract had been harnessed over a long distance and, along with the current, came a new industrial revolution in Western New York. Very soon, the power of the mighty Niagara would be felt worldwide, with Buffalo playing a very electrically charged role.

The first current of Niagara power flowed to a fleet of streetcars in Buffalo. Their movement at the flick of the switch signified much more than a mere crosstown ride. With the age of hydroelectric power came a variety of industries to the area, taking advantage of the plentiful, low-cost power that still attracts many industrialists

Left: Buffalo's baseball team posed for a studio photograph after winning the championship in 1898. Buffalo was one of the first American cities to have a professional baseball team. Courtesy, Buffalo and Erie County Historical Society

Below: Uniformed guards and the electric-powered police patrol wagon are pictured during the 1901 Pan-American Exposition. Courtesy, Buffalo and Erie County Historical Society

Opposite, top: The Electric Tower seen at left was the focal point of the brilliantly illuminated Pan-American Exposition. Courtesy, Buffalo and Erie County Historical Society

Opposite, bottom: The 409-foot tall Electric Tower was designed by John Galen Howard for the Pan-American Exposition. The cupola was adorned with a winged "Goddess of Light," and its base featured an elaborate display of fountains. Courtesy, Buffalo and Erie County Historical Society

to this day.

Several years later, a monument to this accomplishment was erected in preparation for the grand Pan-American Exposition to be held in Buffalo. The Electric Tower was the exposition's centerpiece. One wall of the 375-foot-high creation appropriately incorporated a 70-by-30-foot waterfall, a veil-like cascade that magnificently wedded the significance of Niagara Falls and Buffalo as the world entered the twentieth century.

At the Top of the New Century

Buffalo's title as Queen City of the Great Lakes was never grander than at the turn of the century. The Pan-American Exposition was the ultimate trade show, conceived by the local industrialists who wanted to show the world how far Buffalo had progressed.

It began on May 1, 1901, for a six-month engagement of elaborate exhibitions, thrilling shows and rides, and a variety of concerts, parades, and dances. The overall consensus of the time held that Buffalo was a "city of enterprise, stability, and business energy."

At the century's turn, the population approached the 400,000 mark. The city was regarded as the chief commercial center

LANDING DOCK ON THE EARTH OF THE ARIEL NAVIGATION CO.

Among the highlights of the Pan-American Exposition were exhibits predicting what the future might be like. This exhibit featured a "trip to the moon" via airship. Courtesy, Buffalo and Erie County Historical Society

between New York and Chicago, making it a convenient point of exchange for more trade and traffic than any other city in the country.

The city claimed to be the main shipping outlet for the products of the fertile Northwest Territory. Iron ore mined in the regions of Lake Superior passed through Buffalo on its way to the furnaces, while the immense coal output of Pennsylvania was transshipped from Buffalo to the West and Northwest. Impressed with the flat topography of the area, the owner of Lackawanna Iron & Steel in Scranton decided that it would be more advantageous to build his new plant near Buffalo rather than in the Pennsylvania hills. In 1905 the $60-million facility opened south of Buffalo, combining iron

This graceful Evelyn Rumsey Cory design was used on countless souvenirs of the Pan-American Exposition. Courtesy, Buffalo and Erie County Historical Society

The Temple of Music, designed by Buffalo architects Esenwein and Johnson, served as the concert and recital center during the Pan-American Exposition. Courtesy, Buffalo and Erie County Historical Society

making, steelworks, coke ovens, and rolling mills. It eventually became known as Bethlehem Steel, once among the world's largest steel plants.

As a manufacturing center, Buffalo's numbers were impressive. Over 4,000 manufacturing plants around the area employed some 150,000 people. Buffalo was the fourth largest flour milling center at the time, its twelve mills filling 9,000 barrels daily and three million annually. Nineteen local breweries produced over a million barrels of beer, making it the city's third largest industry in 1900. No other city in the U.S. had a larger market for horses than Buffalo, particularly in the Thoroughbred trade.

The largest local employer at the time was the packing industry. Over a million hogs were slaughtered annually in the stockyards, along with vast herds of cattle and sheep.

The Growth Continues

Buffalo's economy continued to build into the twentieth century

BUFFALO

Right: This view of Buffalo Harbor was taken in the early 1900s. Courtesy, Buffalo and Erie County Historical Society

Right: A worker from the Buffalo Iron Works prepares to deliver his wares in this circa-1917 photograph. Courtesy, Buffalo Area Chamber of Commerce

Opposite: The old Front Street Dock, situated on the Buffalo River between Main and Washington streets, was the hub of shipping activity in the mid-1910s. Courtesy, Buffalo and Erie County Historical Society

as the area became a major transportation center, a hub of not only lake and rail, but also of air and road.

Buffalo was a pioneer of the aviation industry. The Glenn Curtiss Corporation built fighters for World War I, and its successor, Curtiss-Wright, did the same during the Second World War.

The Bell Aircraft Corporation, founded in 1935, built the famous P-39 cannon-firing fighter during World War II, before realizing the potential of the commercial aircraft market. The company went on to build the nation's first jet aircraft, the world's first supersonic jet, and the world's first jet-propelled vertical-takeoff-and-landing craft. Also, Bell pioneered helicopter development and production.

During this century's early decades, more than thirty makes of automobiles were produced in Buffalo. There were steam, electric, kerosene, and gasoline vehicles with names like Thomas-Flyer, Austin-Lyman, Warren Noble, Ess-Eff, the Kensington, and the legendary Pierce-Arrow.

In 1915, as World War I was underway, the Buffalo Chamber of Commerce publication boldly listed the accomplishments of the area to date under the boastful heading, "Buffalo's Bigness Tersely Told."

Among the facts stated were:

—Out of 339 different lines of manufacturing recognized by the United States Census Bureau, Buffalo has 200.
—The Buffalo district is the biggest lumber market in the world.
—Buffalo is the ninth largest manufacturing city in the U.S.
—Buffalo's automobile industry exceeds that of New York City, and its Automobile Club is the largest in the world.
—Industrial Buffalo has a population of more than half a million.
—The Buffalo foundry district is the largest in New York State.
—Buffalo received 5,506,691 tons of iron ore last year and made 1,757,904 gross tons of pig iron.
—Buffalo real estate is assessed at more than $325 million, practically all of it home-owned.
—Buffalo people have $235 million on deposit in Buffalo banks.

The Mid-Century Peak

The port city continued to boom right through mid-century, its industries alternately teaming up and competing. When teamwork was applied, steel mills fed by lake-shipped ore provided the materials for autos, and auto-laden freighters arriving here made Buffalo the world's largest auto-receiving port in 1933.

When competing forces were at work, however, the railroads reduced lake shipping tonnage and, in turn, the railway passenger trade yielded to the overwhelming popularity of the family car and

Alling and Cory

The name Alling and Cory has been synonymous with high-quality printing paper since its inception.

One of Buffalo's oldest, sturdiest buildings was constructed to house The Alling and Cory Company when it first opened a facility in the city in 1911. The structure is made of reinforced concrete—the first of its kind in Buffalo—and is now an official historic landmark. The exterior of the six-story office-warehouse facility has changed little in 75 years, but the city surrounding it, and the company inside it, have experienced enormous growth: Today Buffalo is an important American center for printing and advertising, and Alling and Cory has evolved into a major paper and packaging supplier for those industries.

Though Alling and Cory first came to Buffalo in 1911, the company's history begins almost a century before, in 1819, when Elihu F. Marshall, a cousin of Chief Justice of the Supreme Court John Marshall, founded a small stationery and book shop in Rochester. From all reports, the store was a hub of political activity. In 1825, French general and statesman Marquis de Lafayette addressed a massive rally outside the store. Washington Hunt, a partner of Marshall's in the 1820s, later was elected governor of New York.

In 1834 Marshall sold the store to one of his clerks, William Alling, who managed the business until his death in 1890, when Alling's son, Joseph T. Alling, and Harvey E. Cory took over. The firm was incorporated as The Alling and Cory Company in 1908.

Since that time, as the printing industry has expanded across the Lake Erie corridor through New York, Pennsylvania, Ohio, and West Virginia, the name Alling and Cory has become synonymous with high-quality printing papers. Printers, graphic designers, artists, advertising agencies, and other printing professionals look to the firm for all their printing paper needs.

Over the years packaging materials have become another important Alling and Cory product line. Wrapping, bundling, and banding films; interior packaging; and all types of containers, closures, and protective covers—the company's expert packaging specialists offer a vast array of modern packaging products and services for all industries.

In the 1960s and 1970s Alling and Cory was one of the first distributors to stock a wide selection of business products for automated offices, including paper, toners, and developers for copying machines; rolls and tapes for business machines and telecommunications

equipment; and supplies for word-processing equipment. Some of these supplies are used for the firm's own computer system—a centralized state-of-the-art information system that provides up-to-the-minute data on inventory, pricing, shipping, and individual account status.

Though Alling and Cory now has 19 distribution centers located in five eastern and midwestern states, it is proud that it has been able to maintain its local heritage. The Buffalo operation has always been staffed with hometown people, and the firm's employees at all levels have been active in civic and charitable organizations, such as the United Fund, Goodwill, and the Greater Buffalo Chamber of Commerce.

Throughout Alling and Cory's 75-year history in Buffalo, the company has adapted to the needs of the area. To assist in the city's World War II effort, paper stock distributed by the firm was used by local companies to manufacture military manuals, maps, and food and munitions packing for soldiers overseas. During the area's postwar heavy-industrial economy, the company embarked on an expansion of its maintenance products division, which provides a full range of paper towels, toilet tissue, and other maintenance products for industrial as well as office use. And as Buffalo has moved into the Information Age, Alling and Cory was there again, providing not only its computer supplies and printing papers for many high-tech firms but also a full line of technical and specialty papers.

Quietly yet forcefully, The Alling and Cory Company has become a vital link—between its nationwide network of paper manufacturers and its hundreds of Buffalo customers and clients, and between a long, successful past and a bright future for the city of Buffalo.

Above: President William Howard Taft, posing in the foreground, spoke at a dinner celebrating the merger of Buffalo's Chamber of Commerce with the Manufacturers' Club. Courtesy, Buffalo Area Chamber of Commerce

Opposite: Lafayette Square is pictured in about 1920. Courtesy, Greater Buffalo Chamber of Commerce

the speed of airplane travel.

Still, Buffalo's prominence as a major U.S. city grew in even bigger proportions right through the decade following World War II.

In 1945 a record 257,340,677 bushels of grain were processed. By 1951 Buffalo did 77 percent of the nation's grain milling, its thirty-one elevators offering a storage capacity of fifty-seven million bushels at a time.

During the mid-1950s when teens began to "Rock Around the Clock" and their parents enjoyed the calm reassurance of the Eisenhower administration, Buffalo really hit its stride. Its list of achievements made it one of the most booming cities in the country:

—The latest census figures placed Buffalo as the fifteenth largest city in America.
—It was the nation's biggest inland port, and twelfth largest overall.
—It was the second biggest rail center in the country.
—It was the nation's sixth largest steel producer.
—It was America's eighth biggest manufacturing center.

The Niagara Hudson Building at the corner of Washington and Genesee streets looks much the same today as it did in 1923. Only the name has changed; it is now known as the Niagara Mohawk Power Corporation. Courtesy, Greater Buffalo Chamber of Commerce

The era's most impressive industrial statistic, though, was Buffalo's importance as the largest flour and feed milling center in the entire world. Not only did this industry keep the local economy well-fed, but it literally fed the people living among the ruins of Western Europe during the immediate post-war years.

By the end of the 1950s, however, Buffalo's prominence would begin to sink into a canal system called the St. Lawrence Seaway.

The irony of it was overwhelming. Buffalo's industrial lifeblood had been nurtured with the opening of the first canal system. Now, 135 years later, its importance would be submerged by a new waterway, the advocates of which promised boom times for all.

Since this new sophisticated canal system never reached Buffalo, though, the local economy quickly began to dry up. During the seaway's first full season of operation in 1959, Buffalo's grain shipments—the area's greatest industry—dropped 45 percent below the average of the preceding twenty-five years.

Over a century of Buffalo progress and prominence would dissipate in less than two decades. It was truly the end of an era.

Right: The ship China *of the Erie prepares to unload at the old Bennett storage elevators, seen here in about 1930. Courtesy, Buffalo and Erie County Historical Society*

Below: This circa-1922 photo shows where the new Barge Canal, which replaced the historic Erie Canal, entered the Niagara River. Courtesy, Greater Buffalo Chamber of Commerce

CHAPTER THREE

The Queen City Dethroned

When the St. Lawrence Seaway first opened on April 25, 1959, the local press optimistically predicted that it would increase waterfront commerce. After the official opening ceremony in Montreal two months later which was attended by President Eisenhower and Queen Elizabeth, the *Courier-Express* editorialized that, "while the people of the Niagara Frontier and all along the vast stretch of water to the far reaches of the Great Lakes are cognizant of the realities of it [the Seaway], only with yesterday's ceremonies is it likely that word went out to all nations that new 'seacoasts' have been opened to admit world commerce to the interiors of the United States and Canada.

"Familiarity and nearness to the scene," the editorial continued, "are likely to blind those who live in this region to the tremendous importance of the Seaway's development."

Well, in truth, Western New Yorkers were quite cognizant of the grim realities that the seaway development represented. They knew full well that the Port of Buffalo's nineteenth-century importance as the link between the East and the far Midwest had slowly diminished with the building of each new waterway.

The decline in shipping volume began with the development of the Panama Canal and Mississippi River systems which offered alternative routes from Europe to America's interior and the West. Then, with the opening of the Welland Ship Canal in 1932, Buffalo lost even more trade as lake ships bypassed the port on the way

Opposite: This view of lower Main Street depicts Buffalo in the 1950s, a decade of transition for the Queen City. Photo by Maurice Fitzgerald. Courtesy, Buffalo Area Chamber of Commerce

This Buffalo Evening News *photo of the port terminal on Furhmann Boulevard shows the steamer* J.P. Schoellkopf, Jr. *poised for unloading. Courtesy, Buffalo and Erie County Historical Society*

to Lake Ontario.

By 1954 virtually every interest group in the city—businesses, banks, utilities, labor, politicians, newspapers, and social and civic clubs—knew that the proposed St. Lawrence Seaway would deliver the severest blow of all to local waterfront economy.

Despite legislators' predictions of increased employment, new industries, and world trade benefits as a result of the seaway, these interest groups knew that St. Lawrence would steer oceangoing vessels away from Buffalo. After going through the seaway in Montreal and exiting from the Welland Ship Canal in Port Colborne, Ontario, ships would then sail west toward Great Lakes ports in Cleveland, Detroit, Chicago, and Duluth, instead of turning east toward Buffalo, the only port at the eastern end of Lake Erie. The same would be true for oceanbound vessels coming from the Midwest.

Ever since the St. Lawrence Seaway project was first promoted by the Great Lakes Tide Water Association in 1919, the Buffalo Chamber of Commerce actively opposed it through countless meetings and distribution of literature. Their cause was succinctly made on the occasion of the chamber's centennial: no city or community of interest cares to see the efforts of a century and the expenditure of millions upon millions of dollars in investments come to naught through a diversion of trade into other channels.

Still, despite the widespread area opposition and fierce lobbying efforts, the inevitable happened. Legislation to authorize seaway construction was enacted in May 1954. Although President Eisenhower dedicated it as "a magnificent symbol to the entire world of the achievements possible to democratic nations peacefully working together for the common good," the St. Lawrence Seaway did absolutely no good for the Queen City of the Great Lakes—a queen unceremoniously dethroned.

The Seaway Locks Out Local Trade

The first industry to sink in the seaway shift was the building, selling, and repairing of ships. With the closing of the American Shipbuilding Company in 1962, a 150-year-old Buffalo industry suddenly disappeared.

The severest loss, however, proved to be that of Buffalo's preeminence as grain storage capital of the world.

For the past three decades, access to the Welland Ship Canal had diverted the transshipment of most Canadian grain from Buffalo. Now, as the 1960s unfolded, storage in Buffalo's innovative grain elevators rapidly dwindled as millions of tons of

Midwestern grain were instead shipped to Montreal via the seaway.

In the first full season of seaway operation, Buffalo's grain shipments dropped 45 percent below the average of the preceding quarter-century. Now, more than another twenty-five years later, local grain volume is barely 20 percent of what it used to be. Employment in the industry has gone from 4,800 before the seaway opening to under 1,000 in the 1980s. Abandoned grain elevators began to stand like hulking ghosts along the waterfront.

Buffalo's preeminence as the world's largest flour milling center also faced hard times as mills closed throughout the 1960s. In 1981 Standard Milling, a Kansas City-based company, closed its local plant, the largest in the city. Nevertheless, a daily capacity of ten million bushels still maintains Buffalo's lead in U.S. flour production.

The Great Lakes Dredge and Dock Company takes on the task of deepening the entrance to the Buffalo River and Buffalo Harbor in January 1955. Courtesy, Buffalo Area Chamber of Commerce

Barges such as those pictured here in about 1960 had for many years delivered grain to Buffalo's thriving mills via Lake Erie and the Niagara River. Courtesy, Buffalo Area Chamber of Commerce

Besides the seaway diversion, Buffalo's grain storage and flour milling industries suffered even more when the Interstate Commerce Commission revised its rate structure so that it became far more economical to ship grain on railroads directly from the Midwest to ocean ports along the East Coast.

By this time, all of the local mills were owned and controlled by outside interests, national corporations that remained apathetic toward the city's seaway and rate structure struggles.

Although local organized labor, the Buffalo Chamber, and area legislators made valiant efforts to maintain the local grain industry, the *Buffalo Evening News* pointed out that without corporate backing the city had no chance of winning the rate restructuring case. "Big companies with nationwide or worldwide operations have told their local executives to steer clear of the problems of an individual city," the *News* concluded.

As a result, the Port of Buffalo's role continued to decline throughout the next two decades. By 1979 a total of only sixty-eight vessels arrived at the Niagara Frontier Transportation Authority's port all year. By comparison, just a little over a century earlier, sixty-eight vessels arrived at the port each day.

Peak Times Despite the Seaway

All was not sunk in the Seaway during the 1960s. In fact, quite the opposite was true for the dominant heavy industries. With a combined employment total of nearly 60,000, the 1950s and 1960s were peak decades for steel and automobile manufacturing. Anyone who had Bethlehem Steel, Republic Steel, Ford, or General Motors imprinted across their paychecks had the strong feeling of job security.

The steelmakers were enjoying a period of unmatched profit and productivity. Meanwhile, the automakers' hopes were small—on small cars, that is. With the compact size hitting big in the 1960s, local auto workers were hoping that increased production of such small cars as the Ford Falcon and Chevy Vega would keep the demand going for the engines, axles, radiators, tires, and windshield wipers that made up an integral part of the Buffalo economy.

Although the Vietnam War is a bad memory for many, it boosted local employment in the mid to late 1960s, just as employment rose during World War II. At the height of the Vietnam fighting, generous defense spending expanded the economy and pumped up purchasing power. In the process, area unemployment rates reached an all-time low of 3.8 percent in 1968. As author Goldman described:

This view looking north on Main Street in 1962 features the former Liberty Bank Building on the west side of the street and the Adam, Meldrum and Anderson Company department store on the east side of the street. The modern Tishman Building can be seen in the next block. Photo by Maurice Fitzgerald. Courtesy, Buffalo Area Chamber of Commerce

Opposite: Buffalo City Hall, in the heart of the Queen City, remains the same as in this 1955 photograph. Courtesy, Greater Buffalo Chamber of Commerce

Everybody was optimistic. The steel industry was enjoying a period of unmatched profit and productivity, "in step," as one spokesman for the industry put it, "with the quickened pace of progress in Buffalo."

The automobile industry also looked indomitable at the end of the 1960s. . . . "If you've got any faith in this country at all," the president of Bethlehem Steel said in 1970, "you can't help but believe that a tremendous decade lies ahead."

The tide quickly turned, however, and within a year or two industry in Buffalo, particularly steel and automobiles, entered a period of deepening economic crisis from which it will never recover.

Just as economic momentum continued unabated, suddenly—within a brief year or two—the balloon burst. The comfort of job security and sizable paychecks were dealt the cruelest of blows. Instead of the Seaway rerouting being blamed, trends in the national economy were held responsible for the sudden decline.

Faced by aggressive foreign competition and a drop in domestic orders, steel production was the first to fall. In 1971 half of the 18,000 employees at Bethlehem were permanently laid off. By 1977 the entire American steel industry faced financial collapse, with the older Northeastern factories particularly in peril. Five years later, the two leading steel companies in Buffalo—Republic and Bethlehem—would close most of their local operations.

The local General Motors and Ford plants suffered fewer layoffs than their counterparts across the nation, but, increasingly, a beleaguered auto industry built new plants in other parts of the U.S.—particularly the Midwest—instead of the Niagara Frontier.

Of course, since the steel and auto industries depended on each other for a substantial percentage of business, their tandem downfall was inevitable.

By 1975 the local unemployment rate hit its postwar peak of 12 percent. Layoffs in the steel and auto industries continued into the early 1980s, testing the morale of those hardworking laborers who grew up, family upon family, generation upon generation, firmly believing that the sweat and toil of steelmaking and automaking yielded good union-standard pay and job security.

This steadfast belief in the work ethic has always been Buffalo's greatest strength. From the rebuilding of Buffalo in the 1820s, to its rebirth in the 1980s, Buffalo's work force has been the engine of growth. Businesses in Buffalo today rely on the city's reputation for an honest day's work for an honest day's pay, a reputation that goes back to the melting pot of immigrants who helped build—and rebuild—the city.

Local corporate personnel were also not immune to the economic

scene of the 1970s. The appeal of the Sun Belt, as well as the appeal of states with more liberal corporate tax laws than New York, attracted a variety of locally based businesses. Corporate bases shifted south.

A number of other area businesses felt the drain of jobs and dollars on the local economy. Many familiar names began to disappear from view as entire chains of retail and wholesale department stores, restaurants, shops, and service organizations either closed or consolidated. Along with them, such venerable institutions as the Buffalo Philharmonic Orchestra, the Museum of Science, the zoo, and the historical society teetered on the brink of bankruptcy.

Although Buffalo's economic decline over the past several decades was related to the much broader industrial decline around the country, it was little consolation to those thousands of unemployed who grew up believing in the sweat-of-the-brow work ethic.

The shadow of automation loomed over the area's antiquated physical plants. The workers in those plants were increasingly skeptical about their future. Still, that indomitable work ethic would not be stilled by the coming of the high-tech age. As long as there was determination, Buffalo's work force would retrain, regroup, re-whatever, in order to continue making a living for themselves and their families. For the camaraderie of the Buffalo work force is a kinship in itself, a "family" determined to maintain its standard of living in this aptly named "City of Good Neighbors."

Declining Population

In 1950 Buffalo was America's fifteenth largest city, with a population of 532,000. However, by 1960 it had slipped to twentieth and, by 1970, twenty-ninth. As Buffalo entered the 1980s, its position had dropped to thirty-sixth, with a population shrunken to 357,000.

A 12 percent drop in population between 1970-1975 reflected the downward turn of the auto and steel industries as many were forced to go where the work was.

Of course, the industrial woes contributed significantly to the decline, but there were also other factors coming into play.

The postwar flight to the suburbs was a national phenomenon which was greatly in evidence locally. In the process, racial boundaries began to be drawn, creating segregation and tension throughout the 1960s.

The original intention wasn't to create dividing lines. With solid jobs in the booming auto and steel industries and generous federal subsidies which were made available in the 1950s, many Buffalonians sought their dream houses. However, most land in the residential areas of the city had long been developed. Consequently, developers were discovering the wide open spaces surrounding the city. They built new residential communities—rows upon rows of handsome new ranch houses, split-levels, etc.—to which many city dwellers flocked.

Between 1950 and 1960, for example, over 80,000 white Buffalonians—nearly 20 percent of the 1950 population—took advantage of generous federal subsidies and moved to the suburbs. Within the same decade, the city's black population nearly doubled to 70,000. The ghettoization of blacks blanketed Buffalo's East Side. Such largely integrated neighborhoods as the Ellicott District, the Fruit Belt, and Hamlin Park experienced this population turnover.

Fueled by the prosperity of the auto and steel industries in the 1960s, even more white Buffalonians flocked to the suburbs, creating further segregation and increasing racial tension throughout the decade.

In addition to the suburban moves, declining birthrates across the nation throughout the 1960s and 1970s figured into population

Opposite: Lafayette Square is seen here in about 1950. Courtesy, Greater Buffalo Chamber of Commerce

declines. Also, restrictions on immigration into this country cut down on the number of newcomers who built up city populations like Buffalo's so dramatically in the late nineteenth and early twentieth centuries.

When the Erie Canal opened in 1825, the Irish had become the first to establish Buffalo's first true ethnic neighborhood, servicing the canal and its related industries. They worked hard loading and unloading lake and canal boats. Many of them worked as "scoopers," shoveling grain from the holds of lake boats that carried wheat and rye from western farms. Even as late as 1940 when most of the "scooping" was done mechanically rather than by hand, nine of every ten members of the local Grain Shoveler's Union were Irishmen. They had been joined by the many Poles, Italians, Germans, and Jews who settled in Buffalo over the next 125 years. When quotas became much more restrictive, Buffalo's melting pot began to cool. The downtown retail district suddenly was no match for the convenience and security of the growing variety of suburban shopping malls with their acres of free parking.

The rise of suburban multi-screen movie houses, restaurants, and clubs pulled the plug on downtown nightlife, once a thriving center for film premieres and big-name entertainment.

Although planners and downtown business groups launched major revitalization programs to avert the deterioration of the central business district, other planning decisions greatly undermined downtown survival attempts.

It is generally agreed that the two biggest blows to downtown development were struck by those public officials who decided that the new football stadium and the new university campus should be erected in the suburbs instead of downtown.

Today, over a decade later, Rich Stadium has largely contributed toward the substantial development of the Orchard Park area, as the sprawling State University of New York at Buffalo campus has toward the growth of the Amherst area. One can only speculate what the presence of either or both of them would have done for downtown.

That's not to negate the pivotal role which the stadium and university played in the development of the metropolitan area. A major educational institution and a major-league stadium have generated many jobs, revenues, and prestige for Greater Buffalo. The university has also played a significant role in the downtown renaissance of the 1980s. And on the sports scene, a new stadium is finally being erected in the heart of downtown Buffalo. Although Pilot Field will be the home of a minor-league baseball team (the Bisons), hope is strong that the city will be a serious contender when the major leagues expand in the 1990s.

Above: This demonstration in front of City Hall depicts Buffalo's involvement in the civil rights movement of the 1960s. Courtesy, Buffalo and Erie County Historical Society

While the suburbs were being embraced in the late 1960s and early 1970s, however, downtown was being forgotten. Buildings that once were busy centers of commerce were being abandoned and used as chalkboards for graffiti artists and targets for vandals.

Soon, though, a refreshing, revitalizing wind would begin to blow off the lake and waft through the downtown area. Not, however, before one of the harshest winds of all—the Blizzard of '77—would blaze a trail of destruction across a city that was already down on its knees.

Between January 28 and February 2, 1977, the Greater Buffalo Chamber of Commerce reported a total economic loss to the area of $221,490,000. In the middle of that six-day period, Mayor Stanley Makowski called the White House and desperately informed an aide to President Jimmy Carter that "this city is fighting for its life, and we're in a position where we can't help ourselves any longer. We need financial assistance."

The Blizzard of '77 swept over much more than the walkways, roadways, vehicles, and buildings around Greater Buffalo. It also piled up huge drifts of debt in the business and service sectors.

In its wake, however, the city would begin to dig out from under its icy blanket of metropolitan misery.

CHAPTER FOUR

The Renewal of a Great Lakes City

Yes, just as do other areas of the world, Greater Buffalo has weather. Unfortunately, most outsiders think that Buffalo has only one kind of weather: snow, and lots of it. The Blizzard of '77 put Buffalo into the national consciousness, via network newscasts and Johnny Carson's monologues. The lesser Blizzard of '85 didn't help matters any.

Actually, Greater Buffalo's snowfall usually is typical of any Northeastern area. A much more realistic perception of Buffalo's climate is one of moderation. Many people enjoy the four distinct seasons that are available. Yes, the winter brings snow, but it also brings some of the finest skiing and other winter sports available anywhere—and at very reasonable prices. Spring is exhilarating while summertime rarely becomes unbearably hot. Usually, the 70-85-degree range is perfect for summer picnicking and swims. Then there's the spectacular fall with the colorful arrays of trees and hills that surround the area.

The geographical location of Greater Buffalo is not particularly susceptible to damaging hurricanes (like the Southeast), tornadoes (like the Midwest), or earthquakes and mud slides (like the West Coast).

In fact, a quality-of-life survey published in the authoritative Rand McNally *Places Rated Almanac* in early 1985 ranked Buffalo fourteenth out of 329 metropolitan areas in the U.S. And, yes, ratings were based on climate and terrain, as well as housing,

Opposite: Buffalo takes on a soft pink glow on a winter afternoon. Photo by Joe Traver

Autumn leaves carpet Cazenovia Park. Photo by Joe Traver

health care, transportation, education, the arts, recreation, and economic outlook.

Still, a substantial portion of Buffalo's image seems to be framed in icicles. As the area continues to dig out from this frozen misconception, the spring-like rejuvenation of the economy also continues. Hopefully, this will overcome the "snow job" Buffalo has been given in cheap jokes and references over the past decade.

The Waterfront Resurfaces

Industry prospered along Buffalo's waterways for decades, building up the economy but also breaking down the quality of the water itself. As in other cities around the country, industrial waste and domestic sewage had been polluting Lake Erie, the Niagara River, and the New York shore of Lake Ontario.

Experts located the sources of the pollution in the 1970s and aroused public opinion to clean up the waterways. The best argument was the concern for public health and safety. A new

Above: A young couple enjoys the sun and some ice cream at the waterfront marina. Photo by Joe Traver

Above, right: Generations of Buffalonians have learned to skate on Delaware Park Lake. Photo by Joe Traver

sewage-treatment plant was the answer for one source of the pollution. In the Buffalo River, dredges were deepened and the channel was widened to increase water flow while preventing the buildup of pollutants.

The dumping of toxic wastes began to be regulated by New York State authorities, with the federal Clean Waters Act of 1972 providing additional regulation. Also, treaties between the U.S. and Canada established a policy that prevented either country from polluting international waterways in ways that would be detrimental to the other.

By the 1980s, Buffalo's waterways were sufficiently clean to become inviting for recreational purposes. The Erie Basin Marina is a testimony to that as boaters and riverfront strollers again enjoy the waterfront accessibility and view.

Development along the waterfront has paralleled the water

The industrial waterfront and Skyway are featured in this aerial
view. Photo by Lester J. Kuhn

Mader Construction Corporation

When a company is able to increase its volume of business by a factor of 100 in just 35 years, it has indeed achieved a substantial measure of success. Mader Construction Corporation today counts its volume of business as a construction contractor in excess of $30 million annually.'

The business was founded in 1951 as Edward Mader and Company and was headed by Mader. Later the name of the company was changed to the Mader Plastering Corporation and then to the Mader Construction Corporation.

In 1984 the firm was restructured under its present ownership. James E. Biddle is president, Harold F. Keller is a vice-president, as is Henry A. Finke, who is in charge of the company's office in Rochester, New York. Additional offices of Mader Construction Corporation are located in Baltimore, Maryland, and Orlando, Florida.

The firm does a large volume of repeat business—a strong indi-

---

Located on 10 acres in suburban West Seneca, Mader Construction Corporation occupies this 14,000-square-foot office building and an additional 25,000 square feet of warehouse space on the premises.

cation of the high quality of its work. Among the companies that Mader has served on more than one occasion are the John W. Cowper Company, Inc., Siegfried Construction Company, Inc., and Frank L. Ciminelli Construction Company, Inc.

In the mid-1950s Mader Construction did a substantial volume of work in the plastering of home interiors, but since that time has not engaged in any residential work. Today the bulk of its work is primarily in the interior finishing of walls and ceilings in commercial buildings.

Mader Construction's largest project involved the complete interior renovation of the Erie County Medical Center in a series of contracts over a five-year period. The company's largest single contract, also involving walls and ceilings, came from Buffalo General Hospital in the amount of more than five million dollars. That project was completed in early 1986.

Other large projects that the firm has completed or are currently under way include a 27-story hotel in Orlando, Florida; a hospital expansion at the University of Tennessee; and two build-

Mader Construction Corporation completely renovated the exterior of Cathedral Park Office Building, once a run-down, 11-story warehouse.

---

ings at Epcot Center at Disney World in Orlando, Florida.

The company's impressive list of clients also includes numerous buildings at the Main Street and Amherst campuses of the State University of New York at Buffalo; the Marine Midland Center; the Hilton, Marriott, and Hyatt hotels; the Goldome bank building; the Manufacturers and Traders Trust Company headquarters building; and the Rochester, New York, Convention Center.

Mader Construction also performed the exterior renovation of the Cathedral Park office building at 37 Franklin Street, as well as work on the renovation of Memorial Auditorium.

The company does a considerable amount of preliminary work with general contractors in design and budgeting. It also has a good rapport and works closely with such nationally known architects as Cannon Design, Kideney Associates, and I. M. Pei.

Biddle emphasizes that although Mader Constructon Corporation has done a considerable volume of work outside the Buffalo area, the firm "fully intends to continue its operations in the Buffalo area." The company's first offices were located at 609 Indian Church Road; it now occupies an impressive building at 2730 Transit Road.

Right: A crew team works out on the Black Rock canal at sunset. Photo by Joe Traver

Opposite, top: The USS Sullivan *and* Little Rock *dock at the Buffalo Naval and Servicemen's Park. The Skyway is in the foreground. Photo by Peter R. Barber*

Bottom: Buffalo mayor James D. Griffin gestures expansively at the revitalized waterfront at the Erie Basin Marina. New housing is under construction in front of the city skyline behind him. Photo by Robert McElroy

Downtown Buffalo Management Corporation

Lights. Action. Bring your camera! It's the Main Street Pedestrian Mall, and it's anything but ordinary.

Vital statistics: 99 feet wide and 1.2 miles long, six inbound and six outbound Light Rail Rapid Transit stations in an above-ground fare-free zone, three major department stores, 130 light poles, 260 banners, 23,599 periwinkles, 100,000 granite paving stones, hundreds of shops and restaurants, and more than 20 events that annually draw hundreds of thousands of people downtown.

Picture yourself on an inbound car of the Light Rail Rapid Transit. As it climbs up from the underground portion of the line, a multicolored stretch of Main

The amateur and professional alike get the opportunity to play for an appreciative audience on Main Street.

Main Street visitors enjoy the food, music, and festivities of the downtown Buffalo scene.

Street greets you. Like masts in a concrete marina, 130 light poles hung with pairs of three-foot by nine-foot banners line the mall from the theater district to the Memorial Auditorium. Against backgrounds of different colors, patterns of circles, stars, and bars—three to a banner—boldly guide the eye to the waterfront. Giant steel arches curve gracefully overhead, one as high as 66 feet into the air. And light is everywhere, as neon and incandescent fixtures of all kinds illuminate Main Street from Goodell Street on the north to Scott Street on the south.

Such brilliance underscores the mall's role as the staging ground for Buffalo's downtown renaissance. Offering a triple bill of fun, food, and free rides on its very own people mover, the mall has just about everything Petula Clark

ever mentioned when she sang the words to "Downtown."

But it's not just bulbs that light up the strip. At Tupper Street in the heart of the theater district a 100-foot light tower acts as a beacon for theatergoers and strollers. A pair of 60-foot light towers at Mohawk and Eagle streets carry the theme of "Lights on Buffalo" to the retail district. All in all the mall at night is a dramatically lit stage, with world-class entertainment provided by events ranging from NHL hockey and college basketball at the Aud, to Bison baseball under the lights at Pilot Stadium, to first-run plays at the theater district's five live theaters.

But take a sunlit look at the mall and you'll find that last night's light show is evenly matched by the color and activity that goes on during the day. A series of arbor-like "parkettes" branch off to the east and west from Main Street, offering an open green door to passers-through and a bench-lined oasis to those more inclined to a pause. Located on Mohawk and Eagle streets, Roosevelt Plaza, Theater Square, and at the crown jewel of the Pedestrian Mall, Lafayette Square, these little parks are the ideal spot for sitting and reading, enjoying a bite to eat, or catching one of the many street performers who entertain visitors downtown. Landscaped and decoratively lit pedestrian paths lead visitors and shoppers from ample parking areas on Pearl and Washington streets.

The green in these parkettes— and along the entire length of the mall—comes from some 350 trees, including 112 maples in 6 varieties, 41 honey locusts, 119 lindens, and a variety of pears, pines, beach plums, and spruces. Along with hundreds of shrubs and other plants, pairs of flower-filled hanging baskets on Main Street's light poles add a garden-like atmosphere to the mall. And those 23,000-plus periwinkles dot the landscape with summer-long bursts of color.

Behind the scenes of this color and fun is the organization responsible for managing, maintaining, and promoting the Pedestrian

With the downtown Buffalo Country Market, every Thursday—Spring, Summer, and Fall—the country comes to Main Street.

Mall, the Downtown Buffalo Management Corporation. A not-for-profit organization representing mall-area property and business owners, the DBMC is headquartered at 671 Main Street in the city's theater district, where it operates a tourist and information center.

DBMC executive director Charles Breihof states, "You see people returning to downtown every day. The new Pedestrian Mall is building a healthy economy for downtown as it regains its place as a hub of retail activity, and is creating the lively atmosphere at the same time. In doing so, it has also set the stage for a wide variety of DBMC-sponsored or cosponsored events."

Every Thursday, from June through October, part of the Pedestrian Mall metamorphosizes into the Downtown Buffalo Country Market. Here, along with a variety of fresh Western New York produce, you might encounter a costumed character dressed as an apple or another known as Mr. Country Market Corn. But these aren't the only costumed characters or added attractions the mall has to offer.

At the annual Friendship Tree

lighting ceremony at Main and Tupper streets in December, you may catch a costumed snowman joining Santa Claus in the caroling. In September a three-act extravaganza of dining, play-going, and celebrating is on the bill as *Curtain Up!* marks the opening of another exciting live theater season. For those who like it hot, there's the annual officially sanctioned Northeast Regional Chili Cook-off and Bluegrass Festival in August. And for those who like it served at less than three alarms, delicacies of all kinds and those who enjoy them are abundantly present (over 200,000 of the latter) at the popular two-day Taste of Buffalo in July. Clown Day, the flower show, downtown days, art and craft sales, street performers, and the popular annual CityFest are just a few more examples of the more than 20 annual events that have brought Western New Yorkers to the Main Street Pedestrian Mall by the hundreds of thousands.

In 1901 the Pan American Exposition brought light to Western New York in a way that woke up the world. Inspired by that success, Buffalo has "tripped the light fantastic" to make the Main Street Pedestrian Mall the lodestar of twentieth-century renaissance, an entertaining and colorful people place that's brought the action back downtown.

The Pedestrian Mall provides many places to rest and chat during or after a busy day.

Sun worshippers enjoy the sun at lunchtime on the marina. Photo by Joe Traver

cleanup. In the early 1970s, initial plans were already drawing praise in national publications. *House and Garden* referred to the opening of the Shoreline Apartments as "a village in the heart of the city," noting the city's foresighted move to a new kind of urban living. This domestic urbanization has now extended to elite townhouses along the waterfront and apartment complexes along Main Street. Geared to the young professional, these developments offer the convenience of being within walking distance of the downtown workplace while being able to take advantage of the growing urban renaissance.

The decaying warehouses at the foot of Erie Street were replaced in the late 1970s by the Erie Basin Marina—a storage port for local boat owners—and the adjacent parkways. With the addition of historic naval ships which anchor at the Buffalo and Erie County Naval and Servicemen's Park, waterfront life at the turn of the decade was a scenic delight. Indeed, many longtime Buffalo residents visiting the waterfront for the first time in years are delighted when they gaze upon the splendor of the harbor.

With the addition of new office buildings, a trendy upscale restaurant, a sprawling hotel, and new townhouses and condominiums that are part of the $100-million Waterfront Village, Buffalo's harbor—still considered to be among the Great Lakes'

Right: A campaign to clean up Buffalo's harbor has brought it back from decades of industrial misuse. Photo by Joe Traver

Above: Sunset is a good time to try the fishing in LaSalle Lake. Photo by Bill Wippert

SIEGFRIED CONSTRUCTION COMPANY, INC.

Interior of the five-story glass atrium in the Hyatt Regency Hotel, Buffalo.

The Great Depression of the 1930s was scarcely an auspicious time to form a new company, much less a general construction firm. Unemployment was rampant. Bread lines formed for the hungry. Hundreds of banks closed their doors permanently. President Franklin D. Roosevelt tried to reassure the nation in his fireside chats broadcast by radio.

This gloomy picture, however, did not daunt N. Osborne Siegfried when he formed Siegfried Construction Company, Inc., in May 1934 at 6 North Pearl Street in what was once his father's home. He built a few homes on the lakeshore and gradually branched out. His brother, Cyrus S. Siegfried, joined him in the business in 1936. Both men are now deceased, but they left behind a glorious heri-

tage. Today Siegfried Construction has offices in Boston and Delray Beach, Florida, in addition to its headquarters in Amherst.

By its very nature, construction is a seasonal business, and the company's employment figures vary from around 200 to 600 workers in the field. The firm's construction activities are mainly in New York State, Georgia, Florida, Ohio, Pennsylvania, Massachusetts, and Connecticut. In Florida and Georgia alone, it has some $80 million worth of construction in progress. Its construction volume over the years probably exceeds one billion dollars.

Siegfried Construction works closely with architects and the customer to keep the construction job on time and within budget. As Mason H. Holmwood, president and chief executive officer, says, "This approach results in a more efficient project. It gives the owner an accurate cost pic-

ture before the start of the job, and assures maximum quality and satisfaction in minimum time. The tougher the job, the better the chance we have in getting it. This results in repeat business."

The firm's largest single construction job was the $70-million sewage treatment plant for the City of Buffalo that took place from 1975 to 1978. The company's winning bid on the project was eight million dollars lower than the next lowest bid, much to the concern of Siegfried. However, in a bold move, Ernest A. Bouchard, executive vice-president, took the problem straight to the workers, and with their help the job was completed successfully.

Perhaps Siegfried Construction's most challenging project was literally raising the roof as a single unit on Buffalo's Memorial Auditorium in 1970 and 1971. That project was part of an overall modernization and expansion of seating capacity for the Buffalo Sabres national league hockey team and other events. The entire roof slab covered 71,600 square feet, equivalent to 1.645 acres, about the size of a football field. The roof weighed an estimated 2,200 tons. The job went off without a hitch on May 27, 1971. The expansion of the auditorium provided 4,819 additional seats in a second balcony, bringing seating capacity to 15,172.

Siegfried Construction was also the general contractor for the conversion of the 15-story Genesee Building in downtown Buffalo into the modern 400-room Hyatt Regency Hotel. The Genesee Building had been declared a national historic monument and was saved from planned demolition in December 1981 by preservationists and other concerned citizens. At one point the firm's leaders suggested a major cost savings of some $250,000. Other savings advanced by the company also were implemented. The Snyder-Darien Corporation was the developer of the project, a shining jewel at Genesee and Main streets.

Siegfried Construction has also undertaken considerable construction work for the Niagara Frontier Transportation Authority. The authority is responsible for building the 6.4-mile Rapid Transit System, which will run from the foot of Main Street to Bailey Avenue at the city line, largely in a subway mode. The firm performed the cut-and-cover work for 1,900 linear feet of the Rapid

Aeration tanks measuring 400 feet wide by 1,040 feet long at the Buffalo Sewage Treatment Plant.

Transit System in 1978 and 1979. It also built the Humboldt and Amherst passenger stations and the maintenance, repair, and storage facility at the foot of Main Street.

In addition, the company is the construction manager for the 1.2-mile Pedestrian Mall in the downtown area. The mall is expected to cost roughly $30 million and is planned for completion in the summer of 1986.

Among the firm's other construction projects were the *Buffalo News* office and pressroom buildings and several parking ramps in downtown Buffalo. It also constructed some $70 million worth of senior citizen housing in Massachusetts and Michigan.

Other large projects were the Durez Plastics plant in North Tonawanda followed by work on another Durez facility in Ohio. The

same chain reaction occurred with General Electric—an assignment for that company's plant in Auburn, New York, was followed by another project for its Anniston, Alabama, facility. Such efforts are further evidence of satisfied customers.

As one might expect, the company also built its handsome four-story headquarters building at One Towne Centre in Amherst, leasing part of the facility to six tenants.

Today Siegfried Construction Company, Inc., is owned by some 50 current and retired employees. The firm calls its far-flung building activities "constructioneering," a blend of sophisticated skills and know-how and meticulous workmanship in which it has built its reputation as one of the finest general contractors in the Northeast.

Right: A harborside restaurant provides a landlubber's view of the Jafco Marina. Photo by Joe Traver

finest—is dramatically more active and aesthetically pleasing today than in its previous industrial incarnation.

Downtown Comes Back Up

Before the 1960s, a trip downtown was an exciting adventure. It seemed as though you could get anything you could ever want amidst the bustle of the department stores and shops. The theaters downtown were the only places you could catch first-run films, sometimes even with a live appearance from the films' stars. When the Three Stooges made a feature film comeback in the late 1950s,

Below: Young Buffalonians gather at the Erie Basin Marina for a weekend excursion. Photo by Joe Traver

FERGUSON ELECTRIC CONSTRUCTION COMPANY, INC.

In the early 1930s young Whitworth Ferguson had become vice-president and chief engineer of Buffalo's major electrical contracting company. Although he was proud of his rapid advancement in the large firm, he remained restless. Despite the gloom of the Depression, he strongly believed that the city could support another electrical contracting company, one that specialized in engineering.

On a hot August day in 1935, Ferguson Electric opened for business with headquarters in a small office on Oak Street, 10 employees, and one truck.

Now, over half a century later, Ferguson Electric is Western New York's largest electrical construction firm. With offices and warehouses at 333 Ellicott Street in Buffalo and 2701 Lockport Road in Niagara Falls, the staff has grown to over 250 employees with a large fleet of trucks, having served more than a thousand customers whose electrical requirements have exceeded $500 million.

Although it is one of the largest electrical contractors in the state, the firm has chosen to concentrate most of its efforts in Erie and Niagara counties, giving power to some of the area's most prominent buildings and businesses over the years.

Ferguson Electric's greatest challenge, though, was harnessing the mighty power of Niagara Falls in one of the most spectacular displays of generating hydroelectricity. While the initiating of the massive Niagara Power in 1956 sparked the annals of electrical history, that's not implying that more commercially oriented projects didn't present substantial challenges of their own.

The company was the prime electrical contractor for the $210-million Phase I & II expansion and Phase III renovation of Buffalo General Hospital, installing 16,000 lighting fixtures, 65,000 lamps, 85,000 feet of electrical conduit, and more than four million feet of wire.

Ferguson Electric also provided the electrical installation for Buffalo's tallest building, the 40-story Marine Midland Center, with a plaza that has the area's largest electric snow-melting facility.

Other local landmarks that are powered by the company's electrical expertise include the 27-story Main Place Tower, the sprawling Amherst campus of the State University of New York at Buffalo, the local plants of General Motors and Ford Motor Company,

Harrison Radiator, Occidental Chemical, Anaconda Brass, General Mills, Millard Fillmore and Veterans Hospitals, Shea's Buffalo Center for the Performing Arts, and Buffalo City Hall.

Outside the area, the Ferguson reputation has extended to delicate electrical construction work on the nuclear reactor at the Massachusetts Institute of Technology, as well as more industrialized projects for Wisconsin Steel in Chicago and the Ford Stamping Plant in Cleveland.

Today Whitworth Ferguson, Jr., carries on the reputation established by his late father, advancing the company into its next 50 years with the development of new methods of electrical installations.

Computer, robotics, and fiber optics are a major part of today's high-tech emphasis. Because of today's more sophisticated relaying and power transmission, added concentration has been placed in the areas of preventive maintenance and energy management.

Realizing that such high-tech emphasis requires constant training updates, Ferguson Electric's journeyman employees participate in a thorough continuing education program. In fact, recent contract negotiations with the Brotherhood of Electrical Workers resulted in only one added cost to the labor contract—for the continuous training of journeymen and apprentices, as well as employees of the electrical contractors.

From the huge hydroelectric power project at Niagara Falls to the most routine installation of lighting fixtures, Ferguson Electric continues to power Western New York with the most advanced technique and quality control in the industry.

The current officers of Ferguson Electric Construction Company, Inc. Standing (left to right) are Whitworth Ferguson, Jr., president and director; W. Richard Duffy, executive vice-president and director; and Hans E. Haage, comptroller and director. Seated (left to right) are Donald R. Ferguson, secretary; Robert A. Fredricks, vice-president/engineering; and Donald A. Reiter, vice president/Niagara Falls office. The portrait to the left of the photograph is of Whitworth Ferguson, Sr., founder.

Balling Construction, Inc.

Henry Balling, Sr., was probably on the receiving end of some "constructive" criticism when he decided to launch Balling Brothers at the height of the Great Depression. But fortunately for Buffalo, he didn't pay much attention. The small masonry firm he formed with his seven brothers prospered. And today the successor of that fraternal concern, Balling Construction, Inc., is a General Contracting and Construction Management firm that has played a leading role in the development and revitalization of the city of Buffalo.

Still a family-owned enterprise, Balling Construction is as much a reconstruction company as it is a construction company. With Henry Balling, Jr., presiding, much of the firm's recent work has been the renovation of older buildings in Buffalo. The landmark Guaranty Building and Theater Place are two examples. And more recently, the firm has served as construction manager for Ansonia Centre and the former Courier Express Building, which is now used by the Diocese of Buffalo as the new Catholic Center. In short, wherever you look, the creative impact of Balling Construction can be seen all over the city. However, evidence of the company's work isn't limited to either the downtown area or to the recent past.

Following World War II the then-still Balling Brothers went to work on many projects for the Catholic Diocese of Buffalo. A dozen-plus parish churches, including St. Gregory the Great in Williamsville and Our Lady of Pompeii in Lancaster, were built by the firm. Our Lady of Victory Hospital and high schools, including Turner, Neumann, O'Hara, Timon, St. Mary's, and Gibbons, were also constructed by the Tonawanda-based organization. Balling Construction has served

Ansonia Centre—a $6.2-million apartment complex in the Theater District of downtown Buffalo, at Main and Tupper streets. Balling Construction, Inc., is a general partner/constructor of the facility, which opened in 1986.

higher education as well, constructing Villa Maria College, Hilbert College, and eight buildings at Canisius College.

Incorporating under its present name in 1952, Balling Construction's work was largely in the private sector through the 1950s and 1960s. But gradually during that period the contract pendulum began to swing more toward the public sector, with the company working on projects for the state, county, and city. Today the pendulum appears headed back toward the private sector, with the firm taking on the various roles of developer, general contractor, and construction manager in that context.

The last of those roles, construction management, has become an important area for the company. Balling Construction today believes that its future in the construction industry lies in the further development of this role.

In essence, construction management offers clients closer working relationships with their builder through cost control, value engineering, and schedule controls with the use of the latest research and developments in building materials, energy conservation, and mechanical technology.

During the 1980s Balling Construction expanded into the real estate development field, particularly housing, including Bishop Gibbons Apartments and the recently completed 59-unit Ansonia Centre at Main and Tupper in Buffalo's Theater District. Built in large part because of Balling Construction's belief that housing is one of the things the downtown Buffalo area needs most if it is to recapture of its past glory, the project has proven a resounding success. In doing so, however, various practical challenges had to be met. For instance, the company had to design a way of fitting four floors of living space into the

Balling Construction, Inc., is the general contractor for the Theater District Station, a $7-million project that, upon its completion in 1986, will be the major station on the NFTA downtown aboveground transit line.

shell of what was originally a tall, two-story structure. The firm's ability to do so reflected both its commitment to getting the project off the ground and its ingenuity once it was under way.

More recently, Balling Construction has begun the process of renovating the old Presbyterian Nursing Home at Delaware and Bryant. The company's mandate is to return the site, which originally contained luxury apartments, to its former role. There, too, it has taken on a project that few construction firms would have either the desire or the expertise to even consider.

But housing projects are not

the only feathers in Balling Construction's hard hat. Perhaps its most famous downtown work was the restoration of Louis Sullivan's Prudential/Guaranty Building.

On that project, the firm coordinated the reconstruction of what must have seemed, at times, like a giant jigsaw puzzle. Subcontractors responsible for everything from terra-cotta to carpentry came under the company's wing, and the result was a long but exciting period of "near-residence" while work progressed on the $11-million project.

Balling Construction, Inc., was the construction manager for the Wyoming Correctional Facility in Attica, New York. A $26-million project, it was built in 1984-1985 in a time span of nine months.

Also of note is the company's work to save the Allentown Theater, and its role in the restoration of the Connecticut Street Armory. In the case of the theater, Balling Construction provided both men and materials at greatly reduced cost to help stave off threatened demolition of the landmark. The armory was the victim of a different fate: Ravaged by a spectacular fire in 1982, Balling Construction helped restore the masonry of the building's red sandstone exterior, a job that harkened back to the

original stock-in-trade of Balling Brothers.

Looking to the future, Balling Construction plans to continue to emphasize its expertise in both contracting and construction management. Using modern construction technology and computers has enabled the firm to remain innovative and competitive. But regardless of how high-tech its techniques may get, Balling Construction, Inc., can always be counted on to build, while not necessarily bigger, certainly better things for Buffalo.

Left: One M&T Tower was an early part of Buffalo's renaissance downtown. Photo by Envisions Co.

for instance, Curly, Larry, and Moe delighted about 2,000 kids at the old Century Theater.

By the 1970s, however, that magical aura of downtown Buffalo was gone, replaced by many examples of decay and abandonment. Despite imposing contemporary office buildings like the Marine Midland Tower, One M & T Plaza, and the Erie Savings Bank tower, the business district was losing huge chunks of retail stores to thriving suburban plazas and malls. Nightlife was practically nonexistent, except for the Studio Arena Theatre, a few porno and kung-fu movie houses, and a handful of bars and topless joints.

To combat this blight, plans began to take shape in the late 1970s which would transform Main Street between Goodell and Scott streets into a downtown transit mall—a mall that would blend a rapid transit line with pedestrian activity. Storekeepers along the line would be encouraged to extend their trade into the pedestrian mall with sidewalk bazaars and enclosed terraces that could be opened in nice weather and closed during the winter months.

The idea was that even in bad weather transit riders would see people and activity along the downtown route and be drawn inside. With such a plan formulated on paper, the next step was to initiate what would be the largest construction project in the city of Buffalo since the building of the Erie Canal in 1825.

Above: The newly opened LRRT station at Amherst sports distinctive mural art. Photo by Joe Traver

Right: Construction of the rapid transit tunnels was a laborious process. Courtesy, Greater Buffalo Chamber of Commerce

Light Rail at the End of the Tunnel

The Niagara Frontier Transportation Authority, a state-mandated agency that provides and maintains air, surface, and water transportation for Erie and Niagara counties, began construction of the $530-million light rail rapid transit system on April 2, 1979. The initial 6.4-mile route from the foot of downtown to the state university campus on Main Street symbolized a giant step toward reviving a sagging downtown while turning the city into a major metropolitan center—comparable in sophistication and foresight to other cities with rapid transit.

Hopes are riding high for the NFTA's $42 million Pedestrian Rail Transit Mall. Its potential to return downtown to the busy center of shopping and strolling activity that it once knew has been referred to as the key to the economic revitalization of downtown Buffalo.

Stretching 1.2 miles through the city's central business district, it is the longest pedestrian/rail transit mall in North America. The idea is to stimulate foot traffic in the heart of the retail and entertainment blocks. Downtown Buffalo Management Corporation, the city hall agency created to maintain the cleanliness of the downtown area, also stimulates a variety of traffic-building events. These include A Taste of Buffalo, a weekend event each summer

when area restaurateurs offer their specialties in booths along Main Street, and Curtain Up!, the festive fall opening of all the theaters and nightclubs in the Theater District, complete with a formal dinner and live music under a tent right in the heart of the district.

Each of the six above-ground transit stations has a theme—such as the footlight ambience in the Theater District—while the eight underground stations, spanning Allen Street to the university's South Campus, offer a diverse blend of architecture, featuring a variety of artistic designs that make the system among the most aesthetically pleasing anywhere.

Beyond this 6.4-mile beginning, the overall success of the system is keyed to its future extensions. The corridors which studies have defined as offering the most potential include the Northern Corridors (consisting of the Amherst and Tonawandas extension), the Southtowns Corridor, and the Cheektowaga Corridor.

Studies have also shown that rapid transit has spurred private development in many cities across the U.S. and Canada. According to an NFTA report, the other advantages include:

Above: "A Taste of Buffalo" brings area restaurateurs and enthusiastic patrons downtown for an annual celebration of regional fare. Photo by Robert McElroy

Opposite: The fountain across from the NFTA terminal is a cool afternoon spot. Photo by Envisions Co.

—The attracting of new business and industry and the expansion of job opportunities.
—Enhancement of real estate values throughout the region.
—Removal of deteriorating or neglected properties.
—Accessibility to employment opportunities for the disadvantaged.
—Reduced travel time and cost.
—Significant energy savings.
—A broadening of tax bases.
—The demand on the market for labor, contractors, subcontractors, and services will create new programs to develop small and minority business enterprises.
—Planned future extensions to the initial line will create a continuing opportunity for an increased work force.
—A new sense of pride in the area as developments occur.

Indeed, the grand opening of the system in May 1985 surprised the many people who doubted the value of a transit system originally scheduled to go only 6.4 miles along Main Street. Those people who complained of the six years of construction inconveniences slowly began to realize the potential of the system to elevate Buffalo into the realm of such sophisticated subway cities

THE JOHN W. COWPER COMPANY, INC.

For more than 70 years, as Western New York's largest general contractor and construction manager, The John W. Cowper Company, Inc., has been responsible for building the Buffalo area's most impressive structures.

The firm was founded in 1915 by John Whitfield Cowper. Born in Suffolk, Virginia, in 1871, Cowper was a self-made man. He chose a challenging path to success through hard work and the high standards of personal integrity so

An interior view of the Summer-Best Street Underground Station of the Niagara Frontier Transportation Authority's Light Rapid Transit System.

necessary in the construction field.

The early years of the business linked the Cowper organization to Buffalo's best-known buildings. In 1921 the firm completed the construction of Foster Hall, the first structure on the campus of the University of Buffalo, now the State University of Buffalo. Seven years later Cowper was chosen to build a 28-story office and bank building for the then Marine Trust Company. In 1929 the company began work as the general contractor of the historic landmark, Buffalo City Hall.

The John W. Cowper Company was organized to furnish business and industry with complete ser-

Norstar Bank's corporate headquarters.

vice, from the birth of an idea through the planning and engineering stages, followed by the construction of a complete facility ready for operation. It has been a tenet of the firm to help its clients' ideas advance from the drawing board to reality.

Following this concept, the Cowper organization, in the 1960s, pioneered the relatively new field of construction management. This concept focuses on fulfilling the owner's needs by managing costs and schedules, and providing value engineering. This method provides the owner with the most cost-effective plan for the construction of a facility. The John W. Cowper Company is one of the largest construction managers in the nation.

Overall, the firm is engaged in general contracting, construction management, and building development. It has the personnel, equipment, and knowledge of all facets of the business and can perform any aspect of a project that a client may request.

During the 1960s and 1970s Cowper continued to carry out some of the most ambitious construction projects in the Buffalo area. Among its accomplishments

are the Buffalo City Court building, the Marine Midland Tower, the 80,000-seat Rich Stadium, the M & T Bank headquarters building, the Empire of America Federal Savings Bank building, and Main Place Mall in the downtown area.

Since 1980 Cowper has been responsible for a host of major projects, including the Norstar Bank Building, the Goldome bank corporate headquarters structure and renovation of its adjoining gold-leaf-domed building, and the tower addition and renovations to Buffalo General Hospital.

Cowper also was the major contractor for Buffalo's Light Rail Rapid Transit System, including construction of the LaSalle Street, Utica Street, and Summer-Best underground passenger stations; the Auditorium District, Seneca, Church, and Lafayette and Huron aboveground passenger stations and pedestrian malls; and several sections of the cut-and-cover rail tunnel.

In addition, Cowper has been named construction manager for Buffalo's new 20,000-seat downtown baseball stadium, Pilot Field, and has provided extensive pre-

construction services for the project.

The scope and diversity of the firm's construction activities are broad. It has built industrial and chemical-manufacturing plants, office buildings, shopping malls, schools, health care facilities, colleges, institutional buildings, correctional facilities, hotels, multiple housing units, power plants, railways, sewage treatment plants, Army cantonments, airplane hangars, highway bridges, research centers, and stadiums.

Cowper is active primarily in the Northeast, mid-Atlantic, and Midwest. It has completed projects throughout the United States.

Recognizing that the construction market will increasingly seek companies with a broad range of capabilities, resources, and sophistication of management skills, Cowper merged with Harrison Western Corporation of Denver, Colorado, in January 1984. As plans are formed for the future, the heritage, pride, and high professional standards of The John W. Cowper Company, Inc., will continue to be the principles that place it in the forefront of the construction industry.

The Marine Midland Center bank and office building.

Main Street sights include the grand old Goldome Bank building on the right and the new Goldome Center on the left. The spired Niagara-Mohawk building is in the background. Photo by Robert McElroy

BUFFALO URBAN RENEWAL AGENCY

THE CIMINELLI COMPANIES

Ciminelli Construction erected the 10-level addition to the Erie County Holding Center (at right), shown as part of a night-time Buffalo skyline.

Impact.

Condense the significance of The Ciminelli Companies into just one thought and that word perhaps comes closest to the target. For a quarter century Ciminelli has had an increasingly strong impact on the changing face of Western New York.

There is probably no single area in the region where Ciminelli has not carried out a construction or real estate development project contributing to local commercial and industrial progress. And, as the economic development of the Niagara Frontier continues to unfold, the Ciminelli name remains closely associated with the region's economic strides.

Some examples?

*In suburban Amherst, New York State's fastest-growing community, Ciminelli is moving ahead with development of a 56.2-acre mixed-use site near Essjay Road. Plans include creating a 30-acre office park.

*Also in Amherst, Ciminelli has taken the lead in developing more than a half-dozen other properties. These include One John James Audubon Parkway, where Ciminelli is developing a prestigious 22,000-square-foot office building in the heart of Audubon Office Park.

*In Buffalo, Ciminelli is planning to preserve the city's nearly century-old Cyclorama, a unique, 16-sided building that once housed the Grosvenor Library Reading Room. Plans call for converting the structure into a modern office building that will soon house Ciminelli corporate headquarters.

*Elsewhere in the city, Ciminelli recently completed construction of the Regional Energy Management Center for Niagara Mohawk Power Corp. Designed and constructed under Ciminelli management, the center houses a state-of-the-art complex used to monitor the utility's entire Western New York region.

*At Greater Buffalo International Airport, Ciminelli is developing Buffalo Air Cargo Center, a multimillion-dollar project on a 35-acre site. The center will be operated by Prior Aviation to speed the flow of bulk air cargo to and from aircraft.

Impressive undertakings, yet those are just a few of the scores of ambitious construction and real estate development projects that have been tackled by an organization that grew out of what was once a small residential contracting firm.

The Ciminelli organization's roots can be traced to Bond Con-

Frank L. Ciminelli, president of The Ciminelli Companies.

President Ronald Reagan dedicating Santa Maria Towers on September 12, 1984. The 11-story high rise was constructed by Frank L. Ciminelli Construction Co., Inc.

struction, a concrete and masonry firm that Frank L. Ciminelli helped found in 1954. Frank L. Ciminelli Construction Company—the first segment of what eventually became The Ciminelli Companies—was established little more than a half-dozen years later.

The new company soon cut its teeth on major projects such as construction of the $15-million Ford Motor Company Stamping Plant in Lackawanna. Since then, Ciminelli has participated in projects serving diverse needs ranging from industrial use, to health care, to transportation. They include the South Campus Station of Buffalo's Light Rail Rapid Transit System, downtown's Norstar Building, renovation of the North Grand Island Bridge (southbound), and the Santa Maria Towers high-rise, to name just a few.

In recent years Ciminelli has become increasingly involved in real estate development. Ciminelli Development Company was formed in 1982; Ciminelli Real Estate Corp., a brokerage firm, was established in 1985. Development and brokerage activities have been pursued largely in response to the dramatic increase in the number of businesses seeking to satisfy their long-term needs by using a reliable builder and developer.

The development of Goldome Park is a case in point. The site of a long-vacant high school, the 23-acre property was acquired by Ciminelli and subsequently transformed into a streamlined office complex for Goldome F.S.B., the nation's largest mutual savings bank. The key to the project was successfully executing a "fast-track" construction program specifically to meet the tenant's strict scheduling requirements.

Recognizing early the potential for developing "build-to-suit" space in the controlled environment of commercial or industrial-oriented business parks, Ciminelli developed Mid County Business Park in 1972. Mid County was among the area's first industrial parks. Ciminelli continues to operate the Orchard Park site, which

Goldome Park in Amherst was developed by Ciminelli on a 23-acre site near the Youngmann Memorial Highway.

features eight individual facilities on 40 acres.

Another example of business park development is the conversion of the former Acme supermarket headquarters and warehouse at Broadway and Bailey Avenue. The idle 340,000-square-foot building was subdivided for use by individual tenants who now employ much of the facility for a variety of light-industrial and commercial enterprises.

While growing substantially in its diversity and size (Ciminelli also has offices in Tampa, Florida, where it engages in construction and development), the organization has one characteristic unchanged over the years—its basic philosophy. Pronounced by Frank Ciminelli, it's a philosophy dictating that Ciminelli isn't out to be the biggest—just the best—and that its success rests on its ability to successfully meet client needs. It's a philosophy that's served Ciminelli well in the past—and one that promises a solid foundation as Ciminelli enters its second quarter-century.

as Toronto and Boston.

Far from being merely an expensive metropolitan toy, the Light Rail Rapid Transit System and the pedestrian mall today stand as thriving symbols of a city that is shedding the antiquity of a bygone industrial economy and is, at last, facing the wave of the future.

The Theater District and Other Showplaces

Downtown Buffalo was once an exciting place after dark. The premier nightclub was the Town Casino, with legendary local impresarios attracting some of the biggest names in show business. A typical ad for the nightspot would read like this one from April 4, 1949:

OPENING TONIGHT! SOPHIE TUCKER,
Last of the Red-Hot Mamas
with songs specially written by Jack Vellen

IN PERSON! ONE WEEK ONLY! Extra added attractions...

CHANDRA KALY DANCERS
World's Greatest Interpretive Dancers

CHARLIE KARTS
Wizard with the cards

GENE ARCADE
Sensational new singer

PLUS A HUGE ALL-STAR VAUDEVILLE SHOW

Billed as the "home of the revolving bar," the Chez Ami was also a popular supper club featuring a similar vaudevillian array.

Theatrically speaking, there was the Erlanger and Shea's Buffalo, a grand movie palace which often featured vaudevillian shows. Those who see reruns of the old Burns and Allen TV series will note that the curtain behind George and Gracie's routines at the end of each show prominently features the Shea's Buffalo name. They were among the headliners, as were such others as a young Frank Sinatra when he was appearing as the vocalist with Tommy Dorsey's band around 1940.

Movie theaters such as the 20th Century, Hippodrome, Great

Left: Shea's Buffalo is being restored to an earlier grandeur. Photo by Joseph M. Cascio

Below: Buffalo's Main Street Theater District is undergoing renovation to recapture the excitement of years gone by. Photo by Susan Gawlick

Stimm Associates, Inc.

The Buffalo City Court parking ramp was constructed well ahead of schedule due to an innovative method devised by Stimm Associates—the concrete slabs were poured from the top down!

All over Western New York, from the Erie Basin Marina to the Light Rail Rapid Transit System to dozens of roads and bridges, the sure hand of Stimm Associates has been at work. Yet the company's start in the construction industry came in the form of a first project that was somewhat less than glamorous: It built a garage.

In 1921 Howard F. Stimm, a civil engineer for the Erie Railroad, launched a general construction firm with two associates, incorporating it under the name of H.F. Stimm, Inc. The Great Depression raged during the company's infancy, but unlike many other businesses, Stimm held its own. Its early contracts were for building railroad tracks, trestles, and bridges. And as trains were the prime movers of goods during those days, Stimm construction was vital to the survival of the area's commerce and to its continued growth. This experience later won the firm the contract for the building of Penn Central's monumental Frontier Yard on Buffalo's east side.

Although it had been engaged to a small extent in mill construction and modernization for General Mills and Pillsbury, the company's work in the industrial market expanded greatly during World War II, paving the way for heavier industrial construction.

Fostering such diversification was the reorganization of H.F. Stimm, Inc., in 1958 to form a subsidiary, Stimm Associates, Inc. This division of the firm was designed to handle general contracting, while the parent company continued the engineering and development work. Both corporations were located in the Ellicott Square Building in downtown Buffalo until a 1970s move to the company's present location at 2572 Walden Avenue in Cheektowaga.

Expanding and growing ever stronger in the 1950s, Stimm Associates broke new ground when it was named one of the first contractors on the Niagara Thruway project. Displaying an unusual degree of skill, Stimm engineers constructed the so-called "bathtub" section of the thruway that passes under the International Railway Bridge adjacent to the Black Rock Canal. Built below water level, not only has the section never flooded, but it also paved the way for Stimm Associates to win a variety of major contracts in the public works field.

In 1967 the firm lost its venerable founder. After guiding the company for a half-century and achieving personal recognition as a leader in his field, Howard Stimm died at the age of 72. His entrepreneurial spirit, however, lives on.

In 1969, under the direction of its new president, B. Roy Ertell, Stimm Associates chartered a new affiliate, Stelco, Inc. Located on Walden Avenue just behind corporate headquarters, Stelco's job is to handle all of the company's construction and rigging equipment. And handle them it does. Found in its "modest toolsheds" are devices of all shapes and sizes, including earth-moving rigs, pan loaders, large bulldozers, excavation equipment, a family of back hoes and graders, waterworking equipment, and even barges.

Stimm Associates has put this equipment to work in a variety of ways on a variety of projects. In the area of roads and bridges, the firm is responsible for building the North Grand Island "sister" bridge, two sections of the Kensington Expressway, and through joint ventures, two sections of the Aurora Expressway and portions of the LaSalle Expressway. Further proving the skill of its "bridge

game" was its construction of the double-loop Scajaquada Expressway pedestrian overpass. But perhaps the company's most famous bridge-related feat was raising a 360-foot truss span on the Peace Bridge to replace main bearings. What made the accomplishment remarkable, in addition to the ingenuity and daring of the job, was the fact that Stimm Associates was able to do it without stopping traffic.

Innovations of other kinds have also marked the firm's progress over the years. In 1972 Stimm Associates built the first precast, post-tension concrete structure in the area when it constructed the $3.3-million, 240,000-square-foot City Court parking ramp on Niagara Square. Another company milestone was the Pillsbury flour mill complex. Damaged in an explosion, the structure was completely renovated by Stimm Associates.

One of the few local firms to build tunnels, Stimm Associates has bored under Buffalo in a big way; using a special boring machine from Switzerland, the firm bored 1,500 feet out in the Niagara River to construct a raw water intake tunnel for the Erie County Water Authority. More recently, the company used special equipment to cut through the limestone underlying Main Street in order to build a portion of the Light Rail Rapid Transit line for the Niagara Frontier Transportation Authority. Stimm Associates and its joint-venture partner were given the tasks of constructing two 500-foot platforms out of solid rock, then connecting those platforms with a main escalator shaft to the above-ground College Station at Main and Delavan.

However, tunnels aren't the only unusual thing the company has been called on to build. It also had the chance to emulate nature in building a lake on the campus of the State University of New York at Buffalo. To do so, all it

The lighthouse is a striking part of the beautiful Erie Basin Marina, a project completely constructed by Stimm Associates.

had to do was "dig a hole." But in this case, the hole contained more than one million cubic yards of earth, which had to then be moved and stockpiled for later use in shaping the college campus.

Today Stimm Associates, Inc., is one of the largest general contracting companies in Western New York, with clients throughout the region, the Southern Tier, Syracuse, Canada, and Rochester. Annual sales top $25 million, and Stimm employs 30 engineers, architects, and others in its permanent office staff and up to 300 people from the building trades.

Stimm's skilled construction work covers the entire gamut— earth moving, foundation piling, structural concrete, engineering and design, installation and rigging, steelwork and masonry, electrical, plumbing, heating, and other finishing work.

From humble beginnings some 65 years ago as a small railroad contractor, Stimm Associates, Inc., has played a major role in progress seen across the Niagara Frontier. It is a company that has built the roads and bridges we need, the furnaces and mills that fuel our economy, and the parks we love. And it has built them well.

Above: A snowstorm wraps Buffalo in a soft glow. Photo by Robert McElroy

Opposite, top: The 1984-1985 production of Anything Goes was a joyous bright spot in the Studio Arena Theatre's season. Courtesy, Studio Arena Theatre.

Opposite, bottom: A Chorus Line dazzled audiences in Buffalo's refurbished Theater District. Photo by Joe Traver

Next page: Main Street is being spruced up in an effort to attract patrons to a glittering new Theater District. Photo by Joseph M. Cascio

ECOLOGY AND ENVIRONMENT, INC.

E & E specialists performing a detailed engineering characterization of the disposal lagoon as part of the $50-million project to clean up the Bridgeport, New Jersey, Superfund site.

"Not long ago, we thought of the environment simply as natural surroundings, and of ecology as the study of the interrelations between wildlife and those surroundings. Now that advanced technology has brought together increasing numbers of scientists of many disciplines to achieve a common understanding of ecological processes, we have a much more comprehensive view of ecology. That view transcends physical and biological considerations to encompass the totality of man and the environment, including his socioeconomic well-being and health."

With this philosophy, Gerhard J. Neumaier joined with Frank B. Silvestro, Gerald A. Strobel, P.E., and Ronald A. Frank in 1970 to found Ecology and Environment, Inc. Under their continuous leadership, E & E now operates worldwide to combat problems of environmental degradation. Its staff of 600 represents 70 scientific and engineering disciplines.

While serious problems of air and water pollution still exist, contamination of groundwater resources by spills of hazardous materials and disposal of hazardous chemical wastes has become the nation's primary environmental concern. E & E has employed its multidisciplinary capabilities to analyze the hazards and risks of handling natural gas, petroleum, petrochemicals, toxic materials, and other hazardous substances since 1972. E & E's analyses assist design engineers in site and facility planning, and help management to reduce the risk to employees and the public from processing, transporting, and storing hazardous materials. Its spill emergency response services have been mustered to respond to several thousand incidents involving petroleum products and hazardous chemicals in all 50 states.

Company specialists have investigated more than 5,000 hazardous waste disposal sites for industrial and government clients across the United States and Canada. They review current conditions, determine the extent of contamination, and design and manage engineering programs to mitigate problems. The firm also provides long-term monitoring of air and water quality. Such services are offered to owner/operators of underground storage tanks, as well, as part of a federal program to control pollution from leaking tanks. E & E also manages the removal of asbestos installed in buildings.

E & E's field efforts are supported by its Analytical Services Center in Cheektowaga. Its laboratories are fully equipped to assess the chemical and biological attributes of air, water, and soil samples in compliance with government regulations. It assists industry to obtain required air

quality and wastewater discharge permits, and conducts waste treatability studies.

E & E has conducted environmental studies for projects ranging from the construction of the massive Trans Alaska Pipeline System to the transformation of Buffalo's Main Post Office into Erie Community College. Besides its work throughout North America, E & E has served clients in Puerto Rico, Trinidad, Bolivia, Colombia, Venezuela, the Ivory Coast, Saudi Arabia, Qatar, Indonesia, and Japan. The company is building its new, environmentally sophisticated world headquarters at 368 Pleasant View Drive in Lancaster.

E & E conducts hydrogeological studies at hazardous waste disposal sites throughout the United States, such as this one in southern Illinois.

Lakes, Vogue, Shea's Teck, and Basil's Lafayette attracted many downtown. Jazz clubs such as the Royal Arms were also a big part of nightlife, featuring some of the genre's biggest names such as Buddy Rich and Lionel Hampton.

Into the 1960s and 1970s, however, the bright lights of downtown went out one by one, until many of these entertainment venues became a sad array of vacant and dilapidated buildings. They were victims of the mass exodus from downtown after sundown, a result of ghetto fears and the suburban pull. Just about the only staple of downtown nightlife was the Studio Arena Theatre, which occupied the former Town Casino at 681 Main Street from 1965 to 1978.

Again, the blizzard seemed to be a dividing line between the depths and a new horizon. The resurgence of nightlife actually began very slowly several months prior to the snow disaster. The Friends of Shea's Buffalo Theatre mightily volunteered their efforts to restore the grand movie palace back to its former glory days. When the theater opened in 1926, it was hailed across the nation as one of the country's grandest theatrical palaces. Indeed, the regal accoutrements—from the palatial lobby to the dazzling chandelier above the audience—were breathtaking. After decades of legendary live performances and movie premieres, the Shea's of the 1970s had a crumbling interior and a program of cheap kung-fu movies.

After the yeoman efforts of the volunteer group, the first stage of restoration was completed. The grand reopening occurred on the theater's fiftieth anniversary in an extravaganza appropriately headlined by the ageless George Burns who fondly recalled his frequent Shea's performances with Gracie.

A year after the blizzard, the Studio Arena Theatre moved from

Opposite: Theatergoers enjoy before- and after-theater dining at Theater Place. Photo by Melissa C. Beckman

Right: Workmen put finishing touches on the award-winning Prudential Building. Photo by Joseph M. Cascio

its quarters in the old Town Casino location to a larger, more modern theater across the street which formerly housed the Palace Burlesk, the nation's last new burlesque house when it opened in the mid-1960s.

In October 1979 Precinct Three headquarters of the Buffalo Police Department moved into the old Greyhound Bus Terminal, recently vacated due to the opening of the new NFTA Terminal several blocks south. The precinct move helped maintain a greater police presence along the block, making the area safer for strolling theatergoers.

Mayor Griffin's administration began to refer to the block as the Theater District and vowed to return it to its former prominence. Millions of dollars of publicly supported investment in the area

John Chew
Developments Limited

An exterior view of the Lake Front Commons, an $8-million, 78-town house development, with Buffalo City Hall in the background (to the right).

John Chew, a highly successful entrepreneur with a notable renovation of one of Buffalo's historic mansions to his credit, has recently undertaken a major construction program on Buffalo's waterfront.

His initial venture was to purchase and completely restore the 90-year-old former Birge mansion at Two Symphony Circle near Kleinhans Music Hall. He maintains offices in the Birge building and also leases space to several companies.

Chew's new project involves the construction of what eventually will be 78 town houses on the Buffalo waterfront. The Birge renovation, coupled with the town house construction program, will represent a total investment of more than nine million dollars.

Other property developments under way include a marina on the mighty Niagara River in Fort Erie, Ontario, Canada, and the future calls for yet another Buffalo waterfront development that will include rental properties.

Chew's company, John Chew Developments Limited, acquired the Birge mansion when it was put on the auction block by the City of Buffalo on April 8, 1982.

Its previous owner had failed to pay an accumulation of $44,602.57 in back taxes, including city taxes dating back to 1975, county taxes, and even $19.68 for the city's ill-fated 1976 occupancy tax. The bidding opened at the exact amount owed in taxes and, with no other bidders, an offer of $45,000 by Chew and Richard Hardoby was accepted. Chew is now the sole owner, and he and his wife currently occupy one of two town houses on the property.

Construction of the mansion was initiated back in 1890 by George Birge, president of Birge Wallpaper Company and co-founder of the former Pierce Arrow Motor Car Company. In 1938 the Birge family sold the mansion to the Sisters of Divine Child for use as a convent and school. The Buffalo Elks Lodge 23 purchased the building in 1957; that organization in turn sold it to the Richmond Land Company in 1974.

Chew first became interested in the mansion while jogging along Richmond Avenue. Because of the vandalism and small fires that had been set inside, the building had fallen into disrepair. In addition, portions of the structure, such as brass hardware and marble mantels, had been stolen. "I would go running by, and it appeared that something should be done," Chew says: "After a while, it gnaws at you."

Architect John Kloch of John Edward Kloch Associates was given the task of designing the plans to restore the mansion to its original state. Because the building is in the Allentown Historic District, it is automatically on the National Register of Historic Buildings. As a result, renovation and repairs must be conducted under strict guidelines.

Plaster cornices and moldings in the rooms had to be skillfully recreated by local craftsmen. Original filigree plaster ceilings had to

The Birge mansion on Symphony Circle in Buffalo. This national historic building restoration by John Chew Development Limited is an architectural award-winning restoration.

be cleaned to specifications, and French doors were repaired and refinished. The loggia, a two-story enclosed courtyard, is where one tenant currently houses his showroom of computer equipment. On the second floor, eight Tuscan-order columns surround the oval room. Other rooms renovated include the drawing room, library, and dining room.

The restoration of the Birge mansion is significant in that it has had an uplifting effect on West Side residents. Old, quality buildings, some say, influence the quality of life in the neighborhood, providing a sense of continuity and history—a way of measuring accomplishments through the decades. In another sense, Chew points out, the 25-percent investment tax credit that the federal government allows for the restoration and preservation of significant structures doesn't make restoring a bargain option, but it can make it a viable one.

Chew, a mechanical engineer, approaches his waterfront residential development with extensive experience gained in marketing positions with the Carborundum Company in Niagara Falls and with J.H. Williams Industrial Products, Inc., in Buffalo. He also held a marketing and engineering position with General Motors Corporation's Harrison Radiator Division in Lockport, New York.

The Lake Front town house development that Chew is building on the waterfront is on the last tract of undeveloped, privately owned land between the Peace Bridge and the Naval and Servicemen's Park. The six-acre site is adjacent to the existing Waterfront Village housing development. Plans call for the construction of 78 town houses, with the first phase to be completed in 1986. They will be compatible with existing housing in the area.

The brick town homes will have either two or three bedrooms

An interior view from a town house living room overlooking the lake.

with central air-conditioning; wood-burning fireplaces; a fully equipped kitchen complete with range, dishwasher, garbage disposal, and refrigerator; and an attached two-car garage. The dwellings will also be prewired for security systems.

The first phase will consist of 20 town houses, followed by a second phase of 30 units and a final phase of 28. They were designed by John Edward Kloch Associates and are being built by CCC Construction Company, Inc., of North Tonawanda. The firm of Holcberg, Deck and Cohen, Limited, is the sole sales agent for the Lake Front Commons development.

The homes are priced from $89,000 to $115,000. The cost, substantially lower than other comparable dwellings in the immediate waterfront area, is attributed to the town houses' slightly smaller size, as well as to low-interest financing from the city. The Buffalo Development Companies provided a loan of $465,000 at 4-percent interest, well below going rates. In addition, the city will build a roadway connecting the six-acre town house site with Lakefront Boulevard in Waterfront Village.

This project is just one example of John Chew Development Limited's commitment to the development of Buffalo—a commitment that also reflects its founder's pride in the city's rich and colorful past.

Winter brings a stark beauty to Delaware Park. Photo by Melissa C. Beckman

Holcberg, Deck & Cohen, Ltd.

The real estate brokerage firm of Holcberg, Deck & Cohen, Ltd., put out its shingle in early 1984. At a time when many businesses were choosing to close their doors in Buffalo, Carole Z. Holcberg, Joseph A. Deck, and Ronald S. Cohen chose to open theirs.

Combining their individual expertise, Holcberg, a real estate broker; Deck, a developer, and Cohen an attorney, formed a company based on an energetic commitment to the redevelopment of the city and strong belief that they could play a key role in helping to make it happen.

In less than three years the company has become a leader in the city real estate industry. The 32 associates of the firm have earned a reputation as creative innovative marketers of not only commercial and residential properties, but of the city as well.

As distinctive as the firm's attractive red and white signs, are the details and attentiveness Holcberg, Deck & Cohen, Ltd., pays to each property it exclusively represents. From the written history of the property to the original pen and ink drawing by noted Buffalo artist B.J. Rooney presented to each new owner, the firm is steadfast in providing the utmost in service. The epitome of Holcberg, Deck & Cohen, Ltd.'s, belief in a revitalized Buffalo is the company's headquarters at 355 Linwood Avenue. Once a dilapidated brick castle-like carriage house at the rear of an overgrown field, the building has been gutted, renovated, and superbly landscaped, complete with moat and bridge!

Following suit, the company has been involved in the marketing and or leasing of many of Buffalo's most exciting recent commercial real estate developments, including the historic renovation of the former Knights of Columbus on Delaware Avenue; 392 Fountain Plaza, which formerly housed Leonardo's restaurant; the former Hermans Sporting Goods building on Main Street; Theater Place; and the Clinton House Complex on Franklin and North streets.

Located in a carriage house that was once part of the Satterfield estate, the headquarters of Holcberg, Deck & Cohen offers clients a comfortable, unique setting in which to conduct business. Illustration by B.J. Rooney

Holcberg, Deck & Cohen, Ltd.'s, residential division is the exclusive agent for the sale of Lake Front Commons townhouses, Buffalo's most successful waterfront development. In addition, the firm has represented many of Buffalo's finest homes. From the time a prospective tenant, purchaser, landlord, or seller has the initial appointment with a Holcberg, Deck & Cohen associate to the consummation of the transaction, the same high levels of professionalism, energetic creativity, and time investment are put into a $300 a month apartment or office as are put into a million-dollar building or fabulous estate.

Among the firm's successful sales is the 4 Symphony Circle residence. Illustration by B.J. Rooney

One of the firm's many properties is 392 Fountain Plaza, an exciting new office complex. Illustration by B.J. Rooney

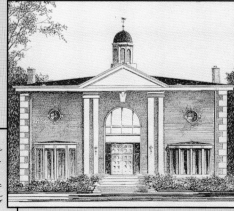

followed. Buildings that were beyond repair were torn down. Renovations were begun on those buildings that were still architecturally sound and significant.

As the 1980s dawned, brighter nightlife prospects began to develop. A number of investors saw the potential. New restaurants opened. A few intimate theaters opened. A handful of bars and nightclubs opened. Through the bulldozing state of transition, some of these pioneers of the renaissance weren't able to hang in there. Other newcomers such as the popular Tralfamadore nightclub continue to brighten downtown. And still others continue to make such plans.

For example, there's the Market Arcade, a structure built in 1892 as upstate New York's first indoor shopping mall. Plans call to convert this boarded-up building into a new complex with three tiers of restaurants, nighttime entertainment, and specialty shops. The upper two floors would include shops where artists and craftsmen would display their works and demonstrate their talents to visitors.

The project also includes an eight-screen General Cinema

The light-rail rapid transit system has brought commuters back to downtown. Photo by Joe Traver

CIR Electrical Construction Corporation

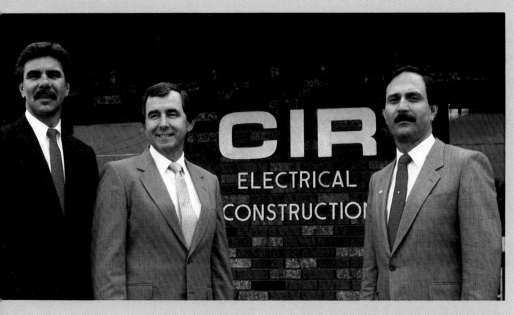

Standing in front of corporate headquarters at 1067 Harlem Road, George R. Schlemmer (right), president and treasurer of CIR Electrical Construction Corporation, is joined in management by partners John L. Chmura (left), executive vice-president, and secretary, and John A. Siuta (center), vice-president.

Starting in 1976 with a $10,000 loan from the late Beatrice L. Schlemmer, CIR Electrical Construction Corporation was formed and has proven itself a bona fide Buffalo success story. Today the company has its own building on Harlem Road in Buffalo and a second office in Niagara Falls, employs an inside office staff of 20, and keeps as many as 150 workers at a time busy on projects all over Western New York.

CIR (the letters stand for Commercial-Industrial-Residential) founder and partner George R. Schlemmer started the business with the conviction that Western New York had room for a new face in the electrical construction field. The fledgling firm's original office was in a small building on Center Street in Hamburg, but as CIR grew, it moved to Seneca Street in West Seneca, and finally to its present 16,000-square-foot location in 1982. Today Schlemmer, the company's president, is joined in management by partners John Chmura, who serves as executive vice-president, and John Siuta, the firm's vice-president.

A number of features make CIR stand out in the electrical construction field. For starters, it's one of the few companies in Western New York to still operate service trucks. In CIR's case, it runs four vehicles, each radio dispatched and operated by qualified journeymen electricians. Energy management is another aspect of the business with which CIR stays completely up to date. Installations range from high-voltage systems to telephone interconnect. And as a value-added service to its customers, the firm also offers a complete design-build capability.

The commitment to service that these practices represent is summarized by the company's no-punches-pulled philosophy of "customer satisfaction comes first and service is our main objective." And judging by CIR's client list, it has taken the right path. Corporations for whom the firm has done work include most of the major local supermarket chains, AM & A's department stores, Fisher-Price, Buffalo Trotting, Westwood Pharmaceuticals, M. Wile, New York Telephone, M&T Bank, Norstar Bank, the Erie County Water Authority, General Motors, Niagara Mohawk, Dunlop Tires, NYSEG, and a number of local malls and school systems, to mention a few.

A typical CIR job has many facets. The CIR project manager, often one of the firm's principals, works with the customer and/or general contractor to coordinate the electrical installation. The project manager will purchase and arrange delivery of supplies ranging from lighting systems and electrical distribution equipment, to conduit and wire. In the recently completed McKinley Mall project in which it acted as the prime electrical contractor, CIR was responsible for all site lighting, building power, fire alarm, temperature control, and a number of specialized lighting systems.

CIR is also a company that is active in the community. Schlemmer has served as president of the National Electrical Contractors Association of Western New York for a number of years; he also served as a director on the Northeast-Midwest alliance of management and labor for the Upstate New York chapter. And the firm itself is active on behalf of the United Way, Catholic Charities, and the Buffalo Philharmonic Orchestra. In short, CIR Electrical Construction Corporation is proud to call Western New York home.

complex on the north side of the arcade and a new hotel, most likely a Day's Inn, on the corner of Chippewa Street.

Surrounding this district are the sweeping new Goldome and Liberty Bank buildings which were erected several years ago and, to the south, the renovated Prudential Building—the Louis Sullivan treasure that was restored to its former magnificence at the turn of this decade. The Buffalo Convention Center, Hyatt Hotel, and more continue to raise the quality of downtown.

For an area that looked like anything but the heart of the city just a decade ago, downtown Buffalo is coming back with a force that rivals any metropolitan area of the 1980s.

"Talking Proud" and Talking Realistic

No doubt about it. The "Talking Proud" marketing campaign launched a few years after the blizzard helped bring Buffalo out from under piles of snow. The high-stepping jingle even made it on

Buffalonians were talking proud as the 1980s began. Photo by Robert McElroy

a Monday Night Football telecast featuring the Buffalo Bills.

In fact, the "Talking Proud" campaign, created by the Buffalo advertising agency of Healy-Schutte & Company, was closely aligned to the playoff-bound Bills in 1980 under coach Chuck Knox. The city promotion was a sleek, modernized extension of the old "Boost Buffalo" campaign of the 1960s. The reasoning behind "Talking Proud" was that there was no better marketing to

*For some Buffalo residents a bliz-
zard is just rollicking good fun.
Photo by Joe Traver*

capitalize upon than a ride on the coattails of a successful major-
league sports team. The home team.

After Knox left and the Bills' fortunes went on the downswing,
such marketing was withheld until a significant portion of the city's
rebuilding was completed, and until Buffalo again had a contending major-league sports team.

Still, community boosterism continues to infiltrate many sectors
around the country. Educational institutions and new and expanding high-tech firms continue to feed diversification. The old
stereotypes seem to be breaking down further every day.

Besides, as one city official put it after the national attention
prompted by the blizzard, the important thing was not what people
said about the city, but that they were talking about the city. And
the talk these days is definitely proud.

CHAPTER FIVE

The Unconventional Convention Site

Buffalo as a convention town? To all the cynics, that once seemed about as unlikely as balmy days in January. Over the past decade, however, the rise of convention centers across the country has been staggering. Municipalities have been dazzled by the economic impact that national and regional conventions can generate, not to mention the more locally oriented events such as trade shows, business meetings, and social affairs.

Because economic belts have tightened across the nation, many companies and social organizations find that they can no longer afford the typical convention towns like Las Vegas, Miami Beach, Los Angeles, New York City, or Chicago. To cut the cost of plane fare as well as the substantial expenses of such "name" cities, many are opting for closer, more reasonably priced alternatives. Yet, at the same time they seek a convention site that offers accessibility and comfort with an interesting array of entertainment and attractions. Buffalo wanted to be such a site. First, though, it needed a convention center.

For years, the Statler Hotel on Delaware Avenue provided that center for business meetings, small conventions, and fancy dress balls. The lobby stroller could catch glimpses of all such functions at one time or another.

When William D. Hassett assumed ownership in the 1970s, he renovated the hotel's lounge, renamed it Statler Downtown, and brought big-name jazz back to the city. Such lively septuagenarians

Opposite: A power boat makes its way upriver along the waterfront. Photo by Dennis R. Floss

Opposite: The distinctive Buffalo City Hall glows at dusk. Photo by Robert McElroy

as Earl "Fatha" Hines and Joe Venuti—the fathers of modern jazz piano and violin, respectively—often played the intimate room, as well as such younger but no less vital figures as Stan Getz and Modern Jazz Quartet members John Lewis and Milt Jackson. Hassett even began a nationally distributed record label offering such greats as Tony Bennett, Bill Evans, and Marian McPartland recorded live in performance at the Downtown Room.

When Hassett sold his interest in the hotel and the Hilton association left, the new owners eventually embarked on a renovation plan that converted the downtown landmark into a modernized office building called Statler Towers. After all, the size of the facility could never really seriously compete with the space options of an actual convention center in accommodating major conventions into the city.

Therefore, it was decided that the building of the Buffalo Convention Center downtown was a necessity. From its opening in 1978 through the mid-1980s, the Buffalo Convention Center functioned primarily as a community center for various trade shows, regional business gatherings, social affairs, and everyday business meetings. As such, it has served as a needed focal point of downtown activity.

Now, with the addition of over 1,200 hotel rooms downtown and a total of over 3,000 within a half-hour drive, the center is primed for major national conventions. Slowly, the convention center is beginning to realize the purpose of its name.

Although its location right in the heart of downtown has not made nearby parking particularly plentiful, the opening of the rapid transit line—situated just a block east—continues to help alleviate the crunch by allowing visitors to use parking ramps all along the downtown route. Plus, more parking ramps are slated to be built around the new downtown baseball stadium currently in progress. Added to that are the shuttle buses that the various hotels operate to accommodate conventioneers.

And, of course, the Buffalo Convention Center is just steps away from the new pedestrian mall, offering visitors a delightful opportunity to exit a convention event and almost immediately encounter the festive atmosphere of sidewalk merchants and outdoor events that will increasingly populate the mall area.

The Chamber's Convention Push

The Convention and Tourism Bureau, an independent organization, helped the city solicit business for the Buffalo Convention Center when it opened in 1979. However a small staff and a

The Hyatt is an impressive redevelopment of a landmark downtown structure. Photo by Peter R. Barber

Above: The new Hyatt Regency will add important hotel rooms downtown. Photo by Susan Gawlick

Right: New light rail rapid transit cars pass the beautiful Goldome Bank. Photo by Peter R. Barber

City Hall and the city court building flank the Mohawk parking ramp. Photo by Envisions Co.

miniscule budget severely hampered their efforts.

In 1980 the Buffalo Area Chamber of Commerce (as it was then known) saved the organization from folding by taking it under its wing. It was renamed the Convention and Tourism Group. William Hanbury was put in charge to pull together the human and financial resources necessary to make a serious attempt at convention solicitation.

From 1981 through the present, a slow but steady progression has been realized each year. "Buffalo is a sleeper," assessed Roger L. Schutt, who has been vice president of the group over the past year. "It hasn't realized its full potential in the convention and tourism markets. Because the industry is still in its infancy here, we could not compete as effectively with other destinations that had budget, staff, and resources considerably larger than ours. To be more competitive, we need more people out there selling the area, better audio-visual materials, better marketing resource materials, and we need to be at more trade shows and events. Basically, we need to be more visible and do more face-to-face selling."

With the combined efforts of the Chamber group, the Convention Center staff, and the various hotel marketing staffs, there have been over 100 conventions held in Greater Buffalo in 1986. Schutt would like to see the growth pattern average 15 percent each year.

The resources that the Convention and Tourism Group uses in

Above: The convention center houses frequent trade shows, such as the annual computer expo, sponsored by the Greater Buffalo Chamber of Commerce in conjunction with Southex Exhibitions. Courtesy, Greater Buffalo Chamber of Commerce

Right: The Buffalo Convention Center's modern interior and complete facilities provide a range of services. Courtesy, Greater Buffalo Chamber of Commerce

Opposite: The McKinley Monument is illuminated by night on Niagara Square. Photo by Dennis R. Floss

"Once they've been here and are somewhat surprised by all the things we have, our chances are very, very good that we will win the convention bid."

Ms. Evans added that tapping a local support group often leads to regional or even national convention business. For example, Herb Knoll, president of Buffalo/Niagara Sales and Marketing Executives, wanted to interest the national arm of the organization in holding its convention in Buffalo in 1988.

In order to outbid such places as Houston and New Orleans, Mr. Knoll felt the need to do an extended marketing push for the city. Before the general convention in the summer of 1985, he had an audio tape produced focusing on the advantages of the city as a convention site. This was sent ahead before the Buffalo delegation's arrival. Then, when they arrived, they had a strong video presentation to complement the audio tape they had presumably already heard. To top off the presentation, Mayor James Griffin and County Executive Edward Rutkowski made guest appearances at the convention, pushing the wonders of Buffalo.

Going all out with the elaborately produced presentations and the live appearances of two top officials from Buffalo so impressed the

Left and right: Honeymooners and families can't resist the fascination of a trip to Niagara Falls. Photos by Joe Traver

Below: Buffalonians sip drinks and watch the city slip by as the Miss Buffalo makes its way up the Black Rock canal. Photo by Joe Traver

HYATT REGENCY BUFFALO

The new $40-million Hyatt Regency Buffalo stands out as a modern-day example of splendor in the resurgence of downtown Buffalo, thanks in large measure to the Hyatt Hotels Corporation and Buffalo entrepreneur Paul L. Snyder. The 400-room facility is owned by Snyder interests and managed by Hyatt.

A unique architectural triumph, the Hyatt Regency Buffalo combines the 16-story French Renaissance style of the former Genesee Building with a new 11-story tower and a 5-story glass and steel atrium. When the hotel opened on February 15, 1984, it marked the first time in the nation's history that a

The 400-room Hyatt Regency Buffalo, which opened in February 1984, marked the first time in the United States that a large office building had been converted into a luxury hotel.

large office building had been converted into a luxury hotel. Oddly enough, hotels had occupied the corner of Main and Genesee streets since the beginning of the nineteenth century.

It is more than coincidence that the Hyatt Regency is located across from the Convention Center, which is scheduled to be connected to the hotel via a glass-enclosed skywalk. The hotel also conveniently abuts the surface section of the Light Rail Rapid Transit System along Main Street.

The Hyatt Regency Buffalo's 400 guest rooms range from singles to multiroom luxury suites. The seventh floor is reserved for nonsmoking guests. In addition, there are nine rooms on floors three through 11 equipped for the handicapped. Health-related facilities include a rooftop glass-enclosed swimming pool and whirlpool, an

exercise room, and a sauna.

The Hyatt Regency Buffalo offers to its guests an array of dining experiences. E.B. Green's is a 120-seat specialty restaurant with an open-hearth kitchen and wine room. It was named for the late Edward B. Green, architect of the Genesee Building.

The Bakery Restaurant, located in the atrium, features fresh-baked delicacies and unique food offerings, from early-morning breakfast to late-night snacks. It is supplemented by The Cafe Petit. The Sun Garden Lounge on the mezzanine overlooks the atrium, Main Street, and the Rapid Transit line.

The two top floors of the hotel house the Regency Club, separated by a special elevator with a pass key for privacy. The Regency Club is devoted to luxury service and is called a hotel within a hotel. It features concierge service, a private lounge, continental breakfast, and other amenities.

The Hyatt Regency Buffalo can accommodate large groups for special occasions. The Grand Ballroom, with its 16-foot ceiling, can seat up to 1,000 people for banquets and about 2,000 for receptions. It is the largest hotel ballroom in Western New York. Also on the mezzanine level are the Regency Ballroom and Niagara Room. In addition, there are six meeting rooms of varying sizes and two boardrooms.

The development and construction of the Hyatt Regency Buffalo provided a unique opportunity for students at the Cornell University School of Hotel Administration to observe and become involved in the early stages of the development of a major hotel. In a sense, the facility became a real-life learning laboratory for the students.

139

Right: A balloon festival adds color to Darien Lake amusement park. Photo by Joe Traver

Opposite, top, left: Two girls, laden with balloons, walk down Delaware Avenue during the annual Allentown Art Festival. Photo by Joe Traver

Opposite, top right: The rising sun casts a brilliant light on the docks of the Buffalo Yacht Club. Photo by Dennis R. Floss

Opposite, bottom: Sailboats pass the Coast Guard Lighthouse in a Wednesday Night Regatta. Photo by Gertrude M. Maloney

organization that the decision was made for the Queen City in 1988.

"There's nothing like having a local hometown hero to sell the city for us," according to Ms. Evans. "That's how we've won several conventions over the past year."

Currently, the Greater Buffalo Chapter of the American Red Cross is attempting to bring the organization's national convention here in 1992. The local Red Cross chapter was among those groups that prefer to take a more aggressive leadership role in soliciting convention business for the area, using the resources of the Greater Buffalo Chamber of Commerce's Convention & Tourism Group for coordinating support. The chapter produced a videotape presentation introducing their national board in Washington, D.C., to Greater Buffalo's scenic treasures and urban renewal, also reminding them how significantly the local chapter serves not only the community but the entire organization. The presentation reportedly was received very well, turning a number of heads in Buffalo's direction.

Working in unison with the Greater Buffalo Chamber of Commerce Convention & Tourism Division and local hotels, Lynn Evans solicits a wide variety of business, from the national level to the regional, including trade shows.

In addition to wining and dining a group representative, the convention solicitors tailor wining/dining packages to the convention delegates and their spouses. They arrange special tours of the area to fit the interests of a particular group, introducing the visitors to anything from a big-league hockey game to a tour of the Fisher-Price toymaking operation. Ultimately, those wide-ranging options convince the convention solicitees that Buffalo is anything but boring—a particularly important point to those spouses accompanying delegates.

Just how valuable is a major convention to the area? "Very valuable," replied Ms. Evans. "From hotel rooms to meals to shopping to entertainment to the use of the convention center itself, the average total per day comes to over a hundred dollars spent by each delegate."

As an example, she said that when the annual convention of the National Organization for Women (NOW) comes to Buffalo in 1988, about 3,000 people from around the country will congregate, spending approximately $300,000 in the area.

A Tough Marketplace

The general consensus is that the new and improved Buffalo has every right to realize the potential of convention business. Naturally,

A solitary runner takes advantage of the last rays of the setting sun. Photo by Joe Traver

the competition is fierce. Lynn Evans, among others, is out there in the field seeking what is known as multi-property business. That is, those conventions that need more than one hotel to house its delegates.

Anyone who has lived in Greater Buffalo for a while knows how much farther their dollar can go. This is a point that does not escape the cost-conscious convention planner. "Many associations and regional meeting groups just don't have the money," explained Ms. Evans. "In many instances, the delegate will have to pay for his own hotel room or has to pay the cost of attending this meeting. That's when they become particularly price-conscious. And that's where Buffalo succeeds. We are one of the least expensive convention destinations in the country."

A group is likely to come to an area where the largest local support group is located. "If over 50 percent of a group's membership is in New York City," reasoned Ms. Evans, "they're going to much prefer to hold their convention there, rather than spend a lot on plane fare and travel." Accessibility is a prime attraction of Greater Buffalo, she claims, particularly for state groups. Still, despite the low cost, accessibility, and the surprising variety of interesting sights, how weighty is that negative image of Buffalo to the uninformed?

"Ten years ago, I might have said the same thing, 'Are you crazy? Hold my convention in Buffalo?'," acknowledged Ms. Evans. "Now I simply say 'Come and see.' If somebody has that negative image, I really urge them to come see for themselves."

When visitors do come to the city they are impressed by the tremendous construction going on. They see Buffalo's commitment to growth, and realize the city truly is a work in progress. By the time of their convention (usually three to five years from that first visit) the new Buffalo will be ready and waiting.

Anticipation

Buffalo has hastened to add hotel rooms to accommodate the anticipated influx of conventioneers. The Hyatt Regency, the Buffalo Hilton, and the new Day's Inn form the new hotel nucleus of the 1980s downtown.

While convention bookings have not yet acheived the high levels they are expected to reach, the trade show business has grown significantly.

"We're now doing about thirty shows a year," said Melvin P. Florczak, director of the convention center, "which not only draw many thousands in attendance, but also make use of hotel rooms,

143

A farmer feeds his sheep in Elma, just outside of Buffalo. Photo by Joe Traver

because many of those involved come in from out of town and stay overnight." The trade shows range from the computer technology shows to home shows in which an entire model home is constructed right on the main exhibition floor.

There's no denying that a steady stream of major conventions can do wonders for the local economy. People like Lynn Evans try to convey to the outside world what insiders already know: that Buffalo is really a charming, homey, colorful place, with wide appeal.

An aggressive marketing campaign—one that's consistent, creative, and very targeted—must be devised to get that word out, to fight that uphill battle against images of the weather, to fight the misconception of a dying industrial town, and to emphasize more of the artistic value, the educational expanse, the rise of the medical, financial, and high-tech industries here. The icing on the cake is the rapid transit system and a pedestrian mall to compete with the sophistication of all the other major metropolitan areas around the country.

The Greater Buffalo arts and tourism industries have joined together to create a "cultural/tourism" action plan using the area's cultural resources to attract more visitors. Sandra S. Hillman, the person most often credited with the resurgence of Baltimore, has been hired as a consultant to the project. She and a steering committee of ten representatives from the arts, tourism, and travel industries in Erie, Chautauqua, and Niagara counties will develop a marketing plan that will encourage tourists to come here, remain in the area longer, and travel throughout the region within a 150-mile radius. The goal is to increase public awareness and to attract visitors here on a year-round basis—a goal close to the heart of a convention-minded city.

Then, of course, there's the Buffalo Convention Center as a community meeting place, whether it's the culinary appeal of a private banquet, an early-morning business meeting, or the annual

M&T Bank

With more than four dozen offices, M&T Bank serves more than 325,000 households and 13,000 businesses throughout Western New York.

Aboard a Buffalo-bound locomotive during the winter of 1856, two young businessmen pondered how to create adequate banking facilities in the booming lake commerce and grain center they called home. On that ride Pascal P. Pratt and Bronson C. Rumsey, both recognized civic and business leaders, decided to head up an effort among the business community to found a bank that would accommodate the 20-year-old city's growing business and manufacturing base.

Their idea gathered steam when prominent businessman Stephen Van Rensselaer Watson, manufacturer Sherman S. Jewett, and merchant William H. Glenny backed the idea and were among others who comprised the institution's first board of directors. With the then-significant sum of $200,000, Manufacturers and Traders Bank, known today as M&T Bank, was incorporated.

Less than six months later the fledgling institution opened its doors for business in a rented storefront at 2 East Swan Street in downtown Buffalo, and made immediate and dramatic progress. In its first year its capital increased by 250 percent. And over the next five decades its expanding volume of business prompted the bank to relocate no less than four times to larger offices, culminating in an 1899 expansion that saw the construction of an imposing three-story, gray-granite building at Main and Swan streets.

During that first half-century M&T's financial support to small and growing enterprises was the fuel that fired Buffalo's nineteenth-century boom years. In particular, it was instrumental in the growth of several large area industries, including railroad construction, leather goods manufacturing, and grain milling.

As the bank moved, so also did it grow through mergers. In 1902 M&T merged with Merchants Bank of Buffalo; in 1916 it absorbed Third National Bank. Benefiting from the prosperity of the post-World War I era, the institution, in 1925, merged with the Fidelity Trust Company, a major financial underwriter for the Peace Bridge construction project and a pioneer in branch banking. This historic merger established the well-known name of Manufacturers and Traders Trust Company.

During that period, as Buffalo businesses shifted from predominantly port commerce to industrial ventures, the bank supplied the financial support necessary for this economic diversification. The institution also provided assistance to out-of-town corporations that were establishing Buffalo-based plants, all against a backdrop of the accelerating pace of the bank's mergers and acquisitions.

The stock market crash of the late 1920s and the ensuing Great Depression came hard on the heels of this steady growth. Like other banks during those dark days, M&T brought some stability to both companies and individuals. But it wasn't until World War II that the area would again experience a significant economic upswing. As they had in the mid-nineteenth and early twentieth centuries, expanding businesses once again looked to M&T for the financial backing required for the production of war goods. From 1942 to 1946 deposits doubled, the institution expanded its branch network to suburbs and outlying counties, and it ventured into additional mergers.

While rapid growth underscores almost every decade of the bank's history, no event highlights M&T's success so visibly as the 1967 construction of its 21-story multimillion-dollar headquarters building on Main Street in downtown Buffalo. Designed by the internationally acclaimed architectural firm of Minoru Yamasaki & Associates,

State-of-the-art systems ensure bank products and services are constantly enhanced to meet changing needs of the marketplace.

The striking white One M&T Plaza, completed in 1967, was the first major new structure to be built as part of downtown Buffalo's renaissance and served as a cornerstone for the city's future development. Courtesy, E. Demme

Inc., One M&T Plaza was created to reflect the institution's unique "warmth and strength." Its construction also signified the first commitment by a major corporation to the then-nascent downtown Buffalo renaissance. The building occupies a full city block bounded by Main, Eagle, Washington, and North Division streets.

The striking white high rise also provides a dramatic backdrop for the bank's popular noon-hour summertime entertainment series. Begun in 1969, this series attracts 200,000 people during its three-month summer season and features local and national talent drawn from the ranks of amateur and professional entertainers. The M&T Bank Plaza Event Series is one of the largest corporate-sponsored outdoor entertainment events in the United States.

M&T has also established itself as a leader in the development and support of Western New York's many cultural, civic, and

charitable organizations through substantial financial commitments, as well as through the encouragement of personal commitments on behalf of hundreds of M&T employees.

The bank's leadership looks to the future as an era for controlled expansion and refinement of products and services to meet the changing financial needs of individual and commercial customers alike. Progressive new financial services augment the traditional bank services through state-of-the-art delivery systems, trust services, broad-based investment services, and capital equipment leasing, as well as through the area's largest venture capital company. First Empire State Corporation, M&T's parent company since 1969, is optimistic that recent and future policies will help to establish M&T Bank as the "best regional bank in the United States."

As such, it has a running start. By the mid-1980s the institution had attained a position of financial strength unprecedented in its history, and was closing in on an asset figure of three billion dollars, with more than four dozen banking offices and 2,000 employees serving more than 13,000 corporations and 325,000 households in Western New York.

The Plaza Event Series, initiated in 1969, is one of the nation's largest corporate-sponsored outdoor entertainment programs. Courtesy, J. Eberle

Today's emphasis on fundamentals epitomizes the bank's 130-year-plus commitment: to provide both an enterprise of sound banking principles and the business wisdom to offer a high ideal of service to the community. This charge echoes one spoken in an animated conversation some 130 years ago between a pair of entrepreneurs riding the rails between New York and Buffalo. The skyline that marked their destination and fired their ambitions has risen considerably in the interim, visible today in the form of the many businesses that M&T Bank has helped to build from the ground up.

Support of Western New York's active civic and cultural organizations is one form of community reinvestment emphasized by M&T Bank. Courtesy, ArtPark.

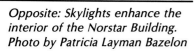

Opposite: Skylights enhance the interior of the Norstar Building. Photo by Patricia Layman Bazelon

Right: Marine Midland Bank, successor to Marine Bank, the first commercial bank in Buffalo, is one of the largest commercial banks in the country. Courtesy, Greater Buffalo Area Chamber of Commerce

master plan?

"No, you can't anticipate that kind of a pattern," replied Mr. Kenzie during a recent interview from his top-floor office in the new twelve-story Goldome Center. "We grew as a result of unusual opportunities that we were ready to take advantage of. It was a time in the early 1980s when banks were basically going broke because of the rates. We bid and won Western [Savings Bank] in an open-bidding contest and we did the same with the two New York City banks. We went to Florida at a time when you could do that sort of thing, providing you put bad banks with good banks. All of those windows have opened and closed. The fact that we were ready to go through them when they were open is the reason why we've reached this point today."

"Most of our [Empire's] growth, development and acquisition has been done with sweat equity," claimed Paul Willax. "Most of the subsidiaries we've either formed or bought have been either very small or very troubled turnaround situations that we were able to buy at the right price." As an example, he refers to Gallery of Homes, Inc., one of the country's largest real estate franchising companies with over 475 offices in forty states and Canada. "That was a million-dollar acquisition in an industry where those firms that are functioning well are selling anywhere from $80 to $220 million," he explained.

According to Mr. Willax, such "sweat equity" dealings have

157

expanded Empire in size, geographic reach, and diversification of services. In the process, the independence of the Buffalo-based bank has been preserved, while the full-service bank of the future has been created.

Full-Speed Ahead into Full-Service

What does all this mean for the Buffalo consumer? It means

Below: The Erie Savings Bank Tower soars into the Buffalo sky. Courtesy, Greater Buffalo Chamber of Commerce

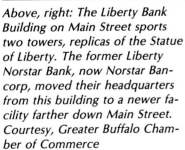

Above, right: The Liberty Bank Building on Main Street sports two towers, replicas of the Statue of Liberty. The former Liberty Norstar Bank, now Norstar Bancorp, moved their headquarters from this building to a newer facility farther down Main Street. Courtesy, Greater Buffalo Chamber of Commerce

unparalleled products and service. As the customer walks through an Empire of America Lobby, she approaches a sleek aluminum and plexiglass modular unit called a Moneyplex center. She activates a video terminal which conveys a range of information on financial planning, presented in concise ninety-second segments by no less than the bank president himself.

The compact Moneyplex centers also contain real people, including a full-service brokerage, superior to the limited-service discount houses that have popped up in other banks around the country. It's part of the push toward complete financial services developed by Empire of America. The video spokesman dispensing the initial investment advice is Paul A. Willax.

Goldome

The original Buffalo Savings Bank building, in the foreground, and Goldome's new 12-story headquarters building light up downtown Buffalo's Fountain Plaza.

Goldome opened its doors for business as Buffalo Savings Bank on July 6, 1846. At the time of its opening, the bank held a mere $18,585.57 for 149 depositors in a small office at Main and Erie Streets.

Today, with more than $14 billion in consolidated assets and 4,800 employees, Goldome is the largest mutual savings bank in the nation. Its operations stretch south to Florida and west to California. It has subsidiaries in real estate, finance, electronic banking, insurance, and computer leasing.

In November 1983 Goldome completed construction of its new 12-story, $55-million headquarters building in downtown Buffalo—the catalyst to several hundred million dollars of additional Fountain Plaza revitalization. It adjoins the bank's Beaux-Arts building at Main and Genesee streets, which was opened in 1901, the year of the Pan American Exposition in Buffalo.

The bank has taken the deregulation powers that were granted in 1981 and used them effectively

to expand its product offering and geographic presence. Goldome is the largest consumer and commercial lender among thrift institutions in the nation. Goldome Realty Credit Corp., a wholly owned subsidiary, is the 11th-largest mortgage banking company in the nation. In 1985 it originated $1.7 billion in residential and commercial mortgages and had a servicing portfolio of $7.5 billion. Goldome Realty Credit Corp. has expanded significantly in new markets. Through 20 offices, the company operates coast to coast.

In 1985 Goldome acquired Neptune Computer Holding Ltd., a Stamford, Connecticut-based company that leases data-processing equipment to large corporations throughout the country.

Goldome has been in the forefront of developing more cost-effective alternative banking delivery systems. Through the institution's unique KWIK-LINE telephone banking service customers can open or renew accounts, make investments, and apply for loans without leaving their home or office. The system serves customers five times as fast as a bank branch at about two-thirds the cost. Goldome also is a leader in electronic banking. Instabank, a Goldome subsidiary, operates a shared network of 450 electronic

banking facilities. Goldome customers have access to more than 2,000 automatic teller machines and point-of-sale locations through Instabank and other shared network facilities throughout the Northeast and Florida, including the multistate New York Cash Exchange network.

Goldome Agency, Inc., offers a full line of insurance products, including life, accident, and health insurance, as well as tax-deferred annuities. In addition, Goldome is one of the largest providers of Savings Bank Life Insurance in New York State. Goldome Premium Finance, Inc., serves general insurance brokers and agents whose businesses and individual clients need to finance the cost of their insurance premiums.

Goldome Credit Corporation provides equity financing for homes in the Southeast and home-improvement financing through an interstate network.

Another subsidiary, Realty World Franchise Corporation, added 34 offices to its statewide roster in 1985. The company provides training, marketing, and nationwide referral services to independent real estate agencies across New York State.

The magnificent vaulted ceilings can be viewed from the second-floor reception area of the bank's Beaux Arts building, which dates back to 1901.

The impressive Goldome Center is one of downtown Buffalo's newest landmarks. Photo by Patricia Layman Bazelon

Empire of America Federal Savings Bank

It's popularly called the Big E. And for good reason. Empire of America Federal Savings Bank is among the largest thrift institutions, as measured by total assets, in the United States.

The Big E is recognized as an industry pacesetter that takes full advantage of advanced technology in the wide range of financial products and services it offers.

Typical of Empire of America's advanced technology is its use of audio and video communications via the first satellite transmission system purchased by a bank.

While the Big E's resources include state-of-the-art advanced technology, the bank values its heritage as a people's institution, working one-with-one to help customers meet their financial goals. That tradition is the foundation on which Empire of America continues to build.

What began September 1, 1854, accepting deposits as small as ten cents per transaction, grew by the second half of the 1980s into a financial network with assets in excess of $8.8 billion and 143 full-service branches. Empire of America has become the second-largest mutual savings bank in the United States and the nation's 13th-largest thrift institution.

The original Erie County Savings Bank, with a single office in Buffalo, is today's Empire of America with deposit facilities across New York State and in Texas, Florida, Michigan, and California. The Big E also does business through subsidiaries and affiliates in more than 35 additional states and extends services into Canada.

The Big E, looking with anticipation toward the twenty-first century, is more than the conventional notion of a bank. Empire of America is Brandywine Enter-

prises, Inc., and Brandywine Realty, Inc., Florida real estate development and real estate firms; Empire Agency, Inc., a general insurance agency representing multiple companies and offering a complete line of life, accident, health, home owners, and auto insurance, as well as tax-advantaged investments through a variety of underwriting companies; Gallery of Homes, Inc., one of the nation's largest real estate franchising companies with more than 375 offices in 40 states; Empire National Securities, Incorporated, a full-service securities broker/dealer registered with the Securities and Exchange Commission and a member of the National Association of Securities Dealers; Empire of America Realty Credit Corp., a fully integrated mortgage banking operation with 18 offices located strategically throughout

---

Empire of America Federal Savings Bank was co-sponsor of the Empire State Games held in Buffalo in August 1986. Shown here is the closing tribute ceremony. Photo by Bob Koch

the country; Empire of America Relocation Services, Inc., the fifth-largest executive relocation firm in the country; Levy, King & White Companies, Inc., a full-service advertising, public relations, and marketing firm with offices in New York State and Florida; Macrotel Inc., a specialist in researching and developing state-of-the-art electronic communications systems for business and financial applications; Metroteller Systems Incorporated, an electronic funds transfer operation servicing more than 80 financial institutions and offering customer access to funds in more than 6,000 retail "in-store" banking facilities and automated teller machines; Sherwin-Greenberg Productions, Inc., a full-service film and video production house in Buffalo that also provides satellite communications services through a mobile ku-band system, the first ever acquired by a bank; and Smartline Corporation, a direct telephone banking and telemarketing sales system offering a complete package of convenience-oriented delivery services to the bank and to other businesses.

This impressive range of customer-focused financial products and services is largely the result of a series of deliberate moves to strengthen the Big E in the mar-

The Empire of America corporate headquarters building at One Main Place, Buffalo. Photo by Paul Pasquarello

kets it serves and seeks to serve.

In 1981 Empire of America adopted a ten-year strategic plan designed to overcome the problems confronting the entire thrift industry and to position the Big E as a strong and aggressive competitor in the financial marketplace of the 1990s and beyond.

That transition plan concentrated on three admittedly ambitious objectives: expanding market coverage into areas with dynamic growth potential, diversifying operations to provide a competitive range of affordable financial services for those markets, and growing to a size that will make the Big E a dominant force in the sophisticated asset and liability marketplaces of the nation.

Advances generated by that strategic plan led to Empire of America's reaching fiscal objectives a full four years ahead of its own demanding schedule. In 1985 the bank enjoyed the beginning of a projected profit trend, and cumulative bottom-line perfor-

mance was $240 million ahead of the target set for that point.

Empire of America has literally put financial services in people's homes in the communities the bank serves. Both customers and non-customers may borrow audio and video tapes from the Big E's lending library. The tapes are from the nationally syndicated television series, "Minding Everybody's Busine$$," featuring chairman Paul A. Willax as producer-host, and authorities discussing such critical topics as financial planning, taxes, and investments.

Empire of America's concern and support for the communities it serves go beyond commercial interests. The Big E takes pride in its reputation as a respected corporate citizen whose contributions make its communities enjoyable places to live, to work, and to do business.

While the bank's involvement extends to all areas it serves, nowhere are its contributions to quality of life more evident than in its Western New York headquarters community. Empire of America's Buffalo-area sponsorships span the spectrum of community activities.

Big E-sponsored events have ranged, for example, from the cultural Buffalo Philharmonic Orchestra summer concert series, through the family-recreation Labor Day at the Buffalo Zoo and the teen athlete Big E Relay Carnival, to the public-service recognition YMCA Salute to Young Leaders.

Empire of America inaugurated the annual Toy Depot to benefit The Children's Hospital of Buffalo. Through public sale of Christmas toys at discount prices, the event saves money for holiday shoppers while it adds to the hospital's financial support. The Toy Depot proved so successful in Buffalo that, under Big E sponsorship, it has been introduced to other communities in support of institu-

Shoppers crowd the lobby of the Buffalo Convention Center, waiting for the doors to open for the Big E's second Toy Depot in 1986. Almost 20,000 people attended the three-day sale of discounted new and quality used toys, which benefited the Intensive Care Nursery of the Children's Hospital of Buffalo. Photo by Bill Wippert

tions there. Empire of America was also a corporate sponsor of the Empire State Games held in Buffalo.

The Big E is headquartered, along with most of its subsidiaries and affiliates, in One Main Place in downtown Buffalo. Empire of America Federal Savings Bank has solidified its pledge to 21st-century Buffalo and will continue playing a major role in its home city's ongoing renaissance.

The Big E fully intends to build upon the values of its heritage to enhance its recognition as an industry innovator and leader, as well as a leading corporate citizen.

Taking tradition to tomorrow, Empire of America Federal Savings Bank reaffirms its commitment to Buffalo, its headquarters city, to the communities the bank serves across the United States and in other countries, and—most importantly—to the customers who have truly built the Big E.

"This is in response to changing customer needs," he explained. "What we're trying to do is keep our customers as they become more sophisticated about investing." As one of those rare bank presidents blessed with a natural camera presence, the youthful executive is the most visible symbol of Empire. His friendly, low-key personality injects a reassuring tone to everything from bank advertising campaigns to a syndicated cable television series entitled, "Minding Everybody's Busine$$."

"I think one of the most important things a business can do is to develop some sort of personal relationship with its customers, even if you have to use television to do it," observed Mr. Willax. "By and large, people like to know who they're doing business with. The comment I get more than anything else [from passersby] is, 'Hey, you've got my money!' That's very revealing. They're giving you that responsibility. And I get the message. That isn't just an offhanded thing for them to say."

In contrast to Ross Kenzie's direct route to the presidency, Mr. Willax aggressively worked his way up in the management ranks since he joined the former Erie County Savings Bank in 1967. Considered to be the architect of the expansion to Empire of America beginning in 1981, his rise to the top paralleled his experience in the National Guard. Enlisting as a private in 1957, he currently holds the rank of brigadier general.

Although different in character, both bank presidents share the keep-and-expand-the-customer-base philosophy. According to Mr. Kenzie, expansion for Goldome doesn't mean a shift upscale in clientele. "That's not the customer who made this bank," he stated, describing the bank's primary customer as the "pale blue-collar type."

Mr. Willax is convinced that a combination of video and computer technology is an important part of financial planning for the general bank customer. "We can use it at this point almost like a medical workup," he observed. "Like medical technology, we can arrive at a diagnosis for a person's situation, but then the actual treatment still has to be given the personal touch."

This drive toward complete financial services for the masses has triggered banks to form a wide variety of subsidiary operations, including insurance, securities brokerage, real estate brokerage, and secondary market concerns.

Metroteller, an Empire subsidiary, was the first electronic banking system developed in the country. The in-store banking concept took off from the first retail location opened in January 1976. After it quickly began to spread across the country, Joe Wolfson, Metroteller president and co-developer of the concept, pushed his firm to become the first shared system in the country,

The handsome new Goldome Center houses financial and professional offices downtown. Photo by David A. Kogut

billion, making it the eleventh largest mortgage banking company in the U.S. The subsidiary also acquired Bankers' Funding. Corporation, a California-based mortgage banking company, and opened a regional office in Chicago.

Goldome's dramatic rise in such a short period has generated a wealth of remarkable achievements. It holds a position among thrifts as the largest consumer lender in the U.S. And its commercial lending and equipment lease financing portfolio have also brought it over the billion-dollar mark, a significant part of that attributed to the acquisition of Neptune Computer Holding, Ltd., a Connecticut-based company that leases data processing equipment to Fortune 1000 companies nationwide.

Other area banks are equally aggressive in pursuit of the consumer and commercial markets. In May 1986, Empire of

Chemical Bank

Chemical Bank's Western New York regional headquarters is located in this historically designated building in the heart of downtown Buffalo on Niagara Square.

Chemical Bank, the sixth-largest bank in the nation, is an international financial services organization with assets of $57 billion. Serving corporate and institutional clients worldwide, it is also one of New York State's premier retail banks.

The institution is number one in serving small and mid-size businesses in the downstate area, an expertise it brings to its Buffalo customers as well.

Part of the Community

Chemical came to Buffalo in 1973 with financial services specifically tailored to the community. Staffed with local financial specialists who know the region, its industries, and its needs, the bank's two offices and operations center are part of the parent company's Regional Bank, which has dedicated its resources—and its people—to

serving customers throughout the New York State area.

A recent Public Securities Association study ranked Chemical as the leader in underwriting New York State general obligation bonds. It is a leading bank in the area for municipal financings, with a specially designated department to serve the municipal marketplace.

The bank is also an active participant in Buffalo community and civic programs, sponsoring special events, supporting community programs, and making philanthropic contributions. Chemical believes that the most appropriate role for a major bank is that of an actively concerned corporate citizen, balancing the claims of customers, shareholders, employees, and communities so that all are equally well served.

History of the Bank

Chemical Bank was chartered in 1824 as part of the New York Chemical Manufacturing Company, which had been founded by

a small group of leading New York merchants to produce chemicals and dyes. However, the banking business soon outstripped the chemical-manufacturing business, and in 1844 the chemical operations were liquidated and the company was reorganized as Chemical Bank.

From its beginning the institution was an active participant in the economic development of the state; its early activities included investment in the building of the Erie Canal.

Nationally chartered in 1865, Chemical grew from a small commercial bank serving New York's mercantile community into one of the nation's largest banks, with a strong correspondent business. During the first decade of the twentieth century the institution opened its first domestic branch, expanded overseas, and acquired or merged with several major New York banks. By 1968 it had incorporated a holding company— Chemical New York Corporation— allowing Chemical to purchase

companies specializing in consumer loans, mortgage banking, and commercial financing.

Helping Business Grow

In recent years the bank has been a leader in technological innovations, especially in electronic banking for both business and the home. In 1985 Chemical helped found the first major automated cash machine network in the New York metropolitan area, the New York Cash Exchange (NYCE), which now has 60 cash machines in Buffalo.

The bank has brought together under one roof a variety of sophisticated resources for its commercial customers, developing practical credit plans to match business cycles, short- and long-term projects, and the best-possible repayment schedules.

Customers considering plant expansion, new construction, leasehold improvements, acquisition, equipment purchase, or major rehabilitation work with knowledgeable account officers to explore various financing options. Those options include business term loans, commercial mortgages, construction loans, working capital, leveraged buy outs, import and export letters of credit, and asset-based financing.

Domestic and International Services

With a global network of 400 offices and 1,400 correspondent banks, Chemical serves its international trade customers with speed and reliability. Services include import and export letters of credit, documentary collections, foreign exchange services, and foreign credit information.

The bank's trust and investment services include setting up and monitoring employee pension plans, as well as helping individual consumers meet personal financial

From the convenience of the office, Chemical's exclusive new PRONTO BUSINESS BANKER allows clients to enjoy instant, electronic access to all their Chemical Bank accounts.

goals. Products range from retirement asset management and investment counseling to estate administration and custody service.

Chemical offers Buffalo businesses many innovative ways to improve cash flow. They include factoring, a flexible financial tool that can turn receivable into cash sooner, and commercial financing, a direct-lending relationship that gives a company a continuous source of working funds while it continues to administer credit, collection, and receivables. Investment banking services are also available; businesses of every size can take advantage of access to capital markets, sophisticated lending arrangements, interest rate swaps, and interest rate caps.

Products For Today's New York Businesses

The institution's computerized cash-management system Chem-Link, is used by more than 1,700 corporations in 35 countries to monitor, analyze, and move funds with ease and speed. In addition, Chemical has a lockbox operation in Buffalo run exclusively for the benefit of area businesses. The bank's automated lockbox processing service is one of its most popular financial products, giving

customers access to detailed receivables information with quicker availability of their cash.

Chemical also offers PRONTO BUSINESS BANKERS, the first electronic banking and information service designed for small businesses. The system lets clients conduct most of their banking transactions on an office microcomputer, printing out hard copy as required.

Other cash-management services include DirectLink, which sends detailed balance and transaction information from all of a company's financial institutions straight to its in-house computer in machine-readable form. TradeLink is a new investment service that lets customers manage their companies' money market program using a terminal in their own office. And PromptPay allows businesses to collect and disburse funds electronically at a prearranged time, simplifying payroll, pension, annuity, and dividend disbursements.

Commitment to the Future

Chemical Bank is proud to be serving the Buffalo business community, helping to keep the commercial sector strong and employment steady. The Western New York region is an excellent business and consumer marketplace, and Chemical Bank is committed to being an active participant in its healthy and diversified economic growth.

America announced plans to become a publicly held company that will sell common stock to the public, converting from a mutual savings bank to a stock savings bank in the process. According to Paul Willax, the decision was made to infuse the organization with the capital necessary to support the tremendous amount of expansion that helped the bank grow to become the nation's second largest mutual savings bank within a four-year span.

The growth also generated an eighteen-million-dollar profit for the bank in 1985—a bottom-line return that was four years ahead of the transition plan instituted in 1981.

To continue to fuel that bottom line, as well as to increase the bank's net worth, the chairman said that the sale of stock would help support future savings growth, expand the bank's lending and investment capabilities, and add more services to compete more effectively with other financial institutions.

That last service-oriented point succinctly captures the thrust of the Greater Buffalo banking market of the 1980s—and beyond.

Banking on the Renaissance

Robert P. Fine is a senior partner of Hurwitz and Fine, PC, a successful Buffalo law firm that does business with a cross-section of local businesses, a number of which have sought expansion.

As their legal representative, Mr. Fine feels that currently the area is in the enviable position of having more buyers than sellers. He credits the financing efforts of the Erie County Industrial Development Agency with fostering a great deal of business expansion. It's the local banking industry, though, that impresses him.

"They have become so much more aggressive in recent years," he explains. "The banks are extremely willing to take a growing business and help it to expand and prosper. The banks really seem keyed into the area's comeback."

Beyond the average consumer, the competitive banking arena has boosted business significantly in the 1980s. More and more businesses are finding a willingness and flexibility in discussing financial assistance.

David Elias, an often-quoted financial expert and chairman of the rapidly growing Buffalo-based investment firm David Elias, Inc., agrees with Mr. Fine.

"For our own clients, we're finding that banks like M & T, Goldome, and Empire are willing to bend over backwards to help," he states. "When I used to go to New York City on business, I used to get comments like, 'Oh, you're from Buffalo. What kind of financial business do they possibly have up there?' That was, of

course, before the expansion of Goldome, Empire, and the rest. Now they look at you with new respect."

The Buffalo banking community, meanwhile, continues to make significant strides in taking care of its own, particularly in the downtown renaissance. Goldome recently announced a four-million-dollar plan to renovate the Western Building at Main and Court streets and create up to 200 new jobs over the next two years. The project will accommodate an expansion within the bank's consumer lending, life insurance, and strategic investment operations. The building, which will be renamed Goldome Court, was part of Goldome's acquisition of the Western New York Savings Bank in 1982. In addition to its headquarters at Fountain Plaza, the bank also owns a computer center on Delaware Avenue downtown.

M&T Bank continues to modernize and expand its branches and services. As the top Small Business Administration lender in New York State for 1985, Marine continues to emphasize support for the area's small businesses—which is also a priority at Key Bank. Empire has leased an additional 72,000 feet of downtown office space and the out-of-town banks are considering more branches.

More and more it appears as though banking has become the major investment in Buffalo's future.

Buffalo's financial community has wholeheartedly supported the downtown redevelopment. Photo by Lester J. Kuhn

173

Merchants Insurance Group

In 1918 Urban Jehle, a successful Buffalo grocer and president of the New York State Retail Grocers Association, was looking for a way to lower insurance rates on the delivery trucks for his store and those of other members of the association. With the support of his colleagues, Jehle sought the help of J. Roger Young, a Buffalo insurance agent; Owen B. Augspurger, a local attorney; and Clifford W. Brown, a civil engineer, in forming a company to handle the insurance on the trucks. They named the resulting company The Merchants Mutual Liability Insurance Company.

Since that first year of business in 1918 when the company took in $117,210 in premiums and reported assets of $91,789, Merchants, now known as The Merchants Insurance Group, has grown to become a major regional insurance carrier. The company, working through the Independent Agency System, serves more than 800 independent agents throughout the Northeast in providing quality service and competitively priced insurance products for policyholders in more than 13 states. Headed by president and chief executive officer James F. Marino, Merchants remains headquartered in Buffalo, where its Western Region office is located, and maintains regional offices in Hauppauge, Long Island; Moorestown, New Jersey; and Manchester, New Hampshire.

Throughout its 68-year history, the company has enjoyed periods of steady corporate growth. At the end of 1986, for example, Merchants projects that its written premium volume will reach $145 million, with assets for the entire corporate group, including Merchants Mutual Insurance Co.

and the Merchants Insurance Company of New Hampshire, totaling approximately $295 million.

The company's growth has been guided by the principle of

QualiSCI—quality service through commitment and innovation. This fundamental principle oversees the thousands of transactions between the company and its agents, and represents Merchants' single-minded goal of providing consistent, unparalleled service to its agents and their customers.

In achieving success in the in-

surance industry, Merchants has had to plan for the future, as well as meet the present needs of its agents and their customers. The introduction in 1984 of the Agency Automation Program—the Merchants Edge—has provided the company with the competitive edge to continue its growth and firmly establish its position as a

leader in the industry.

The automation system, provided by Merchants to qualifying agents at no initial cost, allows the agents to significantly increase sales and operational efficiency by giving them precise, up-to-the-minute information 24 hours a day. The Merchants Edge allows agents to interface directly with

the company's mainframe computer to continually update data on rating, quoting, direct billing, claims, and other services.

In return for this service, the company requests that agents guarantee placing a certain amount of business with the Merchants Insurance Group. Merchants surpassed its first-year goal of placing 100 automation systems throughout the agent network by installing more than 130, further strengthening the partnerships with these agents.

The company's Promise to Agents guarantees that the Merchants Edge system delivers the fastest turn-arounds in the industry on quotes, rates, endorsements, and policies. Agents are able to provide the highest-quality homeowner, automobile, and commercial insurance, thus improving client relationships, increasing sales and strengthening the company.

The Merchants Edge automation system is a prime example of the company's commitment to providing quality service to its agents and customers and increasing overall growth.

This commitment also extends to the home base of Western New York. Merchants has sponsored and supported many community events, including Studio Arena Theater, the Buffalo Sabres, the Buffalo Zoo, the Buffalo Lighthouse, the annual Salute to the Waterfront, and many other civic groups and organizations.

Merchants is proud to be a member of the Western New York community, and pledges to continue to be a leader in the insurance industry, both in Western New York and throughout the Northeast.

A leader in the insurance industry, The Merchants Insurance Group offers diverse, up-to-the minute insurance programs to its policyholders.

CHAPTER SEVEN

The Higher Reach for High Tech

In recent years, "high tech" has been a term brandished about as freely as "yuppies" and "synergistics." But to what exactly does it refer? Complicated electronic "stuff" like the guts of a computer? Chemical formulae with equations as long as a lecture-hall blackboard? The engineers, chemists, et al., who build this "stuff" and the people who put it to use?

Sure, and then some. It's all a matter of perspective. An observer 145 years ago would have considered Joseph Dart's grain elevators along Buffalo Harbor to be a marvel of high tech. Another observer earlier this century would have regarded the intricate workings of local steel mills and automaking plants to be the sweat-stained results of high tech.

Indeed, the Niagara Frontier has been home to many young entrepreneurs and their bold ingenuity almost since Buffalo became a city in 1832, a time when only twenty-four states constituted the United States. Consider this historical spectrum of area accomplishment:

—Buffalo was the first city in the country to light its streets with electricity.
—AM&A's became the first commercial establishment in the country to use the new power.
—The country's first steel casting for commercial use was successfully made at Pratt & Letchworth in Buffalo, which was used in the construction of the first steam locomotive built in Buffalo.

Opposite: Occidental Chemical Corporation maintains administrative offices as well as a research and development plant in Niagara Falls. Photo by Envisions Co.

177

Opposite: Wilfred J. Larson, president of Westwood Pharmaceuticals, poses in the company's laboratories on Forest Avenue. Photo by Joe Traver

Left: A worker checks resistors on a high-tech assembly line. Photo by Joe Traver

—Cornelius Vanderbilt's new railroad brake design was first manufactured at Buffalo Brake Beam Company.
—The first conversion of bulk freighters into self-unloading ships, which could unload faster than conventional vessels, was accomplished in Buffalo at American Steamship Company.
—The first revolving refrigerator for better blood storage was produced in Buffalo at The Jewett Refrigerator Company.
—The first completely American-designed diesel engine was built in Buffalo at The Worthington Company.
—Bell Aircraft Corporation constructed the first aircraft to break the sound barrier—the X-1, piloted by the legendary Air Force Captain Chuck Yeager.
—Rich Products Corporation developed a way to freeze food without crystallization, allowing frozen food to be eaten without defrosting.

Now Buffalo is entrenched in an era when progress and output are measured in terms of tiny microchips. If you're talking computerized industry today, you're talking about practically every existing company. Because everyone's workplace has been technologically enhanced to some degree, the real measure of an area's high-tech significance is in research and development—areas in which Greater Buffalo is among the most innovative in the country.

Moog, Inc., for example, has built its reputation on high tech. In

Moog Inc.

Wearing the clean-room uniform of a surgical-style gown, cap, mask, and gloves, a Moog technician assembles a valve that will blast into outer space aboard the *Voyager 2* space probe. The time is the mid-1980s.

Wearing oil-soaked chinos and a faded work shirt, William C. Moog, Jr., labors in his basement workshop to develop what will soon come to be known as the electrohydraulic servovalve. The time is the early 1950s.

While the contrast between those two scenes is one of both time and technological advancement, perhaps the experience of the last 35-plus years can be put into one simple statement: Bill Moog built a servovalve, and that valve built Moog Inc.

The story begins in 1948. That year research engineer Bill Moog was asked by his then-employer, Buffalo's Cornell Aeronautical Laboratories (CAL), to design a prototype mechanism for the automatic steering of missiles. But, as luck would have it, Moog's valve was well ahead of its time. Not realizing the invention's enormous potential, CAL offered manufacturers a license to produce the high-performance valve,

A complete fin actuation system, including high-pressure gas bottle, control electronics, and four servoactuators, being developed for the GBU-15 guided weapon system.

but no takers came forward. No takers, that is, until Bill Moog himself answered opportunity's knock, took a leave of absence from CAL, and descended into his basement workshop to perfect the device that converted electrical command impulses into hydraulic power.

With zero capital, Moog set up a laboratory and then convinced a Batavia machine shop to manufacture the parts for his invention. Working 18 hours a day, week in and week out, it was only a matter of months before he sold his first four valves to Bendix Aviation. In short order, seeing the enormous marketing edge Moog's invention gave them, Bendix placed a repeat order for 75 servovalves. Moog's business was airborne.

Following that initial success, Moog moved his business to rented space in a vacant airport hangar in East Aurora. In 1951 his brother Arthur and colleague Lewis H. Geyer joined him to form Moog Valve Company, Inc., under which name the firm reached sales of $200,000 by 1952. Just two years later the Moog Valve Company was selling valves to aerospace firms such as Boeing and Baltimore's Martin Company (the predecessor of today's Martin-Marietta), grossing annual sales well into the millions of dollars, and finding its products included as standard equipment on half the nation's fighter planes and 70 percent of its guided missiles. After a major plant expansion and diversification into the industrial market, the firm changed its name in 1959 to Moog Servocontrols, Inc., and sold common stock. In 1966 Moog Servocontrols, Inc., was renamed Moog Inc., to reflect the company's expertise in expanding

The Moog Inc. complex in East Aurora, New York.

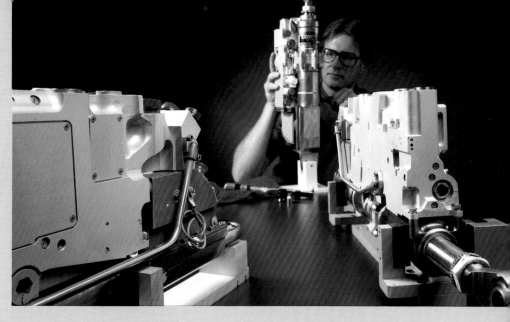

controls technologies.

Today Moog Inc. is a *Fortune* 1,000 company and a world leader in the design and manufacture of a variety of electrohydraulic and pneumatic motion-control devices and systems. Moog-designed and manufactured precision controls are an integral part of missile guidance systems, aircraft flight controls, life support systems, and automated industrial machinery.

Just as it has grown in the number and range of its product offerings, so too has Moog expanded on a geographical scale. The firm has worldwide sales, service, and research divisions with 13 overseas subsidiaries in West Germany, England, France, Japan, Ireland, Italy, Brazil, the Philippines, Spain, Sweden, and South Korea. The corporation also has manufacturing operations in Florida, and a research facility in California. And just as impressive as the global breadth of its operations is its financial strength: Net sales reached the $240.3-million mark in 1985, with 74 percent of that amount coming from government contracts.

As one might expect from a company founded by an individualistic entrepreneur, Moog Inc. has retained an individualistic ap-

Seven Moog actuators control the active flight surfaces on the LAVI fly-by-wire aircraft.

proach to doing business. The firm has a decentralized organizational structure that is divided into four operating groups: Aerospace, Industrial, Carleton, and International. These groups are further broken down into divisions, each of which is responsible for its own product development, manufacturing, sales, and service.

Open communications and creativity are also encouraged among Moog's 3,500 employees—2,700 of whom work at the company's Buffalo area facilities. In 1984 the corporation was rated among the 100 best companies to work for in America. According to founder, current president, and chairman Bill Moog, "Work in an atmosphere of mutual trust and confidence can be a more rewarding and satisfying experience for everyone."

Instances of this emphasis on each employee's sense of responsibility and ingenuity abound. For example, a technician testing a vital component for one of NASA's spacecraft is solely responsible for the quality control of his or her own work. There have never been time clocks at Moog facilities; employees report their own performance and take rest breaks and personal days when needed.

The complexity of the projects the firm undertakes makes teamwork essential. For instance, Moog supplies the servoactuators for the V-22 Osprey helicopter jet,

the atmospheric control system for the Space Shuttle, a rapid response servo system for fighter pilot G suits, and servoactuators for the B-1 bomber. It is also the prime contractor in the design of thermal management controls for space stations. The company's control systems are used on every U.S. strategic ballistic missile, including the Peacekeeper MX.

The rolling countryside south and east of Buffalo is also witness to another measure of Moog's progress—its new Missile Systems Division and corporate offices. Comprised of a series of four octagon-shaped buildings with interconnecting corridors, the complex forms an octagon-shaped courtyard in the middle. Through the extensive use of glass throughout, every person working in the complex has a clear view of the outside. Its architectural design has brought international attention to Moog—in this instance for pure aesthetics on a large scale rather than for the ingenuity of its minute parts in rockets and robots.

The unique ambience at Moog Inc. is largely the result of the spirit of the man who took a working idea and built a high-tech organization around it. The advancement, growth, and prosperity the firm has experienced are outgrowths of Bill Moog's vision that if employees are respected, they put respect back into the company. Its diverse, state-of-the-art product line, long-tenured employees, and strong stock prove that a unique corporate mind set can indeed promote success.

Surgically clean thruster valves are assembled for Peacekeeper's Internal Measurement Unit.

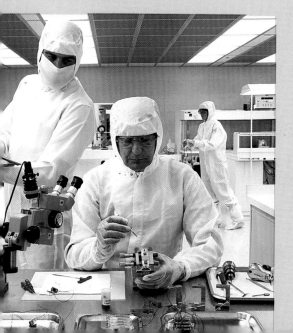

181

the late 1940s, a young engineer named William C. Moog created a device for the automatic steering of missiles and aircraft. His electrohydraulic valve soon became an indispensible component of the aerospace industry. In 1951 Moog rented a corner of an unused airplane hangar just outside East Aurora, a New England-like village twenty miles southeast of Buffalo, and opened for business as the Moog Valve Company. Thirty-five years later, Moog buildings are sprawled throughout East Aurora—with manufacturing operations in Tampa, Los Angeles, Canada, England, Ireland, France, Italy, West Germany, Sweden, Japan, Australia, and Brazil. At the end of 1985, Moog realized record sales of $240.3 million.

Buffalo is home as well to companies such as Westwood Pharmaceuticals, Inc., which have developed their own research labs for commercial purposes. For example, the most recent new product to emerge from the five-million-dollar research center the company established locally in 1983 is Lac-Hydrin, a unique prescription

Opposite: Marvin Trott, of Trott Electronics, holds a speedometer that his Buffalo company manufactured for the new Buffalo light rail transit system. Photo by Joe Traver

Right: High technology has taken the place of steelmaking as the premier industry of the area, and Moog Electronics has long been in the forefront of that change. Courtesy, Greater Buffalo Chamber of Commerce

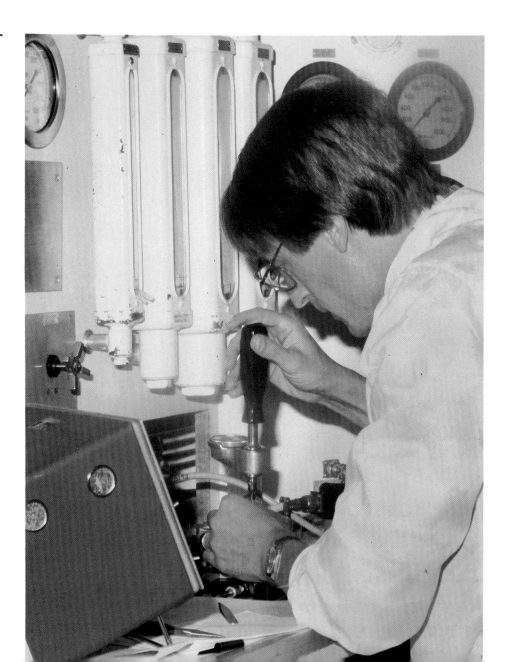

Calspan Corporation

Calspan Corporation, one of the nation's most diversified research and development companies, has a well-earned reputation for technical excellence. For over 40 years it has applied technology to the needs of the nation, combining the theoretical and experimental talents of its staff with extensive facilities to analyze problems, test new concepts, and produce valid and useful solutions.

The firm had its start in 1946 as the Cornell Aeronautical Laboratory when Curtiss-Wright donated its Buffalo research facility to Cornell University. Operating as a tax-exempt unit of the university, the laboratory steadily broadened its interests from aeronautics and associated sciences to become the multidisciplinary organization it is today. In 1972 the firm changed its name to Calspan Corporation

and began operation as a public company in which Cornell University had a major interest. Calspan was acquired by Arvin Industries in April 1978.

In addition to its headquarters buildings and facilities on Genesee Street near the Buffalo Airport and its Flight Research hangar at the airport, Calspan operates the Franklin Research Center Division in Philadelphia, Pennsylvania; government-owned flight dynamics test facilities for the U.S. Air Force at the Arnold Engineering Development Center in Tennessee; wind tunnel facilities for the National Aeronautics and Space Administration at the Ames Research Center in California; and special-

An aerial view of Calspan Corporation, one of the nation's largest independent research and development organizations.

emphasis technical centers throughout the nation. Calspan recently reached an agreement in principle to acquire the Systems Research Laboratories, Inc., in Dayton, Ohio.

Calspan's diversified technical staff and facilities offer its customers a balanced program of analysis and experimentation in such areas as systems analysis; aerosciences; electronics; computer and information sciences; transportation and environmental sciences; structural, mechanical, and nuclear engineering; and full-scale simulation.

Among its many facilities are a transonic wind tunnel in which most of the nation's and many foreign aircraft have been tested, hypersonic shock tubes and tunnels, a 33-acre vehicle research facility, a manned, real-time electronic warfare simulator for testing electronic warfare systems, underground ballistic ranges, and a 700-acre test site in a rural area a 700-acre test site in a rural area of Western New York for experimental evaluation of chemicals, aerosols, and explosives.

A pioneer in the field of in-

Calspan's manned real-time electromagnetic environment simulator, which is used to test electronic warfare systems.

flight simulation, Calspan operates a number of owned and bailed aircraft that have been developed to simulate the flying qualities of many different aircraft. In addition to their use for training military pilots, these aircraft are used as research tools to simulate the handling qualities of advanced aircraft design. For example, before the first space shuttle was built, astronauts were practicing landings of the shuttle in Calspan's Total In-Flight Simulator. After the first mission, pilots informed Calspan that the simulator flights were amazingly accurate.

Other in-flight aircraft simulators include a Learjet Model 24, owned by Calspan, used to train Navy and Air Force test pilots, an Air Force NT-33A variable-stability aircraft, and the variable-stability X-22A. The latter, bailed to Calspan by the U.S. Navy, is used to investigate the handling qualities of vertical- and short-takeoff and landing aircraft.

Calspan also is engaged in several joint ventures. One, the Dynaspan Services Company with the Dynelectron Corporation of McLean, Virginia, provides engineering analysis, operation, and

maintenance services to the U.S. Army at the White Sands Missile Range. The others are nonprofit joint ventures—one with the State University of New York and another with the University of Tennessee—bringing together scientists and engineers with expertise in specialized areas to perform research that could benefit from the synergistic effects of their joint efforts. These nonprofit ventures represent a rare combination of industry and academia working together, using the facilities of both organizations.

Calspan also is proud of its contributions to the communities in which it operates. Typical of these efforts are its continuing support of civic endeavors, such as the Buffalo Philharmonic Orchestra, the Niagara Frontier Industry-Education Council, Boy Scouts, Junior Achievement, science and career fairs, and courses conducted by staff members at local universities and colleges.

Calspan's more than 40 years of research and development for government and industry have contributed not only to the nation's defense but also to the safety and well-being of the civilian population.

Calspan's Learjet, one of the company's variable stability aircraft, is used as an in-flight simulator.

product for moderately-to-severely dry skin.

Perhaps the most significant development in the high-tech realm, though, is in the joint efforts of the university and the industrial sector.

The sprawling State University of New York at Buffalo campus has been one of the biggest influences in the bleaching of the local blue collar into a predominantly white one. As one of only fifty designated research universities in the nation, the University of Buffalo has proved to be an invaluable source of emerging technology, engineering and managerial expertise, personnel, laboratories, and libraries. Combining the work on campus with local industry off campus, however, needed a special approach. That is the core of recent high-tech research and development in Buffalo.

Henry P. Semmelhack is president of Barrister Computer Systems, a successful Buffalo company that designs computer systems for law firms. Photo by Joe Traver

Technology Transfer

That's the term used to describe the pipeline of knowledge, insight, and practical hands-on experience—the transfer of high tech from the research stage into commercial ventures.

The Calspan-University at Buffalo Research Center was among the first to realize the importance of getting industry and university people working together in a technology transfer. Calspan is an outgrowth of the Cornell Aeronautical Laboratory (CAL) of Cornell University which, in 1948, became a wholly owned, non-profit research subsidiary of the university. In 1972 the non-profit status was dropped and in 1978, Calspan was acquired by Arvin Industries.

Calspan has grown from an aviation research and test facility

Hayes Hall is the most distinctive building on the University at Buffalo's lovely Main Street campus. Photo by Envisions Co.

funded by aircraft company donations to a multidisciplinary, high-tech operation. Its association with UB has delved into the areas of hypersonics, turbine research, and surface chemistry. In recent years, it has become intricately involved with NASA's space shuttle program. According to Dr. Charles E. Treanor, director of the Calspan-UB center, expansion into the areas of artificial intelligence and bio-physics is on the immediate horizon.

The Western New York Technology Development Center (TDC), formed four years ago to both create and maintain technical jobs in the area, has steered companies such as Westwood Pharmaceuticals to university researchers with expertise that the companies could use. At the other end of the spectrum, the TDC has encouraged researchers to patent their work and find companies interested in licensing the discoveries. "We are often described as a broker, a marketer, a liaison, a translator, an expediter," said Robert J. Martin, director of technology transfer at the center.

Located at 2211 Main Street, the TDC is referred to as a technical incubator facility, hosting start-up companies right from their inception. Currently, there are thirteen technical companies in the incubator employing about sixty people and generating about two million dollars in sales. Most are linked to the medical field.

"When we started, we looked around the area and asked ourselves, 'Why aren't there more medically related companies in the area?'" recalled Mr. Martin. "With research facilities like UB and Roswell, there should have been more activity in the biomedical field. In the past, some of the state regulations have stifled

Chemical analyst Hebe Greizerstein runs her own chemical analysis business at the Western New York Technology Development Center. Photo by Robert McElroy

Comptek Research, Inc., located in a new industrial corridor, provides computer-based electronic defense systems for the U.S. military

technology transfer from those institutions. SUNY has now recognized that the transfer of technology from the university to the private sector to foster economic development should be one of its roles. They also realize that the taxpayers should benefit economically from the financial support that they have given the university."

In the process, the TDC identified three major strategies: first, reach out to existing industries in Greater Buffalo, determine what problems they face and match these problems with expertise, either in the academic research community or with a business that would help them solve those problems; second, spend time in the research sector itself to determine technologies that are being developed there that could be spun off directly into Greater Buffalo businesses; third, provide a variety of services to technical entrepreneurs.

Among the companies currently in the incubator are three that are doing medically related work that originated at Roswell Park

American Precision Industries Inc.

State-of-the-art equipment is depositing a precision layer of metallic paste on the termination ends covering electrodes in Delcap's ceramic chip capacitors.

The uncommon achievement of Robert J. Fierle in building a garage-size machine shop into the multinational diversified American Precision Industries Inc., listed on the American Stock Exchange, is extraordinary indeed.

That he did so without any business experience and very little money is a modern-day Horatio Alger story. Through the years survival hung in the balance on more than one occasion.

Fierle was working at the Westinghouse Electric plant at the Buffalo Airport when he spotted a newspaper advertisement offering to sell a small machine shop for

$20,000. He obtained loans from various sources and purchased the financially troubled Amherst Tool and Manufacturing Company of Williamsville in April 1947.

At the outset there were three employees including Fierle. Expansion in the first year meant the purchase of a $1,257 war-surplus machine. The firm put up $257 and a bank financed the rest. Sales that year amounted to $21,468; however, the company lost $63.99.

By 1949 there was more government business to be had, and Fierle decided to go after a piece of it. He made a trip to Washington, D.C., where he was able to spot a flaw in the bid of the apparent winner of a Navy contract. He got the job and turned out the 250,000 pieces without a single reject.

American Precision Industries' operations are currently conducted

by three groups with a total of eight divisions. The Electronic Components Group is composed of the Delevan Division, the Delcap Division, the Resistive Products Division, and the API of Florida Division.

The Delevan Division in East Aurora, New York, is a leading designer and manufacturer of high-reliability coil and inductor products. Those quality components are used in a wide range of industrial, telecommunications, computer, military, aerospace, and business machine applications. Major improvements in product design and automated manufacturing processes have strengthened Delevan's competitive position. With the advent of the new surface-mounted technology, the Delevan

The all-aluminum main body of an air-cooled heat exchanger unit is being placed into a special vacuum furnace at the new Air Cooled Applications Division.

Division has positioned itself on the leading edge of change with its newly designed line of surface-mounted coil products.

At the Delcap Division in Arcade, New York, American Precision Industries believes an opportunity for growth exists in its surface-mounted capacitors. The goal of the recently established division is to develop one of the finest automated capacitor-manufacturing facilities in the nation. The firm has great faith in Delcap's capability to become a major force in the capacitor market.

At the Resistive Products Division, also in Arcade, resistors are a natural addition to American Precision Industries' inductor and capacitor divisions. This combination of product lines will make the corporation a stronger competitor in the electronic component business. The Resistive Products Division's new line of one-quarter- and one-half-watt resistor products utilizes the latest techniques in thin-film evaporator production. Six highly automated production lines are capable of turning out more than 100,000 resistors per hour. Those products then become part of an electronic circuit that is the heart of all electronic systems.

The API of Florida Division, located in Silver Springs, Florida,

Corporate offices are located at 2777 Walden Avenue in Buffalo.

manufactures standard inductive components as does the Delevan Division.

The Heat Transfer Equipment Group is composed of the Basco Division and the Air Cooled Applications Division.

The Basco Division, located in Buffalo, is one of the nation's major producers of heat-transfer equipment. The company uses a comprehensive thermal and mechanical design system recognized worldwide for its innovative approach to heat exchanger performance. A task-oriented management structure makes the Basco Division more flexible, innovative, and efficient in responding to increased competition and customer requirements for energy-efficient products.

The Air Cooled Applications Division, formed in 1985, marked American Precision Industries' entry into the air-cooled heat exchanger market. Today all-aluminum air-to-air and air-to-liquid heat exchangers are custom produced at the division's Lockport, New York, facility.

The Motion Control Group consists of the Deltran Division of Buffalo and the Rapidsyn Division, located in Oceanside, California.

The Deltran Division has attained a reputation as a quality manufacturer of electromechanical clutches, brakes, and related assemblies. Its diverse product offerings include hysterisis, friction, and tooth design. This multiple product capability enables the

Robert J. Fierle, chairman of the board and president.

Deltran Division to service a wide spectrum of sophisticated customers, including the military, defense, and aerospace markets.

The Rapidsyn Division's state-of-the-art step motors are the result of design, engineering, and fabrication practices of the highest order. The organization offers a complete line of step motors, microsteppers, drives, and controls. Today's computer peripheral equipment, robotics, aerospace, and military markets demand reliable motion-control devices that operate with precise incremental positionings. Standard designs include variable reluctance, permanent magnet, and hybrid motors with a variety of step angles and torque values.

American Precision Industries' mission is to continually improve its products and services to meet its customers' needs, which will allow API to prosper as a business and to provide a reasonable return to its stockholders (who are the owners of the corporation).

Under the guidance of Robert J. Fierle, who is chairman and president of the company, American Precision Industries Inc. has indeed traveled the long road to success since its founding in a tiny machine shop back in 1947.

Memorial Institute and the University at Buffalo, one company that is developing and marketing nutritional software, a technology laboratory where body fluids are analyzed for drugs (both therapeutic and abusive drugs), and a small domestic subsidiary of a Swiss company that is developing human implant technology.

"We've had no failures so far," assessed Mr. Martin, "and that's certainly very far ahead of the odds for new businesses, which is a 50 percent average failure rate within the first year."

The TDC director concluded that the technology that has been developed in the area over a long period of time can now be used to establish business in Greater Buffalo that can significantly boost the area's economic development.

"The Buffalo area is changing from the heavy industrial base," Mr. Martin declared. "If we approach this whole technology transfer issue correctly and utilize the strengths we have in the area, a good part of our future economy could be linked directly with developments from our medical community in Western New York."

HIDI Seeking New Business

If you've gotten the impression that the medical research industry

193

Cullen Industries, Inc.

The desiccant packaging industry was seriously concerned. The Sunbelt company that was the sole manufacturer of the only nonwoven fabric that met government specifications for preservation use had decided to quit production.

Hearing the announcement, a young Western New York entrepreneur flew to the manufacturer's headquarters in West Point, Georgia. There he arranged to take over the machinery and technology to manufacture the unique line of nonwoven fabrics back in his hometown of Buffalo, New York. John S. Cullen's acquisition of the West Point Pepperell Lantuck Plant in Fairfax, Alabama, led his company to become the only fully integrated desiccant manufacturing and packaging business in the world.

While that acquisition was made in 1978, the eye for growth that marked that transaction has also characterized the entire history of Cullen Industries, Inc. Some years earlier, while still in his early twenties, Cullen had left Union Carbide's Linde Division to develop and sell hygrostats—getters that provide a controlled level of water vapor in solid-state diodes for automotive alternators, germanium semiconductors, and other

electronic devices. Operating in a small garage workshop, Multiform Desiccants began the production of molecular sieve and silica gel drying and sieving agents used not only for car alternators, but also for chromatographic use, pharmaceuticals, dehydrated foods, refrigerants, and diagnostic instruments.

Encouraged by initial sales, Cullen moved his operation to larger facilities at 2222 Elmwood Avenue. The business occupied a second-story loft and was staffed by part-time help. By day Cullen sold his absorbent desiccants to the makers of automobile and television components and other electronics devices; in the evening he managed production operations. The seeds for success were planted.

Among the infant organization's customers were such big-name companies as Delco Division GM, Motorola, Westinghouse, General Electric, and RCA. Within a year the firm added Aerojet General and Raytheon as customers when it was awarded contracts to devise and manufacture a bagged desiccant for the solid rocket motor used in the Hawk surface-to-air missile. This, in turn, led to other aerospace contracts, including one for the manufacturer of cartridges designed to remove moisture from the aviator's breathing gas then used at high altitudes.

Within a few years Multiform Desiccant Products had increased its payroll to 18 people, and its

The automotive air-conditioner desiccant bag production operation.

sales had risen to $400,000, up from $25,000 in 1961, its first year in business. The purchase of a 2.3-acre lot and 8,000-square-foot building at 70 Chalmers Street enabled the firm to expand and subsequently introduce several new products. These included a filter-drier element that simultaneously filters and dries refrigerants, and molecular sieve and silica gel desiccant papers designed to fit in places bagged desiccants can't. Also during that period of innovation, the company developed an inexpensive DRICAP® desiccator cartridge ideal for pharmaceutical packaging as well as with electronics and optical applications.

Building on this foundation, Multiform Desiccant Products diversified in 1966 with the creation of its first subsidiary, Sterile Plastics Corporation (now called Steri-Plex). Formed initially to meet military needs for disposable kits and devices during the Vietnam Conflict, SteriPlex marked the entrance of the firm into the hospital products industry, a market in

With a projected doubling in volume in profitability, products, and markets by 1991, Cullen Industries plans expansions in machinery, equipment, and facilities such as this new headquarters building.

which it is still active. Now strictly a contract manufacturing operation, SteriPlex produces medical-surgical products, such as sterile disposable kits, components, anti-microbial additive devices, and assembly and packaging. Originally operated in Williamsville, New York, SteriPlex moved, in 1968, to the company's then-newly purchased corporate headquarters at 1418 Niagara Street.

The firm's interest in nonwovens as desiccant packaging cover stock resulted in the 1971 incorporation of Industrial Felt Corporation. That is the entity that purchased the West Point Pepperell Lantuck Plant and was housed in a newly purchased two-story, 52,000-square-foot building near

lion dollars. In 1973 sales volume doubled again with the development of similar products for General Motors—Cullen Industries' first customer and its largest today. Sales continued to double each year through 1975.

This growth necessitated additional plant expansion. In 1975 Cullen purchased the former General Electric building at 960 Busti-at-Niagara, spending more than one million dollars on renovations and additions. That same year operations were consolidated with other nearby Niagara Street properties, resulting in a combined total space of 120,000 square feet. The corporation's payroll also expanded: More than 100 employees, many of

The high-speed dricap desiccant line.

Cullen employees at their sewn desiccant bag assembly stations.

the corporate offices on Niagara Street, just a few hundred yards from the Peace Bridge.

These firms officially incorporated under the name Cullen Industries in 1972, and that same year gained Ford Motor Company's automotive air-conditioner bagged desiccant business, which translated into an annual sales increase from $500,000 to one mil-

them highly skilled engineers, machine operators, and technicians, worked in the company's newly enlarged facilities.

Today Cullen Industries is a corporation with three major subsidiaries: its original venture, Multiform Desiccants, Inc.; Industrial Felt Corporation; and SteriPlex Corporation. Annual sales top $15 million. Although it began as a small venture supplying desiccants for automotive electronic needs, Cullen Industries' product line

now includes five types of desiccants that are marketed throughout North America and in Europe. It is a major supplier to nearly every pharmaceutical company. Such has been the diversification, expansion, and volume of its product lines that Multiform Desiccants, Inc., is the largest manufacturer of its kind in the world.

John Cullen plans to continue the firm's active development and acquisition of directly related products and businesses, with its attendant potential to bring unique, professional, and skilled employment opportunities to his native city. "The many expansions at Cullen are in line with our continuing strategy of concentrating our resources in absorbents and packaging," the entrepreneur explains. And so the man who began his business with rented time on a local pill press looks to the future with the same zeal and enterprise: By 1991 Cullen Industries, Inc., expects to double its volume in profitability, products, and markets with attendant expansion in facilities, machinery, and equipment in greater Buffalo.

Ingram Software, Inc.

The Ingram Software, Inc., management team of Buffalo boosters, from left to right: Ronald M. Schreiber, executive vice-president of product and co-founder of the company; Jordan Levy, executive vice-president of sales and marketing; David Edelman, senior vice-president of corporate development; and Franklyn S. Barry, Jr., president.

Ingram Software, Inc., has a history short on years, but it is a history marked by explosive growth in an industry where survival is reserved for a select few.

This Buffalo success story began in 1982, when a small group of local investors formed Software Distribution Services as a subsidiary of Modern Tek Shop's Inc. The founders were Delaware Camera Mart president Irwin Schreiber; his son, Ronald; Gerald Lippes, a local attorney; and Paul Willax, Empire of America chairman. The following year Franklyn S. Barry, Jr., former president of Fisher-Price Toys, joined Software Distribution Services' growing number of investors and became its chief executive officer.

At that time Software Distribution Services was one of countless small regional companies trying to make the move to a full-service national distributor. With the management team's marketing expertise and internal financing, the firm made the jump and never looked back.

While competitors focused on specific selling points, such as technical support or free overnight delivery, Software Distribution Services developed programs to help retailers grow in a competitive business. It was this approach of responding to customer needs that triggered further growth, moving the company into a spot among the nation's top software distributors. However, if the firm was going to realize its goal of becoming a major factor in the distribution arena, greater financial backing was needed.

Software Distribution Services' reputation among retailers and the April 1985 acquisition of a 50-percent interest in the former Aviva Distributors of Toronto, Canada, attracted the attention of the industry and of Ingram Distribution Group of Nashville, Tennessee. In June of that year Ingram bought out the Software Distribution Services investors, merging its Ingram Software Division with the Buffalo organization. The merger brought about a new name, Ingram Software Distribution Services, as well as the relocation of Ingram Software's corporate headquarters to Buffalo.

Six months later, on December 31, 1985, Ingram Distribution Group announced the acquisition of another software distributor, Softeam of Compton, California, thereby forming Ingram Software, Inc. Ingram Distribution Group also acquired controlling interest in a fourth distributor, Micro D, which continues to operate independently of Ingram Software.

Ingram Software has structured a bi-coastal operation through the complete integration of Softeam, servicing customers in the East from its Buffalo headquarters at 2128 Elmwood Avenue and customers in the West from its Compton, California, facility.

Today Ingram Software is an international, full-service distributor to more than 12,000 dealers worldwide. The company operates as a subsidiary of Ingram Distribution Group, which also operates Ingram Book Company, the nation's largest book wholesaler, and Ingram Video and Ingram Audio, distributors of prerecorded audio and video cassettes. All are subsidiaries of Ingram Industries, a privately held corporation headquartered in Nashville, Tennessee. Ingram Industries is also involved in inland marine transportation, coal production and sales, and the manufacture of petroleum wellhead equipment.

Ingram Software carries more than 4,000 products from over 350 manufacturers, including business, educational, personal productivity, and entertainment software, as well as books and accessory products. It distributes products from most major manufacturers, including Ashton-Tate, Borland,

An Ingram worker prepares a shipment of computer software products in the company's specially developed "Priority-Pacs."

Commodore, Intel, Hercules, Lotus, Microsoft, MicroPro, and Software Publishing.

Distribution centers ship these products from Buffalo, Toronto, and Compton, California. Regional sales offices are located in New York City, Boston, Chicago, Los Angeles, San Francisco, Buffalo, Baltimore, Houston, Cleveland, Nashville, and Atlanta.

Backing up the industry's largest distribution and sales network are extensive sales and marketing programs for dealers driven by the corporate philosophy of "E.S.P.— Excellence, Service, and Professionalism." This approach emphasizes all-out support for the retailers' sell-through efforts, and it remains a key to Ingram Software's success. Other strengths that point to continued growth are the firm's high-powered management team of marketing experts, all Buffalonians, and the solid financial resources of its large

parent company, Ingram Industries.

With 375 employees worldwide, 200 of whom are located in Buffalo, Ingram Software, Inc., long ago outgrew its Buffalo headquarters. After a nationwide search, the company concluded that Buffalo is still the most attractive location for its corporate headquarters and is moving ahead to lease warehouse facilities at the Buffalo Airport Center. The move will accommodate the corporation's future growth and allow it to move a portion of its California operation to Buffalo.

Moog Inc., maintains manufacturing facilities in East Aurora as well as Brazil, Australia, and West Germany. Courtesy, Buffalo Area Chamber of Commerce

Robert J. Martin is director of technology transfer at the Western New York Technology Development Center. Photo by Joe Traver

comprises the most lucrative high-tech advancement, you're right. In fact, another agency working to motivate technology transfer is the Health-Care Instrument and Device Institute (HIDI). Its mission is to introduce new medical/dental/diagnostic concepts to the public's benefit and to create new jobs in the process.

HIDI is most directly linked with the university, having evolved there in late 1983 as part of New York State's Center for Advanced Technology. Located in the Parker Hall complex on SUNYAB's Main Street campus, HIDI is sponsored financially by the New York State Science and Technology Foundation which offers $750,000 per year of potential matching funds for mission-related research.

Research projects have included better hospital beds, better food for cell cultures, and evaluation of skin products. Research sites are located in Roswell Park Memorial Institute; Buffalo General, Millard Fillmore, and Children's hospitals; and the UB departments and schools of chemistry, geological science, engineering, dentistry, and medicine.

According to Dr. Robert E. Baier, director, "HIDI is a facilitating

LTV Missiles and Electronics Group

Sierra Research Division

High tech doesn't get much higher in Buffalo than the technology developed and produced by the Sierra Research Division of LTV Missiles and Electronics Group. There you'll find the stuff of modern military adventure movies. Only, in this case, it's not fiction but rather a fact that Sierra has become a worldwide leader in the design and manufacture of advanced electronic systems for military, civil, and commercial aviation uses.

Sierra Research is one of three divisions of LTV Missiles and Electronics Group, which manufactures missiles, rockets, space systems, and military vehicles.

Sierra Research was formed in 1957, when high technology was on the rise in the United States and throughout the world. Six employees of the Bell Aircraft Corporation (now Bell Aerospace) left that firm to form a small electronics company devoted to the advancement of radar and telemetry, a system of measuring, recording, and relaying information from high-speed aircraft, rockets, and spacecraft. This entrepreneurial sextet named the business Sierra Research Corporation after California's Sierra Nevada Mountains, where they believed they would eventually relocate.

But rather than "California or bust," the group boomed right where it began. Ten years after its formation, the firm had 125 employees at its headquarters adjacent to the Greater Buffalo International Airport. Perhaps even more impressive was the fact that Sierra had racked up annual sales of nearly four million dollars. Ten years later, on the occasion of its

Stationkeeping equipment.

20th year in business, the firm had more than 500 employees and annual sales exceeding $20 million. In 1983 Sierra joined the LTV Corporation, and today about 1,300 employees work in its engineering and manufacturing facilities. In 1985 the company passed a notable milestone by registering sales of more than $100 million.

Sierra Research markets its products worldwide in four different areas: Command, Control, and Navigation (C2N), Advanced Technology Products (ATP), Electronic Warfare (EW), and International Applications (IA). C2N develops and sells existing and new programs, including radar, data links,

flight systems, test systems, and tactical air navigation (TACAN). ATP focuses on systems integration and battlefield electronics, which are concerned with surveillance and targeting. EW is involved with electronic countermeasures equipment and radar

LTV Missiles and Electronics Group, Sierra Research Division, Plant 1, on Cayuga Road in Buffalo.

A model of the airborne platform system.

threat simulators. IA markets Sierra product lines overseas, including avionics, test and navaid equipment, inspection systems, battlefield electronics, and communications.

The true scope of Sierra Research can be seen in its contracts with the U.S. military. A good example of this is the firm's development of a unique airborne electronics system that enables aircraft to fly in close formation under adverse visibility conditions and to communicate without voice transmission. Station-keeping systems are installed on most U.S. Air Force C-130 transports and half of the C-141 transports. In July 1986 McDonnell Douglas announced that it had awarded Sierra a $18.9-million contract to develop and produce advanced station-keeping systems for the C-17 airlifter. Sierra-developed tactical data links are used by the U.S. Navy in its LAMPS Mark III anti-submarine warfare program for the detection and location of enemy ships and submarines.

The company has also been busy on a $34-million Air Force project for two airborne platform/telemetry relay systems. Each system consists of a large, electronically steerable, phased array antenna mounted on the side of a de Havilland DASH 8 aircraft, and will operate out of Tyndall Air Force Base, Florida. The flying data link will relay telemetry, voice communications, and drone tracking data while performing radar surveillance on the Florida Gulf and other areas. It will enable critical Air Force tests to be safely conducted without affecting commercial and recrea-

tional use of the Gulf.

The military, however, is not the only area where Sierra Research expertise is put to use. The firm also manufactures precision airborne avionics equipment used to measure the accuracy of airport navigation aids and instrument landing facilities. The company's tactical air navigation equipment is used worldwide in more than 30 types of aircraft, from small helicopters to Boeing 747s.

In an industry that is constantly changing, Sierra Research is doing the same in order to stay on top. Its advancements in digital electronics and time/frequency technology are addressing many new and developing areas such as electronic surveillance, collision avoidance, integral data transfer, electronic warfare, and image-sensing weapons.

The Buffalo corporation also believes in sharing its success with the community. In 1985 Sierra Research donated $50,000 worth of electronic printed circuit boards to Seneca Vocational High School in Buffalo. The circuit boards are

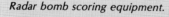

Radar bomb scoring equipment.

Total flight inspection system.

used in mainframe computers and data-collection systems, as well as to teach students how to solder, desolder, and rebuild the boards. Other community activities include strong participation in the Niagara Frontier U.S. Savings Bond Campaign, Employer Support of the Guard and Reserve, and the local chapter of the United Way.

It's a long way from the California mountains to the shores of Lake Erie, but the people at Sierra Research Division wouldn't have had things happen any other way.

Servotronics, Inc.

A unique enterprise, firmly entrenched at the leading edge of technology, Servotronics, Inc., has earned a reputation as "the problem-solving company." Its Advanced Technology Products Group designs and produces a variety of servocontrol components that have broad-ranging applications in aerospace, national defense, commercial and military aviation, and the medical and scientific fields.

Although Servotronics components, such as servocontrol valves, electromagnetic actuators, Apex and Omega metallic seals, and various associated products are all relatively small in size, they are vitally important in function. Each has been developed to solve a specific problem or meet a critical need. The overall performance of complex, multimillion-dollar systems are dependent upon the performance and reliability of the firm's products.

When this nation's huge 12.5-ton space telescope is launched, scientists can probe the unknown depths of the universe some 14 billion light-years away. Servotronics manufactures the electromagnetic actuator that is designed to remotely position a prism to calibrate the giant telescope in orbit.

Business aircraft such as the popular Cessna Citation 3, Gulfstream 3, and Lear Jet depend on Servotronics valves to control fuel flow to their jet engines. Many new-generation commercial aircraft also use the company's controls to regulate cabin air-conditioning and pressurization systems. On the intercontinental Concorde jetliner, a Servotronics pneumatic valve in the thrust reverse system provides deceleration during landing. Other commercial aircraft utilizing the firm's controls include the McDonnell Douglas DC-10; the Boeing 747, 757, and 767; the European Air Bus; and the C-5A, the largest

Dr. Nicholas D. Trbovich, founder, chairman of the board, and president.

cargo jet in the free world.

Servotronics products have long played a major role in the U.S. defense program. Flat armature torque motors help provide directional control for all versions of the U.S. Navy's Standard Missile series. A Servotronics component has been used in the missile since 1966. The Standard Missile is among the most reliable tactical air defense missiles in the world today. These medium- and extended-range missiles are currently operational on some 100 U.S. Navy ships and ships of allied navies. Servotronics also manufactures the coil assembly for the laser-guided Maverick missile.

On the latest military aircraft such as the F-18 Hornet Strike Fighter, the firm provides shear orifice valves for cabin pressurization. Other proven aircraft, including the F-14, F-15, and F-16; the B-1B bomber; and military helicopters, incorporate Servotronics valves and expertise. The General Electric rapid-fire gun drive uses the corporation's pneumatic servovalves. Control units for the turbine drive systems for new torpedo applications are also being designed and supplied.

In developing these and other products for advanced control

systems, Servotronics has consistently demonstrated its uncompromising dedication to excellence and attention to detail. The quality and performance of its products have been recognized by its customers over the years.

To assure continuation of the highest level of quality, reliability, and performance, Servotronics has made a long-term commitment of its efforts and resources. A computer-aided design system provides accuracy of design, with three-dimensional drawings made to scale, and revisions at the touch of a button. Numerically controlled machining centers that accommodate today's advanced programming techniques, fully equipped "white rooms," and rigid quality controls, all contribute to the firm's ability to translate problem-solving designs into finished products—often within stringent time and cost parameters.

The driving force behind Servotronics, Inc., is its chairman and president, Dr. Nicholas D. Trbovich, Sr., who founded the

Servotronics, Inc., corporate headquarters at 3901 Union Road, Buffalo, New York.

company in 1959 at the age of 24. With a strong engineering and management background, including both an M.B.A. and a doctorate degree from the University of Rochester, Trbovich has been awarded more than 30 U.S. and foreign patents, primarily in the fields of electromagnetic technology, fluid power, and consumer products.

After looking at other areas, Trbovich decided to establish his

One of Servotronics environmentally controlled clean rooms and assembly areas, with a collection of Servo Control components and other advanced technology products in the foreground.

expand its facilities. In 1965 the firm moved to its present location on Union Road, consolidating its technology divisions operations as well as its corporate offices.

By that time Servotronics had already established itself among Western New York's growing number of high-tech companies that have contributed substantially to the area's economy. Trbovich is a past director of the Greater Buffalo Chamber of Commerce. He also serves as a director/trustee of various civic organizations and local colleges. In 1967 Trbovich was named as one of the Five Outstanding Young Men in New York State.

The company became a public corporation in 1963, and its shares are listed on the American Stock Exchange. As it approaches its third decade of operation, Servotronics, Inc., continues its strong performance record—and looks optimistically to the future.

business in Buffalo, in a 5,000-square-foot newly constructed building. At the end of its first year Servotronics had five employees in addition to Trbovich, and was becoming well known in the defense and aerospace industries for innovative, problem-solving products. One of the major developments of these early years was a new electromechanical actuator that could operate continuously at 1,200 degrees Fahrenheit in a nuclear radiation environment. For this achievement, the firm was honored with the highest award granted by a leading technical publication.

Servotronics quickly outgrew its original plant, and later leased additional space in the former Wildroot Company building as well as several other locations. In the years that followed the company continued its steady pattern of growth and once again needed to

The United States Navy's Standard Missile contains a multitude of Servotronics products.

IBM

IBM got its start on July 15, 1911, as the Computing-Tabulating-Recording Co. (C-T-R), a corporation made up of three firms that manufactured tabulating machines, scales, and time recorders. Thomas J. Watson, Sr., became president in 1915, and through his business genius the company multiplied countless times during his administration. In 1924 C-T-R became known as International Business Machines, and the following year the first stock dividend was paid.

One of the three businesses that formed C-T-R—the Tabulating Machine Co.—was founded in 1896 by Dr. Herman Hollerith, a native Buffalonian whose home was on the corner of Main and Swan streets. His ideas provided the impetus for growth that began an IBM tradition of producing "firsts" in the industry.

During the Great Depression, when nearly one-quarter of the civilian labor force was unemployed, IBM embarked on a program of expansion. Rather than resort to mass factory layoffs, the firm produced parts for inventory and stored them. It was a gamble that paid off in 1935, when congress passed the Social Security Act, and IBM, in competitive bidding, was selected to undertake one of the greatest bookkeeping operations of all time. Due to the stockpiling of parts, the company was able to build the machines and begin delivery almost at once.

Along with its historic no-layoff policy, IBM places a great deal of emphasis on respecting the dignity of its employees. A quote by Thomas J. Watson, Jr., states that "People occupy more IBM management time than our products." Respect for the individual, outstanding customer service, and a commitment to excellence con-

IBM's waterfront home with city hall in the background on the left. Courtesy, Marc Murphy

tinue to be IBM's basic beliefs.

For more than 70 years the firm and Buffalo have been partners in progress. Locally, its roots date back to 1916, when an office of the C-T-R Co. was opened at 785 Main Street in Buffalo. An IBM retiree, Mary E. McLaughlin, who worked for "40 years, 4 months, and 4 days—all in the same location, Buffalo," stated that when she joined the Buffalo office in 1943 there were only 50 employees. IBM Buffalo currently employs 245 people, including those in its Jamestown location.

Through the years the company has moved to several locations within the city, and currently is proud to be part of the Waterfront Village Complex, which was once an undeveloped stretch of lakefront land. Its three-story office building houses a marketing and service division and boasts a progressive Customer Center. This center provides both the physical facility and personnel for cus-

tomer education, training, and support of IBM products.

Throughout more than four decades of rapid growth and change in the information-processing industry, IBM has been a leader in technical innovation. Its product line spans the spectrum of information-handling systems, equipment, and services. The company develops, manufactures, markets, and services information-processing machines, software and systems, desk-top computers and terminals, office systems, typewriters, printers, copiers, telecommunications systems and products, related supplies, and educational and testing materials.

Extensive programs of education and training for personal and professional growth are available to IBM employees throughout their careers. Statistics on education programs within the company for 1984-1985 report about five million student days worldwide per year, which is an average of 12 days per employee.

IBM supports education in many ways, including grants of cash and equipment to colleges, universities, and educational associations; matching grants; and scholarships to children of employees. In addition, 100 students whose parents are not IBM employees are awarded $1,000 one-time scholarships. Under the Faculty Loan Program, the firm's employees are given paid leaves of absence to teach at colleges with predominantly minority enrollments.

IBM-sponsored programs also promote computer literacy. The firm's activities in this area include the recent donation of personal computer systems, software, and teacher training to elementary and secondary schools in more than 30 states. Another program uses PCs to teach kindergarten and first-grade students how to read and write.

The company continues to expand its purchase of products and services from businesses owned by minorities or women, as well as from suppliers that have a predominantly handicapped work force.

These activities illustrate the fact that IBM and its people have always felt a responsibility for leadership and civic participation by supporting educational, cultural, and social programs in the com-

Susan Wyman (standing on left), IBM advisor to the Job Training Center, and Joan King (seated), acting director of the Buffalo Urban League's Job Training Center, which is located in the Ellicott Square Building. Courtesy, Marc Murphy

munities where they live and work.

In Buffalo this support includes job training for the economically disadvantaged and under-employed individuals, and a broad program of matching grants for education, hospitals, and the arts. Also included are contributions to local organizations through the IBM Fund for Community Service, a program established to encourage and support volunteerism by employees, retirees, and their spouses.

IBM also helped the Buffalo Urban League establish a Job Training Center, which is located in the Ellicott Square Building. The center, which began job training in June 1985, has already realized a significant return on investment in terms of job placement. Support from the Greater Buffalo Chamber of Commerce and the local business community has been instrumental in laying the foundation for a successful program in Buffalo. Since the inception of the first Job Training Center in 1968, more than 60 facilities have been established nationwide with a combined placement rate of at

least 80 percent of the 14,000 individuals trained.

Locally, IBM also supports the chambers of commerce of Buffalo and Jamestown; the United Way; local historical organizations; public television; a Junior Achievement pilot program in which employees taught economics courses to high school students; Career Days for high schools and colleges; Allentown Industries, a sheltered workshop; and Christmas Food Baskets for the needy.

As Thomas Watson, Jr., once said: "I believe the real difference between success and failure in a corporation can very often be traced to the question of how well the organization brings out the great energies and talents of its people."

IBM's new facility on Buffalo's waterfront stands as a tribute to many: its employees—who, over the years, have demonstrated the flexibility and determination needed to adapt and succeed with IBM; to Herman Hollerith—a man whose creative imagination helped lay the foundation of the company; and to the City of Buffalo and Western New York—a community and region that have responded successfully to the challenges of time to emerge vital, aggressive, and dynamic. IBM shares Buffalo's positive outlook for the future and hope that, together, they can continue their combined efforts toward progress.

Account systems engineer Chinappa Mokka is shown working in the Customer Center which overlooks the waterfront. Courtesy, Marc Murphy

agency. We are the network people for local industry, particularly a small start-up industry that doesn't know what resources are available. They come to us and we put them in touch with the marvelous machine that the university, the hospitals, Roswell Park, Calspan, and so on, represent.''

At this writing, there are fifty-two projects in progress at the institute, with research contracts totaling 2.7 million dollars. Both the projects and the sponsors are quite varied. Sixteen of the companies are from the Greater Buffalo area, sponsoring over $450,000 worth of research. Four sponsors are from other parts of New York State, while the remaining fourteen are both domestic and foreign.

''Besides contracts with various local companies like Westwood, Gaymar, and the Medical Foundation of Buffalo, we have compa-

nies that come to us all the way from Silicon Valley," said Dr. Baier. "That gives me a lot of personal delight—I love spending California money."

Dr. Baier has been constantly striving to break down the false stereotype that industry and academia are at odds with each other. "If somebody has a problem—be it a local company or some giant outside firm—they can come to us and not hear something like, 'Well, that's an interesting problem. We'll put a student on it and you can come back in two years.' That's academic business as usual," he said. "Instead of asking [companies] to meet our pace, we will meet theirs. It's really a business arrangement for the delivery of a research project."

With that in mind, HIDI research projects lean toward developing products for the marketplace. Westwood Pharmaceuticals, for ex-

Computer Task Group, Inc.

Three million in 1975, 100 million by 1985, one billion by 1995. That is the revenue goal of Buffalo-born Computer Task Group, Inc, a company that sees a certain full-figured beauty in big business.

However, in the beginning big wasn't beautiful to CTG. In fact, when it was started in 1966 by a pair of ex-IBM employees, the idea was simply to provide computer programming services to the many small companies that had computers but limited staff. But small wasn't where the business was destined to stay.

Founders Randolph A. Marks and G. David Baer soon found it was the big firms that knocked at their rented door. And answering opportunity's knock has paid off: From its first 500-square-foot office at 5586 Main Street in Williamsville, the company's Buffalo presence today includes a pair of Delaware Avenue mansions, as well as two other area locations. CTG also has a network of 50 branch offices in the United States, Canada, and the United Kingdom—with plans to open more in the next few years. And 2,500-plus employees, more than 400 in Western New York, weekly cash paychecks that bear the CTG logo.

How CTG grew into a firm that designs, builds, implements, and maintains information and automation systems for *Fortune* 500 companies is the result of many factors—the phenomenal growth of computer technology, to be sure, being the single largest. But beyond that CTG is an organization that has succeeded in defining both itself and its market to an extent unusual among Western New York businesses. The company's activities on Delaware Avenue are a case in point.

In 1978 the firm bought the former Knox residence at 800

CTG systems professionals provide a broad range of systems development services.

Delaware Avenue. There the green phospher glow of modern computer terminals reflects against polished marble walls as CTG's top management goes about its daily businesss. Notable is the fact that among this group the average age is 44 and the average length of service to the company is 12 years. Both CTG's chief executive officer, David N. Campbell, and its president and chief operating officer, John P. Courtney, joined the company in 1968.

Loyalty to the corporation, as well as business excellence, is also fostered just down the avenue at a second refurbished mansion—now CTG's Institute for Technical and Management Training. There the company makes an annual multimillion-dollar investment

208

in its employees by offering more than 30 different courses in subjects ranging from fourth-generation computer languages and database design to current management theory and selling skills. The institute consists of classrooms, computer labs, residence quarters, and dining and recreational facilities. In addition, employees receive full tuition and can earn college credit for selected courses.

This commitment to its work force is also carried out in the firm's management philosophy, which might best be termed a form of corporate laissez-faire. Employees speak of the lack of constraints and ability to determine their own futures. Company publications are peppered with plaudits for successful individuals. And tellingly, nearly 60 percent of the firm's employees own CTG stock. Corporate benefits are among the best in the business—a not-insignificant factor in making CTG's personnel turnover rate one

The former Knox residence at 800 Delaware Avenue is headquarters for Computer Task Group, Inc.

of the lowest in a high-turnover industry. In 1985 more than 25,000 job applicants submitted resumes to the company.

But beyond this clear identification and fostering of its internal resources, CTG has also been successful in clearly identifying what lies outside. It sees its greatest potential in meeting the internal software development needs of its current *Fortune* 500 clients. To achieve this goal, the firm has carefully mapped out a strategy that emphasizes its expertise in certain specialty areas, including banking and insurance, telecommunications, and industrial automation.

For example, CTG now has industrial automation centers in Pittsburgh, Philadephia, and Detroit, with more centers in the planning stages. From these specialty centers, experts in such fields as artificial intelligence, robotics, and factory automation offer software assistance to customers. Likewise, CTG business experts in other locations offer expertise in manufacturing, retail distribution, and financial services. Because applications software is a key competitive weapon for many of its client customers, the average

CTG systems engineer is as much an intelligence officer as he is a programmer when it comes to the "warfare" of modern information-based business.

The corporation's clients include names with which every Western New Yorker is familiar. Goldome, Norstar, Empire of America, and Marine Midland banks; Occidental Chemical; National Fuel Gas; Niagara Mohawk; Du Pont; Xerox; and Eastman Kodak are among its clients with headquarters or facilities in the nearby area. And on the national level, CTG does work for some of the best-known names in American business, including General Motors, General Electric, Rockwell International, Alcoa, Monsanto, and AT&T.

As Buffalo's manufacturing base has decreased over the last few decades, service industry companies such as CTG have come to the fore as a potent force in the local—and national—economy. And while it still may be a few years (and a few zeroes) away from that billion-dollar milestone, Computer Task Group, Inc., is still the best example we have that geography is no hindrance when it comes to success.

ample, is using the institute to gather data on the ability of its sunscreen products to remain on the skin under varying conditions, such as after water is splashed on a sunscreened arm.

Although Westwood has its own research facilities, the company approached HIDI because the institute has access to special equipment through the vast network of university departments and hospitals. This particular Westwood research is occurring in a clinic called the Instruments and Devices Evaluation Area (IDEA Lab) which HIDI established at Buffalo General Hospital.

Dr. Russell Bessette, director of the IDEA Lab and a surgeon affiliated with the Buffalo Medical Group, recently told a *Buffalo News* reporter, "When companies come to us for testing or research on products, the things that come out hopefully will mean new busi-

Comptek is a Buffalo-based company that specializes in electronic components for the defense industry. Photo by Peter R. Barber

ness for Western New York.''

When HIDI receives matching money from the state, the money goes back into the general research area that originally interested some company enough to draw down the matching funds. The thinking, therefore, is that by developing those areas, perhaps more industrial interest will follow, and the spiral will continue.

Of the total sponsored research at the university, HIDI's share is only a small percentage. Although the total dollar volume of sponsored research for the latest fiscal year was sixty million dollars, much of that money came from federal agencies.

That is where the institute hopes to initiate changes, with the ultimate goal of spawning new companies from HIDI research projects.

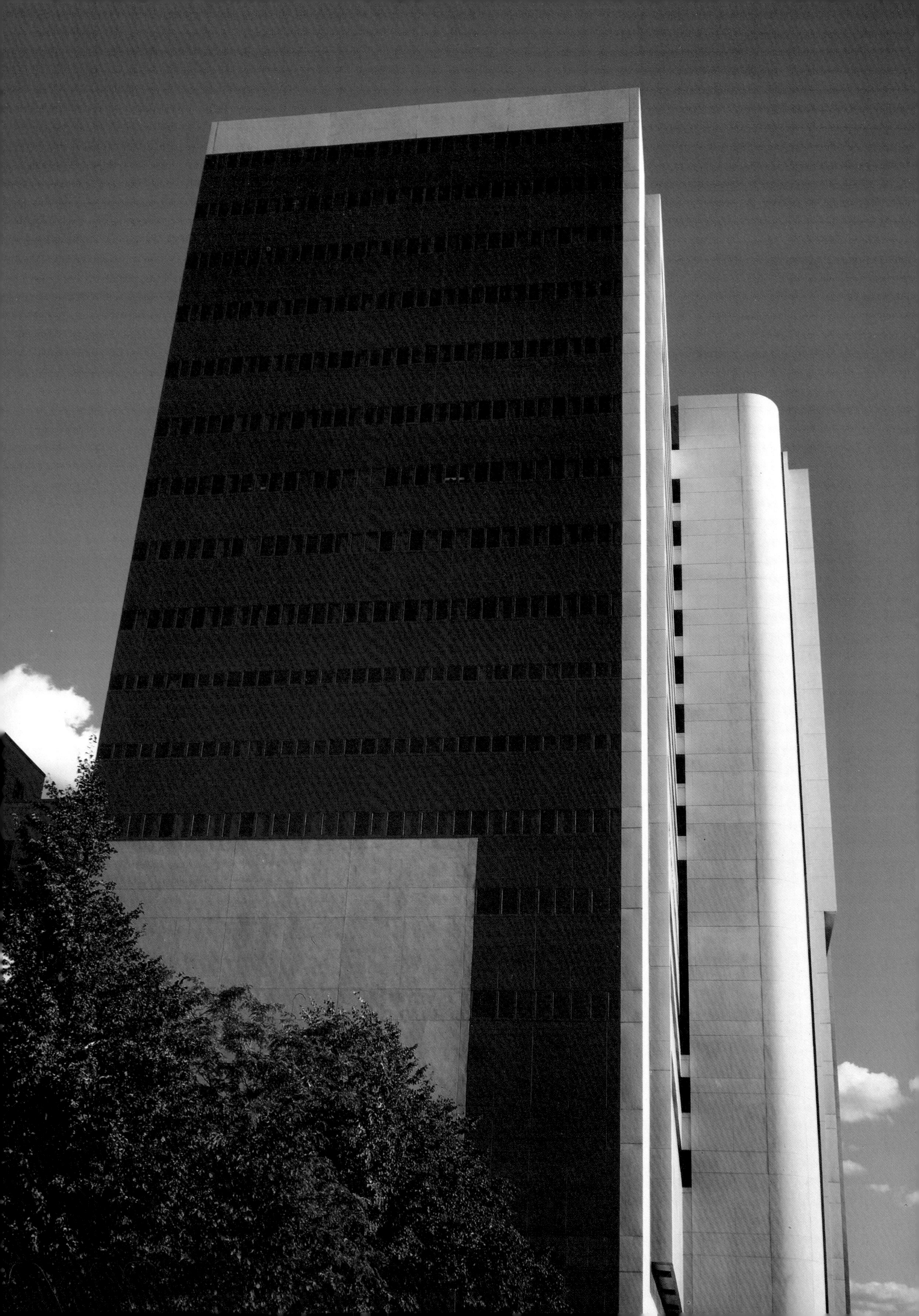

CHAPTER EIGHT

Medicinal Purposes

University at Buffalo president Dr. Steven Sample refers to the area as "an extraordinary center of biomedical research." Others refer to the vast extent of such work as Buffalo's "best kept secret," a "secret" that has grown for over a century with the help of such noted researchers as Dr. Roswell Park who arrived from Chicago in 1883 to fill the University of Buffalo's chair of surgery at the School of Medicine and became, subsequently, chief surgeon at Buffalo General Hospital. His study of malignant tumors led to the establishment of the internationally renowned Roswell Park Memorial Institute for cancer treatment and research.

When Dr. Herbert Hauptman, research director of the Medical Foundation of Buffalo, Inc., was awarded the 1985 Nobel Prize for chemistry, this "secret" industry was suddenly in the spotlight. Medical research in Greater Buffalo no longer had a microscopic community awareness. It was shown for the fertile, wide-ranging field that it is, with far-reaching effects not only locally but internationally.

The local research industry can basically be divided into three sectors: the so-called "pure" research done at places like Medical Foundation of Buffalo and Roswell Park Memorial Institute; the clinical research done in area hospitals like Millard Fillmore and Buffalo General; and the more commercially oriented product development at places like Westwood Pharmaceuticals and Gaymar Industries.

In the thirty years since the Medical Foundation of Buffalo was founded, the contributions that the staff has made to the study of endocrinology—the science of internal glands—have brought it worldwide attention in medical circles, capped by Dr. Hauptman's award for his mathematical technique to determine the structures of molecules vital to life.

Albert Wright III, executive vice-president of administration, has addressed the misconceptions that the general public has about this independent non-profit biomedical research institute. "There are two things we don't do," he stated. "We don't provide health care and we don't produce a product, such as a medication. We conduct research on the basic levels, providing the building blocks for other people to work on. Our major product is knowledge."

He characterized the efforts of the foundation as "quiet research—no sparks and fireworks, but extremely important work."

The research being done in the High Street laboratories is varied.

Below: Nobel Prize-winner Herbert Hauptman poses in his Buffalo office the day his prize was announced. Photo by Robert McElroy

Above, right: Though the lobby of Westwood Pharmaceuticals is thoroughly modern, the company is a century-old Buffalo establishment. It was started in 1876 as a research laboratory. Photo by Patricia Layman Bazelon

One study focuses on the effects of environmental pollutants, food additives, smoking, drugs, and other medications on the production and activity of hormones during pregnancy. Other research programs center on the use of steroids in arthritis, heart failure, stroke, cancer, and other metabolic diseases.

Anti-cancer studies include the search for anti-cancer drugs that have specific sites of action. For example, foundation studies have shown that a major ingredient of birth control pills may be effective in stopping up to one-third of breast cancers which require estrogen to grow.

Although methotrexate is the most widely used cancer chemotherapeutic drug, its effectiveness is somewhat diminished by the serious side effects that occur. Therefore, another area of concentration is on the discovery of a more selective drug that stops the enzyme in cancer cells only, thereby shrinking the tumor.

When it comes to cancer research, however, Roswell Park Memorial Institute is most associated with studies and breakthroughs. It is the oldest and one of the largest cancer research, treatment, and educational facilities in the world.

Its list of accomplishments includes:

—photodynamic therapy, a laser/chemical process pioneered at Roswell, which is used worldwide to treat cancers of the skin, lung, breast, bladder, and head and neck.
—the development of a simple, inexpensive blood test for the early detection of prostate cancer.

Westwood Pharmaceuticals' skin-care products are distributed worldwide. Photo by Patricia Layman Bazelon

Dr. John L. Wright is the director of the prestigious Roswell Park Memorial Institute. Photo by Robert McElroy

—the introduction of a new surgical technique which saves the limbs of over 90 percent of patients whose only other option in the past was amputation.

—the establishment of the country's first Voluntary Plasmapheresis Donor Center for blood platelet collection.

—the development of a treatment that has improved survival rates for childhood cancer from 50 to 70 percent.

—the development of a new photo-radiation therapy to treat skin tumors that might formerly have been diagnosed as inoperable.

According to Dr. Verne Chapman, associate director for scientific affairs, "Roswell Park has a special mission in determining the causes of cancer, as well as in the treatment of the disease."

This mission is part of the legacy left by the institute's founder, Dr. Roswell Park, who recognized the future devastation that cancer would bring upon the world.

In 1898 he developed a cancer research laboratory in three small rooms in the School of Medicine, becoming a pioneer not only in the field of medical research, but also in the present-day structure of government funding of—and community support for—medical research on specific diseases.

"Although our first responsibility will continue to be excellence in research, there are opportunities to forge stronger relations with the university and the local medical community," Dr. Chapman observed. "We have not yet developed active ties with the local

The Roswell Park Memorial Institute has pioneered in laser treatments for certain cancers. Photo by Robert McElroy

business community, but we're looking for ways in which the special character of Roswell Park can contribute to the economic vitality of the Western New York area. Along those lines, we are reassessing and hoping to strengthen the staffing of the institute to improve our capability of attracting research support so that we can maintain the fundamental excellence of the work that is going on here.''

In 1985 T&B Bioclone became one of the first attempts to establish a separate company from Roswell Park research. With the objective of studying better ways to deliver anti-cancer drugs to tumors, T&B Bioclone is an example of technology transfer that paves the way for state-sponsored basic research to venture into the commercial world.

The "technology corridor" along Oak and Elm streets continues to expand. In the fall of 1985, the Oncologic Foundation, a small

The Mentholatum Company, Inc.

The Mentholatum Company, Inc., of Buffalo, with global operations ranging from Australia to Africa and China, began business in Wichita, Kansas, in 1889. The firm was founded by Albert Alexander "A.A." Hyde and is still controlled by the Hyde family, with George H. Hyde as president and his cousin, Theodore A. Hyde, as executive vice-president.

A.A. Hyde had been a banker at an institution in Wichita that failed during a severe depression in the 1880s. Undaunted, he turned to a new venture, the Yucca Company, whose line of products included soap, shoe polish, perfume, and sewing machine oil.

The origin of the formula for Mentholatum Ointment is somewhat uncertain. Hyde and a physician friend developed a prescription to relieve various discomforts that later became what is now known as Mentholatum Ointment. Among its ingredients are camphor, menthol, and petrolatum. Its early trademark was a picture of a nurse with the inscription, "The Little Nurse For Little Ills." Today billions of tins and jars of Mentholatum Ointment have been sold in some 120 countries.

Hyde was a deeply religious man, and his daily routine included prayer and reading of the Bible. He also was a philanthropist who was known not just for tithing, but, in his case, for giving away 90 percent of his income. Various foreign missionary groups, in particular the OMI Brotherhood in Japan, benefited from his support.

About 1912 Hyde sent a missionary to Japan. After two years of providing financial aid, he suggested that the missionary introduce Mentholatum Ointment in Japan and use the proceeds to finance his goal of converting the Japanese to Christianity. The product did well in Japan, and the substantial proceeds were used to create an entire school system, the largest tuberculosis hospital in Japan, and 13 Christian churches.

Thanks to favorable word of mouth from satisfied customers and unique trade incentives in the United States, Mentholatum Ointment obtained retail distribution in the Midwest and the Pacific Northwest. In 1903, as demand continued to grow, a second Yucca Company factory was opened in Buffalo, where The Mentholatum Company, Inc., maintains its world headquarters and a manufacturing plant. The firm adopted its present name in 1906.

Mentholatum Ointment was so successful that it became the corporation's flagship brand, and other products were added later on. Today the firm's sales are approaching $100 million annually. The company has manufacturing facilities in 24 countries and markets more than 50 different products, but Mentholatum Ointment is still the largest seller.

Other major brands in the firm's product line include Mentholatum Deep Heating Rub for muscle aches and arthritis pain; Fletcher's Castoria, the largest-selling children's laxative; and Mentholatum Lipbalm.

During the past 20 years The Mentholatum Company, Inc., has acquired other businesses around the world, as well as various product lines. More than 70 percent of the brands now sold by the firm came from acquisitions. Those products include Fletcher's Castoria, Red Cross Toothache Kits, Snug Denture Cushions, Medi-Quik First Aid Spray, Astring-O-Sol Mouthwash, Cope Analgesic

Theodore A. Hyde (left), executive vice-president, and George H. Hyde, president.

The Mentholatum Company, Inc., with manufacturing facilities in 24 countries, maintains its world headquarters at 1360 Niagara Street, in Buffalo.

Tablets, Thermodent Toothpaste for sensitive teeth, Resinol Skin Care Ointment, Calmol-4 Suppositories, and Unguentine for skin burns.

Among the companies acquired by Mentholatum were a French firm that markets medicinal cosmetics and an Australian concern that produces Laxettes, the leading laxative in Australia, and Stop 'N Grow for fingernail biters.

Mentholatum sells its products through drug wholesalers, food chains, drug chains, and mass merchandisers. Its largest markets are in the United States, Japan, and Nigeria, although the company's products are sold in 138 countries throughout the Free World.

Manufacturing operations are carried out in 24 foreign countries, including Canada, Japan, Puerto Rico, England, France, Australia, Nigeria, and Chile. In addition, the firm has marketing/distribution facilities in Hong Kong and South Africa. The Mentholatum Company products are also exported from the United States, England, France, Canada, and Australia to foreign markets. In fact, more than two-thirds of the firm's sales are in international markets.

The Mentholatum Company, Inc., operates under a number of different business arrangements in the 138 countries where it sells products, including joint ventures, licensing agreements, wholly owned subsidiaries, and partially owned subsidiaries. This flexibility enables the firm to compete in virtually any marketplace.

Through the years sales and profits in the proprietary drug industry have continued to grow. The Mentholatum Company's sales have also shown steady growth and have significantly outperformed industry growth patterns. In the past the firm has carefully avoided head-to-head competition with well-known brands of large multinational corporations. This strategy calls for carefully developing consumer niches that are solid business opportunities, yet not large enough in volume to draw intense competition. This strategy has paid off.

The company places particular marketing emphasis on the mature population—adults 55 years of age and older. Over the next 30 years this will be the fastest-growing segment of the U.S. population. This segment also spends a higher portion of discretionary income on self-treatment and self-medication.

Aggressive expansion of Mentholatum's product line worldwide includes plans for joint manufacturing ventures in India and China. Those two operations would serve markets with a combined population of nearly two billion people. More important, the commitment to quality that has been the foundation of the success of The Mentholatum Company, Inc., since 1889 will continue to be the driving force for the future.

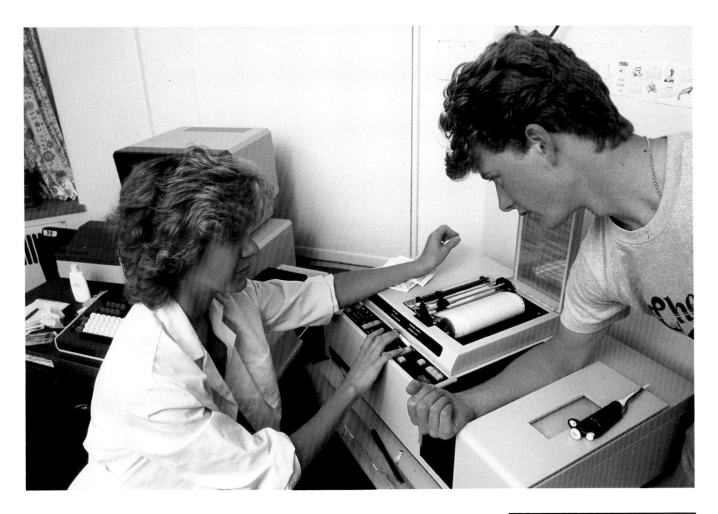

non-profit organization devoted to medical research, moved into the area. It is currently working under a $450,000-per-year contract with Johnson & Johnson to research the use of lasers in cancer treatment.

A technician in a research project funded by Westwood Pharmaceuticals uses a spectrometer to test the skin condition of a patient. Photo by Joe Traver

University at Buffalo researchers recently received a four-million-dollar grant from the National Cancer Institute for a five-year study into whether foods can cause or prevent certain kinds of cancer. It is believed to be the largest amount ever awarded for research into the link between diet and cancer.

University officials described the grant as a quantum leap for local researchers who already won nationwide acclaim when they linked carotene (a pigment found in orange vegetables) with a reduced incidence of certain cancers. They've also found increasing evidence that people who eat a large amount of fats have a higher risk of contracting cancer than those who eat less fatty foods. The goal of this new study would be twofold: to determine whether fats or the calories associated with these fats cause cancer; to see if exercise reduces the chances for cancer and, if so, the type of exercise and the types of cancer.

The work will be especially significant due to the fact that the

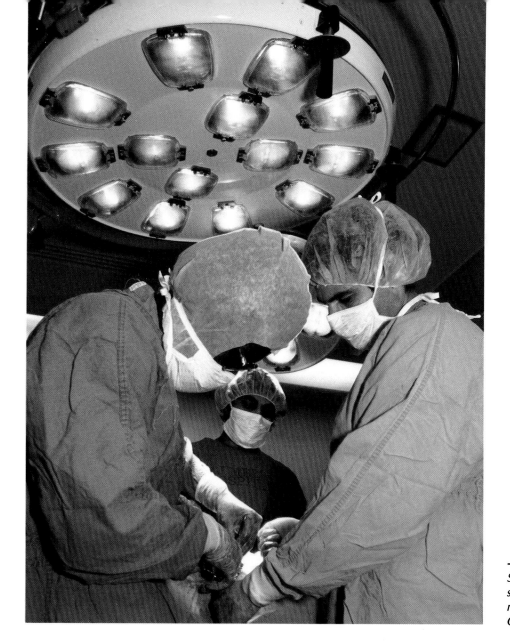

Surgeons perform open-heart surgery at the well-equipped and modern Erie County Medical Center. Photo by Joe Traver

prognosis for some types of cancer is still very poor. Therefore, preventing the disease rather than attempting to eradicate its effects after it invades the body would be a remarkable stride toward eliminating cancer. Among the cancers to be examined in the study are those found in the pancreas, breast, prostate, bladder, and cancers in the gynecologic tract.

Other projects in progress at the university's school of medicine include:

—the development of new radioactive drugs for non-invasive diagnosis of heart disease.
—a probe into the manner by which the human brain interprets what it sees. Through studying the color vision of macaque monkeys, an understanding should be attained as to how the visual cortex—which is part of the brain—creates color vision.
—a study of how drugs of abuse affect the human body and behavior.
—a study of how high blood pressure is affected by alcohol consumption and prostaglandins, a hormone found in reproductive fluids.
—an attempt to identify whether the Hemophilus influenza bacteria, present in lung secretions of respiratory patients, is the cause of chronic lung disease.

Roswell Park Memorial Institute

Roswell Park Memorial Institute, the oldest and one of the largest cancer research, treatment, and educational facilities in the world, traces its origins back to the late 1890s, when Dr. Roswell Park conceived the idea for the development of a cancer research laboratory in three small rooms at the University of Buffalo School of Medicine.

Dr. Park recognized the future tragedy that cancer would bring to the world. Cancer, although a baffling medical mystery when he began, was not one of the most feared and fatal diseases of the day. However, today cancer ranks second only to heart disease as the leading cause of death in the United States.

Roswell Park Memorial Institute is a division of the New York State Health Department. It is unique among research facilities in that it maintains a 258-bed hospital that admits thousands of inpatients and outpatients annually.

But the facility is more than an imposing group of buildings that cover six city blocks. It is the embodiment of a philosophy that links laboratory discoveries with patient care and views professional and public education as essential in fighting cancer. That philosophy is part of the legacy left by Dr. Park.

In the beginning Dr. Park and Edward H. Butler, Sr., publisher of the *Buffalo Evening News,* asked the New York State Legislature to introduce a bill that would provide a $7,500 grant to establish a cancer research laboratory at the University of Buffalo School of Medicine. Butler's political acumen assured that the bill would pass. The grant provided for equipment and maintenance of a laboratory devoted to investigation

Roswell Park Memorial Institute's facilities cover six city blocks.

into the causes, nature, mortality rate, and treatment of cancer. Thus the first facility in the world dedicated specifically to cancer research was born. It was called the New York State Pathological Laboratory of the University of Buffalo.

Dr. Park's research soon grew too large for the laboratory space in the university's School of Medicine. As a result, land was purchased by public-spirited citizens and, largely through the generosity of Mrs. William Gratwick, the Gratwick Research Laboratory of the university was built in 1901. In 1960 the Gratwick Basic Science Building was erected at a cost of $5.6 million.

Roswell Park Memorial Institute provides laboratory research, educational programs, and patient care in 10 major buildings, several ancillary facilities, and three satel-

lite locations comprising approximately 900,000 square feet of space.

Since 1955 the institute has administered a division of the University of Buffalo Graduate School. Staff scientists and clinicians serve as Graduate School faculty members as part of their commitment to the facility's mission as a national comprehensive cancer center. The Roswell Park Graduate Division offers programs in the life sciences, conferring advanced degrees through 10 academic departments. Resident physician and clinical fellowship training programs are conducted in 13 clinical specialties.

Roswell Park Memorial Institute has a long-standing tradition of commitment to public education. The facility is a National Cancer Institute Regional Cancer Communication Office. It conducts education programs in the work place and in the community, and sponsors teacher conferences in addition to distributing health and

Dr. Roswell Park, for whom the institute is named, was a pioneer cancer research scientist at the University of Buffalo around the turn of the century.

science education materials to classroom teachers. The office also operates a Smoking Hotline and an AIDS Hotline.

The institute's basic research programs provide the broad understanding from which clinical programs develop. The fundamental knowledge derived from laboratory studies focusing on the structure and function of the molecule, cell, cell membrane, and biochemical-biomolecular interactions are the foundation for advances in patient treatment and care. Clinical research programs range from preclinical laboratory

studies and national cooperative group trials to improved methodology for the detection and prevention of cancer.

The facility's medical and scientific staff is also deeply committed to professional education and community outreach. One of the strengths of the staff is its full-time commitment to patient care through research, and many of its members are involved in international projects and national clinical cooperative groups, and serve on professional committees and technical journal boards. Staff members also are encouraged to become active participants in the national and international cancer effort.

In order to provide its research staff and students with access to the latest in technology and technical services in a cost-effective manner, the institute has developed a number of core resources.

They include an electron microscopy facility, a laboratory for nuclear magnetic resonance microscopy, a laboratory for nuclear resonance spectroscopy, and a fluoresence-activated cell sorter.

The Department of Laboratory Animal Resources provides for the centralization of animal care and housing for each of the major research buildings. It also manages the Wehr Biocontainment Building, the West Seneca mouse-breeding laboratory, and the Springville Laboratories for the breeding and housing of large animals, as well as serving as the coordinating office for the institute's Animal Care Committee.

In the 1980s work being done at the Roswell Park Memorial Institute and elsewhere is providing treatment for one million cancer patients each year. Despite all that has been done so far, the number of cases is increasing, and more than 390,000 Americans will die of the disease each year. If the current trend continues, one out of every four people in the United States can expect to contract cancer in some form during their lifetime. Despite all that, the prognosis is improving for the cancer patient.

If, 100 years after the founding of Dr. Roswell Park's noble experiment in that small three-room laboratory, cancer is indeed conquered, it will be due in no small part to his foresight and the dedication of those who have followed in his footsteps at the Roswell Park Memorial Institute.

The main entrance to Roswell Park Memorial Institute across from the Cell and Virus Building where scientists conduct research on the inheritance of characteristic traits by people and animals, how normal growth is controlled, and how changes in these processes affect the development of cancer.

223

National Health Care Affiliates, Inc.

When Mark E. Hamister began working in long-term health care facilities in the mid-1970s, few would have predicted that in only 10 years he would be president and chief executive officer of the 18th-largest investor-owned chain of such facilities in the nation.

Hamister, however, simply believes that his business plan is "right on track." Hamister, along with his father, George E. Hamister, and his uncle, Oliver C. Hamister, are the principal owners of National Health Care Affiliates, Inc. (NHCA). Quite naturally, the Hamisters are proud of their success and of their Buffalo roots.

Today NHCA owns and operates 14 long-term care facilities with more than 2,200 beds in New York, Connecticut, Virginia, and Florida. In the Buffalo area, National Health Care operates the Brompton Heights residential care facility at 275 Brompton Road in Williamsville. Brompton Heights offers both private and semi-

National Health Care Affiliates' corporate headquarters is located at 651 Delaware Avenue in Buffalo.

private accommodations, as well as a broad range of activities that includes everything from arts and crafts to luncheons and day trips.

The company is now the 18th-largest health care chain in the industry according to *Modern Healthcare* magazine's annual industry ranking. With revenues

projected at more than $40 million for 1986, NHCA is a force to be reckoned with in the health care field.

The firm's rapid growth is reflected in three consecutive appearances in *Inc.* magazine's survey of the 500 fastest-growing private companies in the nation, ranking 23rd in 1985. NHCA's increase in revenues of 6,026 percent between 1980 and 1984 makes it the fastest growing private company in Western New York.

Hamister attributes the company's growth to its people, from administrators to housekeepers, nurse's aides to vice-presidents—the work force of more than 1,800 employees who have made NHCA a leader in the long-term care industry.

"NHCA is in more than the health care business," says Hamister. "We are in the 'people' business and it is people—residents and their families alike—that the company serves. The elderly have so much to share with us, and we in the field of long-term care are

NHCA's principals and original co-founders (from left): Oliver C. Hamister, Mark E. Hamister, and George E. Hamister.

Florence Parrish and her son, Harold, enjoying Brompton Heights' Annual Miss Buffalo Cruise.

from severe trauma to the predictable signs of aging, staff members must be prepared to adapt and respond to a variety of challenges.

NHCA facilities, led by experienced administrators and a dedicated, knowledgeable staff, epitomize the emphasis on excellence found throughout the organization. Superior quality standards have resulted in accolades from state agencies with whom the company works. In fact, four of NHCA's six Florida facilities have received "Superior"

Brompton Heights, Western New York's premier adult residence, sits amid beautifully landscaped grounds at 275 Brompton Road in Williamsville.

The firm's pride in its Buffalo roots was shown in a renovation and improvement project completed at its corporate headquarters in 1985. A Buffalo Beautiful Award winner, the privately financed $40,000 project involved the installation of heated sidewalks, landscaping, and benches to add a park-like setting, and renovation of the office/lobby area.

From its corporate headquarters to all of its facilities, a dedicated staff helps make NHCA an industry leader. These efforts are applauded through employee-recognition programs that underscore the people orientation of the company.

Various forms of recognition make up the programs. They include attendance awards, employees of the month and year, corporate-wide honorariums, as well as superior license bonuses.

NHCA is dedicated to up-and-coming health care professionals and supports them through an administrator-in-training program. The year-long program, overseen by NHCA regional vice-presidents as preceptors, prepares future administrators through their spending time working in each position within a nursing home, in addition to being admitted as a resident for a two-day period. This learning tool was experienced by Mark Hamister in his own administrative training. Says Hamister, "Living as a resident does is the only way that we can truly become caregivers and understand the true customer needs."

Quality and efficiency of operations have allowed National Health Care Affiliates, Inc., to become an industry leader. The Hamister family and NHCA, like the City of Buffalo, are on the cutting edge of exciting additional growth, change, and excellence. They are proud to be a participant in the revitalization of this fine city.

privileged to have the chance to learn from these people. That's why you will never hear the word 'patient' in any of NHCA's facilities. These individuals are residents who call NHCA facilities home."

The Hamister family is quick to point out that superior quality of care and of life for all NHCA residents is the benchmark that sets the company apart from its competitors. With residents ranging in age from 20 to more than 100, and with health needs ranging

licenses from the state, a recognition received by a scant 20 percent of all facilities in that state.

NHCA's corporate headquarters at 651-661 Delaware Avenue has grown and evolved along with the firm as a whole. Starting with fewer than five employees and rented space in its present building, NHCA now has some 50 people on staff and occupies approximately 17,000 square feet of floor space in the Delaware Avenue complex, now owned by principals of the company.

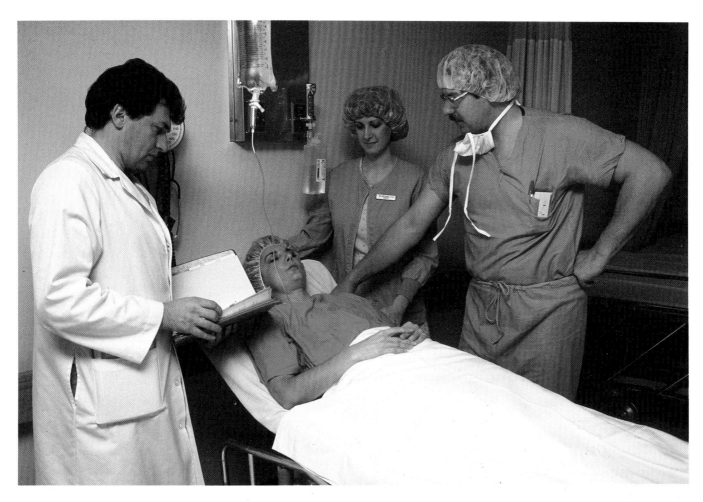

Above: Two physicians and a surgical nurse perform pre-operative procedures at Millard Fillmore Hospital. Photo by Jim Pierotti. Courtesy, Millard Fillmore Hospital, Photography Department

Right: Millard Fillmore Hospital, a pioneer in surgery, brings national attention to the area. Photo by Jim Pierotti. Courtesy, Millard Fillmore Hospital, Photography Department

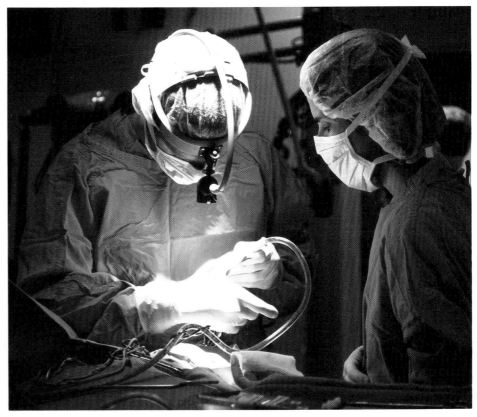

—a study of how certain diuretic (urine-inducing) drugs interfere with the body's ability to properly utilize sugar and energy, thereby developing a way of avoiding such an undesirable side effect in diabetics and others undergoing kidney therapy.

—an investigation into the legal and other problems associated with the re-hospitalization of chronic psychiatric patients.

Again looking ahead to the year 2000, the medical possibilities hold remarkable potential. A new drug to diagnose heart disease? A great advance in kidney therapy? A way to prevent cancer through your diet? The twenty-first century may indeed bring such break-throughs—a direct result of the research and insight of the Greater Buffalo medical community.

Hospitals and High-Tech Care

Over the decades, Greater Buffalo hospitals have contributed significantly to medical science, along with developing a reputation for quality care.

The achievements of Roswell Park Memorial Institute are joined by achievements at Buffalo General Hospital, where the use of a blood dialyzer was pioneered in 1954, as well as a new technique for heart examination. Six years later, the area's first open-heart surgery was performed there.

A pharmacist at Millard Fillmore Hospital carefully fills a prescription. Photo by Jim Pierotti. Courtesy, Millard Fillmore Hospital, Photography Department

Members of several hospitals may unite toward a common goal. At Veterans Hospital in the late 1950s, for instance, Dr. William M. Chardack and Dr. Andrew A. Gage worked with electronics engineer and local inventor Wilson Greatbatch on the development of the implantable cardiac pacemaker.

In 1960 Millard Fillmore Hospital was the scene of the world's first cardiac pacemaker implant and, in 1962, Greatbatch was awarded a patent for his remarkable invention. The heart pacemaker was designated as one of the ten outstanding U.S. engineering achievements of the past fifty years by the National Society of Professional Engineers in 1984. In early 1986 Greatbatch was selected for the National Inventors Hall of Fame. Along with pioneer plant breeder Luther Burbank, he became one of only sixty-four inductees of the elite inventors group. Since that first implant operation at Millard Fillmore Hospital, Greatbatch's invention has helped save and extend the lives of over 350,000 people.

Such high-tech accomplishments have continued at hospitals like Millard where the first CAT scanner in the state was installed in 1972, one of only five operating in the country at the time. To determine exact drug dosage, hospitals around the world are using a computer program for patient drug therapy developed at Millard in

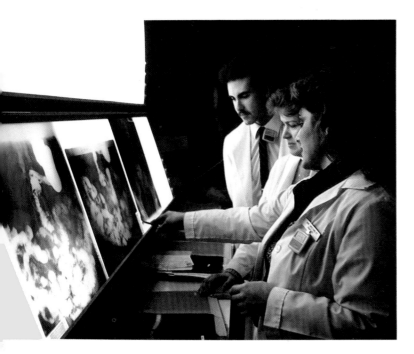

Above: Interns at Millard Fillmore learn the basics of radiology technology. Photo by Jim Pierotti. Courtesy, Millard Fillmore Hospital, Photography Department

Above, right: A cyberscan imager at Millard Fillmore Hospital shows a scan of a human head. Photo by Jim Pierotti. Courtesy, Millard Fillmore Hospital, Photography Department

Right: A patient receives x-rays from a nuclear medicine gamma camera. Photo by Jim Pierotti. Courtesy, Millard Fillmore Hospital, Photography Department

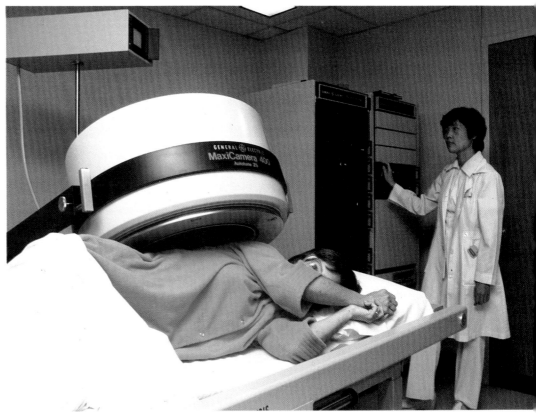

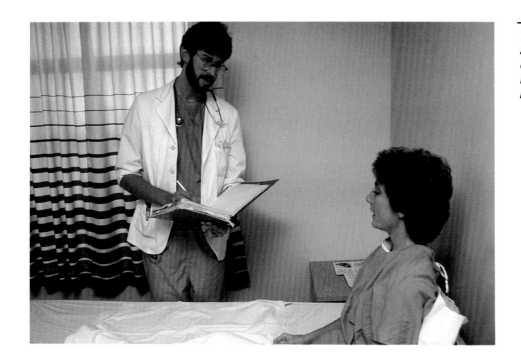

This resident tending to a patient also teaches interns the workings of the hospital. Courtesy, Millard Fillmore Hospital, Photography Department

the early 1980s.

These innovative techniques evolved in Buffalo thanks to a combination of talents: the researchers at the university and the other research centers around the area, and the progressive medical and administrative hospital personnel who offer these researchers practical opportunities to develop their projects.

A prime example of this is the Clinical Pharmacokinetics Laboratory operated by the University at Buffalo. This multidisciplinary clinical and basic research lab has been occupying a part of Millard Fillmore Hospital at Gates Circle since 1972. Within that time span, the unit has become one of the most important drug-testing centers in the country. The computer programs developed by Dr. Jerome J. Schentag and his staff to determine patient drug dosage are used by hospitals around the world. Most of the major drug companies have commissioned the lab to conduct extensive studies of their product developments—an intensive analysis at the experimental stage that is necessary before a new drug is allowed to come on the market.

For granting the space to the Clinical Pharmacokinetics Laboratory, Millard Fillmore's patients get the benefit of having their therapeutic problems treated by the combined efforts of the unit.

Economic Health

The closing of eighty-three-year-old Lafayette General Hospital in early 1986 due to an increasing amount of empty beds symbolized today's threat to community hospitals everywhere.

An official of the Health Systems Agency has stated that the significant drop in occupancy in Greater Buffalo hospitals is attributable to four factors:

Declining population.
Improved medical technology.
Changing reimbursement.
Availability of alternative services to in-hospital care.

Also, third-party payers who pick up most of the country's

The backbone of every hospital staff is its clerical/secretarial staff. Photo by Jim Pierotti. Courtesy, Millard Fillmore Hospital, Photography Department

hospital bills—Medicare, Medicaid, and private insurance carriers—are putting tighter limits on the extent of medical care. These days, fewer patients are hospitalized, while those who are admitted stay for shorter periods of time.

Despite a grim prognosis for smaller area hospitals in particular, aggressive marketing campaigns have been waged by both large and small hospitals in the area over the past several years.

A recent newspaper ad which invites "Discover Columbus" tells the story of the small hospital which has boldly resisted closure recommendations by a Health Systems Agency task force. Although it has voluntarily closed more than a third of its ninety-

Westwood Pharmaceuticals, Inc.

As the population ages and people become more concerned about quality skin care, a company headquartered in Buffalo has the science, the research capabilities, and the product line to help consumers achieve healthier, better-looking skin.

Westwood Pharmaceuticals, Inc., a leader in therapeutic skin care, has roots that go back to 1876, when a patent medicine salesman named Orrin E. Foster founded the Foster-Milburn Company. As medical care evolved in the twentieth century, so did the direction of Foster-Milburn's business. In 1949 the firm's Westwood Pharmaceuticals Division was created to develop and market dermatologic products. In fact, the division's first product, Lowila, a soapless cleansing bar for people with sensitive skin, is still successfully marketed today.

Throughout the 1950s and 1960s both Westwood's sophistication and product line grew. Fostex, Alpha Keri, and Keri lotion appeared in thousands of households nationwide. In the early 1970s the company pioneered sunscreens, adding PreSun to its product line.

The Foster-Milburn era came to an end in 1969, when Westwood was acquired by the Bristol-Myers Company, a multinational corporation that markets pharmaceutical, nutritional, health care, and consumer products worldwide. Bristol-Myers has enabled its skin-care subsidiary to expand its research, and the firm now markets more than 60 formulations of both over-the-counter and prescription products. Its prescription products include Westcort Cream and Ointment, topical steroids used to treat rashes and inflammatory ailments; Desquam-X for the treatment of acne; and Lac-Hydrin, the world's first prescription product for moderate to severe dry skin.

Westwood has come a long way in less than 40 years, and its plans into the 1990s are just as ambitious. The company's motto, "Science Devoted to Better Skin Care," translates into an increasing investment in research and development to produce new, more effective therapeutic products. Moisturel, a fragrance-free moisturizer for those with sensitive skin, and Lac-Hydrin, the state-of-the-art dry-skin therapy, are two examples of products developed by Westwood Pharmaceutical research.

Work continues in the firm's laboratories with more exotic and unique compounds, such as retinoids, nonsteroid anti-inflammatory agents, and photoprotective compounds. Retinoids, chemical derivatives of Vitamin A, hold great promise because they can cause abnormal skin to behave more normally. Nonsteroid

The newest technology enables researchers at Westwood Pharmaceuticals to develop therapeutic skin-care products using computers, robotics, and sophisticated monitoring systems.

anti-inflammatory products could potentially stop inflammation without some of the undesirable side effects of steroids. In addition, research in photobiology may eventually lead to products that will help consumers prevent sun-aged skin so that they can maintain a more youthful appearance. Another priority is finding scientific solutions to the problem of age or liver spots.

Westwood's products can be found in many countries worldwide. In addition to its Buffalo operation, the company has a subsidiary in Belleville, Ontario, which supplies the Canadian market as well as some of its exports.

The firm employs about 800 people, most of whom work in Buffalo, and has more than 200 sales representatives located throughout North America, by far the largest dermatological sales force in the nation.

Westwood Pharmaceuticals, Inc., strives for excellence in all aspects of its business. Extensive research, combined with expertise in topically applied medications, is enabling the company to develop breakthroughs in skin care.

Westwood Pharmaceuticals, which traces its roots back to 1876, has come a long way from this original research laboratory in Buffalo.

three beds, Columbus's president has maintained that the acute-care facility is needed now more than ever, since the closing of Lafayette General has made it the only hospital serving Buffalo's West Side.

Despite the fact that fifty hospitals throughout New York State have gone bankrupt over the past decade, Greater Buffalo hospitals are aggressively taking measures to combat the trend.

At seventy-five-bed St. Francis Hospital, for example, a special "ambulatory surgery" unit was begun in 1985, geared toward operations in which a patient enters and leaves the hospital the same day.

Quick patient turnaround time is also the key to Expresscare, a new service recently instituted in the Emergency Department of Sisters of Charity Hospital.

It's being referred to as the first such hospital emergency service in the area to offer prompt attention to less critical problems. As the hospital's ad campaign states, "Fast, convenient twenty-four-hour care for life's little bumps, bruises, cuts and minor illnesses."

Millard Fillmore Hospital was the site of the first pacemaker implant in the Greater Buffalo area. Pictured, from left to right, are the first pacemaker on through later improved models. Note the decrease in size. Photo by Jim Pierotti. Courtesy, Millard Fillmore Hospital, Photography Department

Then, to relate to anyone who's ever waited long hours in an emergency room for a minor problem to be treated, the tag line reads, "You've Waited Long Enough."

The added service is part of a recently completed $750,000 renovation of the hospital's emergency department. The 1,600-square-foot expansion allows for the simultaneous treatment of both critical and minor emergencies.

Sisters Hospital, which opened in 1848 as Buffalo's first hospital, greatly expanded its capability to rehabilitate patients recovering from surgery, accident, and illness when the million-dollar Physical and Occupational Therapy wing was opened in the summer of 1985. Referred to as the "Rolls Royce of therapy facilities," this 8,500-square-foot wing includes state-of-the-art exercise and therapy gyms where strength is regained in weakened muscles, and a simulated home kitchen where skills are taught to stroke or accident victims.

Sisters also began operation of Greater Buffalo's first hospital-based home health care program, designed to provide a complete program of care for patients in their own home. It's a natural extension of the hospital's long-time commitment to geriatric care. In the mid-1970s, Sisters opened the first hospital-skilled nursing facility and began the area's first clinic specifically for geriatric patients. Now, more than 1,000 such patients are examined and treated there each year.

The reputation and expertise of The Children's Hospital of Buffalo has been so far-reaching that young patients from a wide geographical area are brought there for treatment. For example, since one of the country's first cardiac centers for children was established there in the 1940s, the cardiac unit has become one of the single largest patient groups in the country.

In June 1986, the Buffalo General Hospital dedicated its $210-million medical tower, a sixteen-story, 790-bed facility that repre-

Millard Fillmore Hospital rises beyond Gates Circle. Photo by Joe Traver

Blue Shield of Western New York, Inc.

The innovative atmosphere that made Western New York the industrial frontier for nineteenth-century America was evident also in medicine. While the rail yards in Buffalo connected the Eastern Seaboard to the Midwest via the Great Lakes and the falls at Niagara were being harnessed to help light up the Northeast, the local medical community was establishing world-class credentials.

Roswell Park, M.D., the renowned physician and surgeon, brought attention to Western New York at the turn of the century. Today the sprawling Roswell Park Memorial Institute, operated by New York State, stands as a memorial to this great healer. Hopefully one day soon the center may produce the ultimate tribute to Dr. Park—a cure for cancer.

The State University of New York at Buffalo is home to one of America's great medical schools. Since 1846 this outstanding edu-

Clinical training of physicians—School of Medicine at the State University of New York at Buffalo.

cational facility has produced a stream of top-drawer medical practitioners for Western New York and the rest of the world. The presence of the medical school adds to the quality of life in the Buffalo area.

Children's Hospital is one of the largest and most advanced pediatric medical facilities in the world. Youngsters from every corner of the globe come to Buffalo for the life-saving medical techniques and procedures Children's Hospital has pioneered, including open-heart surgery for infants and small children. Children's is responsible for providing life itself to many youngsters, and a normal life for others who faced restricted life-styles due to heart defects.

Today the medical picture in Western New York is bright indeed. Nearly three dozen hospitals offer outstanding care for Western New Yorkers. More than 2,000 doctors practice in the area, providing a full range of medical specialties. Area residents are blessed with fine medical facilities and practitioners.

The spirit of medical pioneering

The American Falls at Niagara.

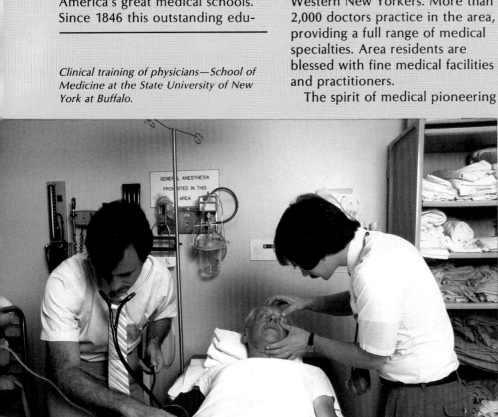

also extends to health care insurance. When the concept of prepaid medical care swept the nation in the late 1930s, Buffalo was once again in the forefront. A group of community leaders formed a not-for-profit medical-surgical Plan to help take the financial fear out of illness. In 1939 they coined a name for their concept and developed a distinctive symbol, superimposing the medical caduceus on a shield. As a result of their efforts, the now-famous Blue Shield name and symbol got their

start in Buffalo.

During the 1940s other not-for-profit medical-surgical Plans across America began to use Buffalo's trade name and mark, and in the early 1950s the national trade association adopted them. Over the years the Blue Shield name and symbol have come to represent the finest in health-care coverage.

The innovative tenor of the 1930s carried through the war years. In the 1950s and 1960s Blue Shield of Western New York, Inc., developed new concepts in health care insurance. By the end of the 1960s Blue Shield dominated the

Western New York market, covering over half of the residents in the eight-county area.

At that juncture a dynamic young executive with an extensive background in commercial insurance and banking was chosen to take over the leadership of Blue Shield of Western New York, Inc. John T. Manyon, C.F.A., became president and chief executive officer of the Buffalo-based Plan in 1967. Over the next few years the pace of progress quickened at Blue Shield.

The revolutionary 50-51 paid-in-full program replaced the traditional indemnity insurance concept.

With 50-51, Blue Shield subscribers could forget about filling out claims and concentrate on getting well. Participating doctors began to deal directly with Blue Shield, accepting 50-51 benefits as full payment for covered services. With the vast majority of practicing doctors participating, 50-51 was an instant success. More than one million Western New Yorkers joined the organization, and the plan recorded the highest market penetration of any large Blue Shield Plan in North America.

Simultaneous with the launch of 50-51, Manyon made a dramatic change in the basis of benefit levels. Most health insurers base their benefits on averages—the "Usual, Customary, and Reasonable" professional charges prevalent in the area. The UCR concept obviously allows the market to drive benefit levels and medical costs. Blue Shield adopted a Relative Value Scale that establishes specific benefits for each covered medical service or procedure. During the 1970s, as inflation drove medical costs through the roof, the rise in Western New York was moderated by these RVS benefit levels. The use of RVS by Blue Shield instead of the prevalent UCR system has given Western New York the lowest health-care costs in the United States. For more than 10 years The Bureau of Labor Statistics has documented this Blue Shield contribution to the area's economic well-being.

In the early 1970s, like most health insurers, Blue Shield required 40 to 45 days to process a claim. Manyon considered that to be an unreasonable amount of time to expect subscribers and participating doctors to wait for their benefits. As a result, he introduced a new data-processing system and soon reduced the waiting period to one week or less. Prompt, fair claims payments made the Blue Shield paid-in-full programs even more attractive to

the medical community, and doctor participation levels soared over 75 percent.

From its inception in the late 1960s, Blue Shield of Western New York, Inc., has provided claims payment services for the federal government's Medicare B program in the area. Its sophisticated claims payment system and cost-containment measures, along with outstanding utilization controls, gave Blue Shield an edge when the federal government solicited bids for Medicare B processing in 45 Upstate New York counties. The Upstate Medicare Division of Blue Shield of Western New York has ranked among the top Medicare B carriers since taking over this widespread area.

Today, with its latest paid-in-full program, 82-83, and a variety of other programs and riders, Blue Shield is the dominant force in the area's health insurance picture; it covers more than twice as many Western New Yorkers as all other health insurers combined. Blue Shield of Western New York processes more than 450,000 claims every month and is entrusted with a half-billion dollars in benefit payments each year.

And that's only the beginning. Blue Shield of Western New York has just launched another new concept—a Comprehensive Health Benefits Program that provides the broadest range of benefits

Roswell Park Memorial Institute for Cancer Research.

ever offered in the area under the Blue Shield banner. It is innovative and flexible, designed for today's changing health care needs. Blue Shield has several other programs under study and plans to bring its heritage of innovation to the alternative care field as well.

Blue Shield of Western New York, Inc., is a major factor in the economic well-being of the community. Its role in protecting against the financial consequences of illness is vital. Its efforts to contain the cost of medical care make the Western New York area attractive to business and industry. As there is much credit to be shared, so also are there many to share in the accomplishments of Blue Shield of Western New York. They include the pioneering community leaders who initiated this concept, the medical community whose support makes Blue Shield work, the dedicated members of the board of directors who give their skills without compensation as a service to their community, and the leadership of Blue Shield of Western New York, Inc., including president John T. Manyon, senior staff members, and the hundreds of employees who show their caring every day for the subscribers they are privileged to serve.

The Children's Hospital of Buffalo.

237

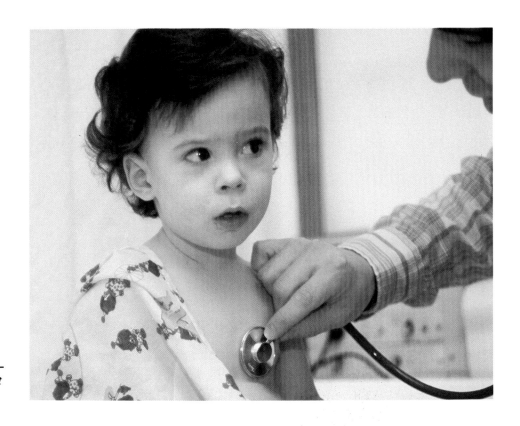

A toddler endures a check-up at a Buffalo hospital.

sents one of the largest construction and renovation projects of its kind in New York State history. All clinical departments—including the hospital's nationally renowned orthopedic, cardiac, and renal surgery departments—were moved into the new facility, along with the installation of over $22 million in state-of-the-art medical equipment.

It is the newest addition to a concentrated area in the High Street section of downtown that brings together medical and research facilities of world significance, including Buffalo General, Roswell Park Memorial Institute, and The Medical Foundation of Buffalo.

There's also been a dramatic rise in health maintenance organizations (HMOs) over the past decade in Greater Buffalo. These family health insurance plans offer area employers a coverage option to give their employees. Health Care Plan was the first. It now has six clinics spread throughout the area, where patients pay a nominal fee per visit. Independent Health soon followed, signing a variety of area physicians and offering its members the option of visiting these physicians in the convenience of their own offices.

The granddaddy of all health insurance plans here is Blue Cross of Western New York which celebrated its fiftieth anniversary in 1986, one of the first such hospital coverages of its kind. It is complemented by Blue Shield of Greater Buffalo, which was developed locally in 1939 to handle members' medical-surgical

Tomorrow's physicians can look forward to first-rate training facilities in Buffalo's health-care institutions.

expenses.

Besides forming an HMO service in recent years to go along with the trend, Blue Cross announced expansion plans during its anniversary year which will require a move from its long-time downtown headquarters into a former department store building near Sisters Hospital.

It's all part of the healthy picture being conveyed by area health institutions, despite certain adverse trends around the nation. The realization is that Buffalo has too strong a reputation in research and care to wind up in an economic sickbed. Thanks to progressive and aggressive researchers and administrators, Buffalo's medical tradition will continue to be an integral part of the area and the world.

Blue Cross Of Western New York, Inc.

Carl M. Metzger served as the first president of the Blue Cross Plan from November 1936 to March 1966.

The Great Depression of the 1930s was the hardest of hard times, a period when many couldn't afford much more than the food on the table and a roof over their heads. Most of all, they couldn't afford to get sick.

Justin Ford Kimball, administrator of the Baylor University Medical Center in Dallas, was deeply concerned about the situation. How could a nation possibly cure its ills if the individual couldn't, he reasoned. As the Roaring '20s became the Depressed '30s, Kimball developed a plan to remedy the situation.

He proposed that if 75 percent of all the teachers in Dallas would contribute 50 cents per month to a common fund, his hospital would consider that as prepayment for any care the participants should need.

By 1936 Kimball's prepayment plan had come clear across the country to Western New York. At that time hospitals throughout the Buffalo area were experiencing many empty beds and unpaid bills. Thirteen general hospitals in

Buffalo and Niagara Falls welcomed the plan. For the first time the institutions would have the assurance that payment for their services would be covered, an assurance also given to the patients. Thus was formed what later became known as Blue Cross of Western New York, Inc., at the time of incorporation on October 21, 1936.

In its first year of operation total membership was 16,219, with $18,000 paid out in benefits. By year-end 1985, with membership over the one-million mark, well over a quarter-billion dollars was paid out in benefits.

The first organization enrolled in the plan was The Mentholatum Company, Inc. Now, 50 years later, Mentholatum—one of the most established names in the health care industry—is still covered by Blue Cross.

Back in 1936 Carl M. Metzger, who participated in the plan's development in Rochester, came to Buffalo and helped to sell the idea to local hospitals and the medical society. He later became the first director of the Hospital Service Corporation of Western New York, the predecessor to Blue Cross.

The first participant to receive the plan's benefit was a Buffalo-

nian admitted to the hospital in February 1937 with pneumonia. Reimbursement by Blue Cross was made in March. By January 1, 1938, Blue Cross had paid out $21,206 for hospital care for 491 members.

Today 38 health care institutions throughout Western New York are participants in the Blue Cross Plan. In 1945 Blue Cross became one of the first plans in the country to reimburse its member hospitals for costs incurred. That same year it formed one of the nation's first medical advisory committees established by a health care plan to review claims.

In 1960 the Federal Employee Program was inaugurated. It marked the first time the federal government had contributed to the health care costs of its employees. The program makes available several different plans, one of which, the Service Benefit Plan, is offered by Blue Cross as well as Blue Shield. Of the approximately 12,000 federal employees in West-

All 38 hospitals in the eight-county Western New York area are participating hospitals. Pictured is Genesee Memorial Hospital in Batavia.

Charles E. Rath, current president of the Blue Cross Plan.

ern New York, 4,000 are enrolled in the local plan.

A social revolution began in 1965, when congress passed the Social Security Amendments that created Medicare. The program provided hospital and medical benefits for persons age 65 and over. When the law became effective on July 1, 1966, Blue Cross of Western New York acquired new responsibilities. The company now offers complementary coverage called Blue Cross Over 65, which helps pay deductibles and larger bills for which the Medicare beneficiary would otherwise be liable.

In 1969 the Blue Cross Prescription Drug Program was inaugurated. Recognizing this as an attractive health care benefit, employers began to include it in their health care package. The popular rider got off to a fast start, generating 35,000 contracts in 1969. As the program expanded, so did the claims, with about 4,000 processed per week at the outset. By 1985 claims

processed grew to an all-time high of 8,402,379, representing $117,376,761 in payments.

In August 1985 Blue Cross began offering Community Blue, a health maintenance organization offering both convenience and choice to its subscribers.

For many years Blue Cross has been active in contributing to the community in the area of health education programs aimed at all segments of the community. In 1976 it inaugurated a series of health care symposiums targeted at business, industry, labor, political leaders, and hospital administrators. Co-sponsored by the Hospital Association of Western New York, the programs have featured many prominent speakers in the fields of fitness, wellness,

Blue Cross president Charles E. Rath (left) presents a $150,000 grant check to J.E. Stibbards, president of Buffalo Children's Hospital, to aid in a pilot project utilizing a magnetic resonance imaging technique. Blue Cross officers Francis E. Hayes and Leo C. Welsh, and Jerald Kuhn, M.D., chief radiologist at Children's Hospital, look on.

medicine, prevention, and other areas of health care. The purpose of these programs is to build community awareness about the importance of pursuing a healthier life-style for better personal health and as a health care cost containment measure.

In addition, Blue Cross has sponsored a number of fitness activities, such as bicycling, skiing, road races, and health fairs to encourage the public to participate in some activity, no matter what their preference, in order to maintain a healthy body. Health education has become, and will continue to be, an integral part of Blue Cross of Western New York's overall health-care program.

In its 50-year history, there have been only three presidents of Blue Cross of Western New York, Inc. In addition to Metzger, who served from November 1936 until March 1966, Richard J. Noonan held the office from March 1966 to March 1973. Charles E. Rath, the organization's current president, was elected to that post on March 16, 1973.

CHAPTER NINE

The Manufacturing Base

As in most other cities that were once industrial giants, Buffalo increasingly reflects the economic shift to more advanced technologies. Although Buffalo business today is a sea of white collars, the blue collar base is still rooted in the local economy. Despite several major factory closings in the past few years, there is still a sufficient industrial foundation in Buffalo, contributing significantly to the Greater Buffalo economy.

The good news at the end of 1985 was that the area unemployment rate significantly dipped to just under 8 percent, the lowest annual rate since 1979 and the second lowest in a decade. While the decline in the unemployment rate was accompanied by an increase in the number of people employed, the increases were realized in the non-manufacturing sectors such as retail trade, health services, construction, banking, insurance, and real estate.

While factory closings and massive layoffs were not prevalent in 1985, Buffalo did suffer the loss of two out of three of the Trico Products plants in the area. The factories will be moved within the next two years to the Texas-Mexico border where the wage rates are a fraction of what Trico employees enjoyed locally.

More Economic ``Drive''

While Trico management may have felt that it had to cut wages

Opposite: Scenes like this were common in the 1960s and 1970s when many of the area's workers were employed by Bethlehem and Republic. The 1980s, however, have seen a shift to high-tech industries. Courtesy, Greater Buffalo Chamber of Commerce

243

Electrical towers are silhouetted by the setting sun. Buffalo was a pioneer in electrical energy, and has benefited ever since from abundant, inexpensive electricity. Courtesy, Greater Buffalo Chamber of Commerce

drastically to compete in the automaking market, the local auto industry has been buoyed by creative sales programs involving rebates, cash allowances, and cut-rate financing. Such price-cutting has generated enough new orders to fill gaps in production schedules, keeping local auto workers and new-car salespeople steadily employed.

Gone are the many layoffs and recalls in manufacturing operations that were evident in previous years. General Motors Corporation paid a record-high total of $663 million in wages and salaries

General Motors' Tonawanda plant is still a major area employer. Photo by Envisions Co.

in 1985 to its Buffalo-area employees. That was a significant jump from the $551.3-million payroll in 1984 and the previous high of $553.9 million in 1979. GM's average area employment climbed to 16,111 in 1985. That was an increase of 950 jobs, or 6.2 percent, from 15,161 in 1984.

Paralleling that rise is GM's plan to spend $340 million to expand and modernize the forty-nine-year-old engine plant in the Town of Tonawanda, which is GM's largest. That figure includes the cost of new machinery installed for production of two new engine lines for 1987-model vehicles.

GM's Harrison Radiator Division in Lockport ended its seventy-fifth year of operation in 1985 by setting production milestones of 200 million motor-vehicle radiators and 75 million air-conditioning systems. Both are used in nearly all GM cars, trucks, and buses.

Over at the Ford Motor Company's stamping plants in the Town of Hamburg, a $117-million retooling program was carried out for the new midsize Ford Taurus and Mercury Sable front-wheel-drive cars that went on sale last December.

The thirty-six-year-old plant provides more metal stamping and sub-assembly work for the new Taurus and Sable car lines than any other Ford plant. As part of the latest multi-million-dollar allocation, two huge transfer processes were installed for the Taurus-Sable project.

Ironically, Trico received an eight-million-dollar contract from Ford to supply windshield wiper blades and assemblies for the new Taurus and Sable car lines. To accommodate this new business, the addition of $900,000 in new tooling was completed at Trico's Elk Street and Main Street plants not long before the closing of both of these plants was announced.

Ford Motor Company's stamping plant is located on the Lake Erie shoreline in Hamburg. Photo by Envisions Co.

The Maturing Process

The employment rolls at the local GM facility increased by nearly 1,000 last year, a sign of increasing strength for the automaker. That 16,111 total, however, still pales in comparison to the record high of 23,462 in 1979.

The 31.3 percent decrease—a loss of 7,351 employees—is symptomatic of the decline of Greater Buffalo's older "mature industries." According to a report by the Western New York Economic Development Corporation, these losses are attributable to a variety of factors. Mature manufacturing companies in Greater Buffalo often occupy obsolete buildings, utilize outdated manufacturing equipment, and operate under outdated management systems and outmoded labor agreements. At the same time, they are beset by foreign and sometimes domestic competition which have none of the above. In the past, local companies with those problems found it easier to relocate their operations to new sites in the South and reorganize their businesses there.

To help prevent these losses, the establishment of a new non-profit corporation—an "industrial effectiveness institute"—has been recommended by the corporation. This institute would concentrate on working closely with the management of individual companies to seek ways of operating more efficiently while keeping competitive with foreign and domestic firms.

The corporation's board would be comprised of executives from the "best-managed" companies in Greater Buffalo. These companies have continuously showed the strength of their commitment

The Kittinger Furniture factory on Elmwood Avenue produces some of the country's finest furniture. Some of the firm's traditional pieces grace the White House. Photo by Joe Traver

Left: George H. Hyde, president and CEO of the Mentholatum Company, uses some of his deep heating rub. Photo by Joe Traver

Below: The Mentholatum Company is based in Buffalo and headquartered on Niagara Street along the Erie Canal. Photo by Joe Traver

General Motors Corporation

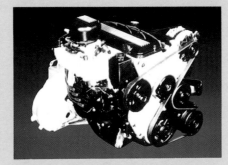

C-P-C Tonawanda currently manufactures four high-quality engine lines for GM: (upper row) The Mark IV and the 2.8-liter V6 60 degree; (bottom row) the 4.3-liter 90 degree and the 2-liter L-4.

General Motors Corporation, the world's leading producer of motor vehicles as well as other products, was incorporated on September 16, 1908. Buick was the nucleus of the company and was soon joined by Oldsmobile, Oakland (now Pontiac), and Cadillac. Chevrolet came on board in 1908.

In the Western New York area GM operates four divisions: the Chevrolet-Pontiac-GM of Canada Group Tonawanda Engine Plant, the New Departure-Hyatt Division Tonawanda Forge Plant, the Saginaw Division Buffalo Plant, and Harrison Radiator, Lockport and Buffalo locations. General Motors is the largest industrial employer in Western New York with approximately 16,000 employees.

The Chevrolet-Pontiac-GM of Canada Group (C-P-C) Tonawanda

Engine Plant is one of the largest engine-producing facilities in the world. The three-plant complex covers more than 2.5 million square feet of floor space on a tract of over 130 acres.

The engine plant began production in 1938, manufacturing front- and rear-axle assemblies and Chevrolet's 216.5-cubic-inch displacement, 85 horsepower, six-cylinder engines at the rate of 75 per hour. With the onset of World War II commercial production ceased and shifted to the production of 14- and 18-cylinder radial aircraft engines under license from Pratt & Whitney. Near the end of the war the first jet

engines were built with General Electric in Tonawanda's Kenmore Avenue facility, and shortly thereafter, axle assembly production was transferred to Chevrolet's Delavan Avenue Plant in Buffalo.

The engine plant was then designated as the Chevrolet Tonawanda Motor Plant, and, as the complex grew, there were many engine lines exclusive to Tonawanda. They included the "W" series "big block" in 1958, which started out at 348 cubic inches and grew into the fabled "409" sung about by the Beach Boys; the flat six, air-cooled Corvair engine in 1960; the powerful MARK IV, a new design "big block" that replaced the "W" series; the aluminum-case four-cylinder Vega engine in 1970; and the "cut down V-8" 90-degree, six-cylinder engine in 1978. As a result of the reorganization of the General Motors car groups in 1984, the Chevrolet Tonawanda Motor Plant became the Chevrolet-Pontiac-GM of Canada Group (C-P-C) Tonawanda Engine Plant.

Currently, C-P-C Tonawanda and the UAW Local 774 work closely together to manufacture four high-quality engine lines: the L-4 (2 liter), V-6 60-degree (2.8 liter), V-6 90-degree (4.3 liter), and the MARK IV (6, 7, and 7.4 liter). More than 1.5 million engines are

With the reorganization of General Motors in 1984, "Chevy Tonawanda" was renamed the Chevrolet-Pontiac-Canada Group Tonawanda Engine Plant. The main administration building for the three-plant complex is located on River Road.

manufactured at the engine complex annually and are shipped to 26 GM assembly plants. Approximately 90 percent of Tonawanda's engines go under the hood of a GM passenger car, with the other 10 percent designated for trucks, marine, and agriculture applications.

Located next to the C-P-C Tonawanda Engine Plant is GM's Forge Plant. This facility was originally intended for the production of aluminum aircraft engine forgings during the Korean Conflict. However, due to the reduction in the war effort, this need was eliminated, and construction was discontinued. Chevrolet Division subsequently completed the facility in 1953 and placed it into

The New Departure-Hyatt Tonawanda Forge, located on Kenmore Avenue, has been in operation since 1953. In addition to Tonawanda, GM's New Departure-Hyatt Division operates facilities in Detroit, Michigan; Bristol, Connecticut; and Sandusky, Ohio.

Harrison Radiator Division of General Motors is headquartered in Lockport, New York, with other manufacturing operations in Buffalo, New York; Dayton and Moraine, Ohio; and Donchery, France.

commercial operation for steel forgings with a primary business of V-8 crankshafts and rear-wheel-drive axles. Additional expansions were made in 1966, 1967, and again in 1972, bringing total manufacturing floor space to the current 394,000 square feet.

With the development of front-wheel-drive vehicles and related

forging components, the forge plant profile has changed in recent years—not only to meet new product demands but also to develop quality standards and hi-tech processing requirements for the future.

State-of-the-art metalworking technology made its debut at the Tonawanda Forge in the early

1980s with the installation of four world-class, high-volume hot-forming lines—the first of which set a world record of more than 82,500 quality forgings in a single day. In 1983 those hot formers were instrumental in the production of the integral wheel-spindle bearing forgings for New Departure-Hyatt Division. In addition to hot forming, close tolerance capacity via both cold and warm forming operational technology has been added allowing for additional growth and opportunity in a highly competitive market, making Tonawanda one of the most advanced operations of its kind in the world.

NDH Tonawanda Forge currently

has approximately 800 employees and works closely with its two unions, UAW Local 846 and IDSC Local 490, to produce approximately 7,000 tons of quality forgings per month, which are then shipped to its 13 major customers, primarily other General Motors manufacturing plants.

In November 1984 the Tonawanda Forge was officially reassigned from the Chevrolet Division to the New Departure-Hyatt Division. This marriage brought new opportunities to the forging business as well as the division by providing additional research and technology along with an application of synergies that will be the key to the success of the plant and direction of the division for future decades.

The New Departure-Hyatt division currently operates facilities in Detroit, Michigan; Bristol, Connecticut; and Sandusky, Ohio, in addition to the Tonawanda Forge. New Departure-Hyatt supplies the most complete antifriction ball and roller bearing product lines in

the United States, as well as forgings for engines, transmissions, axles, drive trains, steering linkage, and suspensions.

General Motors' Saginaw Division operates a major plant on East Delavan Avenue in Buffalo. The facility began as a Chevrolet assembly plant and built its first automobile on August 13, 1923. There were about 400 people on the payroll at the time, compared

Since its beginning as a Chevrolet assembly plant in 1923, the Saginaw facility has been an integral part of Buffalo's East Side community.

to nearly 2,500 today. Assembly operations ceased on July 31, 1941, to convert to defense production. During World War II the plant manufactured components for more than 60,000 Pratt & Whitney 1300-W aircraft engines. More than 6,000 people were employed during that period.

Production of rear axles began in the spring of 1946, along with the manufacture of clutch and brake pedals and body-mounting brackets. The Korean Conflict again wrought change in order to meet military needs. The Wright R-3350 engine and CD-500 tank were both supplied with parts made in the Buffalo plant.

Volume production of rear axles and other components resumed in 1952. Steering linkages and coil springs were then added to the plant's production responsibilities. Between 1965 and 1968 the facility was expanded with the construction of 289,000 square feet of

Harrison Radiator Division was founded in 1911 by Herbert C. Harrison. Today Harrison is a major international producer of heat-transfer products for companies around the world.

floor space. A waste-treatment facility was added in 1968. Today the plant has 1.113 million square feet of space under roof. General Motor's investments in the facility's building and equipment exceed $100 million.

Saginaw-Buffalo turns out thousands of rear-wheel-drive axles daily from its 315-foot-long assembly line. After testing, the assemblies travel to a computer-controlled marshalling area where the rear axles are identified, sorted into storage banks, and held for shipment to GM assembly plants throughout the United States, Canada, and Mexico.

Cooperative efforts between management and the United Auto Workers Union Local 424 have developed in recent years. A result of those efforts is the Quality of Work Life program, involving hourly and salaried employees working together to solve a variety of problems in the work place. Working in teams, employees address areas such as changes in manufacturing processes, environmental issues, working conditions, and even product design. About 15 percent of the work force actively partici-

Harrison incorporates a team philosophy where people work together in a concerted, organized manner to solve problems and achieve objectives.

pates in the program.

General Motor's Harrison Radiator Division traces its roots in Western New York back to August 31, 1910, when Herbert Harrison, with the financial assistance of a few local businessmen, opened a small shop in Lockport, New York. Business was slow at first, and in 1911, 131 radiators were produced. Records show that invoice No. 1 covered the shipment of one radiator to the Remington Standard Company. By comparison, Harrison Radiator now produces more than 200,000 components each day.

Today Harrison Radiator operates five manufacturing facilities devoted to the production of heat-transfer products. The largest is in Lockport, the location of Harrison's world headquarters. Its facilities there blanket more than three million square feet of floor space. Production in Lockport consists of automotive oil coolers, radiators, air-conditioners, evaporators, condensers and heater cores, and industrial oil coolers. During World War II Harrison Radiator turned its experience and facilities toward the war effort and manufactured such products as heat exchangers, oil coolers, intercoolers, superchargers, radiators, and thermostats.

In 1946 a plant in the Kensington section of Buffalo was acquired from the General Cable Company. Staffed with key personnel from the Lockport facility, it gradually took over the production of car heaters and defrosters. Harrison Radiator's Buffalo plant produces heater assemblies, heater-defrosters, and air-conditioning components that are shipped to major GM assembly plants nationwide.

In addition to the Lockport and Buffalo plants, Harrison Radiator operates a facility in Dayton, Ohio, with nearly 1.5 million square feet of floor space devoted to the production of automotive

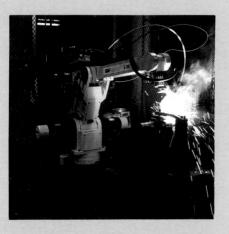

Saginaw Buffalo is the largest private employer in the city of Buffalo. The complex covers 52 acres with 1.13 million square feet of floor space under roof.

air-conditioning compressors. Another facility, located in Moraine, Ohio, produces air-conditioning compressors and accumulator-dehydrators. A 200,000-square-foot manufacturing facility in Donchery, France, turns out heater cores, aluminum radiators, heater assemblies, and air-conditioning assemblies.

With four plants in the United States and a plant in France, Harrison Radiator is in a position to supply quality parts on a worldwide basis. In addition to its own plants, Harrison Radiator has joint ventures or licensing agreements with a number of companies in various parts of the world.

The merger of Delco Air Conditioning into the Harrison Radiator Division of General Motors Corporation in 1981 resulted in Harrison becoming the world's largest manufacturer of automotive air-conditioning compressors and refrigerant controls. In 1984 the division celebrated its 30th year in air-conditioning system production as well as its 70-millionth system produced. That same year the 200-millionth radiator was manufactured—a far cry from the first order of a single radiator shipped back in 1910.

to competitive excellence. They have introduced participative management practices, "team-building" approaches, 'and more flexible production assignments for workers. And because such approaches should reflect the corporate health of their entire home base, these companies have continuously shown their commitment to boosting Buffalo business.

These firms include Chevrolet Motor Division, Dunlop Tire Corporation, Fisher-Price Toys, Graphic Controls Corporation, Moog, Inc., Motorola, Inc., Occidental Chemical Corporation, and Worthington Compressor Division-Dresser Industries, Inc. The mission of this collective board would be to help the older companies adapt to the more competitive way in which the above firms operate.

The need for the institute, the report concludes, is based on a

Above and opposite: Fisher-Price Toys maintains corporate headquarters and plant facilities in East Aurora. Photos by Envisions Co.

belief that the mature companies in the region are its best hope to participate in a large way in the international economy of the present and future. Why? Because these companies represent the roots of the local economy. They are what this area needs to become more of a "headquarters town" once again. After all, corporate bases provide the backbone of an area.

Local Ownership

Changes in ownership of Buffalo companies are frequently in the news. Investor groups, management buyouts, and leveraged buyouts are constantly occurring. However, in most instances, the pieces on the figurative Monopoly game board are being moved by out-of-town owners and investors who make the local purchase and then make the move out of the area.

It happened again in 1985 with Spencer Kellogg Corporation, a resin manufacturer headquartered in Buffalo for ninety-one years. Textron, Inc., the parent company, sold the firm to NL Industries, which immediately announced plans to close the Buffalo headquarters.

Such buying and moving over the years has been one of the primary weaknesses of the area economy. The fact that many Buffalo companies were controlled by absentee owners—that it was not a "headquarters town"—made local businesses susceptible to parent company whims and belt-tightening.

Two recent changes in ownership, however, have gone against that trend. American Brass, headquartered on Buffalo's West Side, was sold by Atlantic Richfield Company of Los Angeles to a local group headed by Randolph A. Marks, a founder and former chairman of Buffalo's Computer Task Group, Inc.

Also, the former Dunlop Tire and Rubber Corporation was sold by Dunlop Holdings, Ltd., of England to an investment group headed by president and chief executive officer Randall L. Clark and comprised of senior Dunlop managers and other investors who purchased the company's United States operations for $118 million, creating Dunlop Tire Corporation. The scenario for this buyout provides inspiration for those hoping to recapture Buffalo's former significance as a "headquarters town." As the 1980s began, the American arm of Dunlop was beset by foreign competition, high taxes, inflation, recession, fuel shortages, and staggering interest rates—factors that closed twenty-two American tire plants over the previous eight years. Throughout the early 1980s Clark consistently denied rumors that the local operation, based in Buffalo since 1923, would be consolidated into the Dunlop facility in Huntsville,

Ford Motor Company

In 1985, as part of Ford Motor Company's $117-million investment in its Buffalo Stamping Plant, perhaps the most dramatic purchase in terms of both appearance and technology were two new computerized transfer presses, such as the one shown here. Weighing more then two and a half million pounds, they are the largest and most complex types of machinery operated by Ford and are used to stamp rear door panels for Taurus and Sable automobiles.

The Ford Motor Company's Buffalo Stamping Plant began operations in September 1950, during a postwar period of expansion in the auto industry. Today the plant produces metal stampings and subassemblies, including such components as floor pans, doors, deck lids, roofs, and quarter panels, for virtually all Ford car lines. The plant receives its sheet steel in coils from virtually every steel company in the country, including a Ford steel-producing facility in Dearborn, Michigan.

The huge plant covers more than 2,466,347 square feet of floor space. This provides for an easy flow of raw materials from receiving through production and on to the shipping dock.

Stampings produced in the plant are shipped out primarily in railroad cars, and trucks. They go to 18 Ford assembly plants in the United States, Canada and Mexico.

During the stamping process, cold-rolled steel coils of varying thicknesses are run through blanking presses and then taken to press lines where they go through from three to eight operations. The plant has 32 major press lines with a total of 161 presses supported by steel grillwork over a 17-foot-deep basement. The major presses weigh from 10,000 to 2.5 million pounds. Dies range from 200 pounds to 80 tons and exert pressures ranging from 75 to 3,000 tons. The bed size of the largest press is 332 inches wide by 120 inches deep. Motors operating these presses vary from 40 to 500 horsepower.

New technology introduced during 1972 plant expansion added two transfer presses, each weighing 2,500 tons and measuring 252 inches by 108 inches; and two high-density stacking systems. One stacking system is 64 feet by 200 feet by 68 feet high. Two 332-inch by 120-inch, 3,000-ton transfer presses were added in 1984. Two larger, more advanced transfer presses were installed in March 1985; these have two 234-inch by 96-inch bolster plates under a split 2,000/1,000-ton ram to produce inner and outer door panels. The two transfer presses also feature transport and color video search systems.

In addition, there are 22 blanking lines, 190 intermediate and small presses, more than 400 pieces of welding equipment, and 232 miscellaneous tool and die machines used in the Buffalo Stamping Plant.

Helping to keep production at a high level has been the success of the Ford Taurus and its sister car, the Mercury Sable, as well as the Ford Escort and the Mercury Lynx. The Taurus-Sable cars have been Ford's best selling line since the Mustang of the late 1960s. The Buffalo plant also produces stampings and subassemblies for the Tempo, Topaz, Thunderbird, Cougar, Capri, Bronco, Continental, and Mark 7 automobiles and for various truck lines.

As a vital link in Ford's production process, the Buffalo facility and other plants of the Body and Assembly Division slice ribbons of steel and shape cold steel blanks into recognizable forms created by stylists many months before. Each part is contoured to mate precisely with its neighbor in the assembly process.

Using an ultrasonic spot-welding technique, the plant maintains a constant vigil on the quality of welds on its reinforced assemblies to ensure structural durability in the finished product. In addition, sample parts from production runs are checked regularly in precision fixtures in the quality assurance areas scattered throughout the plant. Dimensional accuracy, surface finish, and metal strength characteristics are constantly tested against Ford quality standards.

Production management at the plant has at its command a complete computer system that collects and analyzes more than one million pieces of information daily. The computer can automatically print out reports used in production scheduling, engineering, quality control, and payroll accounting. In addition, computer graphic work stations are used to solve design-intent problems and complete inspection control sheets, general dimensioning points on sketches, and feasibility proposals.

Safer operations and more efficient handling of materials by employees have resulted from automation that has been applied to

---

Two new door assembly lines, one of which is pictured here, have been installed at the Buffalo Stamping Plant at a cost of more than $17 million. Included in this expansion was the purchase of six hydraulic hemming presses, 14 low-profile bridge welders, and various automation and robotic equipment used in the production of door panels for Taurus and Sable automobiles.

most jobs in the plant. At the same time automation has improved the overall quality of the stampings produced.

Ford Motor Company's presence in Buffalo goes back to 1910 when it began production in the old John R. Keim plant, with the late William S. Knudson as director. The facility subsequently became an assembly plant, and because of increased demand, Ford built another plant at Main Street and Rodney Avenue. The company also operated an assembly plant on Fuhrmann Boulevard from 1938 until 1958, turning out nearly two million cars.

The story of automobile production is one of 10,000 chapters, each an adventure in time, material, and ingenuity. The settings are the iron mines, Ford's own steel-making facilities, the firm's manufacturing plants, and the facilities of thousands of suppliers who provide vast quantities of materials for the hungry system.

Despite the loss of steel jobs at Bethlehem Steel, the facility in Lackawanna still maintains a rolling mill which is in high production. Photo by Joe Traver

Alabama.

Then, in 1985, the buyout occurred, assuring that Dunlop would remain in Buffalo. Since then, the company has been in its best financial position in years. Clark has referred to it as the fastest-growing, most profitable tire company in the country. The Syracuse-born executive told an interviewer in a recent *Western New York* profile, "Most of us [in the buyout group] are not from Buffalo. We have invested here because there are real assets in the area. It has one of the best pools of skilled labor in the U.S., limitless energy, water." He added that without the cooperation of the United Rubber Workers Local 135, the union that represents most of Dunlop's workers, the company wouldn't have survived the lean years. During those years, workers agreed to pay cuts offset by productivity bonuses.

Worthington Compressor Operation

Dresser Industries, Inc.

In India, Worthington compressors are used in the production of fertilizer. In New York's Finger Lakes, they put the bubbles in champagne. In offshore drilling rigs off the coast of Louisiana, they provide the pressure that moves oil from beneath the Gulf of Mexico.

Worthington Compressor Operation, a division of Dresser Industries, Inc., has been a major industrial employer in the Buffalo area and supplier to industry for nearly a century. The original brick building that housed the 1889 operation of The Snow Steam Pump Works at Clinton Street and Roberts Avenue still stands today.

Over the years the company has developed through a number of acquisitions, mergers, and name changes, as was the case with the firm's most recent acquisition—by Dresser Industries, Inc., of Dallas, Texas, in February 1985. The corporation's current name, Worthington Compressor Operation,

Worthington compressors are used to treat crude oil feed stocks with hydrogen, resulting in a greater yield of fuel and gasoline from each barrel of oil.

Dresser Industries, Inc., reflects this change in ownership.

Today the firm manufactures a number of different compressor models, reflecting the hundreds of different industries that use compressors as a vital part of their business. As an example, much of the gasoline used in our cars and the natural gas used in our homes has been processed using Worthington products. In addition to the compressors used for oil and gas production, hundreds are in

service on ships in the U.S. Navy.

Typically, Worthington compressors go into action after a gas well has been drilled. The gas pressure must be increased before it can be transmitted through gas lines. Worthington manufactures compressors for that purpose—some are in use on Western New York gas wells.

Another application for Worthington technology is the space program. The company supplied a giant reciprocating compressor weighing 200 tons to produce rocket fuel for the Space Shuttle.

Worthington builds compressors for U.S. Navy combat ships. All new submarines, including the USS. *Buffalo*, have Worthington compressors on board.

Skilled labor, perhaps more than any other factor, is responsible for maintaining the firm's reputation for quality. More than 700 employees, many of whose fathers and grandfathers worked at Worthington before them, are employed in the company's production facilities, which include a 240,000-square-foot foundry. This family heritage has generated strong loyalty among Worthington employees.

In addition to industrial applications, Worthington compressors are used by the military. This oil-free air compressor can be found aboard the Trident submarine.

Occidental Chemical Corporation

Peek into almost any American household and you'll see an abundance of products in whose manufacture Occidental Chemical Corporation has played a key role. The reason is simple: OxyChem products and their derivatives are essential ingredients in the manufacture of literally thousands of different products. The drugs we take to fight illness, the detergents we use to clean our clothes and homes, even the carbonated fizz in our favorite soft drinks—all are products that owe their existence to the work of OxyChem.

The firm's parent company, Occidental Petroleum, is one of the world's largest and best-known energy companies, ranking in the top 20 of the *Fortune* 500. Subsidiary OxyChem, headquartered in Darien, Connecticut, contributes to this success with annual sales of more than two billion dollars.

In Western New York, the company's Durez Plastics Division is headquartered in North Tonawanda, its Research and Development Center is on Grand Island, its Energy-From-Waste facility is in Niagara Falls, and its Detergent & Specialty Products Division headquarters is located in an award-winning building in Niagara Falls. OxyChem began with a small chemical manufacturing complex in New York. How it got there is a story in itself.

Theodore Roosevelt was President of the United States when his close friend, young entrepreneur Elon Huntington Hooker, formed the Development and Funding Company in Brooklyn, New York, in 1903. The firm was founded on an untried invention—a method for inexpensively turning salt brine into chlorine and caustic soda. Called the Town-send Cell, this invention works, loosely speaking, on the same principle as the battery—only in reverse—to separate the chlorine, caustic soda, and hydrogen components of salt water. Although much refined today, this process remains the basis for much of Oxychem's modern output of both chlorine and caustic soda.

Two years later Hooker chose a site on the American side of the Niagara River as the location for his small chemical plant. The reasons for his choice were a matter of practicality—vital resources were close at hand, including water from the river, salt from nearby salt beds, and the abundant electric power generated by the falls. In its first year of operation the plant turned out 1,800 tons of product. By contrast, OxyChem today manufactures more than that amount in a single day.

After Hooker was joined by his four brothers, the business became known as Hooker Electrochemical Company. As the years passed the Townsend Cell was modified for efficiency, becoming basis for the Hooker Type S Cell, a design that remains the standard in the electrochemical industry. By the 1950s the firm's annual sales had grown to $54 million, entirely through internal growth. Subsequent acquisitions and mergers allowed the company to diversify beyond electrochemistry, a development reflected in its change of name to Hooker Chemical Corporation and later Hooker Chemicals & Plastics Corp.

In 1968 Occidental Petroleum acquired the firm, and in less than eight years its sales had tripled. The combination of the Durez Plastics Division, Polymers & Plastics Fabricated Products, Agricultural Products Group, Interore Division, International Group, Olefins Division, and the Electrochemicals, Detergent & Specialty Chemicals Group form the organization that today calls itself OxyChem.

The corporation currently boasts some of the most sophisticated chemical manufacturing technologies in the world, producing fundamental organic and inorganic chemicals and numerous specialty chemicals. OxyChem's Electrochemicals, Detergent & Specialty Products Group is a leading supplier of chemicals such as chlorine, caustic soda, and a variety of phosphorus-based products.

The peek into America's living room, kitchen, or bathroom at the beginning of this profile is now worth a moment's consideration. Oxychem-produced chlorine, for example, is essential to the manufacture of plastics, paper, drugs, textiles, water purification chemicals, and paints. Caustic soda is used in the pulp and paper industries as well as in the manufacture of household cleaning products. And phosphates are used in soaps, detergents, beverages, and metal plating. The company can also develop chemicals to meet specific requirements in an ever-changing and increasingly specialized business environment. In addition, Oxychem exports its products all over the world, including the Middle East and China.

Millions of dollars also flow from OxyChem into the local economy. In addition to providing more than 2,000 high-paying jobs for area residents, the company also supports a host of civic and charitable causes. Niagara University, the State University of New York at Buffalo, the Buffalo Philharmonic Orchestra, the American Red Cross, and many other organizations are regular beneficiaries of OxyChem's generosity.

Economy of a different sort is reflected in the Detergent & Specialty Products Division's Niagara Falls headquarters building. In addition to offering stunning views of Niagara Falls, this innovative structure is one of the most energy-intensive buildings of its kind in the world. Using a system of glass panels, louvers, and computer-driven sensors, the building is designed to trap and release air to control interior temperatures. And it does so with such success that no conventional heating is necessary in winter, nor air conditioning in summer.

Yet another use of the building—one not dreamed of by the energy efficiency experts—was first displayed during Niagara Falls' 1985 Festival of Lights. Using a computer to synchronize music

and more than 1,600 multi-colored lights, "OxyLights^{SM}" turned an entire side of the glass-faced building into a kaleidoscopic holiday light show. OxyLights is even listed in the Guinness Book of World Records.

As for the future, Occidental Chemical Corporation is committed to future growth in Western New York. The firm's research and development staff is currently hard at work on new chemical formulations and technologies, advances that, like Elon Hooker's Townsend Cell, should continue to keep the company in the forefront of the chemical industry.

Dunlop currently employs over 1,000 persons at its Grand Island headquarters and 1.6-million-square-foot manufacturing plant in the Town of Tonawanda. The plant is in the second stage of a $100-million modernization program and makes about 12,500 tires a day.

Economic survival and community pride is generated out of such happy turnabouts. That "home team" spirit is particularly significant for the Buffalo industrial scene because it represents a continued trend toward major employers coming under control of local owners.

On the Waterfront

There's a 1,400-acre stretch of land along the waterfront in Lackawanna, just south of downtown Buffalo, that Goldome president and 1985-1986 chairman of the Greater Buffalo Chamber of Com-

merce Ross Kenzie refers to as one of the "crown jewels" of the renaissance efforts. It's the sprawling Bethlehem Steel complex. Before manufacturing completely ceased there in mid-1983, it was the area's largest steelmaker. Today, the site offers the area's biggest potential for new industrial development. It stands as an example of how, despite the inevitable decline of one of the area's mature industries, Buffalo can creatively and flexibly use the vacated site to its economic advantage in the 1980s.

The revitalizing efforts along this site characterize the continued concern for Buffalo's industrial roots. Along a waterfront where blast and open hearth furnaces roared constantly, where ships pulled in and out with the world's largest supply of grain shipments, new industrial development is taking seed in its place, preserving the foundation on which the Buffalo economy rose to world prominence.

Perhaps those observers most interested in such redevelopment

Dunlop Tire Corporation

The story of Dunlop Tire Corporation dates back to 1888 when John Boyd Dunlop, a Scottish veterinarian, invented the pneumatic tire to provide a better ride for his son's bicycle.

Dunlop's tire captured the imagination of the world and provided a major impetus for automotive development, so much so that it was said that Dunlop's invention made the automobile possible. By the end of the nineteenth century Dunlop had established manufacturing and distribution facilities in major countries in Europe and Asia. In 1909 the firm expanded to Japan. Then, recognizing the tremendous opportunity emerging in America, Dunlop crossed the Atlantic, and on March 20, 1923, the first American-made Dunlop tire rolled off the production line on Sheridan Drive near Buffalo.

In 1969, in order to expand U.S. production capacity and meet growth requirements, the firm opened a state-of-the-art radial production facility in Huntsville, Alabama. In 1983 Sumitomo Industries Ltd., the Japan-based member of Dunlop International, acquired the Dunlop tire factories in the United Kingdom, West Germany, and France, as well as the company's world technical center in the United Kingdom.

The culmination of the evolution of Dunlop Tire Corporation from an English-based holding company came with the purchase of U.S. tire facilities in July 1985 by a group of American investors, led by the First Boston Corporation and including members of the management team, from Dunlop Holdings PLC, of London, England. Sumitomo Industries also holds an equity share.

Today Dunlop Tire Corporation's headquarters is located on Grand Island in the Niagara River. In addition to its Buffalo plant, the company operates a tire-manufacturing facility in Huntsville, Alabama, and a cord-processing plant in Utica, New York. Dunlop processes its own cord from fiber to finished plies and belts, resulting in complete quality control over the fabrication of casing components.

Currently Dunlop tires are distributed in both original equipment and replacement markets.

The company enjoys an original-equipment position with U.S. passenger car, truck, and motorcycle manufacturers. Dunlop tires are fitted as original equipment on Honda passenger cars built at Honda's Marysville, Ohio, plant. In addition, the firm has long been a major supplier to General Motors' trucks and buses, as well as to other truck and trailer manufacturers. Dunlop tires also are fitted as original equipment on every motorcycle and all-terrain vehicle manufactured in the United States.

The company's passenger car, light truck, medium truck, and agricultural replacement tires are marketed exclusively through a national base of independent dealer-distributors who account for more than 10,000 retail outlets. Dunlop motorcycle tires are sold in the replacement market through a national network of motorcycle parts distributors who supply motorcycle dealers and motorcycle specialty shops. The firm is the industry leader in the motorcycle replacement market.

In addition to the manufacturing and marketing rights for Dunlop tires in the United States and

The Dunlop Tire Corporation of Buffalo, which traces its roots back to England more than a century ago, has its headquarters in this building on Grand Island in the Niagara River.

Canada, the company owns outright its two associate brands, Remington and Centennial.

In addition to its strong original-equipment stance in the United States, Dunlop has key original-equipment fitments in Europe and Japan on the finest models of BMW, Porsche, Mercedes-Benz, Audi, Volkswagen, Opel, Honda, Toyota, Jaguar, Rolls Royce, Peugeot, Renault, and Volvo automobiles.

Included in Dunlop Tire Corpo-

rations's state-of-the-art products are four high-technology market segments. Passenger radials are the bread and butter of the tire industry. Performance radials have created strong consumer demand at three levels: ultrahigh-performance, V-rated tires for vehicles with top speeds in excess of 130 miles per hour; high-performance, H-rated tires for top speeds of 130 miles per hour; and custom performance nonspeed-rated low-profile radials with aggressive treads.

The firm was a pioneer in the development of radials for light trucks and offers a range of highly engineered tires for recreational, commercial, commuter, and off-road applications. Dunlop also offers a wide range of medium radial truck tires for over-the-highway, on off-road applications for all wheel positions.

Once a prototype is built it must undergo a battery of tests for dynamic strength, traction, wear, rolling resistance, high-speed structural integrity, uniformity, and ride and handling. Nine Dunlop technical centers located world wide supplement state-of-the-art equipment in the United States to test Dunlop tires to the most extreme tolerances.

The firm's commitment to the important radial tire segment of the market has been graphically proven with the recent installation of a radial truck tire manufacturing facility at the Buffalo plant.

In today's global market, tire manufacturers and marketers must possess five elements for success: a major supplier position to motor vehicle manufacturers, economies of scale, product and manufacturing technological leadership, insider position, and a common brand identity. Dunlop exhibits strength in all five of these key elements.

States Randall L. Clark, chairman and chief executive officer of Dunlop Tire Corporation, "Today's world of tightly linked Dunlop group companies provides the Dunlop brand name with unique strengths, strengths that assure the company a major role in the tire industry to the twenty-first century and beyond."

Rigidized Metals Corporation

Richard S. Smith, Sr. (1901-1978), founder, whose idea for deep texturing sheet metal for strength, rigidity, and abrasion resistance is evidenced in virtually every metal utilizing industry.

In 1938 a young stainless-steel salesman saw a patterned silver cigarette case in Tiffany's. He walked out of the famous jewelers with a gem of an idea.

The salesman was the late Richard S. Smith. The idea was textured stainless steel. Today the cigarette case that inspired Smith is on display at the headquarters of the company he founded—Rigidized Metals Corporation.

The idea of rigidizing sheet metal with a continuous pattern of dimples that adds strength, rigidity, and abrasion resistance to the metal seems so simple in retrospect that it is hard to believe that no one else had done it prior to 1938. But a major impediment to the acceptance of the idea was that no one in the metals industry

Richard S. Smith, Jr. (left), son of the founder and current president of Rigidized Metals Corporation, and Hugh Perry, who joined the company in 1942 as its first employee, inspect a Rigid-Tex facing on a hollow metal door.

at that time believed a practical process for deep-texturing sheet metal could be developed. It took Smith years of effort, during which time his idea was rejected by several major steel producers, to turn his idea into a reality.

And what a reality it is! Today Smith's idea, called Rigid-Tex, can be found on airplanes, buses, subway cars, and elevators, fire engine panels, cargo containers, conveyor systems, space heaters, and even the curtain walls on modern skyscrapers. Smith's invention proved itself not only versatile, but also adaptable to changing times. In the energy-starved 1970s the firm developed solar Rigid-Tex, a version of the metal designed specifically for solar collector panels.

The remarkable story of Rigidized Metals is in many ways the story of the man who founded the company. An entrepreneur who personified the American Dream, Smith was a hard driver whose stamp on his business was

as indelible as the Rigid-Tex metal patterns he created.

Every year at Thanksgiving each Rigidized Metals employee receives a turkey or a ham. At Christmastime, employees are given a bonus of $20 for each year they have been with the company. Both are traditions begun by the firm's benevolent founder.

But Rigidized Metal's generosity includes more than its employees. Friendship House in Lackawanna and Citizens for Mental Health of Buffalo are just two of many worthy causes the company has supported through the years.

Today the firm, headquartered at 658 Ohio Street, carries on under the direction of Richard S. "Sky" Smith, Jr., son of the founder and the company's current president. Privately held, Rigidized Metals Corporation also owns two smaller metal-finishing companies in Windsor, Ontario. Sky Smith believes, and with good reason, that there will always be new uses, new applications, and new ideas for using Rigid-Tex. Accordingly, the firm's motto is "Where in the year 2000?"

Where indeed? If in the year 2000, or even next week, you pump some gas, make a call from a pay phone, or take an elevator ride, run your finger over the dimpled surface at hand—and consider the man who put a new wrinkle in the modern world.

A customs inspector at Peace Bridge checks goods destined for the US. Photo by Joe Traver

A Purolator Courier driver poses in front of her big rig. Photo by Joe Traver

are the members of the labor organizations, the growth of which paralleled Buffalo's industrial climb: the steelworkers, the railroad unions, the longshoremen, the grain millers, the building trades unions, the chemical workers, the autoworkers, and the electrical workers. This is a heritage of skilled workers who've endured monumental setbacks in the turn of the local economy over the past twenty-five years. For them, such revitalization efforts bring a degree of much-needed hope.

In September 1984, Bethlehem began a four-year demolition project of that Lackawanna site, during which time 70 percent of the buildings will be razed so that the property can be converted into an industrial park.

The new industrial park will join more than twenty industrial parks across Greater Buffalo catering to a wide variety of manufacturing, warehousing, and distribution needs. The former Bethlehem site is an especially desirable location because of its water, rail, and truck transportation links.

Buffalo Crushed Stone, Inc., a West Seneca firm, has purchased 153 acres of Bethlehem property. Renaming it Gateway Trade

Marlette National Corporation

Although the name is new, Marlette National Corporation has deep roots in the Buffalo area.

Marlette National began here more than 60 years ago. It was then that Elmer Lincoln Marlette moved his family to Buffalo from Milwaukee. Full of confidence in Buffalo's industrial base, he opened an electroplating concern with his son Newton. The firm, known as Marlette and Son, operated out of a small building at 98 Clinton Street.

As the years passed the company grew. It was the first firm in the region to offer chromium plating. Soon it was doing a great deal of that plating for an important customer, The Pierce Arrow Motor Car Company.

Edward N. Marlette, Newton's eldest son, joined the company after his father's death in 1941. For the next four years the firm was busy with work related to the war effort. In 1947 the company was incorporated under the name Marlette Plating Co., Inc., and experienced steady growth under the leadership of Edward and his brothers, John E. Marlette and Richard T. Marlette.

The three brothers began a program of expansion and diversification. Buffalo Bumper Exchange, one of Marlette Plating's major divisions, was started in 1959.

Buffalo Bumper began with a simple idea: Damaged automobile bumpers could be straightened and replated. The end product would be indistinguishable from a brand new bumper but far less expensive.

The idea took hold and Buffalo Bumper began selling its replacement bumpers well beyond the city of Buffalo. Today the company also distributes all types of new automobile parts, including fenders, radiators, and headlights. In addition, Buffalo Bumper has become a prime electroplating source for some of North America's largest heavy truck manufacturers.

In the meantime, Marlette Plating, the parent company, continued to expand. In 1981 it relocated to its present headquarters on Rano Street in Buffalo. The 180,000-square-foot facility is ideally suited to the company's future growth plans.

Marlette Plating's focus was large-scale production metal finishing. Early on it had been an industry leader in automated plating lines.

In 1985 the company acquired National Finishing Corporation. The two companies had long been friendly competitors. While National had also been a large-scale production house, it had several areas in which it specialized. One of the most important was the plating of precious metals,

The automated plating line. Marlette National Corporation, an innovator in plant automation, advanced technology, and new techniques and applications, makes the complex jobs routine.

Marlette's commitment to investing in the future includes this new, sophisticated pollution-control equipment for water treatment in-house.

particularly for high-tech industries. Parts plated by National Finishing even went to the moon.

Edward N. Marlette, Jr., joined the company in 1971 and his brother Michael followed in 1979. Today the corporation offers a full range of metal finishing services, including chrome, copper, cadmium, nickel, zinc, tin, silver, gold, and aluminum anodizing among many others.

Over 60 years and four generations much has changed. Marlette Plating Company and its subsidiaries—Buffalo Bumper and National Finishing—are now Marlette National, one of the largest, most versatile plating, finishing, and related services company in the nation. Marlette National Corporation and its 250 employees are proud to be part of Buffalo's industrial past—and its future.

Winfield Industries

When he started out in business in the early 1960s, Mason Winfield pinned his hopes on a pin—a plastic bowling pin. However, turning his pin into a commercial success proved more difficult than convertng a 7-10 split. It was time for a new idea. And so began a pattern that Winfield has followed ever since.

Winfield simply took his existing technology and applied it to a new market, making polyurethane feed and squegee rolls for X-ray developing machines. And since then the company has survived in much the same way: When markets have shifted or disappeared, the firm has applied its technology to new challenges and products. The result is a thriving concern, specializing in liquid cast elastomeric materials, which now makes plastic parts for everything from guided missiles to business machines.

Winfield Industries' fortunes originally soared with the discovery that it could blend liquid polymers in such a way as to produce a material that could absorb shock without rebounding—ideal for use in railroad coupling shock absorbers. Business was good during the late 1960s, and the company was subsequently purchased by C/R Industries of Chicago.

With the railroad business chugging along nicely, the X-ray machine manufacturer unexpectedly made the use of Winfield's urethane obsolete. The result of that apparent setback was, in fact, a step forward: Winfield used the opportunity to devise a method to cast liquid silicone rubber, which allowed him to maintain the business.

During the 1970s Winfield Industries' growth necessitated a move to its present 45,000-square-foot location in Buffalo's Kensington district. The company

Products developed through Winfield's application of advanced chemical technology to plastics fabrication can be found in missile systems, mining, medical diagnostic, office equipment—and even railroad shock absorbers.

changed hands and prospered, but it continued to search out new markets for its products. Consequently, business and duplicating machines have developed into major markets, as has the military. The low-resiliency polyurethane originally used in railroad couplings is now built into the base of portable metal shelters used to house radio equipment. Parachuted to the ground, these military structures have their landings cushioned by blocks of Winfield urethane.

In 1982 Winfield Industries was sold to its present owner,

A. Douglas Oak, a businessman with a background in aircraft and defense work. Oak's expertise, in combination with the firm's continual upgrading of technology in the area of liquid elastomers, has allowed it to continue its success. Today it is a leading producer of plastic parts for the Peacekeeper Missile and Trident Submarine Missile programs, as well as for a number of other far-ranging and unusual applications.

The changes in fortune that the company has weathered are not atypical of the basic changes that Buffalo has—and will—face. In the case of Winfield Industries, flexibility and creativity have combined with high-quality products and performance to ensure its success. It believes that, using the same qualities, Buffalo can do the same.

New industry stands side-by-side with the old to preserve Buffalo's legacy as a major manufacturing center. Courtesy, Greater Buffalo Chamber of Commerce

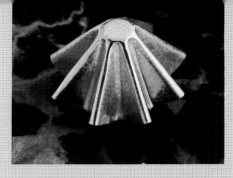

The Renaissance Crown®, a significant development in dentistry.

Williams Gold Refining Company, Inc.

Precision precious metals for electronics.

A nationally recognized leader in the use of precious metals and gold in dentistry and electronics, Williams Gold Refining Company, Inc., has a history and outlook as rich as the element upon which its fortunes were built.

During the 1898 gold rush in Canada's Klondike, Alexander D. Williams, son of a gold miner, unearthed what was believed to be the single-largest piece of gold ever found in the Yukon—the so-called Lodestar, a 26.25-ounce nugget of 80-percent pure gold. Fortified by his strike and his working knowledge of precious

metals, he formed Williams Gold Refining Company in Kansas City in 1907. Five years later Williams moved the operation to Buffalo, where it has remained ever since. By the 1920s Williams Gold was a leading producer of gold alloys for dentistry.

During that decade Alexander's son, Reginald V. Williams, working with a professor at Princeton University, developed the first commercial application of induction melting. It was not until the 1970s that its use became common and now is recognized as the best way to produce consistent, high-quality, homogeneous specialty alloys.

As the company grew, heavy

emphasis was put on both research and education. In the 1930s Williams Gold instituted one of the first such education departments in the nation—and one that is still operating today—to teach new procedures to dentists and dental laboratory technicians.

Today, under John A. and R.V. "Vic" Williams, Jr., the third generation of the family to lead the firm, Williams Gold has expanded its precious metals manufacturing expertise, and has become the number-one dental lab supplier in the United States, as well as a major supplier of alloys for the electronics industry. Most recently, the company introduced the Renaissance Crown®, a dental restoration for replacement teeth that has the potential of totally changing the present lost wax casting method which has been used for 80 years to make dental bridges.

Over the past 30 years Williams Gold has grown from 70 employees and one million dollars in sales to 315 employees and sales of more than $90 million. A plant in Fort Erie and 45 employees serve the firm's Canadian markets, and licenses in South America and France have become important in foreign distribution.

Headquartered at Main and Hertel in North Buffalo, Williams is a business that's brought both prestige and prosperity to itself and to the city it calls home. And while it's been run by family members since its inception, the firm credits much of its success to the dedication of its employees. Further advancements in the dental and electronics business should help Williams Gold Refining Company, Inc., continue to grow, and keep this high-technology company here on the Niagara Frontier.

The Curtis Screw Company plant
is located on the Erie Canal.
Photo by Lester J. Kuhn

273

Lake boats unload grain at Cargill Mills and grain elevators on the Buffalo River. Photo by Dennis R. Floss

Above: The Buffalo Skyway and a General Mills plant at left form a background for Crawdaddy's Restaurant in this view across the marina in Buffalo harbor. Photo by Joe Traver

Right: Scrap concrete, to be used as an artificial reef to promote marine life, is being loaded onto a barge in the Port of Buffalo. The operation is being supervised by State University of New York officials. Photo by Joe Traver

276

The Mohawk, *a tugboat based in Buffalo, pushes a barge down a section of the Erie Canal between Buffalo and Rochester. Photo by Joe Traver*

Center, the company not only is optimistic about attracting renewed industrial activity to the area, but long-range plans call for the opening of the beach south of the plant property in Woodlawn, along with the construction of a marina and a restaurant. Included in that development plan is the seven-story former Bethlehem Steel office building and its surrounding 150 acres in the Town of Hamburg.

The Niagara Frontier Transportation Authority (NFTA), which owns some 600 acres of prime lakefront property, is negotiating with Buffalo Crushed Stone to relocate the Port of Buffalo to the Bethlehem site. This would allow a consolidation of the port activities in Buffalo to a port site that is considered superior in size, protection, and depth to the current port.

Because the Port of Buffalo now operates at a loss, the consolidation would also ensure that the city gets the most out of its port potential. In 1985, the Port of Buffalo handled 205,000 tons of cargo while the Bethlehem port, now operated by Buffalo Crushed Stone, handled 125,000 tons. With a new contract for 160,000 tons of limestone coming through on its way to New York State Electric & Gas Corporation's generating plant in Somerset, the Bethlehem port is

Opposite: This view looks east from the air over the Niagara River, across the Peace Bridge. At the bottom is the main span and truss over the New York State Barge Canal, with the Niagara extension of the Thomas E. Dewey Thruway running alongside. Photo by Joe Traver

Below: A customs inspector at Peace Bridge checks goods leaving Buffalo for Canada. Photo by Joe Traver

This aerial view stretches south to the harbor. Photo by Peter R. Barber

doubling its tonnage.

As for the rest of the former steel plant property, Bethlehem is leasing a building where General Electric Corporation is refurbishing New York City subway cars in a contract with the New York City area's Metropolitan Transportation Authority.

Bethlehem is also leasing space to Pillsbury Company which needs an area to transfer goods from rail to truck. And the fifteen small companies which make up the Foreign Trade Zone are being consolidated into one building on the Bethlehem property. Buffalo's Foreign Trade Zone offers relative freedom from various government restrictions, thereby permitting a company to examine, store, stock, exhibit, manipulate, grade, clean, pack, mix, or sell—wholesale—without duty or government curtailment. Government paperwork is negligible for importers wishing to export.

Bethlehem is currently moving ahead with the second phase of its redevelopment plan, involving the formation of a joint venture company with Buffalo Crushed Stone and a developer not yet

Western New York Foreign Trade Zones Operators, Inc.

Western New York Foreign Trade Zones Operators, Inc., serving international commerce and trade, has brought to Buffalo, to Erie County, and to Western New York a concept that created many new jobs and is helping business and industry compete more effectively in a global economy.

All this came about when the Western New York Foreign Trade Zones Operators, Inc., opened for business on May 28, 1976, as the 23rd foreign trade zone in the nation.

John J. Palisano, president of Lincoln Storage Company, had the vision to become interested in that new venture and established the operating corporation. His involvement in the transportation and warehousing business has roots that date back more than 70 years through the Palisano family.

He selected George K. Keitner, A.C., as vice-president and executive director for the company. Keitner is a former customhouse broker in his native Hungary, an educator, an author of four textbooks, and a former instructor at Niagara University in Niagara Falls, New York. He is also a well-known authority in the field of free trade zones and other customs-related subjects.

As an alternative to paying duties on foreign goods immediately upon their arrival from abroad, special procedures are available for the deferral of duty payments. A more recent and increasingly popular alternative procedure for reducing customs costs under United States law is the use of "foreign trade zones," the domestic version of free trade zones available throughout the world.

Foreign trade zones are an area within the United States but outside customs territory, where foreign and domestic goods may generally be stored, processed, or manufactured duty free. Goods subsequently entering the U.S. market from a zone for import into the United States are subject to duty. No duty is charged if the goods are reshipped from the zone to a foreign country.

United State zone legislation is based upon a concept adopted by Northern European countries. It involves the designation of sites, in or near customs ports of entry, as areas outside customs territory for purposes of entry procedures. The sites remain subject to other national and local legal requirements.

Western New York Foreign Trade Zones Operators, Inc., is a company that is operating, maintaining, and administering such a foreign trade zone. It currently has two activated site locations in Erie County. Site 1 is located in the Gateway Trade Center on Lake Erie, a short three mile drive from the Peace Bridge. Site 2 is located in the Amherst International Park, adjacent to the Greater Buffalo International Airport.

Using the foreign trade zone at or near a final market as a distribution and storage point can considerably reduce the time lag between order and delivery. Goods can be stockpiled in the zone pending an anticipated increase in price level or quota changes and released when advantageous. Merchandise can be released into national territory or reexported in quantities or lots that are larger or smaller than the orignal shipment. The processing of foreign goods in the zone can sometimes result in savings on host country duties and taxes by providing a different basis for duty assignment.

Funds are not tied up in the payment of customs duties, import taxes, or the posting of bonds or other security while goods are held in the zone. In some cases, the zone can accommodate trade activities, particularly for the transshipment, reexportation, and staging of goods for later shipment across national or customs boundaries.

Merchandise in the zone is not subject to federal excise taxes, and export status is accorded when goods are placed in the zone for export. Normally, state and local excise taxes on personal property, such as inventory taxes, do not apply to goods that are in the zone for bona fide customs reasons. The locations of Foreign Trade Zones No. 23, Site 1, and Site 2 at the eastern tip of Lake Erie are at the center of a 500-mile circle containing the great commercial and populated centers of northeastern United States. Within the 500-mile radius of the Buffalo area are 55 percent of the total U.S. population, 60 percent of the total personal income of the United States, 61 percent of the Canadian population, and 85 percent of Canadian manufacturing activities. The unique geographic location on the Canadian border attracts a large number of Canadian and overseas companies to Buffalo and Erie County with their operations. Canadian firms use the facilities of Western New York Foreign Trade Zone Operators, Inc., not only to enter the U.S. market, but also to export and reexport to Canada and other nations.

Amherst International Park at 60 Earhart Drive, Amherst.

Joseph Davis, Inc.

This fabrication of a large tee or fishmouth branch shows the company's special fabrication and welding capabilities using state-of-the-art welding procedures.

Joseph Davis, Inc., founded by the late Joseph Davis at the outset of the Great Depression in 1932, is a major general mechanical contractor serving the heating, refrigeration, ventilating, air-conditioning, process piping, plumbing, and fire protection fields.

In 1932 Davis quit his job with a heating contractor and opened for business in a tiny office in downtown Buffalo. Since then the firm's growth pattern has been a steady upward curve.

A major portion of the company's business is in Western New York. However, it has branched out into eastern Ohio, northwestern Pennsylvania, West Virginia, Indiana, Texas, and Louisiana.

Joseph Davis, Inc., is also the parent company of Davis Refrigeration Company, a division whose roots go back to the year 1904. In addition, a wholly owned subsidiary, the Kiphut-Neumann Company, Inc., handles a major portion of the plumbing business in the area. An affiliate, Davis-Ulmer Sprinkler Company, Inc., serves the fire protection industry. Joseph Davis, Inc., has a warehouse and fabrication complex on the east side of Buffalo, with a National Fabrication Agreement and a modern, well-equipped fabrication shop. Joseph Davis' customer's needs are well served with high-quality welding fabrication, complying with several certified codes. It has an in-house Quality Assurance Program, with welder certification forming a major portion of the QA Program.

Joseph Davis, Inc., provides a complete design-build concept wherein the firm offers its clients a complete package of design, construction, start-up, and operation and maintenance instruction —a so-called turn-key process. The company enjoys such major national accounts as General Motors Corporation, Ford Motor Company, Niagara Mohawk, E.I. du Pont de Nemours & Company, and many, many more.

Among the many major projects that Joseph Davis, Inc., has successfully completed are portions of the enormous Niagara Hydropower project; the Nine Mile Point nuclear power station along Lake Ontario; the New York State Electric and Gas steam power station in Somerset, New York; the Niagara Mohawk steam power station in Dunkirk, New York; the Huntley station in Tonawanda, New York; and the Buffalo General Hospital.

Company executives emphasize that now more than ever, peak efficiency must be paramount in the design, construction, operation, and maintenance of HVAC&R systems. Steadily increasing demands for greater output from these systems, complicated by today's critical need for energy conservation, have presented a new challenge to contractors in this field.

Davis engineers, always alert to new technological developments, have met this challenge by taking advantage of new materials, latest technology, and modern equipment. The company's approach to these problems is demonstrated by an impressive variety of successfully completed projects, ranging from simple boiler room installations to the most sophisticated HVAC&R system for large commercial, institutional, and industrial establishments. Many projects employing multiple-unit installations, miles of piping, and networks of advanced control stations have been built and placed in operation by Davis experts, adding to the firm's established reputation for total systems capability.

Expert designers formulate plans for complicated, completely automated mechanical systems through a range of temperatures below minus 100 degrees Fahrenheit, to installations utilizing steam at pressures up to 1,000 pounds per square inch. Davis designers capably design and install waste-treatment, water-purification, plumbing, and fire protection systems of a complex nature in any type of building, including multistory structures. Refrigeration for the food-processing industry has been a Davis Refrigeration Company forte for many years. This firm also specializes in refrigeration for the liquefaction of such gases as chlorine and phosgene.

Many millions of feet of process piping have been fabricated and installed by Joseph Davis, Inc., in chemical, pharmaceutical, and food-processing plants, as well as in refineries, breweries, and paper, copper, and steel mills, modernizing these plants for greater reliability, better quality processing, and more efficient production.

The firm's performance on these types of complex jobs is notable for the continuing number of repeat contracts with several of the world's largest manufacturing companies. Particularly well known for its work in the construction of boiler and power stations, Davis has installed literally hundreds of packaged and field fabricated boilers.

Utilizing the latest technology, modern material-handling equipment, and heavy-duty construction equipment, the company has been chosen for the modification of high-pressure utility plant systems handling valves and components weighing 25 tons and more. This type of work is routine for the firm's experienced personnel. One project in particular called for the installation of eight million pounds of pipe serving 12 hydropowered generators, each rated at 2,500 megawatts.

The firm takes great pride in the systems and services it has provided for the improvement of the environment. It has for many years pursued the development and installation of industrial and municipal purification systems that have proved highly successful in the detoxification of oils, acids, alkali, iron oxide, mercury, and other chemical wastes. The purification of air-particulate discharge from process and utility exhaust gases is another area where the company's state-of-the-art technology has been much in demand. Installations have included electrostatic precipitators, scrubber systems, and bag houses complete with components and controls.

Such complex projects vary widely in application and demonstrate the firm's diversity in both techniques and processing systems. The Joseph Davis, Inc., team possesses all the modern skills and equipment necessary to upgrade environmental quality at any industrial site.

Corporate executives, ever cognizant of the need to improve the industry, emphasize educational programs for its team and con-

The latest rigging technology is demonstrated in this helicopter lift of an air-conditioning unit onto the historic Albright-Knox Art Gallery in Buffalo.

stantly look for and train young engineers to maintain the company's integrity and follow the path formulated by its founder. The firm, recognizing its place in the civic family of Buffalo, maintains close membership in many technical and civic organizations, thus returning to the industry and community services to show its appreciation for the community in which it operates.

Corporate headquarters housing Joseph Davis, Inc., the Davis Refrigeration Company, and Kiphut-Neuman Company, Inc., is located at 120 West Tupper Street in downtown Buffalo. The corporate offices are located in one of Buffalo's oldest estate mansions, dating back to 1838. Through the years many renovation projects have taken place to preserve its historic architecture.

Breaker *clears Buffalo Harbor of ice in early spring. Photo by Joe Traver*

located. The three companies would jointly attempt to develop and market the industrial park, with the developer constructing new buildings to suit industrial tenants on the cleared lands.

Energy

At the end of Buffalonian Grover Cleveland's second term as the country's president, an event occurred that would change the face of Greater Buffalo. It would brighten the streets, homes, and plants, and energize the economy. The momentous event happened at midnight, November 15, 1896, when the roaring natural energy of Niagara Falls was harnessed and transmitted for the first time to Buffalo. That twenty-mile current represented the first time that electricity had been transmitted over a long distance.

The first to receive the power were the streetcars of the Buffalo Street Railway Company. Since then, a wide variety of Greater Buffalo industry has greatly benefited from the inexhaustible power and cheap energy derived from the geographical proximity to the cataract and the subsequent power project that was built around it. Greater Buffalonians have traditionally enjoyed the lowest electric bills in the state and perhaps the nation.

The newest power surge in local electricity is the multibillion-dollar Nine Mile 2, a massive nuclear power plant in Oswego, east of Rochester along Lake Ontario. Local utilities Niagara Mohawk and New York State Electric & Gas have a combined 59 percent

284

Buffalo's fireboat, the Edward Cotter, *clears its pumps with a water spray while on a winter training exercise. Photo by Joe Traver*

Pratt & Lambert, Inc.

The Pratt & Lambert Calibrated Colors® system is designed to satisfy even the most discriminating consumer with an exclusive array of interior and exterior decorating palettes.

Pratt & Lambert, Inc. of Buffalo, which had a modest start in Long Island City, New York, in 1849, today ranks among the nation's largest paint manufacturers and is a leading producer of coatings and adhesives.

The firm was launched as A.W. Pratt & Company with partners Alfred W. Pratt and his brother Charles, who invented a paint drier that was a revolutionary development in its day. Henry S. Lambert joined the partnership in 1874, and the company was incorporated under its present name in 1885.

The decision to locate Pratt & Lambert's plant headquarters in Buffalo was made in 1902, when New York City and Chicago constituted the company's major markets and Buffalo was considered to be midway between the two cities. Another important factor was Buffalo's low-cost transporta-

tion. At the time imported raw materials could be shipped by canalboat to a dock at the rear of the factory along Scajaquada Creek. Today Pratt & Lambert consists of five operating divisions.

The Paint Division is a national producer of architectural finishes for consumer, contractor, and maintenance markets. Production sites are located in Buffalo; Orange, California; Fort Erie, Ontario; and at shared facilities in Wichita, Kansas, and Memphis, Tennessee.

The Pierce & Stevens Division is a national manufacturer of specialty coatings and adhesives. Headquartered in Buffalo, the division has additional plants in Chicago, Illinois; Philadelphia, Pennsylvania; San Jose, California; Fort Erie, Canada; and Dallas, Texas.

The Southern Coatings Division manufactures a broad line of product finishes and corrosion-control systems, together with specialty products and paints. It is headquartered in Sumter, South Carolina, with a branch plant near New Orleans, Louisiana.

The Industrial Coatings Division is a national manufacturer of factory-applied finishes for a variety of markets, particularly those

Through internal growth and acquisition, Pratt & Lambert has become a leading diversified producer of architectural finishes and industrial chemical specialties.

requiring protection and/or decoration of metal surfaces. Its major production facility is in Wichita, Kansas, with additional plants in Buffalo, one of which is shared with the Paint Division.

The fifth division, United Paint Company, is headquartered in Memphis, Tennessee, and serves the mid-South with architectural finishes through company-owned outlets and independent dealers.

Overall, Pratt & Lambert's activities are carried out at 14 plants in the United States and Canada, together with nearly 50 other facilities that function as distribution centers and retail stores. In addition, there are licensees in Costa Rica, West Germany, Japan, and South Africa.

In 1985 the firm acquired Spatz Paints, Inc., a St. Louis-based producer of coatings for medical and industrial gas cylinders, fertilizers, and liquid propane gas equipment. That same year the company also purchased United Solvents of America, Inc., an Orlando, Florida, marketer of paint sundries, automotive after-market products, and related items.

Today Pratt & Lambert, Inc., is headed by Raymond D. Stevens, Jr. who serves as chairman, and Joseph J. Castiglia, president. Its common stock has been listed on the American Stock Exchange for more than 60 years, longer than any other company whose stock is currently traded on the exchange.

Lucidol Division of Pennwalt Corporation

Lucidol has been part of the Buffalo scene for 60 years.

In 1926 several Dutch chemical engineers opened a small factory in Buffalo to manufacture benzoyl peroxide bleaching compound for the large flour-milling industry that was centered in the area. It was the first business of its kind in the United States and its organization marked the birth of this country's multimillion-dollar organic peroxides industry.

Today the Lucidol Division of the Pennwalt Corporation is the largest producer of organic peroxide chemicals in the United States. Most of the items produced by Lucidol go to the plastics industry for use in the manufacture of large-volume plastics such as polyvinyl chloride (PVC), low-density polyethylene, polystyrene, polyacrylates, and in the curing of polyesters to make reinforced fiberglass.

Lucidol has been, and continues to be, an important part of the growth of the plastics industry. In fact, without organic peroxides, many plastics cannot be made.

While Lucidol's headquarters is in Buffalo, the bulk of the firm's manufacturing is done in plants in Geneseo, New York, and Crosby, Texas. It also has worldwide interests in peroxides with seven plants around the globe.

The largest and most modern research facility of its kind in the organic peroxide industry.

Over the years Lucidol's commitment to quality, safety, and the advancement of peroxides and their uses has been demonstrated by its role in the industry. To date the company has introduced more new peroxides than the rest of the industry combined.

The following are evidence of Lucidol's many industry milestones and contributions to the plastics industry:

*In 1937 the firm introduced the first peroxide for PVC, one of the earliest thermoplastics, now commonly used for food wrap, home wiring, and drain, waste, and vent piping.

*A few years later Lucidol developed the first liquid peroxide marketed in the United States, t-butyl hydroperoxide. This eventually became the building block for the production of peroxyesters, raw materials vital to the growth of the plastics industry.

In 1946 the company pioneered the first benzoyl peroxide paste product, offering a safer alternative to the polyester/fiberglass industry.

Two years later Lucidol introduced the first liquid peroxyester, t-butyl perbenzoate, still today used in more types of plastics than any other peroxide. In 1953 in Geneseo, New York, Lucidol built the first peroxide plant to use remote control for personnel protection.

The firm's research center, located in suburban Buffalo, was built in 1961. This is the largest

Richard A. Schwab, president, flanked (left to right) by Sanford Stromberg, marketing manager; Bernard Kelly, vice-president/manufacturing; and Robert Bitten, vice-president/marketing.

peroxide research facility in the United States.

The technical breakthroughs and expanding capabilities Lucidol continues to provide have proven invaluable to customers in many ways. No other peroxide manufacturer offers the wide selection and flexibility of its full product line, its sophisticated distribution capability, and its commitment to providing technical and safety literature.

Lucidol's efforts for peroxides for the future reflect such concerns as making better use of raw materials, getting more out of available energy, and providing more saleable and more efficient products.

Lucidol believes that what it pioneered yesterday has helped to set plastics industry standards today and will help to ensure a better tomorrow.

Snyder Corp.

Sensitivity to consumer needs in the hospitality industry is credited for the success of the Snyder Hospitality Group. The group's growth is evidenced in the Hyatt Regency Buffalo (shown here), and the Hyatt Regency Rochester, slated for a September 1987 opening.

pizzas, Freezer Queen Foods grew to a leader in the frozen foods industry, doing $100 million in annual sales when Snyder sold it to Nabisco, Inc., in 1970.

Today Snyder Corp. is one of the city's most dynamic and rapidly expanding business empires. The conglomerate maintains interests in commercial hospitality, consumer products marketing, international trade, real estate development, and parking facilities management.

The objective of the Snyder Hospitality group is to seek out opportunities in the hospitality industry where the needs of consumers are not being met and develop an approach to service that market that is superior to those of competitors.

The cornerstone of the hospitality group is the $41-million Hyatt Regency Buffalo, built in a prime downtown location on the city's new $530-million rapid transit line. The luxurious hotel is considered a key element in the

It was a May weekend in 1958 when shoppers in a Buffalo department store noticed a young man in a white apron cooking sandwich steaks in an electric frying pan. He was passing out free samples. The shoppers loved the steaks, but barely gave the man a second look.

They should have.

Today that man in the white apron—Paul L. Snyder, founder of the Snyder Corp.—is one of Buffalo's most controversial, recognizable, and successful business moguls.

The Mansfield, Pennsylvania, native first came to Western New York as a scholarship player on the University of Buffalo football team. In 1957, after finishing college, he turned his energies and marketing instincts—and a very small initial investment—into a frozen foods company called Freezer Queen Foods. From its beginnings as a tiny operation specializing in sandwich steaks and

This renovated, historic mansion, built in 1895 and designed by renowned architect Stanford White, is the firm's corporate headquarters.

AirPark International is a leader in innovative parking facilities development and management.

management, facilities marketing, and facilities management.

This has made the Snyder Resource Group a significant player in this rapidly growing field. Whether it is the development of a $72-million theme park (Darien Lake); a $40-million, 400-room luxury hotel (Hyatt Regency Buffalo); or the renovation of a 2.5-million-square-foot manufacturing facility, the Snyder Resource Group brings ideas to life.

AirPark International is a leader in innovative parking facilities development and management. An absolute commitment to service and an intense awareness of customer needs has made AirPark facilities one of the most successful operations of its kind in the eastern United States. By providing such services as timely door-to-door shuttle bus services, 24-hour security, and emergency car repair, AirPark has achieved a distinct differentiation from its competitors.

Snyder Corp. has come a long way from Paul Snyder's humble beginnings as an apron-clad sandwich steak entrepreneur. Today the firm is a highly diversified empire that continues to draw upon the founding principles that were the cornerstone to its original success. Its role as a leader in Buffalo's rebirth illustrates the passion for excellence that has characterized the 30-year history of this dynamic Buffalo organization.

city's renaissance. There's similar excitement brewing in nearby Rochester, where the $40-million Hyatt Regency Rochester is slated for opening in September 1987.

The corporation's plans call for the Snyder Hospitality Group to expand its sphere of influence into all sectors of the hospitality industry.

Snyder Foods is a specialist in the sales and distribution of consumer food products. Its staff controls the core functions of marketing, sales, product development, quality assurance, and administration. Snyder Foods has been successful at combining the aggressive aspects of an entrepreneurial food marketing company with the technological leadership usually found in only large food conglomerates. Looking to the future, Snyder Foods' objective is to acquire and/or develop food products that are unique and segmented from the present com-

modity classes of today's retailing marketplace.

Snyder Corp. has long recognized that opportunities do not necessarily have geographic boundaries. Advances in telecommunications, transportation, and data processing have contributed significantly to easing the barriers of trade between countries. Snyder Trading Co. has developed into a legitimate and successful participant in world import/export trade. By aligning itself with strategically positioned international producers of goods and services, Snyder Trading Co. has been able to enjoy a long tenure of success in the industry.

The Snyder Resource Group takes an innovative approach to the challenge of real estate development. Rather than seeing a project simply in the traditional terms of financing and construction, Snyder has taken the decisive step to provide services covering the gamut of needs that truly define real estate development. This unique holistic approach entails three levels of expertise: project

Snyder Foods is a specialist in the sales and distribution of consumer food products.

investment in the project, along with utilities in Rochester, the Hudson Valley, and Long Island. Although it has been under construction for more than a decade, the plant's projected service goes beyond the traditional scale of a power plant. It has a projected life of forty years and is expected to generate electricity for more than nine million customers throughout the state.

Much of the added low-cost power that will result when Nine Mile 2 begins operation—scheduled for late 1986 or early 1987—will flow upstate to Greater Buffalo and beyond, promising to fill local industry's pocketbook more than ever.

The natural gas industry in Buffalo changed significantly in 1985 when, for the first time in over three decades, about 60 percent of all natural gas sold in the U.S. was free of government price con-

Below: The nuclear power plant Nine Mile 2 in Oswego is scheduled for completion in early 1987. Photo by Envisions Co.

F.N. Burt Company, Inc.

The corporate headquarters in Buffalo, New York.

F.N. Burt Company, Inc., which is observing its 100th anniversary in 1986, has grown over the years to become a major producer of boxes for a broad range of products. It is currently manufacturing boxes at the rate of 250 million per year.

The firm's headquarters and principal plant is at 2345 Walden Avenue in Buffalo. It also operates a plant in Oneonta, New York. F.N. Burt Company is headed by C. Taylor Kew as president and W. Russell Hurd as executive vice-president. The company was returned to local ownership in 1983 when Kew and Hurd acquired F.N. Burt Company from the Moore Corporation Limited of Toronto. Moore had owned the firm since 1909.

The business was founded by Frederick N. Burt in August 1886 at 440 Main Street in downtown Buffalo as a job printing shop that produced printed labels for boxes and legal forms. Burt entered the

paper box business by purchasing drug boxes and attaching his own labels. As the business grew, he developed machines to manufacture boxes, and about 1901 he began producing boxes for such well-known cigarettes as Helmar, Murad, Pall Mall, and English Ovals.

Burt also developed automatic equipment in the early years; this was the foundation of the business and continues to be so. Additional plants were purchased around the city to take care of a growing volume of business. At the time, machines produced only part of the total number of the boxes that were manufactured, with the majority still made by hand.

When Burt sold out to the Moore Corporation, Moore added considerable capital necessary at that time for machine development involving the rapidly growing cigarette-box industry. With this capital additional machines were developed and built in the F.N. Burt Company's plants to completely mechanize its cigarette box production. With its

own automatic equipment, the firm was able to produce more than 200 million boxes a year, or 98 percent of all cigarette boxes produced in the country.

The 1920s were a time of change for F.N. Burt Company. New items were added to its line of packages, including boxes for Christmas presents, candy cream jars, tincture mascara, pencils, ribbon, garters, paint, face powder, hair dye, soap boxes, and slides for birthday candles. A small folding box department also made ice cream cartons, as well as many cartons for the Larkin Company of Buffalo, a mail-order business.

In the 1920s the cigarette industry changed to the so-called "cup" package. This new method of packing cigarettes reduced prices and increased cigarette sales. The Burt set-up paper box business was the loser, and its volume declined sharply. As a result, the company entered the drinking cup and molded products field. For several years it produced cone-shaped paper cups and did a substantial business, but in 1925 this business was sold to a competitor.

In 1923 F.N. Burt Company began manufacturing items out of paper pulp. For about ten years millions of Santa Clauses, rabbits, kittens, puppies, and Halloween lanterns were made through this process. In the early 1930s the firm developed the "50's cigarette box," and the package became quite popular.

During World War II the firm was called on to produce various substitute packages. Lipstick containers were made of paper, plastic, and scrap metal in substantial quantities, replacing metal that was not allocated for this purpose. Millions of talc cans and jar caps were also manufactured under this process.

In 1936 the F.N. Burt Company again entered the folding carton field. At that time the firm selected the lithographic process for its printing method and continues to use it today. The most modern printing and finishing equipment available at the time was purchased, and since then the company has added millions of dollars worth of folding carton lithographic and finishing equipment to its facilities. Today the F.N. Burt Company is considered the leader in the field of high-grade folding carton packages.

The successful package doesn't just happen. It is the result of skilled personnel utilizing the latest production and marketing techniques. As an innovator and problem solver, the F.N. Burt Company brings every talent and tool to bear on each individual project, beginning with a review of customer needs. Once objectives are established, a packaging task force swings into action and concentrates its full attention on customer problems. Structural and graphic designers analyze customer product and packaging needs, creating package alternatives that are tested and refined.

The F.N. Burt Company's complete in-house pre-press capability—including color separations, plate making, and proofing, both photomechanical and press proofs—allows maximum manufacturing flexibility and quick response on last-minute graphic changes.

Ink mixing and color matching are also accomplished in-house to satisfy the most precise color requirements. From single to six-color presses with interstation drying, skilled craftsmen follow strict tolerances for both color matching and registration. Even postprinting operations are done internally. These include bronzing, lacquering, embossing, intricate diecutting, leaf stamping, and high-speed gluing.

The firm's quality control and

C. Taylor Kew (left), president, and W. Russell Hurd, executive vice-president.

assurance is supported by the latest scientific measuring instruments. A computerized management information system is used throughout the inquiry handling, order entry, production, inventory, receiving, and shipping processes.

The company also has the ability to custom design and build package machinery systems to handle standard and special construction for the high-volume user, as well as production jigs and fixtures to fulfill the needs of the small-volume producer.

The F.N. Burt Company has been committed to innovation, quality, and custom packaging for 100 years. This dedication has enabled the firm to become a recognized leader in the product packaging field. Its plants are among the best equipped in the packaging field, but a major strength is its ability to combine a high level of expertise acquired over many years with the most advanced equipment and state-of-the-art techniques available.

In an era when a great many businesses tend to lose their identities when they are acquired by outside interests, the F.N. Burt Company, Inc., takes great pride in having returned the firm to local ownership.

Typical high-quality paperboard packaging by F.N. Burt.

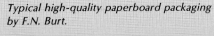

The Niagara Mohawk Building is at the center of this view of downtown. Photo by Joe Traver

trols. The subsequent predictions that fuel bills would immediately rise never materialized in Greater Buffalo, an area where nearly 90 percent of homes are gas-heated. Some have said that the stabilized rates were a result of the natural gas surplus from Canadian and domestic wells.

The entire Greater Buffalo region, particularly Chautauqua County, remains the heart of natural-gas and oil exploration. Independent drillers and exploration companies forecast a steady drilling pace throughout 1986.

And on the oil scene, gasoline pump prices were among the lowest in the country in 1986, dipping down into the seventy-five-cent-per-gallon range. The full-service gas station has disappeared in recent years, replaced by specialty shops featuring products and services such as mufflers, rustproofing, or lubrication service.

It was another changing symbol of how Greater Buffalonians are powered, whether in industry, on the road, or at home.

New York State Electric & Gas Corporation

As the ceremonial ribbon drifted to the floor, Huntingdon Analytical Services, Inc., opened its doors in Middleport. Its new home had stood empty since FMC Corporation closed in the early 1980s, leaving over 100 people out of work. Huntingdon will eventually employ 150 people. It is thanks in part to the efforts of New York State Electric & Gas Corporation's (NYSEG) industrial development department that the British firm ended up in Middleport.

NYSEG's commitment to industrial development is just one illustration that the company is much more than a supplier of electricity to almost 140,000 customers and natural gas to another 19,000 customers in Western New York.

The firm is a vital element in the economic lifeblood of Western New York, employing 300 people in Lancaster, 112 in Lockport, and 213 at Somerset Gener-

Somerset Generating Station, on Lake Ontario northeast of Lockport, is New York State Electric & Gas Corporation's largest generating plant in New York State.

ating Station on Lake Ontario. NYSEG paid $13.6 million in property taxes to Western New York school districts, cities, villages, and towns in 1985. Almost seven million dollars was paid on Somerset Generating Station alone.

But perhaps the largest economic boost to NYSEG's credit came during the construction of Somerset Generating Station, which began producing electricity in August 1984. The billion-dollar project, which included a $350-million expense for environmental protection systems, and the $60-million Somerset Railroad comprised one of the largest construction projects ever undertaken in Western New York. Up to 3,100 workers helped build the 643-megawatt plant and 15.5-mile railroad. The payroll during peak construction totaled more than $175 million per year.

Important as dollars and cents are, NYSEG's involvement goes further. Across the company's service territory, which includes about 35 percent of the land area of Upstate New York, the firm is committed to United Way. In 1986 NYSEG employees contrib-

uted $269,000 to the community service agency. The company contributed another $65,000.

And NYSEG employees contributed thousands of their own hours to United Way agencies, service clubs, chambers of commerce, and other community causes. "We are an integral part of the community," says Robert T. Sorensen, Western Area general manager. "As individuals, we recognize a responsibility that goes beyond providing reliable electric and natural gas service."

The company strives for customer satisfaction with a far-reaching consumer affairs program. For its Project SHARE, Seniors Lending a Hand, and Operation Button Up programs, NYSEG was cited by President Ronald Reagan for community action and volunteerism. The firm has had, for the past three years, the lowest complaint rate of any of New York's 10 major utilities, according to the state Public Service Commission.

Through it all, New York State Electric & Gas Corporation supplies electricity with 99.97-percent reliability and natural gas with virtual 100-percent reliability.

Wehle Electric Company, Inc.

Edwin C. Wehle, founder.

Traveling by shanks mare in 1910, Edwin C. Wehle sold his first electrical supplies—knobs, tubes, conduits, and switches—to a handful of customers along the Southern Tier of New York State. He was the first electrical wholesale distributor—what was then called a "jobber"—in the area. Less than 15 years later he went out on his own to create the Southern Tier Electrical Supply Corporation in Binghamton, New York, the forerunner of the Wehle Electric Company.

Wehle's simple idea was to create a "circle of service" that would provide wholesale electrical parts and 24-hour service throughout western and central New York State. In the person of his son, Richard J. Wehle, and under the name of Wehle Electric Company, Inc., that tradition lives on.

Wehle's electrical wholesale distribution business prospered, and he established three other divisions, in Elmira (1925), in Jamestown (1931), and in Rochester (1934). In 1935 a distributing plant was opened in Buffalo, later becoming the new home of the Jamestown operation and the site of the firm's corporate offices. Shortly thereafter, the venture changed its name to the present Wehle Electric Company. Richard Wehle assumed leadership of the business in 1945, while his father took on its board chairmanship, a post he held until his death in 1969.

Even during the Depression, Wehle Electric prospered. And it has continued to do so. In 1959 the company purchased Sunset Electronics, Inc., launching it into the electronics distribution field. In 1971 Wehle Electric acquired R.C. Neal Co., Inc., a 60-year veteran distributor of industrial supplies, and the year 1978 saw the purchase of Hartford-Healy, a specialty tool house.

Acquisition and customer service went hand in hand for the Ellicott Street-based firm, and with that in mind, Wehle Electric introduced an innovative inventory control system and computerized material acquisition plan. This advanced method, the Wehle Instant Service System (WISS), was billed as "the ultimate money-saving, time-saving" system in the wholesale industry. Begun as a daily direct-purchase program, it reduced the need for customers to maintain high inventories in their own warehouses.

WISS is fully computerized today and serves industry customers nationwide. This computerized warehousing system allows customers instant access to vital product information, and also provides 24-hour service to customers in New York, Pennsylvania, Ontario, Maryland, Ohio, and elsewhere in the United States. On hand to teach customers how to use the system are Wehle Electric experts trained in industrial control system applications. Yet another service of the corporation is maintaining a perpetual inventory system, which eliminates stock-out problems with popular items and keeps outmoded items in stock. This kind of pioneering effort and unparalleled service demonstrates the firm's attention to its 63-year-old motto, "Accent on Service."

That customer-oriented accent is also integrated into the company's operating philosophy, summed up by Richard Wehle: "The only way to build a successful business is to place the right person in every job." Accordingly, Wehle Electric has traditionally prided itself in being not just a business that supplies wares but also as one that supplies information in the form of advice and education for its customers.

To do that, the firm provides ongoing training conferences for salespeople, management, engineers, and other employees. These regular meetings address the day-to-day issues related to both its special technology and its

A small portion of Richard Wehle's extensive whaling collection. It is believed to be the largest private collection in the world.

sales strategies. This direct approach has paid off.

For years Wehle Electric has boasted a high rate of internal promotion among its employees. That is a distinct advantage to a wholesaler and service center with a multimillion-dollar inventory of more than 40,000 different electronic and electrical items, ranging from fuses to engraved signs to totally programmable controllers. However, its internal community is not the only segment of the population to which the company has devoted special attention.

In 1972 a Hurricane Agnes-ravaged Chemung River jumped its banks and turned the town of Elmira into a tossed salad of splinters, mud, and broken pavement. Telephone service was out for weeks. Ten feet of water and a covering of mud laid waste to the complete contents of Wehle Electric's Elmira warehouse. And the company's attitude? As far as it was concerned, the flood was yesterday's news.

The firm's trucks, bulging with emergency shipments from other Wehle warehouses, descended on the city. Rubber-booted company salesmen covered the town with needed parts and advice, and also staffed emergency communications centers to help get the community back on its feet.

Whether responding to an emergency or simply conducting business as usual, Wehle Electric Company is as much a fixture in Western and Southern New York as the electric light bulb. Today, with modern offices and warehouses encompassing 100,000 square feet in its various locations, the firm is considered the state's largest independent electrical wholesaler. The Buffalo offices alone have been enlarged five times to accommodate expanded product lines and growing staff, which today numbers 140 employees. Its four divisions are linked

Richard J. Wehle, son of the founder and president and chief executive officer, amid his whale collection with his dog, Buster Brown.

by an electronic communications system to promptly serve more than 200 leading electrical manufacturers nationwide.

Large as it had become, the company, until recently, had always had a particular problem: Its customers routinely mispronounced the name. The firm soon came up with a simple solution: It developed a trademark whale symbol followed by the letter "E" as a guide to the proper pronunciation of the Wehle name. This, in turn, evolved into the corporate logo and into a whale collection. Housing one of the world's largest collections of whale-related items is a museum in the company's Buffalo headquarters. Encouraged by Richard Wehle, employees and customers alike engage in conservation efforts to save these amazing creatures.

This unusual hobby is just one of the many successes that mark Wehle Electric's long history. When Edwin Wehle built his business, he realized that the sophistication of electrical equipment would continue to advance rapidly. His vision was to supply the technologically advanced wares, and, at the same time, provide ongoing education to customers through knowledgeable service representatives.

From Wehle's first sale in the horse-and-buggy days to the innovative distribution methods made easier by today's computer age, the Wehle Electric Company's trademark mix of service and diverse products will no doubt keep the electronic and supply business humming well into the twenty-first century.

297

CHAPTER TEN

The Professional Community

Western New York's professional community brings a wealth of experience, ability, and insight to the area. The far-reaching reputation of the local medical community, for example, is evidenced in the chapter addressing medical research.

The law community also plays an integral role in the area economy, acting in an advisory capacity to corporations and resolving disputes either by settlement or litigation. Many of the over 3,000 attorneys here act as corporate officers, and some have even become company presidents.

According to George M. Zimmermann, president of the Bar Association of Erie County, this law community is unique in a few instances. "We have a relatively high number of attorneys from elsewhere in New York State, particularly New York City. I think that's true because of the presence of the University at Buffalo Law School to which many students come from all over," he observed. "These students find that they like Buffalo and stay. Also, we have a small enough bar here (2,700 members) so that we generally know each other. That makes it easier and more efficient to do business. That aspect serves our clients well because it enables us to do a lot of things over the telephone. Otherwise, if you were dealing with a stranger, you'd have to put a lot of things in writing."

Zimmermann mentioned that the Bar Association, which is currently celebrating its centennial, is one of a very small minority in the entire country which holds contested elections of its officers

Opposite: Federal Judge John Curtin stands outside City Hall. His strong desegregation rulings changed Buffalo's school systems. Photo by Joe Traver

and directors. "We like to think that gives us a certain enthusiasm and liveliness that might not exist elsewhere," he explained.

The president added that while the quality of legal talent in Buffalo may be high, public perception of the local law community would be similar to that anywhere else—it's mainly word of mouth. "We know that we are not the most popular profession, just because of the nature of the work we do," he said. "We help people who are in trouble, and frequently those troubles are disputes. When I am representing a client, there is usually a client on the other side who is represented by his own lawyer. So, one client knows that there is somebody on the other side who is not looking out for his best interests but is actively opposed to his interests because that's the job he's required to do. By contrast, if I go to a doctor, a doctor tries to help me. At least, there isn't a doctor on the other side trying to make me sicker. For that reason, we're bound to step on toes once in a while because that's the way society operates."

Occasionally, the local law community becomes involved in cases that attract national attention. For instance, there was the "911 case" a few years ago in which the New York Court of Appeals, the state's highest court, decided that municipalities are responsible if they don't handle 911 emergency calls efficiently, making them liable if people get hurt due to negligence in operating such a telephone system. The decision stemmed from an incident in a Buffalo suburb in which a crime victim died in her home while emergency personnel sped off to a similarly named street in the city.

While the history of the bar goes back 100 years, attorneys have played a vital role in the development of the area right from the beginning. As Buffalo became a major industrial and eventually a financial center, new and complex laws and regulations affecting business and labor were of growing concern. Area attorneys rose to the task.

Two local attorneys—Millard Fillmore and Grover Cleveland—even went on to assume the U.S. presidency. Cleveland practiced here in the late 1870s and early 1880s, shortly before he would become Buffalo's mayor and New York's governor. He was a partner in Phillips, Lytle, Hitchcock, Blaine & Huber, which is now one of the nation's oldest law firms, having been established in Buffalo in 1834, two years after Buffalo's birth.

While certain professions here stand out on their own reputation, occasionally the professional community gets an unjust evaluation, particularly when a weighty project is under consideration. It basically comes down to image, which Buffalo is constantly trying to upgrade during its renaissance of the 1980s.

Although perception has improved—Buffalo's medical community, for example, is largely unaffected by the area's image prob-

Opposite: 60 Waterfront Park houses law firms and corporations. Photo by Envisions Co.

301

lems—there are still too many outsiders and even insiders who feel that someone based in Buffalo is not as effective as a ''name'' based in one of the bigger metropolitan centers.

That perception is particularly irritating to Buffalo's architects.

Designs on Buffalo

Buffalo's architectural heritage has been held in international esteem for decades. Three of the world's most historically significant office buildings were built in Buffalo—the recently renovated Guaranty Building, the Ellicott Square Building, and the long-gone Larkin Administration complex.

Buffalo State Hospital, St. Paul's Episcopal Cathedral, New York Central Terminal, and a number of other public and private places have also long been celebrated for their designs.

However, most of the city's architectural masterpieces relied on the creativity of outsiders. Although the most prominent of these was the legendary Frank Lloyd Wright, there were other notable

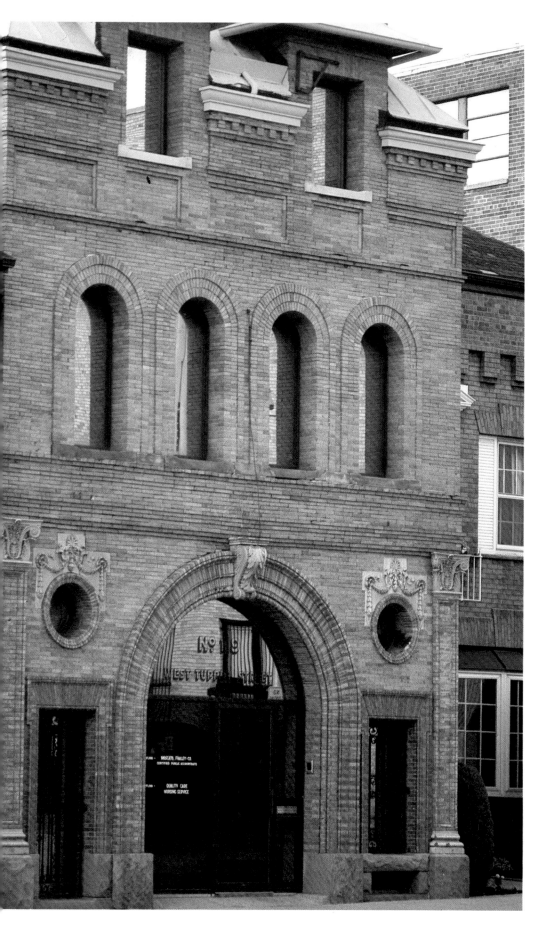

Above: The Buffalo Courier Express Building features this intricate stonework. Photo by Joe Traver

Left: Tupper Street in downtown Buffalo is graced by this handsome facade. Photo by Melissa C. Beckman

Opposite, top: Ellicott Square is one of the world's most historically significant office buildings. Photo by Melissa C. Beckman

Opposite, bottom: The Prudential Building is one of Buffalo's most beautiful, and an award-winner for renovation. Photo by Melissa C. Beckman

outside architects who were imported here—from Richard Upjohn who designed St. Paul's in the mid-nineteenth century to Minoru Yamasaki who designed the towering magnificence of M&T Plaza over 100 years later.

Of course, there have been some local architects of prominence over the years. Edward B. Green, responsible for many of the Delaware Avenue mansions and the Genesee Building (now the Hyatt Regency) downtown, headed a number of local firms from the late 1800s right up until his death at age ninety-five in 1950.

Louise Blanchard Bethune, the first woman architect to practice in the U.S., was a member of the Buffalo firm of Bethune, Bethune & Fuchs, designers of the Lafayette Hotel.

Along with Green & Wicks, the turn of the century produced several other important local firms and individual architects: Essenwein

Buffalo's landmark Episcopal Church stands out from downtown's modern architecture. Photo by Envisions Co.

& Johnson (the Niagara Mohawk building), R.J. Redpath & Son (the main Larkin plant, Alling & Cory warehouse, and structural engineering of Wright's Darwin Martin house on Jewett Parkway), and George Cary (the Historical Society building and the Pierce-Arrow administration building).

Still, the fact remains that whatever architectural significance Buffalo has attained is usually credited to the work of outsiders. Why, then, hasn't this outside influence nurtured a substantial core of renowned local architects?

"For one thing, there was a lack of a training base here down through history," observed Mark R. Mendell, senior vice-president of Cannon Corporation, Greater Buffalo's largest architectural firm. His remarks were made during an interview for *Western New York Magazine.*

"It's not like you have Harvard, MIT, Princeton, or any of the other

Phillips, Lytle, Hitchcock, Blaine & Huber

Founded in 1834 as the one-man law office of Orsamus H. Marshall, Phillips, Lytle, Hitchcock, Blaine & Huber has grown to be the largest law firm based in Buffalo. Its 125 attorneys and 240 other employees perform a wide range of legal services in the areas of banking and commercial law, corporate law, labor, litigation, real estate, trusts and estates, and workers' compensation. Phillips, Lytle's practice covers virtually the entire range of civil matters, including the relatively new areas of energy, environment, and health care.

This broad range of services offered by Phillips, Lytle enables the firm to meet the needs of a diverse group of clients, which includes major financial institutions, colleges, hospitals, public corporations, manufacturers, and service companies, both foreign and domestic. The knowledge and experience gained through handling the legal affairs of these clients also is available to small and medium-size companies. As they grow, these smaller clients, which Phillips, Lytle believes will be the keystone of the future Western New York economy, need the broad range of services offered by a larger law firm.

The varying needs of Phillips, Lytle's diverse clientele requires the firm's professional staff to be equally diverse. Recruiting from the country's top law schools and firms, Phillips, Lytle seeks law students and attorneys who have shown strong scholastic ability and a commitment to the private practice of law. The firm currently has associates and partners who are graduates of more than 30 different law schools.

New associates are required to enter a 12-month rotation through the firm's corporate, banking, and trial departments. This procedure not only familiarizes each attorney with the firm's entire practice, but also develops professional skills that match the diverse needs of Phillips, Lytle's clientele.

The professional obligations of Phillips, Lytle's associates and partners are not limited to work within the firm. In addition to being active in the state and local bar associations and other professional organizations, many of the attorneys are involved in legal scholarship and continuing education. Members of the firm who are recognized for expertise in particular areas of legal practice lecture to various groups throughout the country. The firm also maintains a strong program for providing legal services to disadvantaged members of the community.

The involvement of partners and associates in outside activities extends beyond the legal profession. The firm expects its attorneys to be active members of the community, encouraging them to serve on the religious, charitable, and other community boards and institutions of their choice. In Buffalo, members of the firm sit on more than 60 boards, including every major civic board in the city.

The firm now occupies five floors of the Marine Midland Center in downtown Buffalo, and also maintains offices in Jamestown, Rochester, New York City, and Wilmington, Delaware. All offices are fully equipped with the most modern computer and word-processing equipment, and are linked by an electronic information communications system. Around-the-clock operations are maintained in the Buffalo office.

Phillips, Lytle's corporate practice focuses on the more traditional areas of legal practice. Members' areas of expertise include tax planning for individuals, partnerships, and corporations; acquisitions; sales of businesses, both stock and assets; reorganizations; liquidations and recapitalization; joint ventures; pensions and welfare benefits; contracts, including buy-sell agreements; employment agreements, and license and distribution agreements; insurance; customs and immigration; and the providing of business advice.

The practice in many of these areas overlaps with that in banking, real estate, labor, estate planning, and litigation groups of the firm, and there is much coordination and consultation among members of the firm.

Phillips, Lytle's real estate practice involves joint venture financing and syndication, the representation of buyers and sellers in all forms of real estate conveyancing, negotiation of purchase/sale agreements, institutional and private financing, construction contracts and disputes, representation of developers of condominium and cooperative projects, and the leasing of commercial and residential properties. Staff members also deal in zoning and land use filings, environmental filings and approvals, real estate tax administrative and judicial relief, gas and oil mortgages, and foreclosures.

The Banking and Commercial Law Department, which represents both lenders and borrowers including major banks and other financial institutions, has extensive experience in secured and unsecured commercial and consumer lending and other financing transactions. It also specializes in creditors' and debtors' rights, including reorganization and bankruptcy. It is the only nationally recognized bond counsel in Buffalo, and acts in other capacities in municipal and industrial development revenue bond financing transactions. A significant portion of Phillips, Lytle's practice entails the qualification of clients to benefit from the various state and local governmental development incentives.

The firm's labor practice covers union contract negotiations, grievance handling, the preparation for and presentation of companies' positions before arbitrators, the defense of claims of discrimination before the New York State Human Rights Division and the Equal Employment Opportunity Commission, and representation of employers before various other government administrative agen-

This mural in the lobby of Phillips, Lytle, Hitchcock, Blaine & Huber depicts the city of Buffalo in 1834, the year the firm was founded.

cies, particularly the National Labor Relations Board. The labor and employment practice also involves appearances before state and federal courts, usually in the application for court injunctions in labor disputes, as well as all aspects of Workers' Compensation Law, the Occupational Safety and Health Act, and the federal (ERISA) and state laws governing pensions and fringe benefits.

Phillips, Lytle's litigation practice covers all areas of civil litigation except patent litigation. Key areas of practice are environmental matters, product liability actions, securities and corporate law problems, and commercial litigation involving lending institutions, their lending practices, and individual loans.

The Trusts and Estates Department is involved in adoptions and conservatorships, personal lifetime and estate planning, estate and trust administration, and related tax, corporate, and litigation matters. It handles everything from initial interviewing and drafting of

wills and trust agreements to final accounting procedures. The practice primarily deals with advice to individuals, fiduciaries, beneficiaries, and the representation of clients in Surrogate Court. Computers are used heavily in this practice, both for planning analysis and administrative record keeping.

The Workers' Compensation Department performs defense work exclusively, representing both insurance carriers and self-insured employers in hearings before the Workers' Compensation Board on a statewide basis. It concentrates on the 17 Buffalo and Rochester District hearing points, and appeals to the courts. The department also provides actual claims administration services for a number of the firm's self-insured clients.

Phillips, Lytle, Hitchcock, Blaine & Huber is staunchly committed to Buffalo and Western New York, and will continue to expand and diversify, both geographically and in its legal practice.

Wilson, Klaes, Brucker and Worden, P.C.

The continued success of the firm of Wilson, Klaes, Brucker and Worden, P.C., since its founding in 1961 has resulted from the careful selection and training of talented engineering personnel in the areas of lighting, power, heating, ventilating, air-conditioning, plumbing, fire protection, energy studies, and process systems.

Over the years its strength has been characterized by a stable nucleus of licensed professional engineers, coupled with able technical support personnel. This combination of talent works as an independent and unbiased team to provide depth of expertise on each project. The principals of the firm become personally involved in every project, from the initial design and engineering concept to on-site inspection and follow-up.

The Buffalo-based company, which also has an office in Rochester, is the largest of its kind in the Buffalo area specializing in the fields of mechanical and electrical engineering for the building construction industry. Most of its

Contributions by Wilson, Klaes, Brucker and Worden, P.C., to the revitalization of Buffalo include the Erie County Medical Center (upper left), the Rich Office Building (lower left), and the Rath Office Building (lower right).

work is in Western New York, but its services have been utilized as far away as California.

The firm's clients represent a variety of types, including schools, hospitals, office buildings, shopping plazas, and industrial buildings. The scope of its work is equally as broad, ranging from total electrical and mechanical engineering for the one-million-square-foot Erie County Medical Center to work on a small branch bank.

At Wilson, Klaes, Brucker and Worden energy conservation is not a new topic. The firm used many of today's conservation methods years ago. Energy recovery and variable volume are techniques its engineers employed long before they became popular. The company also evaluates various fuels and equipment combinations, using computer technology when necessary, so that the final design is the most efficient for the particular job.

As an independent consulting engineering firm, the company can offer its clients one distinct advantage—objectivity. This is particularly important when problems are encountered with an existing system. In such cases it is able to evaluate the problem from a point of view other than that of

the owners' maintenance and engineering staff, and without the obvious bias of a manufacturers' representative. The firm will then make a study, analyze the problem, and recommend the most effective solution possible.

Every project undertaken by Wilson, Klaes, Brucker and Worden is a team effort, headed by one of the principal partners as a project manager. The project manager, in most instances, will be on-site, personally conducting tests and making evaluations. Designs are not theorized from behind a desk, but are the result of personal involvement on the job.

When construction of a project is completed, Wilson, Klaes, Brucker and Worden performs a number of follow-up services. They include checking systems to see that they are functioning properly and analyzing fuel consumption against the firm's projected figures. For some jobs, such as its first solar energy system, a comprehensive report was prepared evaluating the system's operation.

In keeping with Wilson, Klaes, Brucker and Worden's professional philosophy of personal involvement by its principal partners, the company's size is large enough to enable it to handle the most sophisticated assignments, yet small enough to maintain personal service. Principals in the firm are Richard N. Klaes, John Brucker, Jr., Arthur F. Worden, John P. Crawford, and Charles B. Hodges.

Hodgson, Russ, Andrews, Woods & Goodyear

Burnt to the ground by the British and the Indians just a half-decade before, the Buffalo of 1817 must have seemed an unlikely place for a young lawyer to hang out his shingle. Yet, within four years of moving to this frontier outpost from central New York, Asa Rice had not only gone into practice for himself, but also had persuaded his brother-in-law, Joseph Clary, to join him. And so began, with the creation of Rice & Clary in 1821, the long succession of related law firms—20 in all—whose present-day incarnation is Hodgson, Russ, Andrews, Woods & Goodyear.

While those predecessor firms may have required aspiring lawyers to work as clerks and kept scriveners on hand to transcribe important documents, such tasks are handled today at Hodgson, Russ, Andrews, Woods & Goodyear by more than two dozen paralegals and a support staff almost six times that size, working on behalf of the firm's more than 100 lawyers.

With its headquarters located in One M&T Plaza in Buffalo, with substantial space in the newly renovated Guaranty Building in Buffalo, and with offices in Fort Lauderdale and Boca Raton, Florida, and Washington, D.C., Hodgson, Russ, Andrews, Woods & Goodyear works in nine principal areas of law: banking, corporate, labor, litigation, real estate, securities, tax, trusts and estates, and environmental.

And just as the practice has produced its share of political and civic luminaries over the years—two U.S. presidents, Millard Fillmore and Grover Cleveland, among them—it also produces work for an equally distinguished

list of clients. The firm is counsel to such well-known corporations as Manufacturers and Traders Trust Company, Computer Task Group, Inc., Westwood Pharmaceuticals Inc., Houdaille Industries, Inc., and Wilson Greatbatch, Ltd.

The firm also does substantial legal work on behalf of a long roster of not-for-profit community organizations. Included on that list are Western New York Public Broadcasting Association, Studio Arena Theatre, the Buffalo Philharmonic Orchestra, Children's Hospital of Buffalo, the Greater Buffalo Development Foundation, and the University of Buffalo Foundation. Similarly, its attorneys also actively participate on the boards of a large number of civic groups.

Hodgson, Russ, Andrews, Woods & Goodyear is located in the newly renovated Guaranty Building (shown here) and One M&T Plaza in Buffalo. The firm also has offices in Fort Lauderdale and Boca Raton, Florida, and in Washington, D.C.

Such civic responsibility is a trademark of Hodgson, Russ, Andrews, Woods & Goodyear and its predecessor firms. In its earliest years it was the work of Rice as part of a select citizens' committee to locate the western terminus of the Erie Canal in Buffalo. In the late nineteenth century John Milburn and Franklin D. Locke were responsible for financing the Pan-American Exposition. And in more modern times George A. Newbury and Laurence R. Goodyear acted as chairmen of what is now Western New York Public Broadcasting Association, and Donald C. Lubick served with the Carter Administration in Washington as Assistant Secretary of the Treasury for Tax Policy.

With such a tradition, no doubt the future of Buffalo, like its past, will continue to see the names of lawyers from the firm of Hodgson, Russ, Andrews, Woods & Goodyear prominently listed in connection with its most significant events.

major schools that are close by," he continued. "The presence of an architectural school of any quality [the State University at Buffalo School of Architecture and Environmental Design] is a relatively recent phenomenon to most of the people here who have been in practice for a long time. Those people may have lived here but, most likely, they didn't train here. They had to train elsewhere at the time and then migrate back here.

"Secondly, the kind of assignments that have been opportunities for greater visionary work to emerge have been associated with a growth environment. The inconsistent pace of activity in the area—where twenty-, thirty-, and forty-story buildings are not constantly being built—doesn't allow for the development of that kind of expertise, especially in a small-firm setting.

"While I can see why an owner sometimes feels compelled to look outside the area for a particular project," Mendell concluded, "there are a number of examples of associated firms locally that may be small but have been quite effective contributors to overall project success."

Cannon Corporation has been the major exception in local business owners looking outside the area for design. Twenty years ago, the firm had about a dozen employees and competed against

Cannon Corporation is one of the largest architectural/engineering firms in the country and has played a major role in the renewal of downtown Buffalo. Photo by Envisions Co.

The Occidental Chemical Company's headquarters in Niagara Falls, a Cannon Corporation design, is renowned for its efficient use of solar energy. Photo by Envisions Co.

the many other "mom-and-pop" architectural firms in the area. Today, the company has 300 employees, of which 200 are in Buffalo, and is one of the country's ten largest architectural/engineering firms with offices in Boston, St. Louis, Washington, D.C., New York City, and headquarters on Grand Island. In 1985 it had designed $260 million worth of property—$20 million more than its record year in 1982.

Cannon projects stretched clear across the country:

—a $100-million renovation to Bronx-Lebanon Hospital Center in New York City;
—the proposed $375-million renovation of Boston Garden;
—the renovation of the National Portrait Gallery at the Smithsonian Institution in Washington, D.C.;
—a $40-million renovation of Cleveland's most prominent downtown landmark, Union Terminal;
—a $30-million bus station/office/residential complex which has replaced a blighted area of downtown Cedar Rapids, Iowa;
—design work at Monsanto Company and the St. Louis University Medical Center, both in St. Louis;
—a proposed $175-million baseball stadium/retail complex which resembles a modern-day version of Chicago's Wrigley Field set against the skyscrapers of San Francisco.

Local design efforts include Cannon's $200-million expansion of Buffalo General Hospital and the Occidental Chemical Company headquarters in Niagara Falls, which has been described as "the largest passive solar collector in the world." The glass-facade structure collects heat in the same manner that a greenhouse does.

Cannon's design projects for downtown Buffalo have played a very significant part in Buffalo's renaissance. The firm won the 1982 Owens-Corning Conservation Award—a prestigious architectural honor—for its design of the Norstar Building. Across the street, Cannon carried out the interior design and associated engineering for the world headquarters of Goldome.

The design for the Niagara Frontier Transportation Authority's Metropolitan Transportation Center in the late 1970s won Cannon the American Institute of Architects' coveted Award for Design Excellence, citing its "striking expression. . .light, airy feeling within the public space and excellent security aspects."

In what architects refer to as "adaptive reuse," the firm restored the former post office and federal building, turning the abandoned eighty-two-year-old Gothic structure into the downtown campus of Erie Community College at a cost that was 25 percent less than new construction.

The renovative *pièce de résistance,* though, has been the modernization and historic restoration of the Guaranty/Prudential Build-

*The magnificent interior of the
Goldome Bank was renovated by
the Cannon Corporation, an
award-winning local design firm.
Photo by Patricia Layman Bazelon*

Nussbaumer & Clarke, Inc.

Creators and their creations. The Nussbaumer & Clarke management team with the Town of Cheektowaga's sewage pumping station in the foreground—a building with a design so advanced that operations can be controlled completely by computer.

Drive into downtown Buffalo along the Niagara section of the thruway. Cross the Lewiston-Queenston International Bridge. Drink a glass of water in any one of dozens of Upstate New York communities. Walk along the property lines of any number of residential subdivisions built in Erie County since the 1950s.

What do they have in common? Surveying, engineering, and architectural work by the consulting engineering firm of Nussbaumer & Clarke, Inc. And if those four examples don't sufficiently impress you with the breadth of this company's expertise, consider the full list of the firm's capabilities: surveying and metering, planning, mechanical engineering, construction services, water treatment, water storage, wastewater treatment, sanitary sewers, storm drainage, transportation, solid-waste dis-

posal, and architecture. This is one company that not only works on solid ground, but under and above it as well.

With their skills as, respectively, an engineer and a surveyor, company founders Newell L. Nussbaumer and Irving Clarke were a natural "team" when they founded their concern in 1933. Today those same skills, plus others are fully represented by NCI's current management: Walter E. Roeder, president, who began with the firm in 1956; Thomas M. Lewandowski, vice-president/engineering; Michael J. Sendor, vice-president/land surveying; Michael J. Miranda, secretary; and David J. Coughlin, controller/treasurer.

However, that team spirit isn't limited to just 9 to 5 at Nussbaumer & Clarke. The conference room in the firm's Deleware Avenue headquarters (NCI also has offices in Oswego and Rochester) shows a dozen-odd trophies proclaiming the firm's prowess in extracurricular activities ranging from softball to bowling. But lest such awards be seen as unrelated to the quality of its engineering

work, it's important to note that a family-like atmosphere is something that is generated consciously by and for the firm's approximately 60 employees. And it's a spirit that extends to its clients as well.

A specialist that knows that there is no such thing as a single recipe for success when it comes to architecture and engineering, Nussbaumer & Clarke stresses to its clients that it acts as "their eyes and ears" during construction, making sure that work proceeds in accordance with contract documents, budget restrictions, building codes, and site conditions.

In the days of the Holland Land Company, land surveyors used chains—often inaccurate because of their tendency to stretch—to determine boundaries throughout Western New York. Today NCI's sophisticated electronic theodolites and distance meters can "read" a distance of five miles in ten seconds with an accuracy of 1/1,000th of an inch.

And such is one measure of the progress in the Buffalo area to which NCI has contributed. Whether in the form of roads, bridges, or water-treatment plants, Nussbaumer & Clarke, Inc., takes pride in its partnership with the Western New York community, and all it has done to make the environment of our area a pleasant one in which to live.

Nussbaumer & Clarke president Walter E. Roeder revisits the site of one of his major accomplishments—the 1961 triangulation and construction surveying of the Lewiston-Queenston International Bridge, a joint venture with Hardesty & Hanover.

ing. Considered to be characteristic of Louis Sullivan's greatest works, Cannon painstakingly restored much of the original architectural detail on the first two commercial floors after years of neglect. The building was honored as Historic Office Building of the Year by the Building Owners and Management Association (BOMA), over competition from all across the country. The award was given by independent architects and BOMA members based on physical attractiveness, community impact, and energy management.

According to Cannon's summary of the project, "Interior marble mosaic ceilings, floors, friezes, and art-glass skylights uncovered during site investigation were cleaned and restored; ornamental stairways connecting (the first) two levels were reopened, reestablishing the circulation plan of 1896; and at street level, the original projected storefront (specifically, the intricate tracery of foliage and geometric designs of the terra cotta facade) has been restored."

The tower of the old post office rises between the Erie County Savings Bank building on the left and the One M&T Tower on the right. Photo by Dennis R. Floss

Acres International Corporation

If you're an international engineering firm that's conducted hydroelectric studies in Alaska, supervised construction of a 300-foot-high dam in Ohio, and designed a chemical plant in Kentucky and a steel plant in Mexico, what do you do for an encore?

Simple. You return to the area where you started out years before, drill more than 40 holes in solid rock, pack them with 9,700 pounds of dynamite, place 111 reinforcing bolts, give the signal, then watch as 25,000 tons of Terrapin Point drop into the Niagara Gorge.

Simple? Yes, it was—at least from the perspective of Acres International Corporation, an engineering firm that has had its United States corporate offices in the Liberty building in downtown Buffalo since 1972. Having already supervised hundreds of civil and industrial engineering projects throughout the world, lowering the "boom" on the shaky tip of the Niagara Falls, New York, tourist lookout was all in a day's work. But it was also a spectacular way to raise the public's awareness of one of the most ambitious international corporations in Buffalo.

Founded in 1924 by Canadian engineer Harry G. Acres, the company's first project was on the Sir

The new administration and engineering office complex for Buffalo Color Corporation.

Rock removal and restoration of the viewing area at Terrapin Point, Niagara Falls.

Adam Beck hydroelectric power project in Niagara Falls, Ontario. From that beginning Acres has gone on to build a firm of crack engineers that tackles projects throughout the world. Today the company has offices in Washington, D.C., and Anchorage, Alaska, in addition to its office overlooking Main and Court streets in Buffalo.

At its Buffalo location more than 130 employees, including nearly 70 engineers, oversee everything from hydroelectric projects throughout the country to the conversion of salt mines in Louisiana for the United States Strategic Petroleum Reserve Program.

Accordingly, Acres International has the capability to provide a full range of planning, engineering,

and construction management services on projects of all kinds, from the design of manufacturing plants and power-generation systems to waste management and environmental assessments.

In the Western New York area, the firm has been particularly active in industrial and chemical engineering, providing services to a large number of local manufacturers. And even though an increasingly larger share of its market is outside the Buffalo area, the company purchases directly for clients several million dollars of equipment and materials annually from local suppliers for projects throughout the country.

Acres International Corporation made some noise with its work at the Falls. Yet, like many others, this is essentially a quiet company, one that goes effectively about its business both in Western New York and throughout the United States.

Cannon's original feasibility study and preservation analysis of the structure staved off demolition threats in 1976. Ten years later, the historic building is a commercially viable property again, with the third through thirteenth floors having been converted to Class A office space.

At one end of the downtown renaissance, Cannon helped preserve history. At the center—Lafayette Square, to be precise—it will take a step into the future by designing the permanent light show that will be part of the Main Street Transit Mall.

The Smaller Firms

Opposite: The intricate detailing of the Prudential Building makes it a renowned landmark. Photo by Robert McElroy

Cannon's local staff of 200 is many times that of the other design firms in the area. One insider referred to the local architectural community as still a cottage industry. There are an estimated 150 archi-

Above: Condominiums go up on the newly revitalized waterfront. Photo by Joseph M. Cascio

tects and about fifty-five firms, most of which have staffs of between three and ten employees.

With a contrast like that, can small firms elbow their way into the forefront of local building? Are they considered to be serious contenders in the bidding races on local projects?

The general consensus among such firms seems to be that local architects are usually overlooked by local developers who allegedly equate talent and skill with architects in the so-called design centers of the country.

317

Hatch Associates Consultants, Inc.

CONSULTING ENGINEERS

Hatch Associates was founded in 1955 and since then has expanded its services to industry and government agencies in North America and in more than 25 overseas countries. Ownership of the firm is vested in the staff which consists of professional and technical personnel with diversified engineering, scientific, industrial, and management backgrounds.

Hatch Associates Consultants, Inc., headquartered in Buffalo, provides a full range of services in the United States. Its parent corporation, Hatch Associates Ltd., is headquartered in Toronto and operates other Canadian offices in Montreal, Hamilton, Calgary, and Vancouver.

Headed by Richard W. Wilson, president, Hatch Associates Consultants moved its offices from Niagara Falls, New York, to Buffalo in 1972. Just two years later the firm had outgrown its limited space in the Statler Building and

Buffalo Light Rail Rapid Transit System looking north at Humboldt Storage and Crossover facility.

Richard W. Wilson (seated), president of Hatch Associates Consultants, Inc., with the firm's senior staff members (from left to right): Richard C. Smith, vice-president; Frank P. Frandina, civil/structural, Rapid Transit; William E. Fischer, scheduling/ project management; Gerald A. Karelus, process engineering/industrial.

took over the entire eighth floor of the Rand Building, directly across from the Erie County Public Library, one of the largest technical libraries in the state.

Since moving to Buffalo, the corporation has experienced a healthy growth in two major areas: rapid transit and consulting services to heavy industry.

In 1973 the Niagara Frontier Transportation Authority (NFTA) reached a critical milestone in the Buffalo Light Rail Rapid Transit project when strong citizen opposition was raised in response to the proposed overhead portion of the transit system through the northeast area of the city. The NFTA came to Hatch Associates Consultants for advice on the feasibility and costs of constructing the line underground. After that

initial study, the firm was appointed, in 1977, as principal consultant for the 3.5-mile rock tunnel section, which included five underground stations. The company's responsibility included design, project management, and construction supervision for that portion of the project north of Ferry Street.

As area residents ride the Light Rail Rapid Transit through the tunnel as much as ninety feet under the surface, there is little evidence of the many problems that were encountered by the designers. Geotechnical exploration discovered large quantities of ground water in the severely fractured permeable rock zones. Should those fractured rock zones be penetrated during construction, the tunnels would have flooded. As a result, a decision was made to lower the groundwater level below the bottom of the tunnels during construction. Wilson and the firm's entire Buffalo staff are proud of the fact that the Association of Consulting Engineers of Canada granted the parent company the Award of Excellence in Civil Engineering for its work on the Buffalo Light Rail Rapid Transit System.

When the Baltimore Region Rapid Transit System required specialized tunneling expertise, it came to Hatch Associates Consultants. And when the Southern California Rapid Transit District required consulting services on tunnel design, it also contacted Hatch Associates Consultants. On the Southern California project, the firm continued on as the section designer of the important

A continuous billet caster at Seattle Steel, Inc.

twin tunnels that will eventually link Los Angeles with Universal City on the 3.25-mile route that passes under the famous Hollywood Bowl.

In the industrial sector, the company has completed more than 250 projects for approximately 100 clients. Many of its clients are prominent firms located along the Niagara Frontier, including Niagara Mohawk Power Corporation, Bethlehem Steel Corporation, SKW Alloys, Inc., Buffalo Crushed Stone, Inc., Allegheny Ludlum Steel Corporation, and Dunlop Tire and Rubber Corporation. The firm also has provided consulting services to departments of the federal, state, and local government, as well as various financial institutions, including Marine Midland Bank, N.A., The Chemical Bank, and Manufacturers and Traders Trust Company. Hatch engineers have provided engineering and consulting services to such faraway places as Sweden, Brazil, Africa, Mexico, Japan, and Indonesia.

When Davis Walker Corporation, the largest independently

Buffalo Light Rail Rapid Transit System inbound platform at Delavan-College Station.

owned wire-drawing company in North America, was considering the construction of a 650,000-ton-a-year wire rod plant, it came to Hatch Associates Consultants. When CEM Associates of Seattle was considering the purchase of Bethlehem Steel's Seattle plant, it also came to Hatch for the feasibility study, and subsequently retained the firm to handle the design, project management, and start-up of a new continuous casting machine. Morgan Guaranty Bank retained Hatch Asssociates Consultants to provide consulting services, and the firm continued to monitor the design and construction of slab-casting machines installed at Bethlehem Steel's plants in Burns Harbor, Indiana, and Sparrows Point, Maryland. The World Bank also has retained Hatch Associates Consultants to provide consulting services for a major steel producer in Indonesia.

Hatch Associates Consultants considers itself a local firm. With its roots firmly planted in Buffalo, the company has made both its name and that of the City of Buffalo known in much of the Free World.

Charles M. Richardson is determined to restructure the image of his profession within the community. As head of his own small firm in Orchard Park, he has experienced the difficulties.

"The problem here is the lack of job opportunities," he said during the same *Western New York* interview. "And when the opportunities do arise, owners tend to go out of town and bring in outside consultants.

"Unfortunately, many of these businesses have mother companies elsewhere. And when they plan to build or expand here, they call in architects from wherever their main office is located."

Richardson claimed that not only does this practice hurt the local architectural community, but the repercussions extend to actual design considerations.

"Buffalo has some very unique design criteria, especially in this climate," he observed. "Unfortunately, when an outsider comes in, he doesn't have a strong feel for our climatic problems. Consequently, many of the buildings fail. The force of the heavy winds and heavy snows aren't considered—conditions that a native Western New Yorker is well aware of."

Richardson also blamed a tendency to commission "name people" for various projects, and for not developing a consortium of local architects to work on larger projects.

"The waterfront was a good example," he recalled. "I was the only local architect among five or six architects on the waterfront project. It was a job that most of the firms in Buffalo could have handled quite easily. Yet, it was not divvied up locally. That took a lot of commissions and fees out of our area."

Just as Richardson has diversified and expanded his business outside the area, Salvatore Catalano of Sargent, Webster, Crenshaw & Folley reported that his firm has done the same. While admitting that "things seem to be perking up locally," Catalano agreed that there's still a tendency here to think that commissioning out-of-town talent is a prestigious move.

John Laping, a partner in the firm of Kideney, Smith, Fitzgerald & Laping, supported that theory. "Owners perceive the out-of-town architects as glamorous—someone who's going to bring something a little different to the community," he pointed out. "What they don't realize is that there's a wealth of talent right here. Our guys stand up as well as anybody across the country."

Mr. Laping's firm was founded fifty-six years ago by James Kideney, one of the more influential practitioners of the art in this area. "If you look at firm names in the phone book, many of those people came out of this office," he noted. "He (Kideney) was very influential in terms of training, in terms of conveying a strong ethical sense of what architecture should be." Among the firm's accom-

Milstein, Wittek & Associates, Architects, P.C.

Milstein, Wittek & Associates, Architects, P.C., is a comprehensive service organization established in 1966. Today the firm is headed by Milton Milstein as president, Warren N. Wittek as vice-president, and Adriana S. Barbasch and Henry J. Kwapisz as associate vice-presidents.

The company offers complete service in the following areas: architectural planning and design; feasibility and economic studies, site planning, environmental analysis, energy conservation, interior design, urban design, landscape architecture, engineering services, cost estimating, and construction administration.

These comprehensive services cover an extensive range of building types and involve both new structures and the rehabilitation of existing facilities. With the advent of an energy-conscious, new-technology era, the firm's designs have met or exceeded new requirements and challenges. It also has won design awards and citations for contributions to the profession and community.

It has to its credits major commissions for office buildings; government buildings; commercial, institutional, and correctional facilities; school, college, and university buildings; campus planning; banks; health care and health science facilities; research laboratories; housing; athletic facilities; and many other building types. Construction budgets range from under $100,000 to over $50 million.

Through such projects it has earned a reputation for high-quality design and construction. The firm strongly believes that its personalized service provides clients with the best level of professional guidance.

MWA has rendered professional services for numerous area structures, including the Edward A. Rath County Office Building, restoration of Old Erie County Hall, Timon Towers for the Elderly,

Timon Towers for the Elderly.

County Hall Annex, Erie County Correctional Facility, the Charles J. Wick Campus Center of Daemen College, the New York State School for the Blind, Olean General Hospital, and various commissions for the State University at Buffalo and Amherst, New York.

Additional commissions for the firm include the Amherst Street Station of the Light Rail Rapid Transit System, Agena Rocket Testing Laboratories for the Bell Aerospace Division of Textron, and special studies for the development of the new Buffalo waterfront.

The firm of Milstein, Wittek & Associates, Architects, P.C., has left an imprint on area architecture that will be admired for many years to come—and continues to strive for a high standard of design.

Edward A. Rath County Office Building.

plishments are Millard Fillmore Hospital and the Buffalo & Erie County Public Library.

One architect who feels that a fair opportunity is afforded to his peers is Milton Milstein, a founding member of Milstein, Wittek, Davis & Associates. His firm designed the Rath Building, part of the State University of Buffalo Amherst campus, and the Alden Correctional Facility.

"I've been practicing in this city for over thirty years, and that's always been the prevailing attitude here among architects," he declared. "But that's not to say that local firms are not engaged for local work. We have been fortunate—I know that others have, too—to be appointed to projects which are undertaken by the city, county, and even the state. On a selective basis, it's a question as

Right: The Buffalo and Erie County Public Library was designed by Kideney, Smith, Fitzgerald & Laping, a local firm. Photo by Peter R. Barber

Opposite: The Rath Building strikes a contemporary note in downtown Buffalo. Photo by Robert McElroy

to whether one fits the qualifications desired. They have used this screening method recently. So, I do feel that local architects have been given the opportunity to qualify. Some have, and some have been less fortunate.

"This attitude, I think, is reflected mainly by the private sector. The city, county, and state make an effort to seek out the local architects for the commissions that are available.

"The Light Rail Rapid Transit System is an example where at least eight local firms have been involved. And these are all architectural firms. Then, there are the local engineering firms that were also engaged. So, I think there have been fair opportunities for local firms that can qualify," Milstein concluded.

The blueprint for the local architectural community continues to be drawn. Some see it in black and white, some see it colorfully fleshed out. Whatever the view, it is generally agreed that there really is a wealth of talent in Greater Buffalo, creating a strong foundation upon which local developers can continue to build.

It's symbolic of much of the professional community in the Buffalo area. Talented, very capable, but—like Rodney Dangerfield—often lacking respect simply because of location.

As Mark Mendell told a *Buffalo News* reporter, to land such out-of-town projects as the $375-million Boston Garden renovation and the $175-million stadium complex in San Francisco, "we had to make a tremendous effort to be innovative. After all, people would not normally regard Buffalo as a design center."

Still, as many optimistically admit, the rebuilding momentum in the area is pushing more and more people to discover many of the natural resources right here in Buffalo—the talented architects and other professionals who may not be on the lips of the image-conscious, but offer just as much, if not more, than their peers situated in the country's name-dropping centers.

CHAPTER ELEVEN

Spreading the Word

As in a growing number of other cities throughout the country, Buffalo became a one-newspaper town a few years ago, when the *Buffalo Courier-Express* folded in September 1982.

The roots of the *Courier* went back to 1834 when it was originally called *The Western Star,* one of over a hundred different newspapers that came and went during the first half of the nineteenth century. The *Express* was another, beginning in 1846. From that point on, a fierce competition developed between the *Courier* and the *Express.* In 1869 Samuel L. Clemens, better known as Mark Twain, bought an interest in the *Express* and served as its editor for two years.

The rivalry continued until 1926 when William J. Conners, a former dock worker who built a fortune by acquiring various interests in Great Lakes shipping ventures, merged both papers. He had been the publisher of the *Courier* since 1897.

From 1926 to 1982, the daily rivalry was narrowed to the *Courier-Express* and *The Buffalo Evening News.* Both papers were family-owned until 1977 when, after ninety-seven years of publishing, the Butler family sold *The News* to Blue Chip Stamps, Inc. Two years later, after eighty-two years of publishing, the Conners family sold the *Courier-Express* to the Minneapolis Star and Tribune Company, Inc.

Although the new owners of the *Courier-Express* aggressively tried to cut into the much larger weekday circulation of *The News,* the death knell tolled when the Sunday edition of *The News*—instituted just after the Butler era—began to seriously affect the Sunday circulation of the *Courier-Express,* which had been that paper's leading money-maker for years.

With the demise of the *Courier-Express,* a substantial core of solid reporters, artists, photographers, and production personnel were looking for new employment in the area. Some were welcomed to *The News.* Tom Toles, for example, was chosen to continue the editorial cartoon excellence established by the Pulitzer Prize-winning Bruce Shanks. Today, Toles' *News* cartoons are widely syndicated and even available in book form.

The News has an impressive core of reporters, reviewers, and feature writers. Among them are critic Jeff Simon, whose assessments of film, TV, and music are among the sharpest, most insightful, and knowledgeable in the business; sports editor Larry Felser, whose trenchant commentaries zero in on the human aspect of this sports-conscious town; and reporter Margaret Sullivan, whose weekly column analyzes the character and current events of the area with wit and perception.

In late 1984, two weekly tabloids appeared on the local scene to address the growing wealth of business news around Greater Buffalo. *Business First* is part of a chain of papers published by Kansas City-based American City Business Journals. *Buffalo Business Journal* is a locally owned and operated venture.

Although both have fulfilled a need for the growing business community, *Business First* appears to have gained the edge in the competition. Because the *Buffalo Business Journal* has since gone to a biweekly format, *Business First*'s weekly schedule captures the immediacy better. The *Journal,* on the other hand, relies more on feature-oriented spreads. In fact, *Business First* has occasionally even scooped the daily business section of *The News* on breaking stories.

Other daily papers in Greater Buffalo are found in Niagara Falls, Lockport, and Tonawanda. Just about every town and village in Greater Buffalo has its own weekly community paper. The Bee Group Newspapers has cornered a good part of this weekly market, based in Amherst and spreading into Clarence, West Seneca, Depew, Lancaster, Cheektowaga, and Kenmore-Tonawanda. In some of these towns, they're in competition with locally based papers such as the *Cheektowaga Times* or *Kenmore Record-Advertiser.* While the Bee weeklies have the look of a better organized paper, the content of the homegrown weeklies usually captures the pulse of a locale more accurately.

The Rama Group put out a regional pennysaver publication for years, composed of want ads and display ads. Last year, however, the name changed to *Metro Community News* and the format became more editorially inclined, with more attention to layout. The circulation is now over 14,500 with twenty-four different editions spread across Erie and Niagara counties.

Buffalo readers have also enjoyed an alternative to traditional news reporting. *Second Story* offers a unique insight and point of view on local, national, and international stories. Publisher Jeff Lasser and editor Tim Switala have been valiantly keeping the biweekly alive, injecting it with a *Village Voice* feel in layout and content. *Second Story* rounds out the Greater Buffalo publishing scene.

Fit To Print

That copy of *Reader's Digest* or *Time* you're reading. . .that paperback romance you're engrossed in. . .that Stephen King horror tale that has you on the edge of your seat. . .that ten million bucks you're trying to win from American Family Publishers and Publisher's Clearing House. . .that jar of Mentholatum. . .that bottle of Seagram's. . .that carton of Rich's Non-Dairy Creamer. . .those laughs you're enjoying from the Sunday comics. . .those bargains that are calling you from the K-Mart and JC Penney newspaper supplements. . . The common denominator of those diverse items is all in the printing and packaging, which is produced by Greater Buffalo printers.

Arcata Graphics, Inc., is over a century old and the largest printing firm in the area, occupying a fifty-acre site in Depew on which an 800,000-square-foot facility houses a staff of over 1,800 employees.

Since 1965 the company—which is owned by the California-based Arcata National Corporation—has turned out more than ten million copies of *Reader's Digest* each month. Since the installation of an advanced gravure facility in the late 1970s, it has turned out more than five million color copies of the *National Enquirer* tabloid each week. Arcata also has *Time* on its hands, as well as the popular Silhouette series of paperbacks from Harlequin Romances.

Greater Buffalo Press, Inc., is the second largest area printer, having built its reputation on the funny papers. In 1932 it began color reproduction work and won contracts to print the Sunday comic sections of the *Buffalo Courier-Express* and the *Syracuse Herald.* Soon it began printing the funnies for the *Chicago Times* and the *San Antonio Express.*

Today, the company is one of the top two producers of color comics in the country. Comic book collectors will appreciate the fact that Greater Buffalo Press printed the first issues of *Superman* and *Batman* in the late 1930s and *Mad Magazine* in the 1950s. In the 1980s, the company has diversified into printing four-color advertising circulars for such national retailers as K-Mart and JC

Mike Smith displays his Buffalo-based company's nationally marketed packaging. Photo by Joe Traver

Penney.

F.N. Burt Company's 100-year history has been literally under wraps. In the early part of this century, the company was the leading manufacturer of cigarette boxes. Then, in 1917, it began supplying packaging for the California Perfume Company, which later became known as Avon Products. Still, today, F.N. Burt prints attractive jewelry boxes for Avon. Other clients include Estee Lauder, Seagram's, Schenley's, and Turtle Wax. In the 1920s and 1930s, the firm became the world's largest producer of small paper boxes. Today, F.N. Burt is the leading supplier of high-quality folding cartons.

Miken Systems, Inc., has helped usher in the age of sophistication in soft-cover book design. Covers that are intricately embossed, glossed, stamped, and coated are produced at the

Cheektowaga plant for such publishing giants as Doubleday and Simon & Schuster/Pocket Books. Authors and titles that consistently make the best-sellers list continuously roll off the Miken presses, filling orders that range from 200,000 to two million. Other clients include National Geographic and Fisher-Price.

The name-dropping and sophisticated press work continues throughout the area printing industry: Thorner-Sidney Press, Inc., whose clients include Sony, General Electric, Rich Products, Westwood Pharmaceuticals; Manhardt-Alexander, the oldest printer in the Greater Buffalo area who does press work for Corning Glass Works, Zippo Manufacturers; Mod Pac Corporation, who works for Mentholatum and Westwood; and Hoffman Printing for Syracuse University and Skidmore College.

AM/FM in the AM/PM

The personality of Greater Buffalo radio is what created its rich historical character. Waking up to Clint Buhlman, "your AM MC," each morning from the 1940s through the 1970s on WBEN... hearing "The Hound" howl each night on WKBW as the pioneering George Lorenz helped usher in the rock 'n' roll era in the mid-1950s by breaking the race barriers of rhythm and blues...enjoying the outrageousness of KB deejays in the 1950s and 1960s like Dick Biondi, Joey Reynolds, Dan Neaverth, and Tommy Shannon.

Buffalo had its share of personalities in those olden days of radio. Some went on to national stature: Buffalo Bob Smith, former WBEN announcer, helped create the long-running Howdy Doody TV series that ran on NBC from 1947 to 1960; Jack Paar was at WBEN long before *The Tonight Show* would make him a late-night TV star in the mid-1950s; Fran Striker, a Buffalo scriptwriter, would create the character of The Lone Ranger in 1930 at WEBR, three years before it settled into a thirty-two-year network run on radio and then television.

Today, radio is a whole different ballgame across the country. Personality is played down while "adult contemporary" music is played up. Call-in shows have regained popularity. And sports is always a big potential ratings ticket.

WBEN-AM is generally on top of the ratings heap these days, although the Buhlman era is long since gone. Owner Larry Levite has concentrated on positioning it as the sports station in town, carrying all Bills, Sabres, and Bisons games.

KB radio changed its call letters to WWKB after new ownership took over in 1986. Gone were personalities Tommy Shannon and Sandy Beach (both of whom made comebacks here in the mid-

Greater Buffalo Press, Inc.

President Paul J. Koessler; John W. Koessler, Jr., chairman; and vice-president of sales and marketing John Davis check samples from the firm's newest press installation at Stevensville, Ontario, Canada.

Greater Buffalo Press, Inc., which began business in a tiny converted garage on Hertel Avenue in North Buffalo in 1926, today spans the nation and reaches into Canada with a chain of nine printing plants.

The firm was founded by the late J. Walter Koessler together with his father, John A., and brother, Kenneth L. Koessler. Koessler had never been trained as a pressman and learned his new trade by doing. At that time his work was done on a flatbed press.

The heart of the firm's business in the early years was the printing of small community newspapers. Among them were the *Cold Spring Advertiser* with a circulation of 7,000 and the even-smaller *International Gazette* with a read-

ership of 1,300. Despite its impressive name, the *Gazette* was devoted to printing foreclosure and other legal notices. In fact, it was the tiny *Gazette* that kept Greater Buffalo Press solvent during the early years of the Depression. As the economy worsened, the number of property foreclo-

sures increased, and it was the *International Gazette's* responsibility to publish those notices.

As the economy improved three more presses were added to the Hertel Avenue shop, and in 1932 a move was made to larger quarters at 1245 Niagara Street. That same year Greater Buffalo Press began color reproduction work and received contracts to print the comic sections of the *Syracuse Herald,* later the *Herald Journal* and the former *Buffalo Courier Express.* Three years later the comic section of the *Chicago Times* was added to the company's growing list of assignments.

Printing only one four-color section per week was not economical for most newspapers, a point that Greater Buffalo Press was able to capitalize on. By specializing in color comics, the firm could guarantee its customers a lower price. In addition, identical

A proof press showing yellow, magenta, cyan, and black comic plates for page makeup.

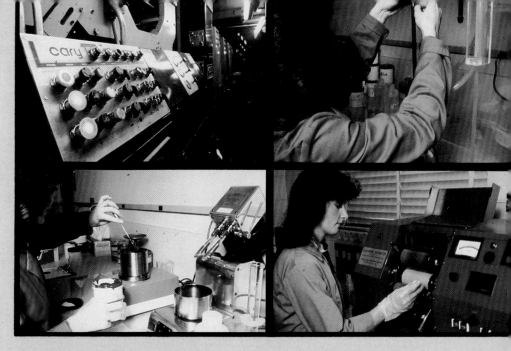

comic strips appeared in a number of newspapers, which meant that the same costly color plates could be used for different press runs.

Business prospered, and in 1936 Greater Buffalo Press moved to larger quarters at 302 Grote Street. That facility still serves as the company's headquarters.

After World War II the firm continued to grow despite a newsprint shortage. Greater Buffalo Press' contacts in the newsprint market were sound, having been established 20 years earlier, and the newsprint shortage actually helped business because publications were eager to conserve their own supplies by having their comic pages printed elsewhere.

The firm's first true subsidiary plant was Great Lakes Color in Dunkirk, New York, some 45 miles south of Buffalo. Today it is Greater Buffalo Press' largest plant, and one of its seven four-color letterpresses, at 147 feet in length, is the largest in the world. In all, the plant can turn out 65 million four-page sections per week.

Southwest Color Printing was

Ink being tested for hue, tack, and viscosity at Greater Buffalo Press' ink-making facility located in Sheridan, New York.

---

opened in 1957 in Lufkin, Texas, some 120 miles from Houston. With the addition of this facility the company not only was able to increase production, but also could supply its southern customers more readily and more economically.

Greater Buffalo Press became international in scope in 1972 when it opened Greater Canada Colour Corporation in Stevensville, Ontario, Canada, just a few miles from Niagara Falls. Other major plants include California Color Printing in Pittsburg, California; Mid-Atlantic Color Printing in York, Pennsylvania; Dixie Color Printing and Southeastern Commercial Printing in Sylacauga, Alabama; and Midwest Color Printing, in Marengo, Iowa.

Over the years Greater Buffalo Press has evolved from solely letterpress work in the form of comic books, Sunday comics, and commercial supplements to a growing emphasis on a diverse offset market that includes news-

paper magazines, high-quality process color newsaper supplements, and other commercial work.

Greater Buffalo Press, a family-owned company, is headed by John W. Koessler, Jr., as chairman and Paul J. Koessler as president. William P. Brosnahan serves as executive vice-president and Kenneth L. Koessler, Jr., is the company's secretary. The firm employs approximately 2,000 people, including about 400 in the Buffalo area.

Greater Buffalo Press, Inc., strongly believes in private support of education. In 1968 the company made a gift of one million dollars to the Canisius College Centennial Campaign in the name of the corporation's founder, J. Walter Koessler. In appreciation, Canisius College named its newest facility at Main Street and East Delavan Avenue the Koessler Athletic Center.

Automatic color separator for comic work developed by Greater Buffalo Press in cooperation with Calspan Corporation, a Buffalo-based high-tech firm.

Giant ink vats at Greater Buffalo Press' Sheridan, New York, facility.

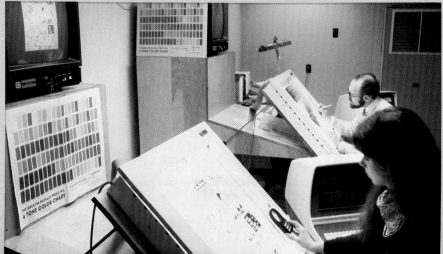

1980s). Only Danny Neaverth remained, celebrating twenty-five years of being one of the zaniest ad-lib minds in the business.

Talk shows are now in at KB. There's Buffalo radio's first midday call-in program with former WEBR host Andy Thomas; in early evening there's Bruce Williams' NBC network call-in show, then late at night there's John Otto, a veteran of over thirty years behind a local microphone.

FM has made big inroads into the market since the 1970s. WJYE-FM took "elevator" music to new heights, being the first in the area to realize the value of billboard advertising. Now, the beautiful music station is usually right behind WBEN-AM.

WBUF-FM's oldies format for baby boomers has proven to be so lucrative that many others have copied the mix of soft-rock memories from the 1960s on up. Former KB personalities Stan Roberts and Fred Klestine have resurfaced on WBUF, as has Sandy Beach on WNYS-FM, which is aggressively trying to cut into WBUF's audience.

The loss of WGRQ-FM was a blow to the loyal young audience who appreciated the mix of personalities with more album-oriented playlists. However, station management deemed that the spending

Above and opposite, left: Radio station WBEN has produced its share of celebrities, including Buffalo Bob Smith of Howdy Doody fame and talk-show host Jack Paar. Today the station concentrates on sports broadcasting and easy-listening music. Photos by Joe Traver

Right: The Buffalo media actively support cultural events such as this production at Shea's Buffalo Theatre, sponsored by radio station WBEN and TV station WGRZ. Photo by Joe Traver

bracket of that audience was insufficient for attracting a wider range of advertisers.

Among the Top Ten stations in the area, only WECK-AM offers a dramatic alternative with its reliance on music from the 1940s through the pre-rock 1950s. Farther down the ratings chart, however, other alternatives do prevail. WEBR-AM's all-news format during the daytime and all-jazz programming after dark has attracted loyal audiences, as has its sister station, WNED-FM, whose all-classical format showcases "beautiful music" in its truest sense.

WBFO-FM, the University of Buffalo station, has the most diverse programming, offering everything from live chamber concerts to traditional folk music, with such National Public Radio programs as "All Things Considered" and Garrison Keillor's phenomenally successful "Prairie Home Companion."

Tuning Into TV

In the developmental stage of the tube, area television stations were judged on their extent of local programming. What native baby boomer doesn't recall growing up with such shows as *Uncle Jerry's Club, Captain Bob, Jungle Jay, Captain Mike* and *Buttons the Cabin Boy,* and, of course, the annual holiday visit of Santa Claus and Forgetful the Elf?

WBEN-TV (now WIVB) was the first area station to sign on in 1948. Program director Fred A. Keller—still a vital artistic force in the community—instituted some daring achievements in those experimental days of live TV. *The Clue* in the early 1950s was the first and only live local mystery series ever done. The yearly visit with Santa (from the day after Thanksgiving to the day before Christmas) incorporated a host of special effects, many quite sophisticated for the time.

Many informational programs filled the airwaves during those early years. Cooking and interview shows abounded with the long-running *Meet the Millers* and *Speaker of the House* on Channel 4, *The Helen Neville Show* on Channel 2, and *Dialing for Dollars* on Channel 7. Personalities also abounded, such as John Corbett, Mike Mearian, Bill Mazer, Liz Dribben, Nolan Johannes, and Bill and Mildred Miller.

While some remnants of that local programming emphasis are still apparent on shows like *AM Buffalo* (the outgrowth of *Dialing for Dollars*) and *Beat the Champ* (the weekly bowl-off that's been a Channel 4 staple since 1957), the measure of today's stations rests primarily on the ratings of their newscasts.

Opposite: WKBW and WBEN helped produce a concert in front of City Hall to benefit the renovation of Shea's Buffalo Theatre. Photo by Robert McElroy

Manhardt-Alexander, Inc.

From close up, a five-color perfector printing press looks as big and sounds as loud as a diesel locomotive. Yet the extraordinary precision—some might even call it delicacy—of the images reproduced by this amazing machine belie its metal massiveness. The creation of such images is the business of Manhardt-Alexander, Inc.

The firm had its beginnings in 1878, when F.P. Manhardt began his family-owned printing enterprise. He brought his sons, Arthur and Charles, into the business, and in 1926 the "Alexander" half of the company arrived in the person of partner I. Lewis Alexander. Keeping with the family tradition of the business, Alexander's son, Melvin, joined the company as a salesman in 1940. He subsequently

became president in 1961, is currently chairman of the board, and continues to be an active participant in the business.

A similar trail to the top was blazed by president and chief executive officer R. Judson Fisher. Joining the firm in 1966 as a salesman, he became sales manager in 1975, executive vice-president and equal partner four years later, and assumed his present position in 1984.

While Manhardt-Alexander's early years were spent in the industrial heart of Buffalo, it relocated to Amherst's Audubon Industrial Park in 1977. Attracted by the additional space and more efficient working atmosphere available in the suburban location, the corporation's business has since grown

Manhardt-Alexander, Inc., makes its home in this modern 30,000-square-foot building located in the Audubon Industrial Park in Amherst. The building features everything under one roof—from a large suite of business offices to prepress, pressroom, bindery, and shipping areas.

significantly. Today some 70 employees enjoy working in spacious surroundings in this bright—a skylight runs the length of the building—one-story structure.

The firm's employees, among whom can be counted a number of father-and-son teams, work with state-of-the-art printing technology that allows them to combine their own individual skills with the powers of the silicon chip. The company's revolutionary new imaging and prepress system is a good example.

Facilitating operations that range from scanning to retouching, this highly sophisticated new system represents the firm's greatest technological advancement. And true to its tradition of leadership in Western New York printing circles, Manhardt-Alexander is the first major printing company in the area to invest in such a system.

Using a color monitor and a "mouse," one of the firm's highly trained operators can create effects normally achievable only by an artist. And what effects they are! Blemishes on a model's right cheek can be removed by "cloning" a patch of skin from the left; disparate pictures from different sources can be combined into a single photographic image; and a variety of air-brush effects are available, as are silhouettes, ghost images, borders, and more.

For Manhardt-Alexander's customers, the benefits of this technology are many. The advanced laser scanner and automatic color-correction system offer greater control over making color separations, and also use less film. The traditionally tedious and time-consuming job of retouching is virtually eliminated. There are fewer size constraints than in the past. And the system can electronically store frequently used information such as logotypes to speed page makeup.

Lest the company's work be construed as all bytes and buttons, it's well worth noting the importance of the personal touch in everything it produces. In addition to the innate craftsmenship exercised in the various production stages of printing, Manhardt-Alexander has its own large in-house design staff, which offers consistently high-quality and award-winning work. And just as craftsmanship is key, so are salesmanship and sales support. While any one of a dozen salespeople may bring the jobs in, it's up to

A client waits in the reception area of Manhardt-Alexander, Inc. Behind him is a large Bas-relief three-dimensional mural representing terms used in the graphic arts industry. Overhead is a skylight that runs the length of the building and provides natural lighting throughout the office area.

the firm's internal sales-service team to keep the jobs moving. And move they do, as this five-person group tracks each and every job, acting as traffic managers, quality-control experts, and inter-departmental liaisons.

As with its imaging and prepress system, sophisticated electronic equipment is also used throughout the Manhardt-Alexander plant. Hundreds of ITC typefaces are available on floppy disc, summoned up at the touch of a button. The stripping and platemaking department uses a computerized platemaker. And in the press-room, computerized machinery controls and records information such as ink specifications and densitometer readings—data that determines whether the ink coverage provided by the press is up to spec.

There, in addition to its one- and two-color presses, the company has a pair of five-color perfecting presses that are the pride of the pressroom. Capable of printing both sides of a 28-inch by 40-inch sheet simultaneously, these sizable machines epitomize

the kind of capital reinvestment that has consistently put the firm at the top of its class.

A 10,000-square-foot bindery, a 1980 addition to Manhardt-Alexander's facility, is where the finishing touches are applied to every job that goes through the plant. Using a variety of specialized equipment, bindery workers cut, trim, and fold press sheets; add covers; and stitch product catalogs. They also die cut orders and strip and string hang tags. Finally, materials are collated, wrapped, and sent on their way to any number of destinations.

And these materials run the gamut from annual reports and catalogs to point-of-purchase materials and brochures from such prestigious customers as Corning Glass Works, Zippo Manufacturing, International Playtex, and Fisher-Price. To service these and many other customers—among whom are many names from the *Fortune* 500—the company maintains offices in New York City, Corning/Elmira, New Jersey, and, of course, Buffalo.

Regardless of where its markets lie, the key thing about Manhardt-Alexander, Inc., is knowing where its heart lies—and that's in producing work of the highest quality. It does so by knowing the ins and outs of that interface between the three-dimensional power of high-speed presses and the two-dimensional images they produce.

WKBW-TV's Eyewitness News anchor team of newscaster Irv Weinstein, sportscaster Rick Azar, and weatherman Tom Jolls have set some sort of a national longevity record. In a business that is high on turnover (particularly in a "stepping stone" market like Buffalo), this team's twenty-odd years together is a truly remarkable occurrence.

Such an established nature has yielded a loyal viewership. The friendly, flamboyant, rat-tat-tat reporting style of Channel 7 has helped it become the top-rated newscast throughout the 1970s and into the 1980s. Only recently has the 11 PM newscast lost its perch

At a concert sponsored by WKBW and WBEN thousands of Buffalonians danced and listened to the Manhattan Transfer while supporting the restoration of Shea's Buffalo Theatre, a treasured city landmark. Photo by Robert McElroy

to Channel 4—and only for one ratings period.

Channel 4's news department tries to sharply contrast Channel 7's more sensationalistic leanings. Carol Jasen and Bob Koop appear to be the most comfortable anchor team in the area, particularly engaging in their handling of segue banter. Veteran sportscaster Van Miller is perhaps the most authoritative figure in local TV sports, and Don Paul neatly combines wit and foresight in his weather reports.

Channel 2's newscasts, meanwhile, have struggled in third place for years. While the criticisms of reporting blandness are true to an extent, Channel 2 has a strong contender in the weekday 5 PM report, anchored by their most credible newscaster, Rich Kellman. And in the all-important sports coverage, Ed Kilgore has built a substantial amount of integrity in recent years. Outside of those network affiliates there are two alternatives on the UHF side of the

Leslie Aires, president of Buffalo Broadcasting and WIVB-TV, pauses in the field of microwave dishes behind the Elmwood Avenue studios. Photo by Joe Traver

dial.

WNED-TV, Channel 17, became New York State's first public station when it went on the air on March 30, 1959. It was among the first public TV stations to remain on the air throughout the summer, and also among the first to broadcast into the weekend.

Among the Public Broadcasting System programs originating from Channel 17 have been *Woman,* the pioneering series on women's issues that made an impact in the early 1970s, and the *Mark Russell Comedy Specials*, live half-hours by the well-known political satirist (also a native Buffalonian) broadcast bimonthly from the Katharine Cornell Theatre on the State University at Buffalo Amherst campus.

WNED-TV has also operated the news-oriented WEBR-AM and all-classical WNED-FM since 1976. Soon, it will begin operating Channel 23, becoming the only public broadcaster in the country

Above: The Channel 4 news team gets ready to go on the air. Photo by Joe Traver

Left: A WIVB-TV cameraman is seen in front of the station's Elmwood Avenue studios. Photo by Joe Traver

WBEN AM & FM Radio

Less than a year after the great stock market crash, an uplifting voice rang out over the Buffalo airwaves. On September 8, 1930, from the 18th floor of the Statler Hilton Hotel, WBEN Radio first went on the air, and it's been a leading force in local broadcasting ever since.

Back in those "golden years" of radio, WBEN was home to such well-known personalities as Buffalo Bob Smith, Mike Mearian, Jack Paar, Foster Brooks, and Clint Buehlman. Today the likes of morning man Bill Lacy and the station's oft-tuned-to traffic copter are more familiar sounds.

Originally owned by the *Buffalo Evening News* (thus the "BEN" in its call letters), WBEN was purchased by its current owner, Algonquin Broadcasting Corporation, in 1978 along with its sister station WBEN-FM, better known as Rock 102. As such, WBEN is the only major broadcast medium in Western New York that is locally owned and operated. "We have strong reasons for Buffalo and WBEN to

prosper," says WBEN president and owner Larry Levite, "because we live here, and our friends and neighbors listen to us."

Local ownership gives the stations the ability to not only be an active part of the community, but also to improve its quality of life. The stations are strong supporters of charity, raising thousands of dollars each year for causes ranging from the American Cancer Society to the Western New York Special Olympics. In addition, they belong to more than a score of local professional and civic associations.

WBEN-AM holds the distinction of being Western New York's top-rated station, and is a true, full-service operation. It offers adult contemporary music, an award-winning news department, a chief meteorologist, complete computerized snow closings, and the only area traffic copter that flies weekday mornings and evenings year-round.

Sports is another forte for the station, which broadcasts from facilities at 2077 Elmwood Avenue. WBEN is the voice of the NFL Buffalo Bills, the Triple-A baseball Bisons, and the NHL Sabres. Add

WBEN Radio's mobile broadcast unit.

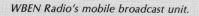

The Rock 102 Robot on location at a local business.

to those events sports talk shows, a variety of coaches' broadcasts, and pre- and post-game shows, and you've got a veritable sports smorgasbord on the air.

On the FM side, Rock 102 is the most listened-to international radio station in the United States, with more than 340,000 Western New Yorkers and 300,000 Canadians tuning in. Attracting this audience are personalities and features such as "American Top Forty" with Casey Kasem, Dr. Ruth Westheimer, "The Comedy Hour," concert specials, news, and album parties.

With the area's top-rated AM station and the most listened to FM station, WBEN Radio has been successful in keeping a half-century-plus broadcast tradition alive, well, and thriving over the airwaves of Western New York.

341

to operate four stations in the same broadcast area. The new station will include general educational programming, as well as more targeted programming for minority groups.

The other UHF affiliate in town is WUTV, located on Grand Island. Most of Channel 29's schedule throughout the 1970s consisted of reruns of old TV series and well-worn movies. In the 1980s, however, new management has brought a flurry of recent blockbuster movies and first-run syndicated programs to creep toward a ratings boost.

Cablescope, International, and Jones Cable provide cable outlets in the Buffalo metropolitan area. They have not only expanded channel selection by offering such premium networks as HBO and Showtime, but also they've pulled in such interesting stations as WPIX in New York, WOR in New Jersey, and WTBS in Atlanta. Plus, they've strengthened their signals to bring in Canadian stations in Hamilton and Toronto—outlets that Greater Buffalonians have enjoyed for years, especially when they can get a sneak preview of an American show before it's broadcast here.

Video Charity

Buffalo appears to be unique among telethon cities across the nation in that just about every pledge made is honored. That gives Greater Buffalo the considerable distinction of having the highest percentage of pledge collections in the country.

The annual Variety Club Telethon is the granddaddy of all local telethons, having begun on Channel 2 in 1963. The following year it was switched to Channel 7 where it has remained ever since.

In that first year, $86,000 was raised. The growth pattern averaged between $50,000 and $100,000 annually during the early years. In the 1970s, a yearly boost of $200,000-250,000 was realized. In 1982, the telethon reached the magic million-dollar mark for the first time and has since honed in on the two-million mark.

One of the longtime Variety Club employees expressed her amazement whenever tabulating pledge checks after a telethon. "I am absolutely amazed by the envelopes that we receive with money stuffed in them," she said. "We wind up with $400 or $500 in cash on the table by the end of the day. This community is very unique. Even when our people are hurting, they realize that there are other people hurting more."

Philip R. Beuth was general manager and vice president of WKBW-TV until 1986 when he departed for ABC-TV in New York City. A longtime Variety Club supporter when he arrived here in 1975, he approached local Variety Club officers with a plan to solicit

WKBW-TV

"Well Known Bible Witness," the origin of the call letters for television station WKBW-TV, Channel 7, traces its roots back to the religious mission of the radio station founded in 1926 by Buffalo native Dr. Clinton H. Churchill, pastor of the evangelical Churchill Tabernacle. The sister television station signed on the air in 1958, and has evolved to become one of the most successful stations of the Capital Cities/ABC Network.

In an industry known for the peripatetic careers of its employees, WKBW-TV has enjoyed success largely because of the great stability of its staff. Many employees have attained more than 20 years of service. The main Eyewitness News anchor team of Irv Weinstein, Rick Azar, and Tom Jolls has been working together since 1965, and is the longest running local team in television history.

WKBW-TV's new home, built in 1978, represents a major investment in the future of Buffalo.

With the acquisition of WKBW-TV in 1961 by Capital Cities Communications, the religious mission was translated into a broad community commitment, and the station established a reputation as a ratings leader in both news and programming. WKBW-TV subsequently introduced popular shows such as "Talk of the Town," "Romper Room," "Rocketship 7," "Buffalo Bandstand," and "Dialing for Dollars," the predecessor of today's popular morning talk show, "AM Buffalo."

As one of the highest-rated locally produced shows in the nation, "AM Buffalo" helped WKBW-TV to climb from the number three spot to the number one spot in the local television ratings, a position it first gained in 1972. A dominant force in the station's ratings climb and leadership position has been Channel 7's award-winning Eyewitness News team, gathering news locally and bringing back the local perspective from as far away as Poland and the Soviet Union.

Community commitment has long been a hallmark of the sta-

tion's management philosophy. For nearly 25 years WKBW-TV has produced live telethons for the Variety Club of Buffalo, and it is now the most successful local telethon in the country, on a per-capita basis. The event raises more than one million dollars annually for the Children's Hospital of Buffalo. On a continuing basis, WKBW-TV also sponsors a number of other community awareness and information programs.

One of the first companies to make a commitment to the resurgence of the downtown Buffalo waterfront, WKBW-TV built its new home in 1978. The stainless-steel facade represents a major investment in the future of Buffalo. In 1985 the station was purchased by Queen City Broadcasting, the principal stockholder being L. Bruce Llewellyn, and the station has continued its market leadership and emphasis on local community service. WKBW-TV has come a long way since the days of Dr. Churchill, but today's television believers tune into their station just as faithfully in the 1980s as they did in the 1930s.

WIVB-TV

The News 4 Buffalo anchor team. Pictured (from left) are Van Miller, Jacquie Walker, Don Paul, Carol Jasen, and Bob Koop.

Channel 4 telecast its first scoop even before it went on the air. The date was May 13, 1948, and the Right Reverend Lauriston Scaife was to be consecrated as Episcopal bishop of Western New York, a ceremony of sight, sound, and solemnity fully worthy of live television coverage.

Indeed, the event was tailor-made for one of today's media events, with dozens of TV photographers and reporters scrambling and bumping for position amid miles of cable.

But on May 13, 1948, Buffalo had no TV station. Not yet. One, WBEN-TV, was to begin broadcasting the very next day. But the news wouldn't wait and neither would the station. Although its official inaugural broadcast was 24 hours away, Channel 4 went on the air live that Thursday afternoon from St. Paul's Cathedral, not only the first telecast in Buffalo, but the first such religious

ceremony ever telecast anywhere in the United States.

Four months later Channel 4 sent the first-ever live video images of Niagara Falls into the nation's living rooms, or at least those with television sets in those days when radio remained the principal mode of electronic communication. It was a pioneering spirit that has remained the channel's hallmark through today and beyond.

When Buffalo's Channel 4 signed on, it shared airwaves with but two dozen other stations in the country. Like many, it was owned by a newspaper corporation, the *Buffalo Evening News.*

Times, techniques, and governmental outlook on communications conglomerates all have changed since those pioneering years, and so too has the corporate structure of Channel 4. Howard Publications of Oceanside, California, assumed ownership of Buffalo Broadcasting Co., Inc., in 1977. Even the call letters soon changed, to WIVB-TV, the "IV" representing the Roman numerals for "4." With a quick flick of the Latin-to-English dictionary, the call letters become W-4-B, short for "We're 4 Buffalo," which has given rise to hordes of wildly enthusiastic station boosters waving four fingers before the camera.

True to its calling of being owned by newspaper companies, Channel 4 has always believed strongly in the importance of local news. News 4 Buffalo's team of professionals has been providing news, weather, and sports longer than any other local TV station, and is reaching more and more homes every day. News 4 Buffalo brings viewers the news they need and want to know, and keeps them abreast of the consumer, health, and lighter sides of life in the greater Buffalo area. Its weather team, WeatherWatch 4, has the latest technology to bring precise forecasts throughout the

day, and News 4 Sports covers everything from the Bills and Sabres to college, high school, and amateur competition. Whether watching News 4 at noon, 6 p.m., or 11 p.m., viewers are assured of the latest information, interesting features, and "live" reports presented clearly and sensibly with them in mind.

The station's dedication to new and modern technology also has the viewer in mind. Two years ago CBS, of which WIVB-TV is an affiliate station, came forward with an advancement permitting transmission of a television signal on blank electronic band heretofore left idle. It was called ExtraVision®, and affiliates could take it or leave it.

WIVB-TV took it. The service makes it possible for viewers with specially designed decoders to pick up news and information at any time of the day or night, through printed messages on the television screen. ExtraVision® is an electronic newspaper of the air—locally, WIVB-TV ExtraVision® carries news and sports, up-to-date weather forecasts, entertainment notes, and consumer tips.

More important, ExtraVision® offers the availability for closed captioning for the deaf or hearing-impaired. At the moment, ExtraVision® is neither widely received nor commercially profitable, yet Buffalo Broadcasting Co., Inc.—WIVB-TV—continues to provide this new service on the cutting edge of communications technology.

ExtraVision® suits the station's historic outlook. Right from the consecration of Bishop Scaife, community service has been a primary objective, with, as in the case of the hearing-impaired, special attention toward those with special needs.

In January 1986 the American Association of Disability Communicators and the President's Committee on Employment of The

Handicapped honored WIVB-TV with first prize in its annual Media Awards competition.

The station was singled out for its half-hour special titled "Breaking Sound Barriers," which seized the moment of the Studio Arena Theatre's production of the play "Children of A Lesser God" and the attention that play calls to the daily struggle of those with severe and/or total hearing impairment.

This honor was not the exception, but practically the rule at WIVB-TV, where the 2077 Elmwood Avenue corridors are lined with awards and tributes from organizations helping those who fight otherwise solitary fights. The station has carried the United Negro College Fund Telethon and the local Black Achievers in Industry Awards dinner for many years. *Buffalo News* television critic Jeff Simon cited WIVB-TV president

Leslie G. Arries, Jr., president and general manager of WEVB-TV.

WIVB-TV employs more than 100 people in its modern offices at 2077 Elmwood Avenue.

Leslie G. Arries, Jr., as the one local TV executive who is genuinely committed to affirmative action and minority hiring.

The station, too, moved swiftly toward eliminating any sexual bias in job assignment. A 1971 advertisement for the station shows not one woman listed among 57 news-staff employees, but within a dozen years the station had named Patricia K. Sroka as station manager, the highest rank ever held by any woman at any network affiliate in Buffalo and among the very few in such a position at television stations across the country.

Mrs. Sroka—who passed away in 1983 and in whose name has been established a scholarship to assist other women interested in broadcasting careers—rose through the ranks at the station, which historically has promoted from within. When Howard Communications took over the property all local management, including president Arries, was retained. At present, station manager Sandy DiPasquale, program manager Quintin Renner, broadcast operations manager Twila Henneberger, and news director Jim Peppard all have risen through the station ranks. Peppard, in fact, formerly served as an officer of the American Federation of Television and Radio Artists (AFTRA) union local.

Broadcast employees of WIVB-

TV are represented by two respected national unions, AFTRA and NABET, the National Association of Broadcast Engineers and Technicians. No other Buffalo-area broadcaster is so widely unionized. One brief strike was settled in the 1970s; all other disputes have been resolved through compromise rather than confrontation.

The station employs more than 100 persons in its modern offices at 2077 Elmwood Avenue. The facility, owned by WIVB-TV, also houses the operations of WBEN-AM and WBEN-FM, wholly separate from the television station although all were once part of the same corporate structure.

While satellite feeds and network links bring the global village into Western New York living rooms via Channel 4, local programming still remains an important part of the mix. Sportscaster Van Miller hosts "Beat The Champ," a successful Saturday bowling show. In addition to a number of regularly scheduled programs aimed at serving a specific audience, Channel 4 often produces music and entertainment specials highlighting local talent. The news department had also won numerous awards for documentaries that both touched viewers' hearts and turned their heads.

None can foretell what the future may hold, except that when the occasion arises, Channel 4 will rise along with it, following a tradition traced to the station's first day on the air—in fact, even earlier than that.

345

Harvey Marshall, chief photographer at Channel 2, is a nationally acclaimed television photo journalist. Photo by Joe Traver

corporate involvement. At first, it was greeted with skepticism. Beuth reasoned that "anyone who does a telethon has to finally come to the realization that the general public alone cannot be depended upon for contributions. You've got to involve companies and give them the opportunity to show their community spirit."

The Channel 7 executive soon convinced the telethon organizers of the corporate value. He got the ball rolling that first year with the participation of Burger King and the Pepsi-Cola Bottling Company. Now, the corporate involvement has spread to an overwhelmingly wide cross-section of businesses.

The most prominent is the local supermarket industry— Tops, Super Duper, Bells, and, to a lesser extent, Rochester-based Wegman's. The store chains ask each of the companies that sell products in their branches to offer cents-off allowances on volume purchases, the savings of which are then turned over to the telethon. The unique promotion has worked so effectively that other Variety Clubs around the country are copying it.

The corporate list also includes a significant portion of the local restaurant, bowling, and retail industry, in addition to *The Buffalo News'* "Kids' Day" promotion, originally conceived by the late *Courier-Express.* "Kids' Day" involves hundreds of community leaders and citizens who stand on street corners to sell special newspaper editions, with the proceeds going to the Variety Club. Corporate fund-raising now accounts for over one-third of the total each year.

The satellite program is another unique aspect of the Variety Club Telethon. The idea began shortly after the initial broadcast when parents of handicapped children at the Rehab Center wanted to do something extra for the following year's effort.

These fund-raising "branches" now number over thirty, stretching across Greater Buffalo, Southern Ontario, and Northern Pennsylvania. They include veterans' posts, Knights of Columbus organizations, and United Auto Workers' chapters. Members of these organizations go out into the communities year-round, holding pancake breakfasts, baked goods sales, carnivals, and a lot of other functions to raise funds. Guests who visit the telethon are amazed at the success of the local satellite program. Efforts to establish them in other areas around the country have generally been disappointing.

Being the only completely local telethon also gives it a unique advantage. Expenses are kept under tighter control, amounting to no more than 11 or 12 percent. Plus, every single dollar goes to Greater Buffalo charities. The major portion goes to the various departments of Children's Hospital and the Rehabilitation Center. Other child-related agencies that share the telethon totals include St. Mary's School for the Deaf, St. Joseph's School for Exceptional Children in Dunkirk, Skating Association for the Blind and Handicapped, Association for the Research of Childhood Cancer, Children's Rehabilitation Camp Fund, *The Buffalo News* Camp Fund and Neediest Fund, Human Growth Foundation, United Cerebral Palsy, and the local chapter of Boys Town of Italy.

As for the array of talent that has appeared on the show for the past twenty-odd years, Beuth claims that the telethon is a very good Buffalo booster through people from Hollywood. "The city gets very good grades from people like Ann Jillian, Ted Knight, John Gabriel, and John Davidson," he said. "It's a very good PR thing for the city because everybody treats these celebrities so well here. Take Hal Linden. I see Hal almost every year and he waves to me and says, 'Heyyy, Buffalo! What a great time! I'll never forget it.' And I heard him tell other people that too."

The firm of Gelia, Wells & Mohr advertises its service in big, bold letters. Photo by Robert McElroy

Since the Variety Club Telethon was established, the other stations have also become committed to various causes. Channel 2 was one of the first four stations to broadcast the Muscular Dystrophy Telethon in 1970, the first year it went beyond its local New York City base. It has since broadcast the event each Labor Day weekend, cutting away from Jerry Lewis's hosting chores for local inserts each hour.

Meanwhile, Channel 4 has broadcast telethons for the Leukemia Society and the United Negro College Fund since 1980. Channel 29 has been involved with the March of Dimes Telethon each summer since 1983. And periodically since the 1970s, International Cable has broadcast telethons for the Arthritis Foundation, Easter Seals Foundation, and a Variety Club satellite broadcast from Sloan, NY.

The telethon concept has proven to be a show of strength in a community that throws any economic struggles to the wind in the hope that those illnesses that particularly prey on the young may one day be forever banished.

Pledges of support for such a cause never go begging in Greater Buffalo.

Advertising!

The sub-head above—complete with exclamation point—is prominently painted across the outside of Gelia, Wells & Mohr Inc. at Main and Harlem in Snyder. To some, it succinctly captures the excitement of marketing. To others, it's just plain gaudy. Whatever

WGRZ-TV

Channel 2's annual Concert in the Sky lights up Niagara Falls.

WGRZ-TV Channel 2 began broadcasting from Buffalo in 1954. That station is still on the air today, providing Western New York with a broad range of information and entertainment programming 24 hours per day.

The news operation at WGRZ is the area's largest, with an exclusive five o'clock evening newscast and the only permanent Niagara County television news bureau in Niagara Falls.

An unmatched dedication to local news coverage finds NewsCenter 2 broadcasting live from a different area of Western New York each Friday. "NewsCenter 2 Neighbors" focuses attention on local issues and individuals often overlooked by major television newscasts.

This commitment to promoting the community is reflected in many of WGRZ'S broadcasts and activities.

Sports fans recognize WGRZ as "The Sabres Station." For 10 years Channel 2 has had the distinction of being one of only two network affiliates nationwide to originate live professional hockey coverage. A rigorous schedule of Buffalo Sabres telecasts emphasizes the road games so local fans can follow the team throughout the season.

In a city with three professional sports franchises—football, baseball, and hockey—WGRZ is the only local station that hosts a weekly sports magazine. "Sports-Extra" gives fans a chance to call in and talk with local players, coaches, and owners.

In December 1985 WGRZ was the first to introduce stereo TV to Western New York with a telecast of the Buffalo Philharmonic's 50th premiere concert. As an affiliate of the National Broadcasting Company, Channel 2 has access to more true stereo programming than any other local television station. Its conversion to stereo broadcasting leads local television into a new dimension of technical superiority.

WGRZ-TV's headquarters at 259 Delaware Avenue.

The station's commitment to quality programming includes a devotion to public affairs. It has a complete, autonomous community programming staff which is responsible for two weekly series, "Buffalo Etc." and "Probe." Another weekly series, "Open Rap," is prepared by the Council of Churches of Buffalo and Erie County and provides young people with the opportunity to converse on current issues and problems of the day. Issues of vital importance to the community have generated a series of award-winning WGRZ public service specials.

In addition, the station has gone to great lengths to get involved in local activities. Hundreds of thousands of viewers look forward each year to Channel 2's annual Concert in the Sky, a mammoth fireworks show staged over Niagara Falls each Memorial Day weekend.

Throughout the year WGRZ personalities rally behind event after event to aid local charities and promote the area. From news to entertainment to community involvement, at WGRZ-TV local broadcasting means responsibility to the needs and interests of the people of Western New York.

New York Telephone

More than 100 years ago New York Telephone introduced to Buffalo an invention that would transform the way Western New Yorkers live and work. Today the company continues to employ new technologies that may revolutionize life in the twenty-first century.

Last century's dramatic invention was Alexander Graham Bell's telephone. In the 1980s New York Telephone's technologies are the digital computer and fiber optics, the building blocks of the communications network and services of the future.

In 1878 the company that became New York Telephone in 1910 opened Buffalo's first central office at Main and Eagle streets. It served 20 customers. To call each other, customers cranked a handle that signaled an operator who

Technicians like Beth Kuhn use video terminals to monitor and update the more than 60 computer-based central office switching systems New York Telephone uses in Western New York.

made the desired connection.

Today New York Telephone's 2,500 employees in Western New York operate a communications network that is a vital and reliable part of the region's infrastructure. Western New Yorkers pick up their telephones and dial more than seven million times a day.

The network that handles those calls is among the most advanced in the state. It represents an investment of more than $900 million in switching, transmission, test, and administrative equipment. To a large degree, the network is an array of computer-based technology.

Today more than two-thirds of the 92 central office switching systems in Western New York are computers, 13 of which are digital devices that process calls as streams of high-speed pulses or digits. With computer-controlled switching, the company is able to provide its basic services more economically. Optional features, such as Custom Calling Services, and new features can be added by changing the programs.

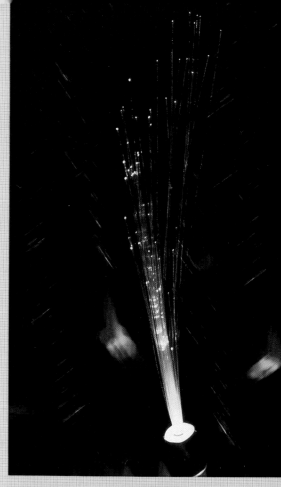

Fiber-optic cables, in which laser-generated light pulses carry calls through hair-thin glass fibers, will be the information highways of the twenty-first century. In the Buffalo area, New York Telephone began using fiber optics in 1986. The company now has more than 1,000 miles of fiber in place and working in Western New York.

There are also digital transmission links—using copper, microwave, and fiber-optic technologies—among all of the company's central offices in Western New York and to many customer locations. This digital network enables businesses to move data quickly and accurately.

A growing part of the digital network employs fiber-optic (light-wave) technology. Laser-generated light pulses transmit voice, data, and video signals through hair-thin strands of ultra-pure glass at the speed of light. Today a pair of fibers can transmit 25,000 simultaneous messages with high degrees of reliability and security.

New York Telephone was the first telephone company in the nation to put fiber-optic technology into commercial use. The company is now one of the largest light-wave users in the country. Its light-wave systems total more

than 1,000 miles of fiber in Buffalo and the metropolitan area.

While technological advances like these have helped the company meet the communications needs of Western New York, they also are the driving forces behind many of the changes occurring throughout the industry.

For much of its history, New York Telephone was part of the Bell System and part of a nationwide regulated monopoly. That all began to change 20 years ago when technological development made it possible—and desirable in the view of policy-makers—to open the business to competition. The process was accelerated in

An environmentally controlled "hut" in Amherst houses fiber-optic and digital transmission equipment. It brings the newest technology to the doorsteps of both businesses and homes. It will provide them with access to such advanced communications as bank-by-phone, telephone catalog shopping, and computer services.

New York Telephone's communications network in Western New York is an array of computer-based technology through which more than seven million messages travel every day. The compact circuit board assistant manager Bill Rybarczyk holds is from a high-speed digital switching system, a key building block for the telephone network of the twenty-first century.

1984 when a court decision mandated the divestiture of the Bell System.

New York Telephone is now a member of the NYNEX family of companies. While it no longer provides telephones or carries long-distance calls to other parts of New York and other states, the company continues to provide and maintain many of the most important parts of telephone service. These services include a package of local calling plans, long-distance calling within Western New York, optional features such as Touch-tone and Custom Calling Services, operator services, and access to worldwide communications networks.

Using new technologies, New York Telephone already has begun to introduce a new generation of communications services. They include the simultaneous transmission of voice and data and the remote reading of utility meters through telephone lines.

Ultimately services like these will lead to the type of network Western New York will need in the twenty-first century when individuals, at home and at work, will depend even more on their ability to communicate—by voice, by data, and even by picture.

To meet the requirements of what is sometimes called the Information Age, New York Telephone today is laying the foundation for an integrated digital network. Its hardware will be the digital switching and fiber-optic transmission systems. But its power will be software—intelligence—that customers will tap to have the network meet their specific needs.

Accessing data bases, paying bills, video conferences, taking polls, catalog shopping, and checking and adjusting thermostats are just some of the conveniences that New York Telephone's network of the future will make possible in Western New York.

A graphic designer adds the final details to a Healy-Schutte & Co. ad. Photo by Robert McElroy

the impression, it's undeniably visible—which symbolizes the whole idea of advertising.

Of the top ten agencies in the area, Healy-Schutte & Co. has long been regarded as having the highest degree of consistent creativity, its art directors and copywriters approaching each project with painstaking detail in both concept and execution. The agency, which expanded to Rochester and Syracuse in late 1983, vies with Levy, King & White (LKW) for second place among area ad firms in annual capitalized billings.

In early 1986, ownership adjustments affected both LKW and the area's largest agency, Faller, Klenk & Quinlan, Inc. (FKQ). Empire of America Federal Savings Bank bought a majority interest in LKW and moved the bank's estimated eight-million-dollar account from FKQ to LKW. A month later, it was announced that Bolling Peterson Advertising would be merged into FKQ.

This was a significant creative move for FKQ. Bolling Peterson was established in 1980 by an art director and copywriter from Ellis,

Above: Levy, King & White, one of the area's leading advertising firms, sports a new entrance on Pearl Street. Photo by Patricia Layman Bazelon

Left: The smartly designed interior of the Levy, King & White building is seen in this vertical view. Photo by Patricia Layman Bazelon

353

Buffalo Telephone Company

A new dimension in communications for people on the move has taken root in Western New York with the operation of the expanding Buffalo Telephone Company. A relative newcomer to the Buffalo area, the firm supplies cellular mobile telephone service to an expanding list of customers in an over 2,000-square-mile area. This innovative communication service began in the spring of 1984. Now customers can dial or receive calls—in their vehicle, boat, home, or wherever they choose to place the cellular mobile phone—from any telephone in the world where direct dialing is available.

The concept of mobile telephones as they exist today originated about 15 years ago. Buffalo Telephone was the fourth such

The cellular mobile system provides instantaneous operation without going through a traditional operator. Subscribers are secure in the knowledge that their office, home, or the 911 emergency number is available to them.

company in the nation to become operational, and it pioneered the cellular system in the Buffalo area. There are now more than 100 cities in the nation that have such a system. Buffalo Telephone offers an array of cellular mobile telephones, including in-vehicles, briefcase-size, transportable, and fully portable models from various manufacturers.

The firm occupies the entire 16th floor of the Rand Building in downtown Buffalo where it has its headquarters, along with six million dollars worth of sophisticated equipment. The location functions much like the central office of conventional telephone companies.

Major users of the cellular mobile phone system are operators of construction companies, small businesses, persons involved in making deliveries, doctors, attorneys, marketing personnel, and those whose time is valuable. The company believes that anyone who spends more than an hour a

On-site use of the cellular mobile phone system by construction companies is just one of its many valuable assets for its subscribers, who include doctors, attorneys, delivery persons, and all those whose time is valuable.

day in a vehicle can easily justify the cost of a cellular mobile phone.

There have been cases in which people were in trouble in boats in Buffalo-area waterways and were able to contact the Coast Guard directly for help. Criminals have been apprehended by persons witnessing a crime who then dialed 911 on their car phones to alert the police. During the blizzard of 1985 Buffalo Telephone Company provided briefcase versions of the cellular telephones to the Erie County coordinator as well as local television and radio stations free of charge.

Features of the telephones include instantaneous operation without the need to go through a traditional mobile-phone operator. There is no waiting for open channels. The voice quality is equal to or better than that in an office or home, and callers can be confident that they will be heard only by the person to whom they are speaking. Each cellular phone has its own unique telephone

number, and each radio unit has its own special serial number. Both of those numbers are transmitted during each call, providing security against theft and use by unauthorized persons.

The Buffalo Telephone Company cellular system is designed to handle up to 100,000 subscribers and is adding new customers at the rate of about 100 per month. By 1990 it expects to have 10,000 to 15,000 subscribers in the Buffalo area. And by the year 2000 company executives believe that roughly 60-70 percent of all telephones will be of this type because it will be "less costly and certainly more flexible." It is also thougnt that a substantial portion

of the anticipated growth will come in the rural areas.

Buffalo Telephone does not have a monopoly on cellular and is licensed by the Federal Communications Commission. The firm estimates that it has an 80-percent share of the market in the Western New York area.

The concept of this type of system in a sense goes back to World War II with the integration of two-way radios into land-line communication in which an operator was required to assist on all calls. In the mid-1960s another system was used in which an operator did not have to push a button. A little later a direct-dialing system was developed in which no operator was required. The problem was that the number of frequencies was limited by the

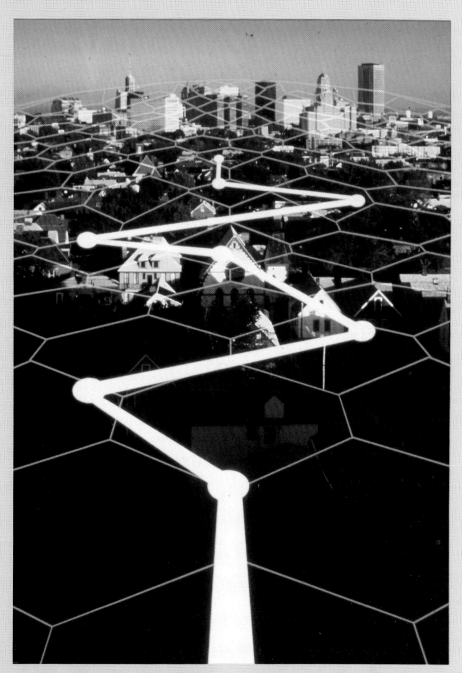

The entire 16th floor of the Rand Building in downtown Buffalo is headquarters for the Buffalo Telephone Company, which supplies cellular mobile telephone service to customers in an over 2,000-square-mile area.

FCC, which meant high prices for mobile telephones.

Buffalo Telephone calls its operation a cellular telephone system, referring to the location of its antennae in Western New York. Cellular technology has moved telecommunications into a new dimension of total accessibility, making it a substantial improvement over previously available mobile systems.

In cellular operation, instead of having one transmitter location, there can be an infinite number of

sites overlapping geographically. Mobile-phone transmissions are handed off automatically, without the customer being aware, from one base station to another. It's all done with a computer, and it's possible to keep adding cells across the continent.

Dennis M. Rooney, general manager and chief executive officer of Buffalo Telephone Company, believes that cellular mobile telephones will be the most significant development in the communications industry that will affect the average person. Says Rooney, "It will alter the life-styles of people for the better in the coming technology explosion. It may well be down the road a bit, but the two-way wristwatch radios used in the 'Dick Tracy' comic strip will become a reality."

Singer & Webb (now the Ellis Singer Group). Within a five-year span, the agency's consistency in generating riveting, high-quality work competed with Healy-Schutte in creativity, culminating in the award-winning "Kiss Your Butt Goodbye" anti-smoking campaign for the American Lung Association, devised by copywriter Mitch Flynn.

Meanwhile, LKW's creative level has been boosted to more of an award-winning stature since the veteran designer/creative director John Webb—a former partner of Ellis Singer—returned to the area at the request of Peter King, LKW chairman and CEO.

Among other ad agencies in the area, M.F.B. Productions has been steadily gaining in reputation, particularly since it began marketing Norstar Bank. The refreshingly personalized, low-key TV commercials have been a welcome change from the usual slogans of commitment found in most bank advertising. And Rob Price Design, a very small ad firm by comparison, has been consistently turning out some of the handsomest-looking marketing pieces in the area.

As for expanse, FKQ has the largest number of offices with branches in San Francisco, California, Charlotte, North Carolina, and Tampa, Florida. LKW also has a branch in Tampa, and its subsidiaries—William Collins Associates Public Relations and Quantum Analysis Marketing Research—have offices in Buffalo and Syracuse.

Also, the concept of agency networking—an exchange of services among member agencies across the country—has been prevalent in the area for many years. This gives local ad firms invaluable information on a particular region when they're dealing either with an out-of-town client or a local client who wishes to establish himself in a particular area.

Ellis Singer is a member of the National Advertising Agency Network (NAAN), begun locally in 1933 and now stretching around the world. Requests for research, store checks, local media advice, etc., are regularly exchanged among members, saving time and the client's money.

The John E. Hayes Company relies greatly on its relationship with the Mutual Advertising Agency Network (MAAN) for input across the U.S. and Canada, and Lloyd Mansfield Company's membership in Affiliated Advertising Agencies International (AAAI) has given the firm a worldwide edge.

Because members of the NAAN, MAAN, and AAAI are not competitive with each other, each firm's principals feel free to discuss mutual problems, ideas, financial data, and other matters. One executive sees networking as the only way that a local agency can compete against the advertising giants— without the giants' tremendous overhead costs.

Faller, Klenk And Quinlan, Inc.

An attractive 2.5-story atrium reception area greets employees and visitors to the headquarters of Faller, Klenk and Quinlan, Inc., at 2401 North Forest Road.

The Faller, Klenk and Quinlan, Inc., advertising and marketing agency has grown from a small one-room office in September 1957 to become, by far, Western New York State's largest advertising and marketing agency with billings of more than $50 million annually. It calls itself a marketing and communications company.

The firm's network of four branch offices spans the nation, from Tampa, Florida, and Charlotte, North Carolina, in the South to San Francisco in the West. To complement its Buffalo headquarters, Faller, Klenk and Quinlan, Inc., acquired the Bolling Peterson Advertising Agency with annual billings of about six million dollars.

Further expansion of all its operations on a fully national scale within the next five years is planned by the company's president and founder, Robert O. Faller. As an example of the firm's growth, billings have multiplied fiftyfold since 1976. Today employment stands at about 170 persons, 110 of whom work in the Buffalo area.

Faller, Klenk and Quinlan's list of clients is an impressive one. It includes Dunlop Tire Corporation, the Snyder Corporation, Pepsi Cola Bottlers, Williams Gold Refining Company, Independent Health Association, MGM, Inc., Good Neighbor Chevrolet Dealers, and Bryant and Stratton.

The scope of the agency's facilities is also broad. It encompasses in-house photography studios, computerized typesetting, word processing linked electronically to typesetting equipment, and computerized media buying. A special computer links the firm to a centralized data bank, putting it on-line with telephone directory publishers for Yellow Pages advertising. Faller, Klenk and Quinlan also has a separate, fully computerized direct-marketing subsidiary with expertise in direct mail, telemarketing, and list processing and fulfillment.

Creative as the company is in its advertising and marketing, it outdid itself when it selected its present location in the Buffalo suburb of Amherst. It purchased an elaborate 14-acre wooded estate, complete with a large heated swimming pool, tennis and basketball courts, volleyball and horseshoe facilities, jogging path, cookout and picnic section, and a carpeted patio area. The opportunity to work in this environment enables the firm to attract high-caliber talent from across the country.

Faller, Klenk and Quinlan has received literally hundreds of awards for its creative ads. It is particularly proud for twice having won the prestigious Effie Award, administered by the American Marketing Association.

Growth is virtually a byword for the firm. In 1985 it completed a $3-million expansion at its headquarters location. Added were 25,000 square feet of office space that will provide for still further growth in its work force. The addition features an attractive 2.5-story atrium reception area.

Faller, Klenk and Quinlan is deeply involved in providing its services to the growing health care field. The firm has five hospitals as clients, including three in the Buffalo area, and also serves several other businesses in various health-related fields.

In the unforgiving world of advertising and marketing, Faller, Klenk and Quinlan, Inc., has demonstrated impressive bottom-line results.

Healy-Schutte & Company

It is believed that advertising had its beginning in ancient times, with vendors walking through the streets, calling attention to their wares. One written advertisement, perhaps the first and about 3,000 years old, was discovered in ancient ruins by an archaeologist; it offered "a whole gold coin" as reward for the return of a runaway slave named Shem.

Today advertising is a highly creative, sophisticated endeavor which, contrary to the belief of detractors, actually reduces the cost of goods and services to the consumer.

One of Buffalo's largest advertising, marketing, and public relations agencies is the highly successful Healy-Schutte & Company. Alden F. Schutte is president and chief executive officer and Thomas B. Healy is chairman of the firm, which is headquartered at 1207 Delaware Avenue in Buffalo. Healy-Schutte also has an office located at 400 Andrews Street in Rochester, New York. Over 100 people are employed in the two offices, with 70 located in Buffalo.

Healy-Schutte was formed in June 1974 through the purchase of a small Buffalo agency that employed eight people and had annual billings of $1.7 million. Since then, Healy-Schutte has acquired two additional communication firms and has grown at an annual rate of more than 25 percent. The agency had total billings of $29 million dollars in 1985.

Healy-Schutte's business philosophy states that marketing, advertising, and public relations are simply creative salesmanship in print and electronic media. The agency believes that in order to develop successful marketing programs, there must be a complete

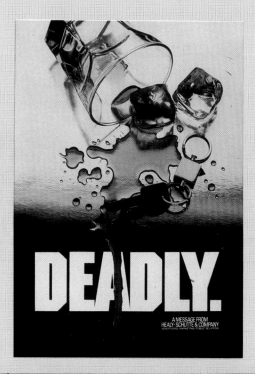

agency effort. A combination of marketing, creative, and media professionals must be clearly focused on communication objectives if a client's needs are to be served effectively. Healy-Schutte also believes that this combined group of talents requires strong leadership and discipline. Thus, responsibility is placed directly on the shoulders of the agency's executive committee.

"We have a simple precept by which our account contact people are expected to function," says Schutte, "which means that the account team that is assigned to any particular piece of business is held accountable for ensuring that the work flow between agency and client is smooth, complete,

correct, on time, within budget parameters, and, most important, RESPONSE focused."

RESPONSE is a copywrited communication system that was created by Schutte in 1976. This unique selling system approach structures the development of distinctive selling ideas for Healy-Schutte clients because it incorporates the following eight basic selling fundamentals into each campaign:

1. First, the agency must identify a specific target audience and then build a strategy that's relevant to that segment both demographically and psychographically.

2. Then, because today's marketplace has no room for "me too" products, a unique and exclusive

position must be found or created for each client's product or service.

3. Each communication must be clear, simple, and succinct. The viewer must take from the ad the intended message without confusion.

4. Time and space are valuable and not to be wasted, so every Healy-Schutte & Company ad offers the target audience an important benefit—a promise right up front.

5. Originality in presentation is essential if a communication is to break through advertising clutter and assure high readership and high message recall.

6. An advertising theme needs to be created that associates the product or service benefit with the client or brand name so they become synonymous to the viewer.

7. In addition, the advertiser's message needs a style or stance—one that conveys the corporate personality and is distinctly different within the selling category.

8. Last, but certainly not least in the RESPONSE doctrine, is dollar efficiency—which is critical to success. A proper ratio must be

determined between production and media expenditures. Both must be cost efficient and realistic for the scope of the campaign.

In the area of research, Schutte says that the company has built a group interviewing system into its operating approach as a partial means of defining advertising objectives. "We conduct research for our own use, not just at client request," he adds. "Since this is largely qualitative research, we use this information to stimulate ideas—to provide a real buyer's perspective to the product, service, or advertising concept under consideration."

Healy-Schutte & Company provides its clients with comprehensive consumer data when requested via the development of in-depth research and its implementation. The firm also provides research management services to those clients who do not have their own in-house capabilities.

Healy-Schutte originated the highly acclaimed and successful Talking Proud campaign for the Buffalo Area Chamber of Commerce in 1981. It received national television exposure, and Schutte personally wrote the catchy "Buffalo's got a spirit" jingle.

The agency has won literally hundreds of awards for its creative product over the years, but takes

Built in 1911, this classic Gothic stone mansion, at 1207 Delaware Avenue, is headquarters for Healy-Schutte & Company.

particular pride in the recognition it received from the McDonald's restaurant chain. Employing over 90 ad agencies throughout the world, McDonald's in 1985 selected Healy-Schutte, along with two other international communication firms, as their stand-out marketing/media leaders. Among other national awards received by the agency are the Effies, which are presented by the American Marketing Association for sales effectiveness. Healy-Schutte has won three of these awards and was the first Western New York agency to receive such an acclaim.

As to the future, Schutte believes his agency's potential for growth is virtually unlimited. "Our goal for 1990 is to reach $50 million in billings, which will probably come through further acquisitions in other cities," he says.

It would be difficult to find offices as elegant yet as practical as those of Healy-Schutte & Company. Built in 1911 by William D. Chapin, the building is a classic Gothic stone mansion whose Old World charm comes complete with imported stained-glass windows, mahogany woodwork, marble, and hand-carved fireplaces. At one time, the home was known for its beautiful gardens, cascading waterfalls, and a small army of servants. The style of this turn-of-the-century building certainly contrasts beautifully to the contemporary quality and standards embodied in the Healy-Schutte organization and the product this ad agency creates.

CHAPTER TWELVE

Retailing to Restaurants

When Buffalo was in its infancy, the public market was the center of the city. Here, people flocked to the various farmers, butchers, and dairymen who sold their produce, eggs, meats, fruits, and vegetables from the backs of their wagons.

By the turn of the century, Buffalo had four public markets. The Elk Street Market was the largest wholesale market in the city, while the Washington Street Market was the largest retailer. On the East Side, the Clinton and Broadway markets accommodated the many Polish immigrants who settled there.

An account of downtown activity at the time characterized the Washington Market—which was located at Washington, Chippewa, and Ellicott streets—like this: "There are three market days each week, Tuesday, Thursday and Saturday, and upon the latter, when the market is open day and night, it becomes so crowded as to be almost impassable."

Today, only the Broadway Market remains, the highlight of the Broadway-Fillmore business district. Increased city funding, an architectural facelift, and tighter security have helped this venerable institution retain the tradition of the public market, while at the same time renewing an area wracked by decay and rows of vacant storefronts, chief of which is the large building at 998 Broadway. That was an address driven into the shopping consciousness of thousands of Buffalonians who regularly patronized Sattler's Department Store right through the 1960s. Now, just as new stores are slowly filling the vacant buildings, there's hope on the horizon that the old Sattler's haunt will be sold, gutted, and returned to the vital core of retailing that it enjoyed for decades.

And, lo and behold, the public market has made a comeback in

Opposite: Rows of charming specialty shops line the historic Allentown area. Photo by Melissa C. Beckman

361

Right: The Broadway Market on Buffalo's East Side harks back to turn-of-the-century shopping. Vendors, such as this European baker, openly display their goods. Photo by Joe Traver

Opposite, top: Accommodating butchers are prevalent at the Broadway Market. Photo by Joe Traver

Opposite, bottom: Because the Broadway Market is located in the city's traditional Polish section, links upon links of homemade kielbasa (Polish sausage) are sold daily. Photo by Joe Traver

the center of downtown. Downtown Buffalo Management Corporation, a city hall development agency, reinstituted the tradition during the summer of 1984 with the opening of the Downtown Country Market.

While one of the primary jobs of this agency is to create a variety of events each year to spark the downtown renaissance, Executive Director Charles Breihof refers to the market idea as the most consistent downtown promotion that his agency has conceived. Whereas an event such as the Taste of Buffalo (bringing many area restaurateurs downtown for an annual celebration of Buffalo dining) requires much effort and expense for something that only lasts two days, the market is a cost-efficient alternative, running Thursdays from May through October.

Here, a steady flow of downtown employees on their lunch hours and coffee breaks happily buy fresh fruits, vegetables, and baked goods from area producers. Plans for 1987 call for the market to settle into a permanent location along Main Street, just south of Court Street, with thirty-five farmers and thirty-five craftspeople offering their homemade goods on Thursdays, as well as on Saturdays in an effort to attract people downtown on a non-workday.

Left: Two women enjoy after-work cocktails on the patio of Carbur's Restaurant in the heart of the downtown Theater District. Photo by Joe Traver

Opposite, top, left: An enthusiastic trio shares one of the many gastronomical delights at the annual Taste of Buffalo celebration downtown. Photo by Robert McElroy

Opposite, top, right: T-shirts make colorful souvenirs of the event that brings together a smorgasbord of Buffalo's delicacies. Photo by Robert McElroy

Opposite, bottom: A Buffalo restaurateur offers a sampling of one of her specialties. Photo by Robert McElroy

Stores and More

The roots of Adam, Meldrum & Anderson Company (AM&A's) go back to 1867 when Robert B. Adam helped usher in the department store age here in Buffalo. Since then, many locally based retail chains have been established here. A national variety store chain originated here during the early part of this century when Seymour Knox, Sr., merged his successful store chain with his cousin, F.W. Woolworth.

Some of the local chains, like Hengerer's, Hens & Kelly, and Sattler's, are just a memory. Others, like L.L. Berger, Sample, and Kleinhans are still very much a retail presence around the area. Then there's the substantial presence of national chains like JC Penney and Sears, and regional chains like Sibley's and Fay's Drugs.

The basis of these stores, of course, is in the small shops that grew around the public markets way back when. Some of these individual shopkeepers are still the retail backbone in area villages and towns. In Kenmore, for example, parents have purchased new shoes for their children at the Kenmore Boot Shop since World War I. In East Aurora, Vidler's 5&10 carries on the tradition of the plank-floored variety store.

Adam, Meldrum, And Anderson Company

Believing in Buffalo isn't difficult for the Adam, Meldrum and Anderson Company. It's been doing that since 1867.

When Robert B. Adam I came to the United States in 1857, he searched for 10 years before selecting Buffalo as the site for his new department store. Adam immediately recognized the industrial and mercantile potential of this young and thriving area. But, most important, he was encouraged by the hard-working commitment Buffalonians had in making their city the best.

Adam echoed this belief in Buffalo. His first store was established on March 21, 1867, dedicated to providing quality merchandise and service at a price the community as a whole could afford. To fully ensure local commitment, Adam, Meldrum and Anderson has remained a locally owned and operated business through the three generations of guidance Robert B. Adam I to III have given.

Robert B. Adam I headed the YMCA for many years, and also served as a trustee of Cornell University and Buffalo General Hospital. His loyalty and service to the community was recognized, and he was named chairman of New York State's important Grade Crossing Commission.

Adam also pioneered the development of the first buying office to provide joint buying power for a group of independent stores located nationwide. His customers appreciated this innovation because it significantly reduced the price of merchandise.

During the presidency of Robert B. Adam II, the nation entered the Great Depression. It took a man of stamina to lead the department store through such a crisis. Both Adam and his business

overcame the country's worst financial disaster as well as pressure from the conglomerate buying power of stronger retail chains.

Robert B. Adam III assumed the presidency in 1945, and to this day the department store remains on top of the retail scene in Western New York, amid off-price, factory outlet proliferation and national chain consolidations. The company has grown from one store in 1867, measuring 22 feet wide by 85 feet deep with 11 employees, to 10 stores in 1986 with more than 2,200 employees.

Robert B. Adam III comments, "We are survivors of the retail shakeout of the late 1970s and early 1980s because we have adhered to our original motto, 'Second to None.' Our objective is still to be the acknowledged leader in the values we can offer customers and the services we can perform for them, and the rewards we offer our associates."

Adam, Meldrum and Anderson's

commitment to downtown Buffalo and its revitalization continues to grow. Recently the company purchased the J.N. Adam Building that the downtown store has occupied since 1960. It also plans to install a covered walkway between its downtown store and the Main Place Mall to offer downtown shoppers the convenience they deserve.

As to the future of the Adam, Meldrum and Anderson Company, Robert B. Adam III states: "With our dominant market share in Western New York, I see a bright future for our company. With the upbeat attitude of our employees, our strong management, and our desire to succeed, I feel confident in being here another 119 years."

Three generations of Buffalo business leaders, Robert B. Adam III, foreground, and his father and grandfather, have headed the Adam, Meldrum and Anderson department store in Buffalo since its inception on March 21, 1867.

The independent little village shops and neighborhood store-keepers have dwindled in the face of the chain stores and the giant malls. The retailing scene began to change when the University Plaza opened where Main Street and Kenmore Avenue meet at the city line north. The year was 1939, automobiles were swarming the roadways more than ever, and the push toward the suburbs was beginning. The suburban plaza concept was taking hold. In a bold move, young Robert B. Adam III—third-generation president of AM&A's—decided to open a branch in the University Plaza in 1947.

Opposite: More and more events are bringing people back to the downtown area. Photo by Robert McElroy

Above: A taste of the "new" Buffalo is being enjoyed by many. Photo by Robert McElroy

This action by downtown's most established department store helped bring the suburban plaza idea into wide acceptance.

Five years later, the opening of Thruway Plaza with its thirty-nine stores and thousands of parking spaces in the center of Cheektowaga sparked the move to the giant suburban plaza.

By 1962, the plaza concept already began to appear outmoded as Amherst's Boulevard Mall became metropolitan Buffalo's first covered suburban shopping mall. Indoor shopping was in! Within a decade or so, shopping malls were found throughout much of

Right: A farmer is all ears at the weekly visit of the Downtown Buffalo Country Market. Photo by Joe Traver

Opposite, top: The Country Market provides weekly fun for all downtowners from late spring through early fall. Photo by Joe Traver

Opposite, bottom: Go ahead, squeeze'em. It's all part of the farmer's market feel at the Downtown Buffalo Country Market. Photo by Joe Traver

Greater Buffalo. Even Thruway Plaza became Thruway Mall.

Today, about a dozen malls attract most of the suburban shoppers. The largest is Eastern Hills Mall in the Williamsville-Clarence area with ninety-seven stores. The newest is McKinley Mall in Hamburg which opened in October 1985. Tapping the growing South Towns market proved to be instantly lucrative for the $50-million mall. In just two months, the merchants of McKinley's seventy-seven stores reported that sales were as much as 100 percent above their projections.

Benderson Development Corporation brought the concept of Factory Outlet Malls to the area in the 1980s with its Niagara Falls and West Seneca locations featuring famous designer stores that offer their fashions and merchandise direct to the consumer, cutting out the distributor and cutting prices in the process.

that helped spur the comeback of that deteriorating section. Soon Burger King, Arby's, John & Mary's, and Wendy's moved downtown to attract the office employee who wanted a quick inexpensive lunch or snack. McDonald's was first again to build in the newly designated Theater District, with portraits of movie stars creating a show-biz atmosphere complementing the theatrical flamboyance of the block.

Courtyard Mall introduced the food court downtown—a collection of fast-food stands under one roof. After the mall had problems keeping its tenants, Main Place Mall took up the food court idea successfully by converting the second floor of the former Sattler's store into a comfortable smorgasbord of stands.

During the rebuilding efforts of the late 1970s and early 1980s, several individuals gamely invested in new bars and restaurants, although some were ultimately defeated by competing with the turmoil of construction and general transition. Reuben's Backstage, for example—which occupied the former Stage Door on Pearl near Chippewa—hung in there until the mid-1980s, offering full seasons of dinner theater.

There were a few attempts to reopen the Old Spain, one of the most popular restaurants of downtown's heyday. Unfortunately, none succeeded until Swiss Chalet took it over after its previous location across the street burned.

The idea of establishing more restaurants along the waterfront in the proposed Marina Marketplace seems to hold great potential! Since the Erie Basin Marina was developed, the rambling, upscale

DeRose Food Brokers

When many businesses were leaving Buffalo for the suburbs, DeRose Food Brokers was traveling in the opposite direction.

That was back in 1977, when the company was one of the largest food brokers in the state outside New York City. Today the corporation is one of the largest food brokers in the country, and a sister firm, Niagara Trading Company, is the second-largest importer of pineapple in the United States.

A Buffalo success story? Every bit as much as chicken wings!

DeRose Food Brokers was the first area company to refurbish a Delaware Avenue mansion for office space. Proximity to the downtown business district and easy access to public transportation seemed critical during the energy-drained 1970s. But it was a deep loyalty to the city of his birth and a vision of a prosperous future that led Michael J. DeRose, chairman and sole owner of DeRose Food Brokers, along with his three sons, Christopher, Michael, and David, to make the Orrin Foster mansion headquarters for a food processing, packaging, and distribution empire that reaches from Thailand to the Atlantic seaboard of the United States.

As a food brokerage company, DeRose Food Brokers acts as a sales organization for food production and processing firms, handling orders, shipping, sales promotions, advertising, and in-store display. Corporations represented by DeRose Food Brokers include Rich Products of Buffalo, H.J. Heinz, Sorrento Cheese Company, Inc., Gioia Pasta Co., Ocean Spray, Domino Sugar, Grandma Brown Beans, Libby, McCormick Spices, Freezer Queen, Mrs. Paul's, Dukkee, Dixie, 3M, and Ore-Ida Potato. Overall the firm

With a deep devotion to the city of his birth, Michael J. DeRose, chairman and sole owner of DeRose Food Brokers, refurbished the Delaware Avenue Orrin Foster mansion for the firm's headquarters.

represents 31 of the nation's largest food companies.

In 1983 an innovative licensing arrangement with Libby made Niagara Trading Company, also wholly owned by Michael J. DeRose, solely responsible for the production, sales, marketing, and distribution of all pineapple products sold under the Libby label for the United States and Canada. Not only did this remarkable deal make Buffalo the center for all transactions involved in the merchandising of the Libby's brand, but it also confirmed the company's commitment to Buffalo when DeRose successfully resisted attempts by Libby to have him relocate his businesses to Chicago.

Part of the immediate future for DeRose Food Brokers and Niagara Trading Company rests on the success of a new brand name—Queen's Pride. Taking its cue from Buffalo's erstwhile sobriquet as the "Queen City of the Great Lakes," the Queen's Pride label is found on products ranging from mushrooms to frozen chicken wings. In particular, the Buffalo-style chicken wings are meeting with increasing success throughout the country. And what would chicken wings be without sauce? Taking flight in the national marketplace alongside Queen's Pride wings is Queen's Pride Buffalo-style Chicken Wing Sauce, bottled locally in Wilson, New York, and Queen's Pride Mustard, bottled in Lockport.

What better way to put the icing on a Buffalo success story than by taking our best to the rest of the country?

Rich Products Corporation

Rich Products Corporation, which traces its roots back to a small dairy on Vermont Street in 1945, today has annual sales of $600 million with 33 production facilities nationwide and in Canada. The company has a line of over 800 products and approximately 6,000 employees. Rich Products Corporation is now the nation's largest privately held frozen-food manufacturer.

In 1935 Robert E. Rich purchased Wilber Dairy, a small facility with two trucks and a horse-and-wagon route. While vastly expanding this operation, in 1945 a twist of fate took the newly established Rich Products into the frozen-food business. Robert Rich took a supply of a refrigerated nondairy whip topping to a restaurant and supermarket trade show in New York City, packing it with dry ice for the ride on a New York Central Railroad train. However, he put too much dry ice in the package, and when he arrived at his destination the product was frozen solid. Although he knew that cream from cows' milk could not be frozen and still whip, he decided to thaw this product and see if it would whip. It did, and to a large degree that product, Rich's® Whip Topping®, was responsible for building Rich Products into the frozen food giant it is today.

The company then focused its attention on developing additional products. In the 1950s the firm introduced a commercial line of frozen chocolate eclairs and cream puffs. In 1961, after extensive research and development, Coffee Rich came onto the market for use as a creaming agent for coffee and tea, on cereals and fruits, and in recipes instead of cream.

Rich Products began a massive corporate expansion in the early 1960s with the construction of a nondairy plant in Fort Erie, Ontario, across the Niagara River from Buffalo. Today it is the only Rich facility that produces frozen dough and nondairy products.

Frozen baked goods were added to the firm's product line in 1969 with the acquisition of the Elm Tree Baking Company in Appleton, Wisconsin. During the 1970s nine plants in various locations throughout the United States were acquired, and for the first time the Rich name appeared on frozen seafood specialty items, soup bases, gravy mixes, powdered coffee creamers, and meat specialty items.

Rich Products also purchased Palmer Frozen Foods at that time, a frozen bakery goods producer and distributor in eastern Pennsylvania. With this acquisition Rich had its entry into the frozen dough market, of which it is now the leader. Next came the construction, and later expansion, of the world's largest dough-producing plant in Murfreesboro, Tennessee, followed by entry into the seafood specialties market with the acquisition of SeaPak Corporation in St. Simons and Brunswick, Georgia, and Brownsville, Texas, from the W.R. Grace Company. Expansion continued unabated in the early 1980s with the purchase of the H.J. Heinz Company's frozen dessert plant in

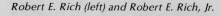

Robert E. Rich (left) and Robert E. Rich, Jr.

Rich Products' corporate headquarters at 1150 Niagara Street, Buffalo.

Lake City, Pennsylvania. Later PREAM®, a nondairy coffee powder, was purchased from Early California Foods Company of Los Angeles.

Rich Products' self-described premier achievement, and an industry first, came in June 1980 when it unveiled its new process that allows foods to remain soft while frozen. The Freeze Flo® process was developed by the company over a seven-year period. While initial use has been limited to frozen dessert items, Freeze Flo's® application to other food groups is virtually unlimited.

That discovery kicked off another expansion wave as the firm moved to bolster production capabilities of its own Freeze Flo® products. Included into this is Rich Fruit Pak Company of Escalon, California, which produces frozen fruits for many different catering uses.

Other additions to the Rich family were Turner Foods of Rome, Georgia; and Casa Di Bertacchi of Vineland, New Jersey, both meat specialty producers, and the former L.J. Harris plant, a major pie producer located in Saugatuck, Michigan. In 1982 Rich Products added Wakefield Seafoods of Bellevue, Washington, the nation's premier packer of frozen crab.

Bakery production capacity was expanded in 1983 with the addition of the Tennessee Doughnut Company of Nashville. Rich Products Corporation also introduced at this time another Freeze Flo-based dessert, Fresh 'n Frosty®, which is a soft-serve dessert treat.

Diners on the outdoor patio of Crawdaddy's enjoy a spectacular lakefront view along the Erie Basin Marina. Photo by Joe Traver

Crawdaddy's Restaurant and The Hatch, a burger stand on the edge of the water, have done remarkable business.

From Weck to Wings

In the beginning, there was beef on weck. Like baked beans in Boston and Creole cooking in New Orleans, the sandwich became a food specialty uniquely associated with Buffalo. This creation of succulent roast beef served in a sliced roll topped with salt and caraway seeds was most likely introduced to the area by German burghers who arrived here during the nineteenth century.

Although it could be found in taverns and restaurants all around the area, the legendary beef on weck could be found in its purest

form at a modest corner tavern called Bailo's on Buffalo's East Side. Here, many b-o-w fanatics considered Bailo's sandwich to be the ultimate, made with heaping mounds of juicy beef and served with thick, log-like steak fries swimming in a sea of gravy.

When the original Bailo's burned down in the late 1970s, a tradition was lost. Still, a reputable beef on weck could still be found at such places as Schwabl's in West Seneca and Otto's in Cheektowaga. As evidence of the sandwich's continuing popularity and close association with the area, the new ownership of radio station WNIA changed the call letters to WECK, distributing bags of kimmelweck rolls as calling cards to its advertisers.

In the 1960s, a new food specialty soon began to surpass the beef on weck in the area. Legend has it that one day in 1964 a truck driver mistakenly delivered a load of chicken wings to the Anchor Bar at Main and North streets, instead of the backs and necks which were originally ordered by owner Frank Bellissimo. His wife Theresa, who did the cooking, chose not to use the wings in spaghetti sauce as others did with this formerly undesirable part of the chicken. Instead, she cut them in two, deep-fried them, and served them with celery and bleu cheese dressing as hors d'oeuvres at the bar.

The experiment soon took wing, one might say, and proved to

Sorrento Cheese Company, Inc.

Sorrento's family of "the best Italian cheese in America."

A fleet of spotless refrigerated trucks outfitted with the latest equipment are rolling billboards for one of the nation's fastest growing cheese makers. But back in the late 1940s Sorrento's cheese was sold to neighborhood merchants and families by the firm's owner, a man who earlier in that same day—much earlier, in fact—met dairy farmers at dawn to buy cans of fresh milk to produce a high-quality blend of soft Italian cheese.

Leaving his job at another cheese factory in 1947, Russo set up his business in the teeming hub of South Buffalo. His dream has become the company's motto: to make the "best Italian cheese in America." Committed to the old world quality he knew as a boy, he named the firm after his birthplace, Sorrento, Italy.

Today, at an expansive plant not far from the site of that original location, company founder Louis Russo can proudly watch as his Sorrento Cheese Company, Inc., processes millions of pounds of milk each day to meet the growing demand for mozzarella, ricotta, and other fine Italian cheeses.

Buffalo's large Italian population and New York State's thriving dairy industry aided Russo in quickly establishing a high customer demand for his specialty products. Within five years the company had expanded both its plant and its payroll—the former by leasing a dairy facility, and the latter by hiring five additional employees, for a grand total of eight. By 1957 Sorrento had incorporated and moved to the South Park location in South Buffalo. Soon the 26,000-square-foot manufacturing and office building was the place of employment for a staff of 20, as well as the nucleus of a burgeoning business whose sales had soared to a record-breaking high.

In the 1960s Sorrento products—mozzarella, ricotta, provolone, Spanish cheese, basket cheese, grated cheese, whey products, and cream—were fast becoming widely recognized for their distinct smoothness, consistency, and taste. In short order another facility was added to the firm's cheese-making operation.

In 1984 Sorrento opened a 75,000-square-foot cheese plant in Goshen, New York, approximately 70 miles northwest of New York City, a traditionally strong market for Sorrento products. Slightly smaller than the sprawling multi-acre parent plant in Buffalo, the Goshen facility easily produces two-thirds of the Buffalo plant's output.

A variety of factors over the years have helped Sorrento grow. Increased consumption of Italian cheese and the ever-increasing popularity of pizza have both been important. However, Sorrento's insightful marketing strategies have also been key contributors to its dramatic growth. Once attracting the industrial and whole-

A member of Sorrento's impressive fleet of trucks makes its way through the New York countryside.

Assistant plant manager, Mike Liuzzi, checks the stretchability and texture of Sorrento's mozzarella cheese.

sale trade, Sorrento's products are now a major factor in the retail market as they are sold to major chains and stores throughout the country.

Sorrento has taken on very much of a high-tech look. The firm has installed state-of-the-art production equipment at all its facilities and maintains the highest possible standards of production. The milk has to be the best; each container is tested for purity and quality as soon as it arrives at the plant. From pasteurization to separation to final packaging, Sorrento cheese is tested at every stage of production to assure high standards of quality and consistency. It's an unceasing operation: Sorrento facilities include tons of stainless-steel equipment which undergoes vigorous daily cleaning as well as sophisticated and well-equipped dairy-testing laboratories that operate 24 hours a day.

Sorrento is fast becoming the first soft Italian cheese manufacturer to have its products sold across the entire nation. Facilitating this wide geographic presence are distribution centers in Chicago and New Jersey. And reflecting

this distribution is the fact that the Sorrento brand can now be found on the shelves of major grocery chains throughout the nation.

In addition to its industrial and retail sales division, the company maintains an expanding food-service operation. Fresh Sorrento products are provided through leading wholesalers to restaurants, pizzerias, schools, hospitals, food co-ops, and government-sponsored programs. Two other Sorrento subsidiaries round out the corporation's local presence: Located on Walden Avenue in Cheektowaga are SCC Foods, which sells a full line of products as well as cheese supplied by Sorrento, and SCC Transportation, which operates and maintains all of the company's popular refrigerated trucks.

Growing from a three-man venture to a major growth company in the industry, Sorrento demonstrates its commitment to the state of New York in a variety of ways. For example, although Sorrento purchases raw materials throughout the Northeast, the majority is obtained from New York cooperatives. Ever mindful of his modest beginnings, Russo expresses his gratitude to Buffalo through generous support of local

charities and by sponsoring a multitude of community programs. At Sorrento there is a strong willingness to give back to the community.

Today, with Sorrento trucks rolling across the nation, it's difficult to imagine the firm's founder, in a day's time, buying fresh milk, making batches of mozzarella and ricotta, and then traveling throughout Western New York to sell that day's production.

However, growth and automation have not changed the friendly atmosphere at Sorrento. A privately held organization with members of the Russo family holding various executive positions, the firm also treats employees and customers as family. Today Sorrento Cheese Company, Inc., is a leader in its industry, where every employee believes in their company and shares the pride of making the highest-quality Italian cheeses. This pride and dedication contributed to sales increasing tenfold over the most recent eight-year period. Another reason for Sorrento's success, according to Louis Russo, is simple: "Consistently give the customer the best quality available and service equal to that high quality." With an eye to the future, you can count on Sorrento to deliver even more of "the best Italian cheese in America."

Sorrento all natural ricotta as it approaches its final stage before shipping.

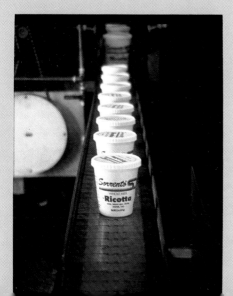

Midday diners enjoy the cozy outdoor patio of one of the charming restaurants along Elm-wood Avenue. Photo by Joe Traver

be an immediate hit. Taverns and restaurants across the area soon added the specialty to their menus and, as the 1970s dawned, thousands of pounds of wings were consumed by Buffalonians weekly. As the word spread, the term "Buffalo-style chicken wings" began to crop up in restaurants across the country. Finally, in 1980, the finger food received the ultimate recognition—a feature story by American food writer Calvin Trillin in the upscale *New Yorker* magazine entitled, "An Attempt to Compile a Short History of the Buffalo Chicken Wing."

This former throwaway food now brought a certain culinary prominence to the area, and a saucy new meaning to the words, "hot, medium, or mild."

Gourmet to Ground Round

Remarkably, no one in the area has yet to take the vast popularity of the chicken wing and turn it into mass acceptance via a nationwide or even a local chain. However, there is a variety of locally based chains here that compete with and, in some instances, surpass such restaurants as Pizza Hut, Denny's, Ground Round, Ponderosa, Kentucky Fried Chicken, and the others.

The largest local chain is Your Host, an expanded coffee shop established in 1944, which is in twenty-four locations around the area. It's the nearest thing to the old Deco shops which made up much of the coffee-shop character of Buffalo in the 1940s and

Buffalonians enjoy a wide variety of dining options. Photo by Joe Traver

1950s.

Many former Buffalonians insist that Buffalo pizza is far superior to those found in other parts of the country. There is an incredible number of pizzerias throughout Greater Buffalo, seemingly on every block of every business district. Santora's twelve locations comprise the largest pizza chain, but this is a highly preferential product. Many have sworn by Bocce Club pizza for years. When a Bocce Club box made an appearance in *Vamping,* a motion picture that was shot in Buffalo, a rousing cheer went up in local movie theaters.

Ever since Ted's Jumbo Red Hots was established near the Peace Bridge entrance along Porter Avenue back in 1927, it's become the definitive area hot dog. Since then, five other Ted's locations have sprung up around town, extending even to a location in Tempe, Arizona.

Since the first Mighty Taco was built here in 1974, Mexican finger food has attracted many Buffalo tastes, so much so that Mighty

Perry's Ice Cream Company, Inc.

Second and third generation—vice-president Dale, chairman Marlo, and president Tom Perry—review packaging for newest flavor of Perry's Deluxe, bringing its total to 48 flavors.

Akron, New York, is one of the many unique communities to be found in Western New York. It has its own fresh spring water supply and its own electrical system, giving both corporate and individual residents the benefits of inexpensive water and power. Akron is a community with a great deal to offer those who live and work there.

One such corporate resident in this unique community is Perry's Ice Cream Company, Inc. And just as Akron is unique, so is Perry's Akron address: One Ice Cream Plaza. That address was not always where Perry's mail was sent, how-

ever, for this is a new address for a business that dates back to 1918.

Company founder H. Morton Perry originally ran a dairy as a one-man operation. After two years he was joined by his brother-in-law, Perry Blackmore, and the dairy business grew. Eventually, in 1932, the Akron School approached Mr. Perry with a request to supply them with ice cream. (The school dietician knew that his mother had a recipe and a reputation for making good homemade ice cream.) Mr. Perry obliged, and with his mother's recipe prepared the ice cream mix on his kitchen stove. He churned the ice cream in an ice-and-salt hand freezer, packaged it, and sold it to the Akron School. Thus, Perry's Ice Cream Company was born.

Mr. Perry's philosophy was sim-

The highlight of a tour of Perry's is sampling ice cream and novelties, such as ice cream sandwiches and creamsicles. The company sells ice cream products to more than 4,000 food stores, institutions, and restaurants.

ple: make the highest quality product possible. He often said, "If my name is on it, I want it to be the best. To be successful, we must manufacture quality products, give quality services, and most important, it must be presented by quality people."

H. Morton Perry's son, Marlo, joined the business after he graduated from Cornell University with a degree in Dairy Science. Shortly thereafter, the younger Perry started to purchase larger ice cream freezers and other equipment. The building of Perry's Ice Cream Company started and has never stopped.

The third generation of the Perry family is currently represented in the company's management by Thomas and Dale Perry, Marlo Perry's sons. Tom started with the firm in 1963 after graduating from Michigan State University with a degree, like his father before him, in Dairy Science. Today he is the company's president and chief executive officer. Dale joined Perry's in 1966 after graduating from Alfred State with an associate's degree in business, and is Perry's executive vice-president and chief operations officer. Together the two brothers have continued the "Tradition of Quality" that their grandfather started in 1932.

Under the brothers' leadership, Perry's soon outgrew its original facility at One Pearl Street in Akron. This led to the firm's development of an ambitious 10-year plan to build its present facility at One Ice Cream Plaza. A new site only a few blocks from the original location was selected for development, and work progressed in three distinct phases.

Phase I was a freezer warehouse with a loading facility to be used as a distribution center, and is 80 feet wide, 100 feet long, and 12 feet high. During this earliest phase of the company's move to its new headquarters, the ice cream was manufactured,

The modern plant and freezer truck show Perry's has come a long way since it was founded by Morton Perry in 1918. The absolute insistence on quality has remained a family tradition.

hardened, and then palletized at the original location, then shipped to One Ice Cream Plaza for distribution.

Phase II consisted of an 80-foot by 100-foot by 24-foot addition to the freezer, and the construction of a dry storage warehouse.

Phase III was more ambitious still—a new, state-of-the-art ice cream production complex completely designed by Tom Perry. The layout of the plant, and its use of energy-saving methods, won Perry's Ice Cream national acclaim. A prestigious national trade magazine, the *Dairy Record,* described the facility as one of the most modern ice cream plants in the United States, and commended the firm's commitment and creativity in utilizing natural resources to conserve energy costs. The natural resources to which the *Dairy Record* referred are yet another element in the uniqueness of Akron, New York.

Years ago gypsum was Akron's main industry. As a result, miles and miles of abandoned gypsum mines, filled with an endless supply of water, underlie the entire community. Knowing this, Tom Perry had wells drilled down into the abandoned mines to pump the cool water into the new facility. Today this natural resource is used to cool the condensers of

the refrigeration system, air condition the plant, and precool the mix product. But cool water isn't the only natural resource underlying Akron. The company also drilled several natural gas wells— with much success. Today these help supply the plant with energy to fire its boilers.

Natural resources aren't the only things that Perry's Ice Cream Company is thankful for, however. It had a founder who had a philosophy of quality products, quality service, and quality people. It's blesssed with a location in Western New York that is within a several-hour drive of a significant percentage of the population of New York State. And perhaps most important, it is thankful for the four generations of the family that have carried on not only H. Morton Perry's name, but also his philosophy. Yes, four generations, for Tom Perry's son, Brian, also joined the company after graduating from Alfred State College with an associate's degree in business.

The Perry family takes pride in having as employees many families in which members of the second and third generation are now at work for the firm. Perry's is family-oriented, not only with the company itself, but with its customers and consumers as well.

As the "consumer" part of the family continues to "Pick Perry's Ice Cream," the growth of this unique business with the unique address in a unique community will continue. And for that, Perry's Ice Cream Company, Inc., is thankful.

Wine-tasting opportunities abound throughout the region, thanks in large part to the wineries that surround Greater Buffalo. Photo by Joe Traver

Taco has expanded to eight locations.

Locally based chains also include restaurants of a finer dining nature. The Turgeon name has operated a number of well-regarded restaurants both in and out of the area for over three decades, the latest of which is the Nickel City Cafe chain which offers a locally oriented menu and decor. Romanello's has been serving the area since 1920 when it established Roseland, a West Side tradition. The Romanello family now operates three locations.

Outside of the chains, a wide variety of individual restaurants abound, covering just about every taste and ethnic flavor.

The downtown renaissance has mixed old favorites like Chef's, the sixty-three-year-old Italian landmark, with new favorites like Harlan's and Shayleen's, fast becoming a gourmet's delight.

Gourmet tastes are also appeased around the area at places like

The Cloister, located on Delaware Avenue where Mark Twain lived while he was editor of *The Express.* The Business Executives Dining Award went to the restaurant as one of the top 100 restaurants in the country for 1985.

Farther north on Delaware is the Park Lane Manor House, the reputation of which was established years ago by internationally renowned restaurateur Peter Gust Economou. Then, it's on to Oliver's in North Buffalo and The Saratoga Restaurant, the latter of which offers a dramatically expanded menu under new ownership.

Gourmet treats also abound in such places as Amherst, with the new Cloud 9 offering an Indonesian-flavored menu that changes weekly, and the traditional fare of Asa Ransom House in Clarence, a charming historic inn that was the site of one of Buffalo's pioneers.

Ethnically speaking, Greater Buffalo is a veritable United Nations of culinary enjoyment. The epitome of French dining is found in the cozy Rue Franklin in Allentown. Also in that section of the city is Towne Restaurant, the Greek menu of which many hold in high regard.

Polish. . .East Indian. . .Caribbean. . .they can all be found in Greater Buffalo, which has truly become a melting pot of tastes. Someone once remarked that a person could visit a different area dining establishment each day for a year and not find an inferior meal. That's probably the best testimony to the culinary expanse and expertise of Greater Buffalonians.

CHAPTER THIRTEEN

Scoring

On a sunny Thursday, July 10, 1986, a group of dignitaries gathered near the downtown corner of Washington and Swan streets, next to an old vacant building. An unlikely meeting place for a governor, a mayor, a president of a multimillion-dollar corporation, and other high-profile types? Not when that same corner would serve as home plate when the $55.7-million baseball stadium opens on that site in April 1988.

The event was the ground-breaking for the long-awaited cornerstone in the downtown revival. Governor Mario Cuomo called the stadium project "a celebration of Buffalo's spirit," lauding Mayor James Griffin's persistence in pushing the project through. He called it an example of "partnership at its best," citing how the Republican-controlled Senate and the Democrat-controlled assembly eventually got together to approve the state's $22.5-million advance for the economic development project. Robert E. Rich, Jr., president of both Rich Products, Inc., and the Buffalo Bisons ballclub, also praised Mayor Griffin for "going the extra mile time and time again."

Also acknowledged at the ceremony were the Common Council which was deeply involved with project development; Pilot Air Freight Corporation, which purchased the naming rights to the stadium (Pilot Field); the business community which bought suites to help finance the project; M&T Bank which purchased project bonds; and area labor unions which agreed to a no-strike clause during the construction period.

The governor concluded his remarks by reminding everyone that he wanted to be invited back at least twice—when the new stadium opens and when the city holds its first major league game.

On this bright summer day, the Buffalo Bisons occupied first place in the Eastern Division of the American Association. As the dignitaries took turns wielding sledgehammers against the vacant building that would be demolished to make room for the stadium,

Robert E. Rich, Jr., president of the Buffalo Bisons, contemplates the future prospects of baseball in Buffalo. Photo by Joe Traver

all things seemed possible and the many sports fans of Buffalo were in their glory.

A Whole New Ballgame

After much wrangling with site location, lease agreement, and state approval, the go-ahead was finally given to the downtown stadium project in February 1986. By the spring of 1988, the Buffalo Bisons should be playing the first game in their new home. Whatever the score, the game will be a victory for the downtown renaissance as well as baseball in Buffalo.

For local fans, it was the biggest coup since club president Robert E. Rich, Jr., brought Class AAA baseball back to Buffalo in 1985 after a fifteen-year hiatus.

Actually, the baseball comeback occurred in 1979 when Mayor James D. Griffin formed a local investment group that paid $40,000

Above: Pictured is the 1986 version of the home team. The former Chicago White Sox farm club signed an agreement with the Cleveland Indians for 1987. Photo by Joe Traver

Right: Robert E. Rich, Jr., Bisons president, has been very active in day-to-day involvement with the club. Photo by Joe Traver

for a franchise in the Class AA Eastern League. Although the ninety investors had the right spirit, they lacked the administrative expertise to keep a ballclub going at the box office.

After four struggling seasons, the franchise was purchased by Rich Products Corporation. With hefty corporate financial support and aggressive marketing, the club went from a total attendance figure of 77,000 in 1982 to a league-leading 200,531 the following year.

In 1984 the 223,443 not only led the league again but had the third highest attendance in Eastern League history. Furthermore,

Opposite: The pitch at War Memorial Stadium will give way to the pitcher's mound in new Pilot Field, scheduled to be ready for the 1988 season. Photo by Joe Traver

Right: A dugout blow-up with former Bison Steve Christmas is captured by the camera. Photo by Joe Traver

it placed the Bisons as one of only two Class AA clubs in the country (Nashville was the other) to rank among the top ten in minor league attendance that year.

With the acquisition of a franchise in the American Association in 1985, the season total of 362,762 was fourth-highest in the league and sixth-highest of all minor league clubs. Locally, it represented the most fans ever assembled at War Memorial Stadium during a baseball season.

Despite renovations to bring the old stadium up to Class AAA standards, American Association officials made it clear that the "Old Rockpile" would not be a suitable home for the Bisons over an extended period of time. The future of the franchise in Buffalo

The Old Timers' Games are always a big draw for those who fondly recall such names as Minnie Minoso—and even for those too young to remember. Photo by Joe Traver

was contingent on the building of a new ballpark.

Proponents of that new stadium, though, were looking beyond pacifying the American Association. They were shooting for the big leagues and all the activity and revenue that is generated in a city with such a franchise.

Ballpark Figures

During Buffalo's eighty-three-year affiliation with the International League, many of the 17,000 seats in old Offermann Stadium were often filled. In the 1959 championship season, an attendance record of 413,263 was set. After Offermann's demolition that year,

however, the move to War Memorial Stadium in the 1960s proved to be the team's downfall. The local franchise was forfeited to Winnipeg in 1970.

In the 1970s, though, major-league baseball took a financial turn for the better, taking all of baseball along for the upswing. That prompted Mayor Griffin to spearhead a movement to bring the game back to Buffalo and a new stadium in the process.

"The interest in baseball has always been here," he said when Buffalo landed the American Association berth. "The results show that we have a great marketing base. We can attract people from as far away as Rochester, Syracuse, the Southern Tier, Northern Pennsylvania, and even up into the Ontario peninsula."

Originally, the mayor pushed for a 40,000-seat domed stadium

to be constructed upon a mainly vacant 13.1-acre site bounded by Washington, Swan, Oak, and Exchange streets in the heart of downtown. After much budgetary compromise, an expandable 19,500-seat open-air stadium was agreed upon at an estimated cost of $54.7 million. According to an economic viability report published by the Downtown Stadium Committee, the construction is expected to create 1,400 jobs and add $59 million in wages to the Buffalo economy.

Once the stadium is completed, the Bisons won't be the whole ballgame. The facility will also be able to accommodate professional soccer, concerts, track events, college football, large convocations, and such special events as the Empire State Games and religious crusades.

As a result, the economic viability report estimates that a total of $2.1 million will be spent directly and indirectly in the area, with approximately 110 jobs created and a net tax revenue of $300,000 per year.

With the arrival of a major-league franchise, the numbers rise dramatically. New total direct and indirect spending by visitors and player personnel would top thirty-three million dollars a year. And that's taking into consideration an expansion team struggling to compete. With a team in the thick of a pennant race, the spending is expected to surpass $50 million.

Over 1,100 new full-time equivalent jobs would be supported by the team's operation, the report continues. Of course, that total would increase proportionately to the public's interest in a contending team.

Significant part-time summer jobs would be available for young people, including minority youth. The report cites an example of a typical night game in Kansas City, during which over 700 people are employed in all aspects of the operations. New wages would total nearly sixteen million dollars from direct and indirect spending. Tax revenues, measured only in terms of sales tax increases to state and local government, would approximate five million dollars per year.

But just how realistic is the arrival of a major-league franchise in Buffalo? The prospects are more optimistic than the casual observer might expect. . . .

The Pitch to the Majors

Opposite: The lighting of the torch signaled the beginning of the Empire State Games in Buffalo. Photo by Robert McElroy

In the fledgling days of the National League just a little over a century ago, Buffalo was one of the eight teams, finishing as high as third place in four of its seven big-league seasons. Four players went on to become early members of the Baseball Hall of Fame. Because the club was in financial jeopardy after the 1885 season, however, management decided to sell the entire team to the Detroit Wolverines of the same league for $7,000. That brought an unceremonious end to Buffalo's stay in the majors.

A hundred years later, many people were predicting the city's big-league comeback. And they weren't all local people championing the cause. New York Yankees owner George Steinbrenner felt that Buffalo had a "better than average chance" of being one of the four cities granted a franchise when the National League expands in the next decade. He based it on the area's reputation as a tightly knit community that identified strongly with its sports teams. Steinbrenner pointed out that in the International League days, Buffalo's attendance figures topped all other clubs of the league, including Montreal and Toronto, both of which made it to the majors.

In November 1985 Buffalo officially entered major league baseball's expansion derby when a group headed by Bisons president Robert E. Rich, Jr., met with baseball commissioner Peter Ueberroth and a committee of owners in New York City. As one of twelve cities making a pitch for expansion, the Buffalo delegation felt there was great interest in the city's potential.

The Buffalo contingent included Rich and Northrup R. Knox, vice president and vice chairman of the Buffalo Sabres. Rich would be the majority owner of a Buffalo franchise while Knox, a likely investor in the venture, would lend his experience as the owner of a major league sports team since 1970.

Contained in the Buffalo media packet was an ownership sketch, noting "Ernst & Whinney will verify the net worth of the Rich family, which is substantially in excess of the minimum requirement stated as a criteria for ownership of a major league team." The Rich family reportedly has a net worth of $350 million, $250 million above the minimum required by baseball.

Because major league baseball takes into close consideration a city's television market, the local contingency clarified Buffalo's relatively low ranking (number thirty-four in the U.S.), noting that the rating doesn't include viewership from Rochester and Syracuse via cable, or the viewership in Southern Ontario. The group contended that such a combined market would rank Buffalo eighth in the country.

Although no definite decisions are expected to be made in the near future, major league baseball is known to be considering an expansion by as many as six teams by the early 1990s—two in the American League and four in the National League.

Considering the heights to which Buffalo baseball has risen in its dramatic minor league comeback over the past several seasons, who's to say that the determination of Robert Rich, Jr., Mayor Griffin, and many other local supporters—not to mention the fans— won't bring the big leagues back to the city? The pitch looks good.

The Most Elusive Goal

June 17, 1986, was a sad day for thousands of Buffalo Sabres fans. After sixteen seasons as a Sabre, Gilbert Perreault announced his intended retirement. *Buffalo News* hockey reporter Milt Northrup wrote that the veteran center "was the rock upon

Seen left to right are Buffalo Sabres veterans Gil Perreault, Lindy Ruff, and Mike Foligno ready to break out on the ice. Though Perreault announced his retirement in June 1986, he has since changed his mind and returned for yet another season, to the delight of Buffalo hockey fans. Photo by Bill Wippert

which Buffalo's first NHL [National Hockey League] team was built. Expansion teams are supposed to be dull and pedestrian at the start, but from the first day he stepped on the ice wearing a Sabres crest, Perreault lent dash, excitement, talent and a flair for the dramatic to hockey in Buffalo. He was the last of the superstars who made Buffalo an exciting pro sports town in the mid-1970s—O.J. Simpson, Perreault and Bob McAdoo. Only Perreault endured. His sixteen years was the longest playing career in a Buffalo uniform for a major-league athlete in this city.''

During his final season, Perreault entered the exclusive club for which every hockey player shoots: the 500th goal. In the entire history of the NHL, only ten others have achieved that goal.

While Perreault was most responsible for spreading hockey fever among Western New Yorkers and continually filling the stands of Memorial Auditorium throughout the 1970s, Buffalo has had a love affair on ice since the American Hockey League Bisons skated around the Aud during the 1950s and 1960s. When the Knox family brought a National Hockey League franchise to Buffalo in 1970, big-league momentum was at its peak. Named the Sabres, the team very quickly generated sellout crowds, prompted by Punch Imlach's

Opposite: Mike Ramsey helps goalie Tom Barrasso fend off an attack by the Washington Capitals in Memorial Auditorium. Photo by Bill Wippert

Right: An unusual overhead view of the Sabres' bench shows coach Scotty Bowman calling the shots. Photo by Joe Traver

colorful coaching, the energetic play of rookie sensation Gilbert Perreault, and the staunch goaltending of veteran Roger Crozier.

Several clever drafts created the famous "French Connection" line of Perreault, Richard Martin, and Rene Robert. This exciting trio of high-scorers led the Sabres to their finest season in 1974-1975 with club records of 354 goals and 113 points. It was a season in which the Sabres thrillingly skated their way into the final series of the Stanley Cup playoffs, while fans camped out overnight at the Aud just to be in line the next morning to buy the limited amount of single-game tickets available. For such devotion, the fans were rewarded with a stunning semi-final victory over the Montreal Canadiens, four games to two, but the Sabres bowed to the Philadelphia

Opposite: Phil Housley glides across the ice. Photo by Bill Wippert

Right: He shoots, he scores! Photo by Bill Wippert

Flyers in the finals.

That was the closest the Sabres have ever come to grasping the Stanley Cup. Since then, the Sabres have skated into playoff after playoff, always a bridesmaid, never a bride. Even with the addition of Scotty Bowman behind the bench, hockey's winningest coach has failed to produce that elusive Stanley Cup.

Nevertheless, for over sixteen seasons, Sabres fans have consistently filled the Aud. Although in recent years they haven't enjoyed sellout after sellout as in the past, attendance has still been among the league's best. For instance, even though the Sabres struggled around the 500 mark during the 1985-1986 season, the

The Sabres provide non-stop action at the Aud. Photo by Bill Wippert

team was comfortably resting on the middle rung of the twenty-one-team NHL attendance ladder.

NHL president John Ziegler has referred to the Sabres as one of the league's ''better operations.'' The Knox family has developed a solid reputation for earnestly trying to put a winning team on the ice. They hired hockey's winningest coach, Scotty Bowman. They spent money on solid trades and draft picks. Everyone is primed to hear Ted Darling, the voice of the Sabres, shout his familiar ''He shoots! He SCORES!!'' for the most elusive goal of all—the Stanley Cup, and all the prestige that it would bring the team and the city. Try as he did, Gilbert Perreault couldn't accomplish it single-handedly. But his legacy will live on, giving the team the drive it needs to reach that goal. And the fans will be there to spur the drive.

From Kemp to O.J. to "Oh, No"

Professional football made its debut in Buffalo on September 8, 1946, with an All-America Football Conference (AAFC) team coincidentally named the Bisons. In 1947 the team's name was changed to the Bills, and by 1950 Buffalo was without a professional football team again, a victim of the AAFC's demise.

In 1960, the Bills were back in business as members of the new American Football League (AFL). With such stars as Cookie Gilchrist and future congressman and presidential hopeful Jack Kemp, the Bills won AFL championships in 1964 and 1965, the only major league championships ever held by a Buffalo sports team. The Bills subsequently made the playoffs in 1966, 1974, 1980, and 1981.

When the AFL merged with the National Football League (NFL) in 1970, the Bills joined the Eastern Division of the American

Buffalo Bills keep close watch on the game from the sidelines. Photo by Joe Traver

O.J. Simpson, the Bills' legendary running back, addresses a packed Rich Stadium on his induction into the team's hall of fame. Photo by Joe Traver

Football Conference. In 1973 two milestones were reached. The Bills moved into 80,000-seat Rich Stadium in Orchard Park and, to celebrate, O.J. Simpson became the first professional football player to rush for 2,000 yards in one season. He shattered Jim Brown's previous mark with a record 2,003 yards on December 16, 1973, in a game against the New York Jets in Shea Stadium. Simpson, who had weak legs and wore braces as a child, went on to become not only the most famous Bill but one of football's enduring legends.

The team slumped in the late 1970s until the beginning of this decade when coach Chuck Knox took the Bills into two successive playoffs, recalling the glory years of the mid-1960s and mid-1970s. The excitement reached its peak in a Rich Stadium game telecast

Right: Former quarterback Joe Ferguson is shown signing autographs after a 1980 game. Photo by Robert McElroy

Left: Byron Franklin also accommodates young fans after a 1985 game. Photo by Robert McElroy

Above: Bills' fans are caught up in the excitement of a playoff game in the early '80s. Photo by Robert McElroy

Opposite, top: Rich Stadium is filled to the rafters with 80,000 fans. Photo by Bill Wippert

Opposite, bottom left: Pop star Olivia Newton-John supports the home team during a concert visit to Memorial Auditorium. Photo by Robert McElroy

Opposite, bottom right: Faithful fans get together at one of the many tailgate parties that occur in Rich Stadium parking lots before home games. Photo by Robert McElroy

Above: A pair of gleeful fans eagerly wait for the Rich Stadium gates to open for a brisk November game. Photo by Joe Traver

Above, left: Six points! Photo by Bill Wippert

Left: Bills quarterback Jim Kelly became the highest-paid NFL player when he signed for the 1986 season. His arrival signaled a resurgence of fan interest in the team. Photo by Joe Traver

Left: The Bills provide exciting NFL action for the region's fans. Photo by Bill Wippert

Bottom: A former Bills quarterback rests during a Bills minicamp in May 1982. Photo by Robert McElroy

nationwide on ABC's Monday Night Football, during which a half-time presentation focusing on the Greater Buffalo Chamber of Commerce's "Talking Proud" campaign brought the area new recognition. The nation saw a vibrant city moving ahead.

By the end of the 1985 season, the club had won only four of its last thirty-two games. That certainly was no reason for "Talking Proud." Even the mayor, in his latest bid for re-election, made a campaign promise "to bring pro football back to Buffalo."

A young Bills fan keeps a close eye on his team. Photo by Joe Traver

Opposite: Jim Kelly's rifle arm and the potential of a Bills' comeback in 1986 prompted a dramatic rise in season tickets. Photo by Joe Traver

Many Bills fans, however, weren't laughing. They just stopped coming. On a typical Sunday at the turn of the decade, it wasn't difficult to fill all 80,000 seats at the Orchard Park stadium. During the 1985 season, the team barely attracted a quarter of that capacity.

"If we field a winning, contending, interesting team, we'll have crowds of 80,000 again," Bills owner Ralph Wilson told a *Buffalo News* reporter. "Losing the last two years is not easy for the fans, it's not easy for anybody. But it's there and we're going to try to correct it."

He reaffirmed his faith in head coach Hank Bullough who took over for Kay Stephenson during the 1985 season, emphasizing the importance of establishing continuity in that position. Wilson also maintained that he had no plans to move the club to another city, citing the stadium lease that he has with Erie County through 1997.

What it comes down to is beefing up team performance and, in the process, ticket sales and all the revenue generated by area restaurants, taverns, hotels, tour buses, merchandising, and the other businesses that benefit from a winning team.

411

Opposite: The youthful participants of the Empire State Games
celebrate the opening of the
multisport competition in Buffalo.
Photo by Joe Traver

Above: Buffalo's Empire State
Games not only drew crowds
from across the area but from
across New York. Photo by Joe
Traver

Enter Empire State & UB

The most exciting area sports news in the past few years has
been Buffalo's hosting of the prestigious Empire State Games and
the University at Buffalo's five-year plan to develop a big-time
sports program at the university.

The arrival of the Empire State Games in August 1985 was a real
coup for the area. For the first seven years of its existence, the
statewide amateur athletic competition was held in Syracuse, primarily because of its central location. However, that became less
of a priority as Buffalo, Rochester, Albany, and Long Island began
to express interest in hosting the annual multisports event. Buffalo
was clearly the most vocal in its bid, beginning to make its feelings
known as early as 1981.

The Greater Buffalo contingent, led by state assemblyman
Dennis Gorski, submitted a painstakingly detailed proposal to woo
the games away from Syracuse. The Chamber of Commerce got
the local business community behind the project, arranged meetings with state officials, and confidently guaranteed financial, staff,

413

and promotional support. With Assemblyman Gorski representing the effort in the state capital, Mayor James Griffin and Erie County Executive Edward Rutkowski pulled things together at the local government level.

Ultimately, a wide assortment of Western New Yorkers could proudly take credit for playing a role in Governor Mario Cuomo's announcement at Christmastime 1983 that Buffalo would host the Empire State Games in 1985 and 1986.

Eugene T. Mann, Norstar Bank chairman and chairman of the local organizing committee for the first games here, said that the reason so much effort was expended was two-fold. "Since the first year of the games, we've sent a number of our young athletes to Syracuse to participate, but everyone loves to have a few home games as well. So, this gives our own athletes the opportunity to show off in their home town," he observed. "Secondly, because

Below: One of the rowing teams in the Empire State Games pauses for a break along the Black Rock Canal. Photo by Joe Traver

our city has had such a tremendous rebirth in the last few years, I think it's important that we show that off as well, to as many people from across the state as we can."

Although the economic impact on the area was projected to be around the five-million-dollar mark, Mr. Mann claimed that the "vibrancy" generated by the visitors here would supersede any dollar figure. "What you have are 6,000 participants who will come here for the games and, following them, you have thousands of parents, friends, and people who are interested in athletics," he declared. "I think we're going to surprise all of those people by showing them that Buffalo is a great sports town and [showing them] what great facilities we have."

The most extensive promotional campaign in the history of the

Opposite, top: A long jumper makes his mark in the Empire State Games. Photo by Bill Wippert

Opposite, bottom: The 400-meter race at the Empire State Games was held on the State University of Buffalo running track. Photo by Bill Wippert

Above, left: Empire State runners are seen in a victorious mood. Photo by Joe Traver

Above: A smiling Empire State winner savors her award. Photo by Joe Traver

games got underway in Buffalo, involving corporate support for the first time. Eight local corporate sponsors backed the games, hyping interest through their advertising while offering discounted tickets for events. The University at Buffalo has been the primary host site for the games, with two-thirds of the participants housed on the Amherst campus and the remaining one-third at Buffalo State College.

A record 172,000 spectators witnessed those first Empire State Games held here as more than 6,000 of the state's finest amateur athletes competed in twenty-seven different sports at sites throughout Greater Buffalo, including UB, Buffalo State, Canisius College, Erie Community College North and South, Memorial Auditorium, Buffalo Convention Center, West Side Rowing Club, Buffalo Gun Club, and a variety of high schools, sports clubs, and parks. Three more sports were added to the 1986 games.

In attracting the hundreds of young and mature athletes from around the state, the Empire State Games have been a model of cooperation between the participating institutions and the sponsoring business community.

The sportsmanship of the games and the excitement they have generated throughout the community characterize the sporting nature of a city determined to be competitive. That determination has spread to the area's colleges as well.

416

Canisius College basketball games provide many exciting moments. Photo by Joe Traver

A university determined to be competitive in sports spurred the University at Buffalo's Intercollegiate Athletic Board to develop a five-year plan to move into a big-time sports program. University trustees voted to lift a nineteen-year-old ban on athletic scholarships to clear the way for raising UB's athletic program to the highest level of intercollegiate competition, known as Division I. The university currently competes in Division III in all sports, except baseball, which is Division I.

The school's Amherst Campus has facilities for a full Division I program, except in football. Plans are to build sports teams in hockey, soccer, basketball, and swimming. The football team would be upgraded to Division I-AA, a lower form of Division I competition that includes the major public universities and all of the Ivy League.

UB president Steven B. Sample said that the decision "allows our athletics to be commensurate with our academic objective to become one of the great public research universities of America."

The program would open the door to a number of possibilities down the road. Perhaps a basketball berth in the North Atlantic Conference, facing such rivals as Canisius College and Niagara University. And maybe an NCAA football team. While many budgetary considerations have to be worked out along the way, dreams of competitive Buffalo teams in all collegiate contests don't seem too farfetched at this point.

CHAPTER FOURTEEN

Living Well, Working Well

The most attractive feature of Greater Buffalo for many is the low cost of living. In 1985, the slim 4 to 4.5 percent rise was the lowest in a decade. This, plus the low interest rates of 1984 and 1985 have increased local home building and buying as more and more people are drawn to the value of living in Buffalo. They quickly discover that the Buffalo area is one of the most affordable places for housing and work space in the country. Goldome chairman Ross Kenzie has said that while the bank has occasionally had problems recruiting new employees into Buffalo, once they arrive they become hooked. "When they experience how economical it is to live here and all the things that are available to them, then they don't want to leave," he pointed out.

Other executives echo that misinformed newcomers are constantly surprised at the quality of life here available at little expense. Even if they leave the company that brought them here, many decide to remain in the area, especially if they've experienced the cost of living outside Greater Buffalo. For example, average housing prices in Houston can run twice that of Buffalo's, and New York City's is about three times as much.

Confirming this observation is the Nationwide Relocation Service index, which annually assesses housing values in 200 markets across the country. It consistently ranks Greater Buffalo within the top ten in regard to the lowest-cost housing at high quality standards.

According to the Buffalo Board of Realtors, low interest rates helped make 1985 the third consecutive year in which sales of one- and two-family homes and condominiums increased. The Greater Buffalo Chamber of Commerce reported that the local home building scene also enjoyed a three-year increase, thanks to a falling interest rate which hit 10.73 percent by the end of 1985. By spring of 1986, interest rates dipped below the 10 percent mark and the demand for housing skyrocketed more than ever.

Again in 1985, both the realtors and the home builders benefited from the State of New York Mortgage Agency's (SONYMA) Affordable Housing Program, financing about 600 home purchases in Western New York. In early 1986, Governor Mario Cuomo proposed spending an extra $2.5 billion over the next five years to help fund new housing in New York State. Of that figure, one billion dollars would be allocated to the SONYMA program.

With such incentives to first-time home purchasers and low interest rates continuing into 1986, Greater Buffalo's reputation for low-cost housing remains one of the best values in the country.

The Move Downtown

"Downtown is becoming an increasingly desirable lifestyle

nationally. Indeed, it is hard to think of any city with an active, attractive downtown that does not have a large resident population."

With that thought, a downtown master plan prepared by consulting firms from Toronto and New York City under the supervision of the city's Division of Planning was issued in November 1985. The goal the consultants set was 150 units of housing developed in downtown Buffalo each year. They said it would create "a sense of activity and interest on downtown streets" and generate more visitors and shoppers to the heart of the city.

The plan calls for "a much broader range of households" than the lower income, non-family, and elderly households currently living in the downtown area. The consultants feel that "the attraction of home ownership and moderate and upper-income households" should be the focus.

Opposite: Relaxed townhouse living is a key part of waterfront development. Photo by Joe Traver

"It is these groups," they add, "who will do the most to transform the environment of potential residential areas and who provide greatest support to area restaurants, stores and entertainment facilities."

The master plan concludes that downtown has opportunities for developing 845 to 1,055 housing units through reuse of existing buildings and 2,100 to 2,300 units through new construction.

The consultants consider the Franklin/Pearl/Delaware area as the top priority for new housing construction and the Theater District as the first location for rehabilitating existing buildings into housing.

Low density housing will be constructed at the outset, "first, because the market evidence suggests initially a stronger townhouse than apartment market; and second, in order to achieve a neighborhood transformation quickly over a wider area."

City planners see the 150-unit-a-year goal as being ambitious but possible. They point to the first test of the downtown housing market already in progress—the long-vacant two-story Ansonia Building at the northwest corner of Main and Tupper streets.

The Ansonia and More

The Ansonia Centre, formerly a commercial structure, was gutted and renovated into retail space on the first floor and fifty-nine upscale apartments on the upper floors. It's a pioneering effort, testing the downtown housing market.

The developers are gearing for a tenant base consisting of a young professional group that works downtown and desires to live at the north edge of the Theater District, across from the Studio

Above: Kite-flying is springtime recreation in the heart of downtown. Photo by Joe Traver

Right: Young people gather for fun at one of the many outdoor events along the Main Street corridor. Photo by Robert McElroy

Above: A young downtown visitor gets a dad's-eye view of activities. Photo by Robert McElroy

Above, right: The annual CityFest downtown brings together many groups for cultural celebration and just plain clowning around. Photo by Robert McElroy

Right: Stylish Buffalo shirts help boost the city's image. Photo by Robert McElroy

Above: The Casino has long been a Delaware Park landmark. Photo by Susan Gawlick

Right: The beauty of the city sky-line is photographed in late fall. Photo by Dennis R. Floss

Left: A toddler is treated to a summertime shower in a Buffalo neighborhood. Photo by Joe Traver

Top: A happy trio gets ready to play. Photo by Joe Traver

Above, left: Characteristic regional architecture is seen in this aerial view of a west-side neighborhood. Photo by Joe Traver

Left: A pint-sized lineup of perhaps future Buffalo Bills are coached in a city park. Photo by Bill Wippert

The Ansonia Centre has been a key element in encouraging downtown residency. Photo by Joe Traver

Arena Theatre, and less than a block from other entertainment and dining attractions.

City hall aided the Ansonia project with a loan of $1.32 million gained in an urban development action grant from the federal government and with short-term construction loans.

The action-grant program is seen to be the key to further downtown housing efforts. The city is counting on nearly a million dollars from the program to help finance the renovation of the Vernor Building at 752 Main into stores and twenty apartments, and over half a million to aid the remodeling of the Roanoke Hotel at 206 South Elmwood Avenue.

In planning the Metro Rail corridor running out of downtown to the north, housing was emphasized. The proposal is that all commercial development along the line have a one-third residential component as a way to increase rail-line ridership. A key part of the plan involves the construction of a roadway along railroad rights-of-way between Kenmore Avenue and Amherst Street to open up as much as fifty acres for potential housing development.

State funding will also figure heavily in a variety of housing pro-

Residents check the lotto winners while waiting for a bus along Elmwood Avenue. Photo by Joe Traver

grams. The Affordable Home Ownership Development Program, a new state program designed to promote home ownership among low- and middle-income persons, is opening funding possibilities. City hall has applied for more than three million dollars under this state effort, with an eye toward funding the proposed fifty-six-unit Rebecca Park development.

In the Pratt-William area of the inner city, more state funding would continue construction of subsidized single-family houses for sale to owner-occupants. Fifty houses have already been built using scattered city-owned lots and federal subsidies, and another twenty-five are in progress at this writing.

At William Street and Fillmore Avenue, another subsidized program—this one church-sponsored—is also in progress. Thirty-nine single-family homes and fifty apartment units for the elderly are expected to be built in Adamski Village. A sixteen-unit single-family development is also being constructed on a site bounded by Oneida, Howard, Bond, and Lord streets.

Along the waterfront redevelopment area near the Erie Basin Marina, top-shelf housing is continuing. Twenty more townhouse units are scheduled at Rivermist; at least sixteen more condominium units at the Breakwaters; and about thirty more condo units at Marina Village.

Gull Landing, a 3.3-acre site on the waterfront, is being planned as a mixed residential and commercial development. On lands east of LaSalle Park on the waterfront, construction of ninety-eight owner-occupied townhouses are in the works.

All of this measures up to a renaissance of lifestyle options deep within the heart of the downtown renaissance. This move back to the city is attracting young urban professionals in dual income families, earning $24,000 to $49,000 a year. They're attracted to the idea of a short walk or subway ride to the office, a brief jaunt to any number of dining options, from gourmet to a burger along the Marina, the proximity of the Theater District and the nightlife, and the close shopping variety of the anchor department stores, Main Place Mall, and the pedestrian mall. They represent the key to a thriving urban center that doesn't become an instant ghost town once the workday ends.

Office Space

St. Patrick's Day is rousingly cele-brated by the Tonawanda Clown Band along the parade route. Photo by Joe Traver

The value of Buffalo's office space is as well regarded as its housing value. According to the Greater Buffalo Chamber, the average office building lease is 22 percent below the national average. And,

Opposite: The rear of City Hall is seen in this downtown view. Photo by Envisions Co.

Above: Some familiar downtown landmarks are pictured at striking angles. Photo by Envisions Co.

while national urban core Class-A rates have consistently risen 30 percent annually, Buffalo's annual increases have been only 6 percent.

Despite that financial enticement, however, office occupancy rates in downtown Buffalo had been falling for more than two years, until a September 1985 survey by the Buffalo Building Owners and Managers Association (BOMA) showed an increase of 2.65 percentage points. The 82.6 downtown office occupancy rate at the time showed the first increase since the building owners started doing a biannual survey in March 1983. Both city planners and BOMA officials attributed it to the rise in bank expansion.

Marine Midland Bank was one of the biggest contributors to the increased occupancy rate when it leased an additional 30,000 square feet of space in the Roblin Building for its expanded credit-card processing operations.

Empire of America Federal Savings Bank moved 35,000 square feet of offices—including some from Amherst—into its Main Place headquarters. Both banks claimed that it was more convenient to move certain operations within easy access. Also, the Cigna Corporation insurance firm moved from a 26,000-square-foot location in Marine Midland Center to a 68,000-square-foot site in Goldome Center.

Further contributing to the occupancy rise are the law firm of Saperston Day Lustig Gallick Kirschner & Gaglione which took 50,970 square feet in Goldome Center, while Shearson Lehman American Express took 14,684 square feet. That made the 368,138 square feet of space in Goldome Center, which previously had been 60 percent occupied, fully leased.

Ironically enough, many building owners blamed the Goldome Center—among other projects—for the previous occupancy declines. Because that building, along with the Norstar Building and several others, were built with the aid of city subsidies, building owners said those properties lured tenants from existing buildings and, in the process, created a glut of office space. That controversy prompted the formation of the Office Space Vacancy Task Force which also came up with some optimistic news in late 1985.

The task force found that the city's "office absorption rate"—the rate by which offices become occupied—has been 262,000 square feet per year since May 1982. That means more and more offices have been opening up downtown, even while the occupancy rate was falling due to the construction of new buildings.

City planners agreed that the absorption rate showed significant growth in the kinds of industries that choose downtown office locations.

Opposite: Buffalo celebrated its sesquicentennial in grand style along Delaware Avenue in 1982. Photo by Robert McElroy

Building & Buying

In early 1986, a survey of forty metropolitan areas by the National Association of Realtors rated the Buffalo/Niagara Falls market as the least expensive place to live in the U.S., based on single-family housing. Statistics compiled by the Greater Buffalo Board of Realtors at that time revealed that the average home in Erie County during 1985 cost between $40,000 and $49,900.

The most popular home buying areas in the city continue to be North Buffalo, the Delaware District, and the near West Side. These areas offer a wealth of stately older homes with such amenities as carved woodwork, several working fireplaces, and solid plaster construction—features that are difficult to duplicate in new homes because of today's prohibitive costs for such workmanship. Greater Buffalo, in fact, has a unique ratio of one new home built to every ten existing homes that are resold. That far surpasses the national average of one for three, making for an abundant local supply of quality existing houses available at a lower cost than it would take to build a comparable one in today's market.

Despite a sharp decline in new housing construction across the nation, building starts in the Niagara Frontier have risen in 1986.

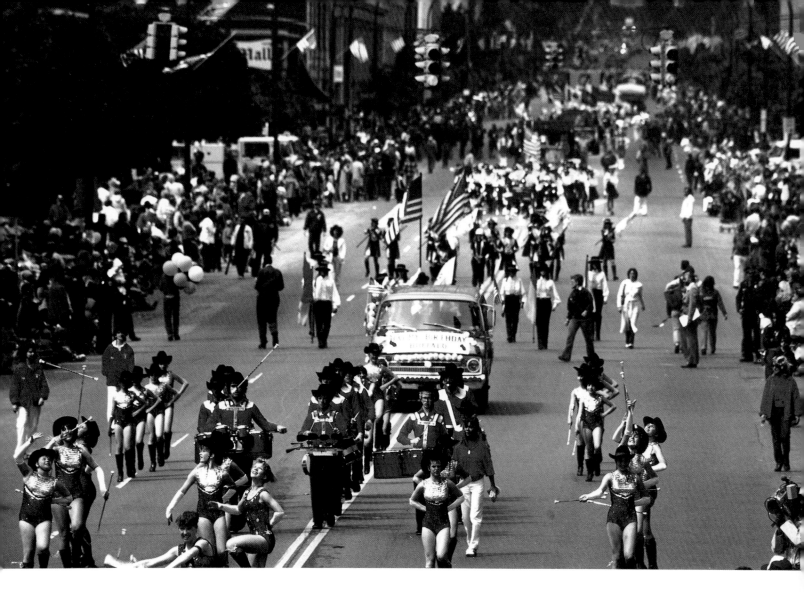

One expert attributed it to favorable mortgage rates and the area's steady transition from blue-collar to white.

While the cost of an average new home in Greater Buffalo is around $125,000, efforts are being made to expand the "affordable" housing market. For example, M.J. Peterson Company produced seventy-five brick Victorian reproduction houses in the Pratt-Willert Park area of Buffalo which cost $65,000 to build. With federal and city assistance, however, the three-bedroom, one-and-a-half bath homes can be developed by the private sector and sold to lower- and middle-income families for $40,000, according to a company spokesman. Fifty more of these homes were slated to be built in 1986.

The higher end of the new building scale is in the prime suburban locations of Amherst and Orchard Park. The presence of the University of Buffalo campus and the expansive Audubon Industrial Park has made the Town of Amherst the leading suburb for new home starts in the last decade. Much of Orchard Park's growth has blossomed since the arrival of Rich Stadium in 1973, particularly in the stately Jewett-Holmwood area where Motown recording star Rick James, a native of Buffalo's East Side, has a home with a built-in recording studio. It was there that he produced his friend Eddie Murphy's singing debut "Party All the Time" in 1985.

The suburbs around Greater Buffalo are filled with variety. The area ranges from the historic village charm of East Aurora and Clarence, reminiscent of New England, to the pastoral splendor of Elma and Alden, the rural beauty of Arcade and Franklinville, and the convenience and accessibility of Kenmore, Tonawanda, and Cheektowaga. Home buyers can choose from the trappings of career success in Williamsville and East Amherst, the rolling hills of Boston, the canal character of Lockport, and the lakeshore view along Hamburg.

The city of Buffalo also has its variety. It offers the historic village charm of Allentown, the quaint homes of which have been lovingly preserved. Authors Samuel (Mark Twain) Clemens and F. Scott Fitzgerald once resided in this section just north of downtown. The magnificent mansions along Delaware Avenue now serve as headquarters for such burgeoning companies as Computer Task Group and Healy-Schutte & Company, as well as the Greater Buffalo Chapter of the Red Cross and Canisius High School. Elmwood Avenue features a combination of preppiness and collegiate style with the rows of specialty shops and pubs affectionately referred to as the Elmwood Strip. The "lifestyles of the rich and famous" are housed in the sumptuous mansions in the Delaware Park and Nottingham-Middlesex areas. Handsome North Buffalo reveals a close-knit character.

The lifestyle options are plentiful all around Western New York, with the homes and surrounding amenities and conveniences geared to anyone's needs.

Above, left: Motown recording star and Buffalo native Rick James, left, is seen relaxing at his Orchard Park home with comedy film star Eddie Murphy. Photo by Robert McElroy

Above: This handsome Victorian is a prime example of the architectural wealth located in Greater Buffalo. Photo by Joseph Cascio

Above: Rows of venerable houses grace a typical West Side neighborhood. Photo by Melissa C. Beckman

Left: The former home of President Millard Fillmore, a Buffalo native, is a city landmark. Photo by Joe Traver

The State University of New York at Buffalo:

NEW YORK'S MAJOR PUBLIC UNIVERSITY CAMPUS

Hayes Hall, on the South Campus of SUNY-Buffalo, is a proud reminder of the institution's 140-year tradition.

The State University of New York at Buffalo (SUNY-Buffalo) is New York State's major public university campus. Its range of academic programs and services is the broadest of any public institution in New York and New England. Nationally, the university ranks in the top 30 of all public and private institutions in terms of the quality of its graduate faculty.

More New Yorkers come from all over the state to study at SUNY-Buffalo at every level—baccalaureate, master's, professional, doctoral, and postdoctoral—than go to any other campus in the State University system. The institution's diversity is represented by the more than 300 registered degree programs offered. Indeed, the university awards more bache-

lor's degrees each year than any public or private institution in the state. SUNY-Buffalo also offers more doctoral degrees than the other three SUNY university centers combined, and is one of the leading institutions in the nation in terms of postdoctoral enrollment.

During the past two decades New York State has undertaken a program to build an entirely new academic core campus for the university while also renovating the original campus to serve as a comprehensive health sciences center. To date, 1,200 acres have been acquired and developed, and 100 new buildings have been constructed. Several additional major structures will complete campus development by 1990. As a result of this investment of nearly a half-billion dollars, SUNY-Buffalo has the most modern physical facilities of any major university in the United States.

A comprehensive research pro-

gram conducted by more than 4,000 full-time and affiliated faculty members generates grants and contracts worth more than $55 million annually. The world's first cancer research center, now known as Roswell Park Memorial Institute, was founded in Buffalo in 1898, and today approximately 20 research centers and institutes are at work on campus. The Ernest Witebsky Center for Immunology is the only university-affiliated immunology center in the nation. In addition, SUNY-Buffalo's Environmental and Hyperbaric Physiology Laboratory contains one of the world's most sophisticated diving capsules.

The university houses the National Earthquake Engineering Research Center, the only one of its kind in the country. The Center for Neurobiology was founded in 1968 by Nobel Laureate Sir John Eccles, and the nation's first Center for Clinical Pharmacokinetics and Biopharmaceutics was established at SUNY-Buffalo six years later. The Periodontal Disease Clinical Research Center, established in 1977, is internationally known for its work, and funding for this program has moved the university's School of Dental Medicine into fifth place among all U.S. dental schools in terms of research grants from the National Institute of Dental Research. The Center for Cold Regions Science and Technology, associated with the Department of Geology's Ice Core Laboratory, is well known for its work in the polar regions of Greenland and Antarctica, and for its curatorship and distribution of ice-core samples worldwide.

SUNY-Buffalo has a strong commitment to assist in the economic revitalization of western New York. This includes major initiatives to use the university's research capabilities and faculty expertise in creating new industries and new jobs. For example, in 1984 SUNY-Buffalo, in cooperation with the Western New York Technology Development Center, established the first high-technology incubator in the SUNY system and 13 new firms were created in the first full year of operation. The university also broke new ground when it established the Calspan-UB Research Center, the first joint venture between a State University of New York campus and a major private corporation. One of the state's new Centers for Advanced Technology, a Health Care Instruments and Devices Institute, has also been established here to promote commercial production of technological breakthroughs developed by the faculty.

Indeed, the faculty of the university have been responsible for many scientific and technological advancements. The implantable heart pacemaker was developed at the university by Dr. William M. Chardack and Dr. Andrew Gage, both faculty members in the Department of Surgery, and by Dr. William Greatbatch, a faculty member in electrical engineering. Dr. Robert Guthrie, professor of

The Joseph Ellicott Complex, on the new North Campus, consists of 38 buildings that provide a living-learning environment for many of the university's residential students.

pediatrics, devised the internationally used PKU test for the early identification of an inherited metabolic disorder.

Dr. Herbert Hauptman, a SUNY-Buffalo research professor of biophysical sciences, and medical and research director of the Medical Foundation of Buffalo, Inc., was co-winner of the 1985 Nobel Prize in Chemistry. The award was given for his development of a mathematical method to determine the three-dimensional crystal structure of biologically important molecules, such as hormones, vitamins, and antibiotics. The technique is now a primary method in producing new drugs and chemicals useful to industry and medicine.

With a total work force of approximately 4,500 full-time employees and 7,500 part-time workers including student assistants and volunteers, SUNY-Buffalo is Western New York's second-largest employer and a major contributor to the region's economy. In fact, the university also generates between 20,000 and 25,000 off-campus jobs for the citizens of Western New York.

In addition to economic benefits and educational services, the institution contributes to the quality of life in the region through such activities as an annual program of 200 concerts, recitals, operas, and other musical performances. The university also has a public radio station, WBFO-FM, and presents theatrical offerings at the Pfeiffer Theatre in downtown Buffalo and an annual Shakespeare program in Delaware Park.

Hundreds of physicians affiliated with the School of Medicine provide care in most major community hospitals. In addition, approximately 40,000 individuals receive dental and consulting services each year in the School of Dental Medicine's public clinics.

SUNY-Buffalo has had a proud history and strong tradition of ac-

A research program, which attracts grants and contracts worth more than $55 million annually, is a key element in SUNY-Buffalo's commitment to economic development in Western New York.

ademic leadership since its founding in 1846 by Millard Fillmore, the 13th President of the United States, and other professional leaders of the rapidly developing settlement of Buffalo. The university began as a medical school, which now is one of the oldest in the nation, having continuously offered the M.D. degree for 140 years.

Today instruction at the university is organized under 16 faculties and schools: architecture, arts and letters, natural sciences and mathematics, social sciences, engineering and applied sciences, law and jurisprudence, management, educational studies, social work, information and library studies, medicine, dental medicine, nursing, dental, pharmacy, health-related professions, and Roswell Park Memorial Institute.

Created by its founders to be "eminently useful to its community," the University at Buffalo has never hesitated to serve the citizens of Western New York. This service is especially important today as the university establishes itself among the very top research universities in the nation.

Opposite: A row of brownstones adds character to a section of Allentown. Photo by Joe Traver

Right: Some of Buffalo's officers pause to chat. Photo by Robert McElroy

Below: Flower boxes adorn the courtyard of an Elmwood Avenue apartment building. Photo by Melissa C. Beckman

Above: This handsome stone building serves as town hall in picturesque East Aurora. Photo by Joe Traver

Left: Bicyclists are silhouetted along a cobblestone road in East Aurora. Photo by Joe Traver

Above: Hand-crafted quilts are perennial favorites at the many arts and crafts festivals held throughout Western New York.

Top: The Amherst Youth Band entertains at a lunchtime concert downtown.

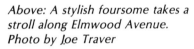

Above: A stylish foursome takes a stroll along Elmwood Avenue. Photo by Joe Traver

Above, right: This columned building is Delaware Avenue headquarters for local developer Paul Snyder. Photo by Joe Traver

Right: Artistic neon lights up the Elmwood Strip after dark. Photo by Joe Traver

Erie Community College

This colorful mural greets students and visitors as they enter the administration building of the North Campus in Williamsville. Painted by an ECC instructor, it highlights pictorially the many facets of Erie Community College.

The City Campus, in downtown Buffalo, is listed on the National Register of Historic Places, and features an expansive atrium, which was used to light the sorting floor of the old Post Office.

Erie Community College has a rich tradition of service to the area, dating back to its founding in 1946. Today, with three campuses in full operation, the institution serves the population of Erie County with facilities designed to meet the post-secondary educational needs of Western New Yorkers.

On April 4, 1946, the New York State Legislature established the New York State Institute of Applied Arts and Sciences at Buffalo as a two-year technical college for high school graduates. The institution offered eight programs when its doors first opened in the fall of 1947.

At the time of its founding Erie Community College was housed in the former office building of the Pierce Arrow Motor Car Company on Elmwood Avenue. In 1953 the name Erie County Technical Institute was adopted when the county assumed local sponsorship of the school under a new state law. At the same time a tu-

ition and fee system was put into effect. In 1960 the institute was moved to a new campus, consisting of eight buildings on 120 acres of land at Main Street and Youngs Road in Williamsville; today that facility is known as the North Campus. The name Erie Community College was adopted nine years later—to more accurately reflect the school's mission.

In 1971 the City Campus was instituted, and the college became the first multicampus operation in the state outside of New York City. The former Bishop O'Hern High School at Main and Riley streets became the City Campus' temporary home.

While various sites were being examined for a permanent downtown location, plans for the South Campus were initiated. In October 1974 the $18-million South Campus opened its doors in Orchard Park. This addition allowed the college to service all Erie County residents with three accessible locations.

In the fall of 1979 the old post office building on Ellicott Street was turned over to Erie Community College for renovation. It later became the permanent site of the

The South Campus, in Orchard Park, features accessibility to the handicapped as this angular view of the campus shows. Home site of the Special Olympics, the Recreation Program at South sponsors a volunteer recreation program for handicapped children and adults.

City Campus.

Erie Community College's three distinctive learning environments service more than 13,000 community residents through various classes and programs. The institution takes pride in offering its students a well-rounded college education, coupled with the skills needed to cope with the complexities of the modern-day world. Today students have a choice of more than 60 academic programs and 15 certificate programs.

In addition, Erie Community College is a leader in intercollegiate sports on the community college level, boasting many national championships. Competition between colleges is available in virtually all major sports for both men and women. An extensive intramural program is sponsored at all three campuses of the institution.

Today Erie Community College, which is part of the State University of New York system, is headed by Dr. Louis M. Ricci, president.

443

Schools & Churches

Admittedly, the University at Buffalo has received considerable mention throughout this book. And with good reasons. The university is New York State's largest educational center, with nationally ranked schools of medicine, engineering, business, dentistry, pharmacy, law, and other professional advanced-degree programs. The name "Buffalo" is being spread to Asia as a result of the university's recent acceptance of one of the largest training grants in the history of the State University of New York system. With this $20-million grant, UB will establish an institute in Malaysia to train engineers and business people and prepare them for schooling in the U.S. The Malaysians preferred UB because they were familiar with the university's management program in China. Plus, UB has a third Asian link: an exchange program of professors from UB and Peking. With such a global reach, UB president Dr. Steven Sample referred to the school "as a major international university with a focus in international education." It is that aspect—in addition to the important research and economic impact to the area—that makes UB stand out.

That's not to imply, however, that higher education in the area is confined to the 26,000 students attending UB. Sizable student populations are also found at seven state and private four-year institutions and six public and private two-year colleges across the Niagara Frontier.

The State University College at Buffalo, commonly called Buffalo State, has been a highly regarded part of the community since it opened as a teacher's college in 1871. Since the 1950s, the college has greatly expanded in size, enrollment, and diversity of programs. Under D. Bruce Jonstone's current presidency, business studies, broadcast journalism, and computer science are among the leading programs. Rockwell Hall, a venerable landmark on Elmwood Avenue and the college's most visible building, is undergoing an eleven-million-dollar renovation which will house a world-class master's level program in art conservation, along with the Burchfield Art Center, which features the works of the late nationally renowned watercolorist—and Buffalonian—Charles Burchfield.

Canisius College, the second oldest institution of higher education in Buffalo (next to UB), has been one of the area's leading private institutions for well over a century. Under Reverend James M. Demske's twenty-year leadership, the Jesuit college has developed courses in computer science, management information systems, and educational computing. Many high-ranking executives across the nation—such as Gene F. Jankowski, CBS presi-

Bryant & Stratton Business Institute

With a baker's dozen of colleges and universities located within its environs, the Buffalo metropolitan area is considered a leading center of higher education in New York State.

Leading the way in the business sector of local higher education is one of those 13 schools—Bryant & Stratton Business Institute. Few people may be aware of it, but Bryant & Stratton not only leads the way in Western New York, but also is the single largest business school in the nation.

For those who like to keep track of Buffalo's biggest and best, that's a pretty impressive position. It was made possible thanks, in part, to the use of three locations within walking distance of its downtown, Main Street location. In addition, Bryant & Stratton operates its Eastern Hills school for the convenience of the total population and the expanding needs of business locations in the surrounding towns.

For the staff of the school,

which is headquartered at 1028 Main Street, the number they're most likely to boast about is how many of the institution's graduates are placed in jobs. In 1985 that figure was more than 1,400—a success rate of 90 percent of those who used the placement facilities. Impressive indeed, and a fitting statistic for a school whose motto is "Learning for Earning."

Bryant & Stratton has garnered these high marks by continually setting standards for business education, from its founding in 1854 right up to the present.

Established by Dr. J.C. Bryant, a noted Buffalo physician, educator, and businessman, the institute was a champion of hands-on career training back in the days when "hardware" meant a pennyweight of nails, not the powerful IBM computers found on today's campuses. The first course offered was bookkeeping. But in a move typical of its drive for innovation, the school's discontent with the established bookkeeping curriculum led it to develop its own system. By the end of the nineteenth century Bryant & Stratton's methodology had become the accepted standard of business and industry.

Now well into its second century of providing quality training,

business and industry continue to be major themes at the school.

In 1983 Bryant & Stratton expanded a curriculum that already included accounting, business administration, fashion merchandising, and seven other specialties by adding a program in electronic technology. Developed in response to research that indicated an increasing demand for highly qualified electronic technicians, the high-tech program is guided by an advisory board consisting of representatives from many of Buffalo's leading research and manufacturing firms. The development of this new program and its administrative structure reflect the school's unique relationship with the businesses and industries that will provide employment for its future graduates not only in electronic technology, but also in the other career-path courses it offers.

Innovation, a close relationship with the business community, a commitment to hands-on training, and a dedication to placing its students in jobs with a future, that is how Bryant & Stratton Business Institute has led the nation in business education since 1854—and no doubt how it will continue to lead in the years to come.

Above: State University of Buffalo students head toward their next class on the Main Street campus. Photo by Joe Traver

Top: The contemporary architectural sweep of Temple Beth Zion is a distinctive feature of Delaware Avenue. Photo by Melissa C. Beckman

dent—are Canisius graduates.

Canisius, Niagara University, and St. Bonaventure are known as much for their NCAA Division I basketball teams as they are for their studies. Daemen, D'Youville, Medaille, Houghton, Trocaire, Hilbert, and Villa Maria colleges form a variety of private institutions that offer a wealth of learning options. Erie Community College is the area's leading public two-year institution, headquartered in Williamsville with branches in the South Towns and in the heart of downtown, magnificently housed in the renovated Old Post Office, a massive Gothic edifice originally dedicated in 1901.

Beneath the college level, Western New York has an extensive system of preschool, elementary, and secondary institutions. Over 350 public schools and more than twenty-five private and parochial schools offer a range of educational programs for students of all ages, levels, interest, and desires. Quality facilities cater to the gifted and the handicapped. A wide assortment of evening courses in colleges and high schools cater to those adults who seek further education. The Greater Buffalo educational system truly constitutes a choice network of learning options.

Religious institutions also play an important role in the area. The Roman Catholic faith is predominant, with the Buffalo Diocese among the largest in the country. St. Joseph's Cathedral downtown is the cornerstone of the diocese. St. Louis Church at Main and Edward is the oldest parish, founded in 1832 when the city was incorporated. Our Lady of Victory National Shrine and Basilica in Lackawanna is architecturally world-famous and its founder, the late Reverend Nelson Baker, is a legendary figure in humanitarianism.

A prime example of the religion's unified efforts in the area is the annual Catholic Charities drive around Eastertime. Known as the

campaign that always succeeds, Catholic Charities always surpasses its substantial goal—money which goes to serve a variety of worthy organizations in Greater Buffalo.

Landmarks of other faiths around the area include St. Paul's Episcopal Cathedral, a landmark in the heart of downtown since 1820; First Presbyterian Church which dates back to 1823; and the dramatic contemporary architectural sweep of Temple Beth Zion on Delaware Avenue. Members of these faiths—along with the Baptists, Lutherans, Greek Orthodox, Serbian Orthodox, et al.—make up an area that is deeply committed to its religious beliefs.

In fact, it symbolizes the commitment and variety of all the many different people and lifestyles that prevail throughout Greater Buffalo. A quality of life. A spectrum of choice.

447

448

CHAPTER FIFTEEN

The Finer Things of Life

Listen only to the bad comics who aim cheap shots at Buffalo and you gather an impression of a city buried in snow. But listen to a Buffalonian—especially someone who has come here from somewhere else—and you get a very different impression. You're talking to a person who is exhilarated by the distinct change of seasons and the surprisingly temperate climate. You're talking to a person who enjoys the snowfall for what it offers—the best skiing this side of Vermont, and a lot more economical. You're talking to a person who is overwhelmed by the amount of cultural options: an evening at the Philharmonic, at an intimate jazz club, at the ballet, or at a stadium rock concert.

Because most students today strive for more than a baccalaureate degree, the University at Buffalo attracts a large segment of extraordinarily bright people at the end of their educational experience. Eventually, their discoveries of the area's cultural, recreational, and overall lifestyle amenities encourage them to begin their careers in Buffalo. Perhaps more than anyone, they represent the career potential, population stabilization, and subsequent economic revitalization of Greater Buffalo. The eighteen colleges and universities within the eight-county area—eleven of them in Buffalo—have played a large role in advancing economic recovery.

Despite demographics indicating a drastic decrease in high school graduates, Buffalo schools have maintained enrollment and

Ski competitions, such as this one held at popular Kissing Bridge just south of Buffalo, attract many participants and observers. Photo by Joe Traver

Left: This trio proves that winter can be fun as they take a slide down a snowy hill at Delaware Park. Photo by Joe Traver

Below: Fresh snow and a sunny Sunday are all this trio needs for a winter frolic in a West Side neighborhood. Photo by Joe Traver

Left: A sunny, wind-blown day in a Lockport park is enjoyed by this pair of autumn revelers. Photo by Joe Traver

Below: The annual pumpkin festival in Collins, just south of Buffalo, is one of autumn's delights. Photo by Joe Traver

Above: Amidst a sea of concert-goers, this fan lets the photographer know how much she's enjoying one of Greater Buffalo's many outdoor performances. Photo by Peter R. Barber

Right: A couple enjoys fishing on a hot summer afternoon from the Front Park pier along the Lake Erie shore. Photo by Joe Traver

Far right: Balancing the bubbly at an outdoor summertime event in Allentown. Photo by Robert McElroy

453

funding through aggressive marketing and specially tailored courses to attract new students.

For example, nearly every school now offers a wide range of night classes and services to accommodate adult students. And for those people wishing to attend college without participating in campus life, Cornell University's School of Industrial and Labor Relations has been operating a successful experiment with classes being taught in the Boulevard Mall branch of Sibley's department store.

State University at Buffalo has not only been striving to become one of the top public universities in the country, but it also has become a force in revitalizing the local economy. To illustrate, UB president Dr. Steven Sample points out that most of the student population comes from outside the region. Considering that a visiting student spends an average of $4,000 per year in various area purchases, that pumps up the Western New York economy by a remarkable $600 million annually.

He observed that many feel UB is ''the essential catalyst for the economic revitalization of this region.'' The president himself works

For decades, this characteristic edifice at the front of the State University of Buffalo's Main Street campus has most readily symbolized the school. Photo by Joe Traver

toward that goal by participating in various economic councils and the Greater Buffalo Chamber. The university also reaches out through a unique management program which teaches American businessmen how to trade with China and the Far East, and through the Center for Regional Studies which provides ideas that foster economic rebirth. UB's sprawling Amherst campus has also reached out in another significant way to advance the downtown renaissance.

The Theater District

By 1990 the cultural life in Greater Buffalo will be greatly enhanced by the presence of a new thirty-five-million-dollar center for the fine and performing arts on the UB Amherst campus. Perhaps more importantly at this point, though, is UB's renewed commitment to the remodeled and renamed Pfeiffer Theatre downtown—formerly the Center Theatre and, before that, the site

Pictured is the lobby of Theater Place downtown, home of several eating establishments, an art gallery, office space, and Buffalo's primary nightclub, the Tralfamadore Cafe. Photo by Melissa C. Beckman

of the old Studio Arena Theatre and legendary Town Casino nightclub.

The importance of the Pfeiffer Theatre is twofold: one, to maintain the university's presence downtown and, two, to spark momentum for the success of the Theater District.

The FNUB Corporation purchased the building from the Studio Arena in late 1985. After having rented the theater from the Studio for seven years previously, the university now has a five-year lease from FNUB, about the time it will take to construct the new Amherst campus center.

Until the two new performance centers are opened on the Amherst campus, major university productions will be held at the Pfeiffer. After that, officials will reassess the production options and the continued presence of UB within the Theater District. Plans at this writing include a possible cooperative venture with the Studio Arena Theatre. When the Pfeiffer was dedicated in April 1986, a joint production of *Fiddler on the Roof* was staged by the university and Buffalo State College.

Although its theatrical scope is undecided once the new campus fine arts center is opened, the Pfeiffer Theatre promises to be among the big three that make up the anchors of the Theater District. Right now, the thinking is to give the theater its own identity and not just make it a rental house. That identity vs. rental policy is of even greater concern at the grand showplace across the street from the Pfeiffer.

Shea's Buffalo

The sixty-year history of this landmark consists of many sparkling opening nights. Legendary showman Mike Shea built the 3,000-seat facility in 1926, giving it a grand opera house quality. He decorated it with priceless European crystal chandeliers, Tiffany-designed interiors, and one of the largest Wurlitzer pipe organs ever built.

When audiences began to drop off in the 1960s and 1970s because of the general downtown tailspin, those exquisite pieces began to fall into disrepair until a group of dedicated volunteers began a major restoration job. The Friends of Shea's Buffalo accomplished a significant amount of their task for a grand reopening in 1976, the theater's golden anniversary. Since then, Shea's has been the shining hope of the Theater District in the downtown renaissance. Touring productions such as *Annie, Camelot* with Richard Harris, and *Evita* have played to packed houses.

Unfortunately, however, there have also been some not-so-sparkling events staged there in the form of increasing financial setbacks. Main Street's messy construction certainly hasn't helped fill the theater's more than 3,000 seats. Neither have expensive, large-scale theatrical events produced by the theater. By early 1985, both factors combined to build a $700,000 deficit.

In the ten years since the venerable theater was renovated and reopened, six people have filled the executive director's chair. At this writing, Stanton H. Hudson, Jr., is presiding. He's in the process of developing a long-range strategy for Shea's that will combine a rental policy with some carefully planned productions of its own, possibly single performances by very established artists.

To keep Shea's budget in the black, Hudson not only has to come up with viable theatrical seasons but he also has to deal with politics. Unlike Buffalo's other major cultural institutions, Shea's is owned by the city. To wipe out that whopping deficit, city hall initiated a series of grants and an agreement under which the city paid off several hundred thousand dollars in back utility bills.

On the road to establishing the theater as a full-scale performing

The marquee of Shea's Buffalo, one of America's grand historic showplaces and the heart of Buffalo's Theater District, asks one of the prime questions of the downtown renaissance. Photo by Joe Traver

arts center, Hudson is determined to come up with a variety of ways for the theater simply to generate a solid fiscal base. That includes corporate affairs, citywide promotions such as moonlight dances held outside the theater, and approaching local performing arts groups to use Shea's as a home base.

Besides continued corporate sponsorship of the theater, Hudson plans to tap into such sources as foundations and government and private grants. Also, the creation of an endowment fund or capital campaign to seek much needed improvements to the sound system and the cramped backstage area are in the offing.

For the time being, though, a cautious approach is being taken to ensure that Shea's Buffalo will light up the Theater District for a long time, and return a piece of the history that it enjoyed as one of the grandest vaudeville and movie palaces of the 1920s, 1930s, and 1940s.

Studio Arena

The Studio Arena Theatre arrived downtown in 1965 after a forty-year history as Buffalo's primary community theater. The first production in its new home in the former Town Casino nightclub was the American premiere of Eugene O'Neill's *A Moon for the Misbegotten,* as staged by Jose Quintero for Italy's prestigious Spoleto Festival. James Daly and Colleen Dewhurst starred.

With this opening, the Studio Arena went professional, becoming one of the most respected regional theaters in the country over the next two decades. World premieres by such noted playwrights as Edward Albee and Lanford Wilson, starring roles filled by such names as Jon Voight, Celeste Holm, Van Johnson, and Betsy Palmer, other roles filled by such newcomers as F. Murray Abraham, Bonnie Franklin, and Roy Scheider all helped build the Studio Arena's formidable reputation over the years.

The Studio's reputation blossomed throughout the country despite the fact that the theater was surrounded by a decaying downtown area. In 1978 it moved to a larger, more modern building at the corner of Main and Tupper where it now provides the anchor for the Theater District concept.

The Studio Arena continues to be the only theater downtown offering a consistent September-to-May season. The productions are impressively mounted, frequently to critical acclaim.

Although the first season only drew 2,600 season tickets, support grew dramatically under executive director Neal DuBrock. His blend of the commercially viable with the occasionally daring stimulated curiosity along with box office receipts. By the 1979-1980 season, the subscription list reached its peak at 13,500.

However, the recession of the 1980s combined with the state of flux downtown began to empty a number of seats. Dwindling attendance, cuts in county funding, and various production expenses ran up a deficit of $900,000 by the theater's twentieth anniversary season.

The turnaround began in the mid-1980s, fueled by the theatrical integrity of artistic director David Frank and the administrative foresight of managing director Raymond Bonnard. As the subscription list climbed back up near the 12,000 mark, the Studio was helping to lead the country's regional theaters out of the financial doldrums. The season-ticket count proved to be the largest subscription audience of any performing arts series in the state, outside of New York City.

"Sure, an increase in public funding would be helpful," managing director Raymond Bonnard said during the anniversary season, "but with the county's financial problems, that's just not realistic. That's why we have to turn to the private sector for contributions. More aggressive subscription drives and appeals for tax-deductible contributions would help resolve this financial situation." With a well-conceived plan and continuity in management, Bonnard saw the solution within reach by the theater's twenty-fifth anniversary season.

"To help us achieve this goal, we must also work on a better awareness and a clearer understanding of the theater's significance here in the community," he emphasized. "We have to develop a higher profile locally and, with that, our national reputation will continue to build."

At the same time, artistic director David Frank commended Buffalo audiences for their taste in theater. He considered local theatergoers to have a wider range of taste than those he knew at the Loretto-Hilton Repertory Theater in St. Louis which he directed for eight years prior to his arrival at the Studio in 1980.

"The economic and sophistication levels are very broad," he observed, "and that's very challenging to come up with something for everybody. Unlike the audiences at Stratford, for example, our production of *A Midsummer Night's Dream* introduced the play to a certain number of people. At the same time, there was a significant number of very sophisticated theatergoers as well."

With that audience range in mind, Frank expressed a strong desire to move the theater into the next decade with works that are both ambitious and exciting, yet accessible to a broad audience.

"I don't want anyone to accuse us of being an elitist organization," he stated. "But that doesn't mean that the work will merely be measured by the number of people who pass through the turnstiles, because that would be contradictory to the basic existence of a non-profit organization.''

Yet, to achieve that goal, the artistic director would like to see the subscription audience distinctly larger so that excitingly varied work can continue to be produced.

''Above all, I'd like to see the theater make its national reputation not so much on its ability to send pieces to Broadway, but in its ability to serve its own community so brilliantly that it takes on national signficance,'' he summarized. ''That would be the ultimate measure of success for this theater.''

As the Studio concluded its twenty-first season, it continued to explore new ways of funding, such as the first joint production—the Fats Waller musical, *Ain't Misbehavin'*—which involved the regional theaters of Syracuse, Rochester, and Buffalo. The success of it prompted discussion of further joint ventures.

The cast of "Ain't Misbehavin'" belts out another rollicking Fats Waller tune during a month-long engagement at the Studio Arena Theatre. The musical proved to be one of the theater's biggest draws of the 1985-86 season. Photo by K.C. Kratt

Buffalo Philharmonic

When it comes to Buffalo's performing arts reputation spreading nationally, the Buffalo Philharmonic Orchestra (BPO) has been in the forefront for years. During the BPO's fiftieth anniversary season, a February 1986 appearance at Carnegie Hall in New York City prompted thunderous applause. The New York Times critic hailed it as "a musical event tinged with greatness."

Over the decades, the orchestra has been blessed with a strong blend of musical talent, under the baton of a variety of prominent conductors, including Lukas Foss, Michael Tilson Thomas, Julius Rudel, and, currently, Semyon Bychkov.

Many astute music lovers around the world consider Bychkov to be the next great conductor. He has conducted orchestras from Seattle to Paris and in 1985 he received a remarkable twenty-five-minute ovation in Germany after conducting the Berlin Philharmonic, an orchestra that many describe as the world's finest.

Such worldly accomplishments, though, don't take precedent over his primary commitment as music director of the BPO. The personable, unassuming native of Leningrad appears to be just as taken with the Buffalo community as the community is with him. "Buffalo audiences are very sophisticated," he said. "It's amazing

The Buffalo Philharmonic Orchestra performs one of its many outdoor concerts during its summer season.

Titled "Rocks, Papers, and Scissors," this Judy Pfaff work is an example of the many contemporary art pieces that are exhibited at the Albright-Knox Art Gallery. Photo by Robert McElroy

how much music they have been exposed to that other audiences haven't. And that's because of its history. The years of Lukas Foss and Michael Tilson Thomas have given Buffalo audiences an enormous exposure to a repertoire that is not standard, that is not known by everyone. New music, contemporary music, the avant-garde. That gives us the opportunity to program just about anything we believe in."

Bychkov's exciting appearances at the podium have generated a resurgence in attendance at classical concerts, ranking alongside the packed houses which greet the pops concerts. The architectural sweep of Kleinhans Music Hall makes it one of the most acoustically sensitive concert halls in the country. The thirty-four-year-old music director is eagerly anticipating a European tour for the BPO in 1988, the funding for which is being aggressively sought. Nothing would help improve Buffalo's image more than a world tour by a world-class orchestra.

Albright-Knox

With a collection cited as "one of the world's top international surveys of contemporary painting and sculpture," the Albright-

Knox Art Gallery is especially rich in American and European art of the past thirty years. These works were mostly acquired through Seymour H. Knox, farsighted patriarch of the entrepreneurial family whom President and Mrs. Reagan honored at a White House ceremony in July 1986 for his contributions to contemporary art.

The distinctive white marble building, designed in the Greek Revival style by Edward B. Green, has been an Elmwood Avenue landmark since 1905. Inside are brilliant representations of Abstract Expressionism, Pop and Op Art, Kinetic Art and Color Field, Conceptualism, Minimalism, and the pluralistic trends of the 1970s, by such contemporary masters as Jackson Pollock, William de Kooning, and Henry Moore.

The gallery's permanent collection offers a panorama of art through the centuries, from a Cycladic idol dated 3,000 B.C. to the revolutionary trends of the 1920s and 1930s as painted by Picasso, Matisse, Rodchenko, and others.

Yearly, the gallery presents ten or more special exhibitions focusing on individual artists or themes of art-historical interest.

The courtyard of the Albright-Knox Art Gallery can be viewed from many different angles.

The Buffalo News has sponsored free outdoor concerts on the steps of the Albright-Knox Art Gallery since the early 1980s. They are held each Sunday afternoon during July and early August and feature the Buffalo Jazz Workshop with special guests. Photos by Peter R. Barber

These exhibitions receive widespread critical attention as they travel throughout the U.S. and Canada. Albright-Knox sponsored an event in 1965 that broke new ground for Buffalo as a contemporary arts center. The controversial "Festival of the Arts Today" was covered by national magazines and major critics throughout the country. Music, painting, dance, film, and theater were among the offerings. Some, such as those featuring nude dancers and electronic artworks, were considered shocking. The gallery hosted most of the events along with the University at Buffalo, Buffalo State College, the Buffalo Philharmonic Orchestra, and the New York State Council of the Arts.

Arts About Town

A number of fine theater groups, musical ensembles, and dance troupes brighten area stages. Veteran director Neal Radice recently opened Alleyway Theater in a renovated space in the old Greyhound bus station in the Theater District. The front of the building is used as a police precinct. His first season featured several original works, from a look into the life of Puccini to a satire on all-American beauty contests. Gary Fisher's Buffalo Entertainment Theatre also provided a forum for Buffalo playwrights, in addition to staging works by such contemporary playwrights as Sam Shepard and Samuel Beckett. Unfortunately, it closed recently after seven struggling years on the edge of the newly forming Theater District. The Ujima Company, led by Lorna Hill, is the premier black repertory group, working from its home called Theaterloft on Elmwood Avenue, which was the Studio Arena's first home in the 1920s.

Troupes such as the Buffalo Ballet Theater and Empire State Ballet delight dance fans throughout the area year-round, with Empire also taking its act to the streets via a caravan stage that is pulled across the state.

The Amherst Saxophone Quartet, which offers brassy renditions of a repertoire ranging from ragtime to classical, has achieved national notoriety, first, when they played with the late ragtime legend Eubie Blake and, secondly, when they appeared on the Johnny Carson show in 1985.

Jazz is a particularly hot attraction in the area. Spyro Gyra, the extremely popular fusion group, was first formed in 1975 as a no-name bar band playing weekly jam sessions at the old Tralfamadore Cafe when it was a modest basement club at Main Street and Fillmore Avenue. Today, many jazz combos can be found in Buffalo. Each summer, for example, *The Buffalo News* sponsors a weekly

Far left: Pop stars like Cyndi Lauper perform in outdoor concerts on the State University of Buffalo campus. Photo by Robert McElroy

Left: Rock star Mick Jagger performs in one of several Rolling Stones concerts held at Rich Stadium. Photo by Joe Traver

Opposite: This picturesque sunset was photographed at the Austin Street boat harbor. Photo by Peter R. Barber

series of free outdoor concerts by the Buffalo Jazz Workshop on the steps of the Albright-Knox Art Gallery.

And, seemingly, there's a rock band born every week somewhere in the area, playing anything from old rock to new wave. Stan and the Ravens, for instance, features Stan Szelest, a local pianist who used to work with The Band before they hit the big time in the late 1960s. Then there's 10,000 Maniacs, a new band from nearby Jamestown that is currently gaining attention on MTV and in *Rolling Stone.*

Seasoning

Because Buffalo's temperate climate highlights the distinct characteristics of each season, a distinct array of pleasures is open to the Western New Yorker. The climate and character of the Buffalo skyline and backroads have attracted the attention of a growing number of filmmakers who are impressed with the wealth of scenic delights.

Independent director Frederick King Keller, born and raised in Snyder, has filmed most of his feature films using area locations. Included is *Vamping,* a suspense film starring Patrick Duffy as a jazz saxophonist on the skids who becomes involved with robbery and murder. After a limited theatrical release the film played

Glenn Close and Robert Redford take a break on the set of "The Natural," the 1983 film that was shot in War Memorial Stadium, among other area locations. Photo by Joe Traver

nationwide on The Movie Channel. Keller's current release, *My Dark Lady,* stars his father, Fred A. Keller, who also wrote the original screenplay. The elder Keller, one of the area's most respected stage actors and directors, operated two celebrated area moviehouses during the 1960s that featured art films.

Many Buffalo summertime locations were used in filming 1983's *The Natural,* an adaptation of Bernard Malamud's novel, starring Robert Redford and Glenn Close. War Memorial Stadium, in fact, was briefly remodeled to give it a 1930s appearance in keeping with the storyline. A few years earlier, Burt Reynolds and Goldie Hawn came to town to film snowy scenes for their romantic comedy, *Best Friends,* utilizing the grand interior of the old Central Terminal.

Western New Yorkers are just as attracted to the seasonal charm and delights of the area. There are more than 500 parks and playgrounds and thirteen state parks in the Buffalo metropolitan area, offering a range of activities from golf and swimming to skat-

Far left: One out away or one run to win? This player was part of the national championship series of women's professional softball that was recently held in Buffalo. Photo by Joe Traver

Left: Rowing is another recreational delight here, thanks to the abundance of waterways. Photo by Joe Traver

Below: The Richmond Avenue Downhill attracts determined competitors. Photo by Melissa C. Beckman

The Buffalo Harbor offers many interesting angles for sunset-watchers. Photo by Dennis R. Floss

ing and tobogganing. Within a ninety-mile radius there are over twenty public and private ski resorts offering challenging hills and reasonable rates. Golfers tee off at over thirty-five area courses; tennis enthusiasts serve at several hundred outdoor public courts or at the dozen or so indoor tennis and racquet clubs; yacht clubs line lakes Erie and Ontario; and amusement parks abound from the space-age rides of Darien Lake and Canada's Wonderland (just outside Toronto) to the traditional charm of ninety-eight-year-old Crystal Beach and its seventy-year-old Giant Coaster with the world's only wooden track.

During the summer months, Artpark in nearby Lewiston has become a center for dance and opera. Located on a beautiful setting overlooking the Niagara River, the spectacular 2,400-seat theater is surrounded by woods, cliffs, grassy hills, and a dramatic plateau. Artpark invites a variety of visual artists from across the country to create large-scale sculpture projects on the open landscape. Craft artists create pieces using both traditional and experimental craft media. And Artpark visitors of all ages get the opportunity to

Above: There she is . . . Miss Buffalo 1985 posing at the Allentown Art Festival. Photo by Robert McElroy

Above, right: A group of young art connoisseurs is seen at the famed Allentown festival, which has become one of the rites of spring every June. Photo by Robert McElroy

Right: The 1985 winners in the annual pumpkin festival in Collins pose with their championship pumpkins. Just imagine the carving possibilities of these monster jack o'lanterns. Photo by Robert McElroy

Following page: Delaware Avenue is filled with thousands of strollers during the annual Allentown Art Festival. Photo by Joe Traver

Johnnie's SUGAR WAFFLES

A horn player limbers up in one of the recital rooms of the Chautauqua Institute, a historic summertime cultural haven just 90 minutes from Buffalo. Photo by Joe Traver

create art themselves, under the guidance of various artists.

Summer in Buffalo also means a sightseeing cruise on the *Miss Buffalo* to take in the city's exciting new waterfront, a stroll along the twenty-three acres of the Buffalo Zoological Gardens which houses 1,200 animals both indoors and outdoors, or a tour of the huge historic ships that highlight the Buffalo & Erie County Naval & Servicemen's Park. And, of course, there's the majestic beauty of Niagara Falls, one of the world's wonders. Visitors have the option of seeing the splendor of this magnificent cataract from both the U.S. and Canadian sides.

Special events are held the year-round throughout Greater Buffalo. The Erie County Fair & Expo each August is one of the county's oldest and largest county fairs. City Fest is one of the newest attractions, a day downtown at the end of August filled with music, magicians, and cafe-style dining. Shakespeare in Delaware Park, sponsored by the UB Department of Theater and Dance, has been a summertime staple for a decade. Curtain Up! in September celebrates Buffalo theater with a formal dinner and a variety of opening performances. The Winter Festival and the Festival of

A cheery balloon seller adds to the delightful ambience of one of Greater Buffalo's many outdoor events. Photo by Robert McElroy

Trees highlight the holiday season both downtown and throughout the Niagara Frontier with indoor and outdoor activities and special exhibits and displays, such as the popular animated Christmas scenes in AM&A's Main Street window.

The Ethnic Heritage Festival in spring at the Buffalo Convention Center offers visitors a look at the customs, entertainment, and foods of the various cultures that make up the Buffalo area. The annual Allentown Outdoor Art Festival, one of the nation's largest art festivals, begins the summer season. For indoor interest, there's the Buffalo Museum of Science which offers an array of natural science exhibits along with a look at the stars in the Kellogg Observatory. The Buffalo & Erie County Historical Society features a vast spectrum of the area's rich heritage. And for a gaze at the entire city, the twenty-eighth floor observation deck of Buffalo City Hall offers a breathtaking panorama.

It's a panorama that combines the historical charm with contemporary interest—a full spectrum of cultural, recreational, and seasonal enjoyment. Western New Yorkers are indeed blessed with an abundance of riches.

476

CHAPTER SIXTEEN

Closing Thoughts on New Beginnings

Opposite: Participants cheer their team at the Empire State Games which came to Greater Buffalo in 1985 and 1986. Photo by Joe Traver

How far have we come? A long way. And we still have farther to go. Buffalo is a city that is turning itself around, rising from the depths to which many American cities sank during the 1960s and 1970s. Rebuilding has progressed considerably over the past eight years, and Buffalo is still very much a city in transition.

Buffalo has many believers. While they may not always be in accord regarding remedies and the renaissance, they are unified in spirit.

Charles M. Mitschow, regional president of Marine Midland Bank, N.A., has said, "As Western New York industry continues to change to a service industry base, the area's business climate should improve as its manufacturing sector trims down to include only the strongest firms. We are definitely on the path toward economic recovery."

Franklyn S. Barry, president of Ingram Software, which has become a leading software distributor around the country, feels that with Buffalo's geographical accessibility and work force, the area has the capability to become a major distribution center. More than 100 million people live within a 500-mile radius, representing almost one half of all U.S. personal buying power and more than three quarters of all Canadian manufacturing activity. He also pushes for a metropolitan form of government to include the entire Greater Buffalo area in the renaissance, an important factor in the economic development of such cites as Atlanta and Nashville.

A hot-air balloon rally attracted many colorful entries to nearby Darien Lake theme park as enthusiasts from across the region rose to the occasion. Photos by Joe Traver

Paul A. Willax, Empire of America chairman and CEO, strongly feels that the key to Buffalo's future is in working with Buffalo's existing businesses on a one-to-one basis. "What Buffalo needs is to keep the businesses that it's got and develop neighborhoods," he observed. "We've got to help the business that's here to get more capital, to develop new products or more efficient ways of doing things. That would make a real strong base here."

Buffalo Philharmonic music director Semyon Bychkov's initial impressions of the area still hold true for him. "I think the most important thing here is the people who live here," he said. "There's a very special kind of friendliness. We know that in our own neighborhood [in Snyder] and on our own street. Our neighbors will come and in-

The steps of Erie County Hall are a familiar downtown landmark. Photo by Susan Gawlick

Next page: A mosque looms in a city neighborhood, symbolizing the variety of religions that are practiced throughout Greater Buffalo. Photo by Bill Wippert

troduce themselves and do anything for you that you might need at the moment. But at the same time, they will be very tactful and not impose themselves on you."

The strong area work ethic continually comes up in conversation. Often it has been accused, though, of not being in tune with high-tech adaptation. UB president Dr. Steven Sample disagrees. "The presence of a major research university such as ours makes a big difference in how an area acclimates itself to higher technology," he reasoned. "We now have the most successful high-tech incubator in the state to nurture the growth of such companies. Over the next few years, we want to point to one hundred new busi-

ness ventures developed here. Sure, some may die, but a few can turn into a Moog or Calspan. No one realized how much entrepreneurial spirit was alive in Buffalo. The depth and breadth of it has amazed everyone.''

Dr. Sample pointed out that a definite transition is taking place in the area, from heavy industry to higher technology. As a number of other observers agree in regard to the area renaissance, Dr. Sample pointed out that rebuilding efforts for the most part haven't been unified. ''Each person is doing his or her own thing in his or her own way,'' he said, adding that a portion of that fragmented working method can achieve some significance.

All seem to agree that the Buffalo area holds great potential and has a good thing going. The major puzzler, though, is how to get the word out to the immediate world. No one has yet achieved the ultimate marketing plan that will cement Buffalo's progressive new image in the minds of people around the country. Little by little, inroads are made through accomplishments of the university, a local company, a local organization, or a local person.

Maestro Bychkov feels that the symphony orchestra's highly regarded history and recent successes do wonders for Buffalo's image. ''Who can represent Buffalo better?'' he asks. ''When you have an artistic organization that you can be proud of, it has a great nobility to it that reflects very well on the community. Because only a community of sophistication and enlightenment would care to support a fabulous symphony orchestra.''

And there are those who feel that a huge advertising campaign should blanket the country—something many times more expan-

Top: Although the Erie Basin Marina may not attract as many visitors in the fall, it takes on a special seasonal beauty all its own. Photo by Dennis R. Floss

Above: Youngsters enjoy a bright winter day skating and sledding along frozen Delaware Park Lake. Photo by Joe Traver

sive than 1980's "Talking Proud" campaign—expounding the virtues of Buffalo. And there are those who counter that the hype should come when everything is done, when all the construction is finished.

Above all, there is impatience in Buffalo, the impatience of a city in transition. The impatience of slow but steady growth.

Such impatience can be healthy as it characterizes a city primed to better itself. Some of it, though, can be defeating. Perspective seems to be the key to the rebirth of Buffalo. Solid economic recovery and development lies in long-term realizations, not short-term perks.

Ross Kenzie summarized it very pointedly. "The renaissance of the thirteenth and fourteenth centuries lasted a couple of hundred

The "Miss Buffalo" sails into port. The boat offers passengers daily cruises during the summer, with frequent moonlit cruises featuring a dance band. Photo by Joe Traver

years. The renaissance in Buffalo is certainly going to last twenty years. We have a lot of people who think it's going to turn around in twenty minutes. It's not going to do that. It's like losing weight— you've got to lose it the way you put it on.''

With that analogy, Buffalo is clearly trimming down, shaping up, and becoming healthy once again. Dieting is not fun, but exercise can be stimulating. And rebuilding efforts are certainly being exercised all around the area. In fact, it already appears as though Buffalo has developed the muscle, tone, and drive to compete with similar-sized cities across the country. And, increasingly, it can also take on some of the giants as well.

And that's a Greater Buffalo in much more than name alone.

Patrons

The following individuals, companies, and organizations have made a valuable commitment to the quality of this publication. Windsor Publications and the Greater Buffalo Chamber of Commerce gratefully acknowledge their participation in *A Greater Look At Greater Buffalo*.

Acres International Corporation*
Adam, Meldrum and Anderson Company*
Alling and Cory*
American Precision Industries Inc.*
Automotive Sound Systems, Inc.
Richard C. and Joan B. Baer
Balling Construction, Inc.*
Balling E. Bingel, Inc.
Blue Cross of Western New York, Inc.*
Blue Shield of Western New York, Inc.*
Bryant & Stratton Business Institute*
Buffalo Fire Office, Inc.
Buffalo Marriott
Buffalo Telephone Company*
F.N. Burt Company, Inc.*
Calspan Corporation*
Central Trust
Chemical Bank*
John Chew Developments Limited*
The Ciminelli Companies*
CIR Electrical Construction Corporation*
Computer Task Group, Inc.*
The John W. Cowper Company, Inc.*
Cullen Industries, Inc.*
Joseph Davis, Inc.*
DeRose Food Brokers*
Downtown Buffalo Management Corporation*
Dunlop Tire Corporation*
Eaton Equipment Corp.
Ecology & Environment, Inc.*
Empire Finishing Systems, Inc.
Empire of America Federal Savings Bank*
Erie Community College*
Faller, Klenk and Quinlan, Inc.*
Ferguson Electric Construction Company, Inc.*
Ford Motor Company*
General Motors Corporation*
Goldome*
Greater Buffalo Press, Inc.*

Hart Hotels Inc. dba/Holiday Inns of Buffalo
Hatch Associates Consultants, Inc. Consulting Engineers*
Healy-Schutte & Company*
Hodgson, Russ, Andrews, Woods & Goodyear*
Holcberg, Deck & Cohen, Ltd.*
Hyatt Regency Buffalo*
IBM*
Ingram Software, Inc.*
Gerald Kelly Associates
Keystone Corporation
Kay Lenahan
Sheldon T. Lenahan
LTV Missiles and Electronics Group*
Lucidol Division of Pennwalt Corporation*
Mader Construction Corporation*
M&T Bank*
Manhardt-Alexander, Inc.*
Marine Midland Bank, N.A.*
Marlette National Corporation*
Medaille College
The Mentholatum Company, Inc.*
The Merchants Insurance Group*
Milstein, Wittek & Associates, Architects, P.C.*
Moog Inc.*
National Association of Bank Women-WNY Chapter
National Car Rental
National Fuel Gas Company*
National Health Care Affiliates, Inc.*
Mr. & Mrs. William E. Neuman
New York State Electric & Gas Corporation*
New York Telephone*
Nussbaumer & Clarke, Inc.*
Occidental Chemical Corporation*
Ohmeda
Peat, Marwick, Mitchell & Co.
People, Inc. services to the developmentally disabled
Perry's Ice Cream Company, Inc.*
Phillips, Lytle, Hitchcock, Blaine & Huber*
Pratt & Lambert, Inc.*
Price Waterhouse*
Production Efficiency Company Inc.
RIBCO, Inc.
Rich Products Corporation*
Rigidized Metals Corporation*
Root, Neal & Company, Inc.
Roswell Park Memorial Institute*

Servotronics, Inc.*
Siegfried Construction Company, Inc.*
Snyder Corp.*
Sorrento Cheese Company, Inc.*
The State University of New York at Buffalo*
Stimm Associates, Inc.*
WBEN AM & FM Radio*
Wehle Electric Company, Inc.*
Mr. & Mrs. Kenneth R. Weishaupt
Western New York Foreign Trade Zone Operators, Inc.*
Westwood Pharmaceuticals, Inc.*
WGR/WRLT Radio
WGRZ-TV*
Williams Gold Refining Company, Inc.*
Wilson, Klaes, Brucker and Worden, P.C.*
Winfield Industries*
J.F. Winske-Dupont
WIVB-TV*
WKBW-TV*
Worthington Compressor Operation*

*Corporate profiles of *A Greater Look At Greater Buffalo*. The histories of these companies and organizations appear throughout the book.

The post office tower is silhou-
etted against the setting sun.
Photo by Dennis R. Floss

Bibliography

The Buffalo News:

Anzalone, Charles. "The Shaping of Things to Come." November 17, 1985.

_____. "Area Colleges Holding Ground in Battle for Students, Financing." January 26, 1986.

_____. "UB Scientists Get $4 Million Grant To Study Cancer-Diet Connection." April 9, 1986.

Argenio, Modesto. "Energy Bills Powered by Nine Mile 2." January 26, 1986.

Buckham, Tom. "Shea's is Banking on its New Director." February 24, 1986.

Carucci, Vic. "Bullough Has Owner's OK." December 3, 1985.

_____. "Wilson Cites Need to 'Correct' Bills." December 3, 1985.

Ciotta, Rose. "Waterfront Awaiting Sharper Focus." January 26, 1986.

DiCesare, Bob. "Buffalo Makes Its Pitch for Major League Ball." November 8, 1985.

Doran, Terry. "UB Plans to Give Old Center Theatre New Life, Name." February 23, 1986.

Ernst, Tom. "Doors Open to a Lot of Possibilities Down the Road for UB." May 29, 1986.

Fairbanks, Phil. "Goldome Bank to Spend $4 Million, Add 200 Jobs at Western Building." June 19, 1986.

Gates, George. "Retail Center is Called Key to City's Revival." November 8, 1985.

_____. "Create 150 Housing Units Downtown Yearly, Study Says." November 10, 1985.

_____. "Ansonia Renovation is Test of Market." January 26, 1986.

Kelley, Jim. "Attendance Drop Fails to Worry Sabres." February 16, 1986.

Montgomery, David. "Smaller High-Technology Firms Helped by Influx of Aid." January 26, 1986.

_____. "HIDI's Research May Spawn New Firms." January 26, 1986.

Northrup, Milt. "Gil's Talent, Dash An Instant Splash." June 18, 1986.

O'Hara, Don. "Dealer Incentives Aid Area Auto Workers." January 26, 1986.

_____. "WNY Business Conditions Near an Eight-Year High." February 14, 1986.

Page, Arthur. "Decline, Fall of Lafayette Hospital is a Warning." February 18, 1986.

Peters, Jim. "MISL Confusion Leads Bellanti to Bow Out." February 19, 1986.

Ritz, Joseph P. "Impact of Trico Move Emphasized in Study." February 13, 1986.

Schroeder, Richard. "Goldome Sets Low-rate Credit Card." May 18, 1986.

Sullivan, Margaret. "Agency Sought to Head Off Loss of Jobs in WNY." February 19, 1986.

Sullivan, Margaret & Anzalone, Charles. "UB Will Launch 5-Year Plan To Enter Big-Time Athletics." May 29, 1986.

Summers, Robert J. "Bright Financial Picture Painted by Area Firms." January 26, 1986.

Turner, Douglas. "Population May Take Positive Turn." January 26, 1986.

Vogel, Mike. "Buffalo: Poised for Rebirth." January 26, 1986.

_____. "Can 'Buffalo Place' Be Eaton Center?" November 30, 1985.

_____. "Then and Now: What Does Our Future Hold?" May 2, 1982.

Warner, Gene. "Sporting Life: Unforgettable Moments." May 2, 1982.

Watson, Rod. "Stadium Provides Plenty of Ground for Political Hardball." January 26, 1986.

Watson, Rod & Raeke, Carolyn. "Stadium Hailed as Symbol of City's Spirit." July 11, 1986.

Zremski, Jerry. "Area Retailers Rebuilding Sales After Mildly Disappointing Year." January 26, 1986.

_____. "Cannon Designing National Stature in Architecture Field." December 15, 1985.

_____. "City's Office Occupancy Rate Turns Upward." December 7, 1985.

_____. "Low Interest Rates Good News for Realtors, Builders." January 26, 1986.

_____. "Trico's Plant Closings to Hit Poorest Areas." February 15, 1986.

_____. "It's Time for the Chamber to Do More Than Talk Proud." February 16, 1986.

Other Books and Journals

Anzalone, Charles. "The Shaping of Things to Come." *Buffalo Magazine of the Buffalo News.* November 17, 1985.

Biltekoff, Judith. "Housing 1986" *Western New York Magazine.* March 1986.

Bisco, Jim. "Anniversary of the Studio Arena: A Theatrical Event in Three Acts and Twenty Seasons." *Buffalo,* March/April 1985.

_____. "Designing the Future" *Western New York Magazine.* June 1984.

_____. "Empire State Games" *Western New York Magazine.* June 1985.

_____. "Home Run to the Majors." *Western New York Magazine.* December 1984.

_____. "100 Years of Bison Baseball." *Western New York Magazine.* April 1985.

_____. "Medical Research in Western New York." *Western New York Magazine.* February 1986.

Brown, Richard C. and Bob Watson. *Buffalo: Lake City in Niagara Land.* California: Windsor Publications, Inc., 1981.

Buffalo Evening News Almanac and Fact Book 1960. Buffalo: *Buffalo Evening News,* 1960.

Buffalo Evening News, various editions, 1945-1954.

Business First, *Top 25 Lists 1984-1985, Buffalo and Western New York.* Business First of Buffalo, Inc., 1985.

The Community and the University. Office of University Publications Services, State University of New York at Buffalo, February 1975.

Courier-Express, various editions, 1952-1981.

Dimock, Mame. "Cultural/Tourism: A

New WNY Partnership.''

Articles. Arts Council in Buffalo and Erie County. Summer 1986.

Evans, Donna. ''Marine Seeking Broader Consumer Base.'' *Business First Magazine.* June 10, 1985.

Goldman, Mark. *High Hopes: The Rise and Decline of Buffalo, New York.* Albany: State University of New York Press, 1983.

Haynes, Richard. ''At Work: City Fortunes Changed With the Times.'' *The Buffalo News.* May 2, 1982.

History of a City, Richard Schroeder, editor, Emily Dwass, text. *Courier-Express,* April 18, 1982.

Hovey, Bradshaw. ''Culture and the Arts.'' *Business First.* December 23, 1985.

_____. ''Theatre District Pieces Fit Together.'' *Business First.* September 30, 1985.

Hyland, Bruce. ''Banking Beyond Buffalo.'' *Business First* June 10, 1985.

Ins and Outs of Buffalo: A Thoroughly Authentic and Profusely Illustrated Guide. Buffalo: A.B. Floyd, 1899.

Metro Rail and You. Niagara Frontier Transportation Authority, 1985.

Metro Rail and You. Public Relations Department of the Niagara Frontier Transportation Authority, 1985.

New York State Department of Labor. *Employment Statistics, 1958-1978.*

''People.'' *Financial Planning.* May, July, September 1984.

''President Rumsey Looks to the Niagara Frontier Future.'' *Buffalo Business.* February 1959.

Progress Report. Town of Tonawanda Development Corporation, 1985.

Prospectus for Opportunity. Buffalo Area Chamber of Commerce in cooperation with the Erie County Industrial Development Agency, 1983.

''Research and Development'' *Western New York Magazine.* September 1985.

Thomas, Scott. ''Banking 1986: A Survey'' *Western New York Magazine,* May 1986.

_____. ''Banking 1986: A Survey.'' May 1986.

Western New York MetroScene. Second edition, 1978-1979.

Index

Windsor Books

ALABAMA

The Valley and the Hills: An Illustrated History of Birmingham and Jefferson County
by Leah Rawls Atkins
1981, 248 pp., $21.95
ISBN 0-89781-031-7

Historic Huntsville: A City of New Beginnings
by Elise Hopkins Stephens
1984, 216 pp., $22.95
ISBN 0-89781-096-1

Mobile: Sunbelt Center of Opportunity
by Cathalynn Donelson
1986, 224 pp., $22.95
ISBN 0-89781-200-X

Mobile: The Life and Times of a Great Southern City
by Melton McLaurin and Michael Thomason
1981, 200 pp., $22.95
ISBN 0-89781-020-1

Montgomery: An Illustrated History
by Wayne Flynt
1980, 196 pp., $24.95
ISBN 0-89781-10-4

Tuscaloosa: An Illustrated History
by G. Ward Hubbs
1987
ISBN 0-89781

ARIZONA

Scottsdale: Jewel in the Desert
by Patricia Myers McElfresh
1984, 136 pp., $22.95
ISBN 0-89781-105-4

Tucson: Portrait of a Desert Pueblo
by John Bret Harte
1980, 186 pp., $19.95
ISBN 0-89781-012-0

ARKANSAS

Arkansas: An Illustrated History of the Land of Opportunity
by C. Fred Williams
1986, 384 pp., $29.95
ISBN 0-89781-182-8

CALIFORNIA

Heart of the Golden Empire: An Illustrated History of Bakersfield
by Richard C. Bailey
1984, 160 pp., $22.95
ISBN 0-89781-065-1

Burbank: An Illustrated History
by E. Caswell Perry
1987
ISBN 0-89781-204-2

Butte County [Chico]: An Illustrated History
by Bill Talbitzer
1987
ISBN 8-89781-208-5

California Wings: A History of Aviation in the Golden State
by William A. Schoneberger with Paul Sonnenburg
1984, 192 pp., $24.95
ISBN 0-89781-078-3

Los Angeles: A City Apart
by David L. Clark
1981, 254 pp., $19.95
ISBN 0-89781-017-1

Long Beach and Los Angeles: A Tale of Two Ports
by Charles F. Queenan
1986, 208 pp., $24.95
ISBN 0-89781-178-X

Merced County: An Illustrated History
by Delores J. Cabezut-Ortiz
1987
ISBN 0-89781-209-3

The Monterey Peninsula: An Enchanted Land
By Randall A. Reinstedt
1987
ISBN 0-89781-199-2

Napa Valley: From Golden Fields to Purple Harvest
by Denzil & Jennie Verardo
1986. 160 pp.. $22.95
ISBN 0-89781-164-X

The Golden Promise: An Illustrated History of Orange County
by Pamela Hallan-Gibson
1986, 432 pp., $27.95
ISBN 0-89781-160-7

Pasadena: Crown of the Valley
by Ann Scheid

1986, 288 pp., $24.95
ISBN 0-89781-163-1

Redding & Shasta County: Gateway to the Cascades
by John D. Lawson
1986, 184 pp., $24.95
ISBN 0-89781-187-9

Harvest of the Sun: An Illustrated History of Riverside County
by James T. Brown
1985, 256 pp., $24.95
ISBN 0-89781-145-3

Sacramento: Heart of the Golden State
by Joseph A. McGowan and Terry R. Willis
1983, 160 pp., $24.95
ISBN 0-89781-066-X

San Bernardino County: Land of Contrasts
by Walter C. Schuiling
1984, 207 pp., $22.95
ISBN 0-89781-116-X

San Diego: City with a Mission
by Dan Berger
1987
ISBN 0-89781-212-3

[San Francisco] International Port of Call: An Illustrated Maritime History of the Golden Gate
by Robert J. Schwendinger
1984, 160 pp., $22.95
ISBN 0-89781-122-4

Santa Clara County: Harvest of Change
by Stephen W. Payne
1987
ISBN 0-89781-185-2

Stockton: Sunrise Port on the San Joaquin
by Olive Davis
1984, 160 pp., $22.95
ISBN 0-89781-093-7

Ventura County: Land of Good Fortune
by Judy Triem
1985, 232 pp., $22.95
ISBN 0-89781-156-9

COLORADO

Life In The Altitudes: An Illustrated History of Colorado Springs
by Nancy E. Loe
1983, 128 pp., $22.95
ISBN 0-89781-051-1

Denver: America's Mile High Center of Enterprise
by Jerry Richmond
1983, 256 pp., $29.95
ISBN 0-89781-082-1 AE

CONNECTICUT

Only in Bridgeport: An Illustrated History of the Park City
by Lennie Grimaldi
1986, 304 pp., $24.95
ISBN 0-89781-169-0

We Crown Them All: An Illustrated History of Danbury
by William E. Devlin
1984, 144 pp., $22.95
ISBN 0-89781-092-9

Hartford: An Illustrated History of Connecticut's Capital
by Glenn Weaver
1982, 192 pp., $24.95
ISBN 0-89781-052-X

New Haven: An Illustrated History
edited by Floyd Shumway and Richard Hegel
1981, 224 pp., $19.95
ISBN 0-89781-033-3

Stamford: An Illustrated History
by Estelle F. Feinstein and Joyce S. Pendery
1984, 192 pp., $22.95
ISBN 0-89781-114-3

DELAWARE

The First State: An Illustrated History of Delaware
by William Henry Williams
1985, 216 pp., $24.95
ISBN 0-89781-158-5

DISTRICT OF COLUMBIA

Washington, D.C.: The Making of a Capital
by Charles Paul Freund
1987
ISBN 0-89781-205-0

FLORIDA

Fort Lauderdale and Broward County: An Illustrated History
by Stuart McIver
1983, 236 pp., $24.95
ISBN 0-89781-081-3

Palm Beach County: An Illustrated History
by Donald W. Curl
1986, 224 pp., $24.95
ISBN 0-89781-167-4

GEORGIA

Columbus: Georgia's Fall Line "Trading Town"
by Dr. Joseph Mahan
1986, 256 pp. $24.95
ISBN 0-89781-166-6

Eden on the Marsh: An Illustrated History of Savannah
by Edward Chan Sieg
1985, 224 pp., $24.95
ISBN 0-89781-115-1

IDAHO

Boise: An Illustrated History
by Merle Wells
1982, 208 pp., $22.95
ISBN 0-89781-042-2

Idaho: Gem of the Mountains
by Merle Wells and Arthur A. Hart
1985, 256 pp., $24.95
ISBN 0-89781-141-0

ILLINOIS

Chicago: Center for Enterprise
by Kenan Heise and Michael Edgerton
1982, 600 pp. (2 Vols), $39.95
ISBN 0-89781-041-4

Des Plaines: Born of the Tallgrass Prairie
by Donald S. Johnson
1984, 136 pp., $19.95
ISBN 0-89781-095-3

Prairies, Prayers, and Promises: An Illustrated History of Galesburg
by Jean C. Lee
1987
ISBN 0-89781-194-1

Prairie of Promise: Springfield and Sangamon County
by Edward J. Russo
1983, 112 pp., $19.95
ISBN 0-89781-084-8

INDIANA

At the Bend in the River: The Story of Evansville
by Kenneth P. McCutchan
1982, 144 pp., $22.95
ISBN 0-89781-060-0

The Fort Wayne Story: A Pictorial History
by John Ankenbruck
1980, 232 pp., $22.95
ISBN 0-89781-015-5

Indiana: An Illustrated History
by Patrick J. Furlong
1985, 232 pp., $24.95
ISBN 0-89781-152-6

Muncie and Delaware County: An Illustrated Retrospective
by Wiley W. Spurgeon, Jr.
1984, 144 pp., $22.95
ISBN 0-89781-104-6

Terre Haute: Wabash River City
by Dorothy J. Clark
1983, 112 pp., $19.95
ISBN 0-89781-089-9

IOWA

Cedar Rapids: Tall Corn and High Technology
by Ernie Danek
1980, 232 pp., $19.95
ISBN 0-89781-021-X

LOUISIANA

River Capital: An Illustrated History of Baton Rouge
by Mark T. Carleton
1981, 304 pp., $21.95
ISBN 0-89781-032-5

So Mote It Be: A History of Louisiana Freemasonry
by Glenn Jordan
1987
ISBN 0-89781-197-6

New Orleans: An Illustrated History
by John R. Kemp

1981, 320 pp., $24.95
ISBN 0-89781-035-X
The History of Rapides Parish
by Sue Eakin
1987
ISBN 0-89781-201-8

MARYLAND
Baltimore: An Illustrated History
by Suzanne Ellery Greene
1980, 325 pp., $19.95
ISBN 0-89781-009-0
Maryland: Old Line to New Prosperity
by Joseph L. Arnold
1985, 256 pp., $24.95
ISBN 0-89781-147-X
Montgomery County: Two Centuries of Change
by Jane C. Sween
1984, 232 pp., $24.95
ISBN 0-89781-120-8

MASSACHUSETTS
Boston: City on a Hill
by Andrew Buni and Alan Rogers
1984, 240 pp., $24.95
ISBN 0-89781-090-2
*The Valley and Its Peoples: An Illustrated History of
the Lower Merrimack River*
by Paul Hudon
1982, 192 pp., $22.95
ISBN 0-89781-047-3
South Middlesex: A New England Heritage
by Stephen Herring
1986, 248 pp., $24.95
ISBN 0-89781-179-8
Heart of the Commonwealth: Worcester
by Margaret A. Erskine
1981, 208 pp., $19.95
ISBN 0-89781-030-9

MICHIGAN
Battle Creek: The Place Behind the Products
by Larry B. Massie and Peter J. Schmitt
1984, 136 pp., $19.95
ISBN 0-89781-117-8
Through the Years in Genesee: An Illustrated History
[Flint]
by Alice Lethbridge
1985, 144 pp., $22.95
ISBN 0-89781-161-5
In Celebration of Grand Rapids
by Ellen Arlinsky and Marg Ed Conn Kwapil
1987
ISBN 0-89781-210-7
Jackson: An Illustrated History
by Brian Deming
1984, 148 pp., $19.95
ISBN 0-89781-113-5
Kalamazoo: The Place Behind the Products
by Peter J. Schmitt and Larry B. Massie
1981, 304 pp., $19.95
ISBN 0-89781-037-6
*Out of a Wilderness: An Illustrated History of Greater
Lansing*
by Justin L. Kestenbaum
1981, 192 pp., $19.95
ISBN 0-89781-024-4
*Michigan: An Illustrated History of the Great Lakes
State*
by George S. May
1987
ISBN 0-89781-181-X
*Muskegon County: Harbor of Promise: An Illustrated
History*
by Jonathan Eyler
1986, 200 pp., $22.95
ISBN 0-89781-174-7
Saginaw: A History of the Land and the City
by Stuart D. Gross
1980, 200 pp., $19.95
ISBN 0-89781-016-3

MINNESOTA
Duluth: An Illustrated History of the Zenith City
by Glenn N. Sandvik
1983, 128 pp., $19.95
ISBN 0-89781-059-7
City of Lakes: An Illustrated History of Minneapolis
by Joseph Stipanovich
1982, 400 pp., $27.95
ISBN 0-89781-048-1
Saint Cloud: The Triplet City
by John J. Dominick
1983, 168 pp., $22.95
ISBN 0-89781-091-0
St. Paul: A Modern Renaissance
by Virginia Kunz
1986, 200 pps., $29.95
ISBN 0-89781-186-0
St. Paul: Saga of an American City
by Virginia Brainard Kunz
1977, 258 pp., $19.95

ISBN 0-89781-000-7

MISSISSIPPI
*The Mississippi Gulf Coast: Portrait of a People: An
Illustrated History*
by Charles L. Sullivan
1985, 200 pp., $22.95
ISBN 0-89781-097-X

MISSOURI
*From Southern Village to Midwestern City: Columbia,
An Illustrated History*
by Alan R. Havig
1984, 136 pp., $19.95
ISBN 0-89781-138-0
*Joplin: From Mining Town to Urban Center, An Illus-
trated History*
by G.K. Renner
1985, 128 pp., $19.95
ISBN 0-89781-153-4
*At the River's Bend: An Illustrated History of Kansas
City, Independence and Jackson County*
by Sherry Lamb Schirmer and Richard D. McKinzie
1982, 352 pp., $24.95
ISBN 0-89781-058-9
Kansas City: The Spirit, The People, The Promise
by Patricia Pace
1987
ISBN 0-89781-211-5
Springfield of the Ozarks
by Harris and Phyllis Dark
1981, 240 pp., $19.95
ISBN 0-89781-028-7

MONTANA
Montana: Land of Contrast
by Harry W. Fritz
1984, 200 pp., $24.95
ISBN 0-89781-106-2

NEBRASKA
Lincoln: The Prairie Capital
by James L. McKee
1984, 192 pp., $24.95
ISBN 0-89781-109-7
Omaha and Douglas County: A Panoramic History
by Dorothy Devereux Dustin
1980, 200 pp., $19.95
ISBN 0-89781-011-2

NEVADA
Reno: Hub of the Washoe Country
by William D. Rowley
1984, 128 pp., $22.95
ISBN 0-89781-080-5

NEW HAMPSHIRE
*New Hampshire: An Illustrated History of the Granite
State*
by Ronald Jager and Grace Jager
1983, 248 pp., $27.95
ISBN 0-89781-069-4

NEW JERSEY
Hudson County: The Left Bank
by Joan F. Doherty
1986, 168 pp., $22.95
ISBN 0-89781-172-0
Morris County: The Progress of Its Legend
by Dorianne R. Perrucci
1983, 216 pp., $24.95
ISBN 0-89781-075-9
*The Hub & the Wheel: New Brunswick & Middlesex
County*
by Gary Karasik
1986, 136 pp., $22.95
ISBN 0-89781-188-7
New Jersey: A History of Ingenuity and Industry
by James P. Johnson
1987
ISBN 0-89781-206-9
A Capital Place: The Story of Trenton
by Mary Alice Quigley and David E. Collier
1984, 160 pp., $22.95
ISBN 0-89781-079-1

NEW MEXICO
New Mexico: The Distant Land
by Dan Murphy
1985, 184 pp., $24.95
ISBN 0-89781-119-4

NEW YORK
Albany: Capital City on the Hudson
by John J. McEneny
1981, 248 pp., $24.95
ISBN 0-89781-025-2
Broome County Heritage
by Lawrence Bothwell
1983, 176 pp., $24.95
ISBN 0-89781-061-9
A Greater Look at Greater Buffalo

by Jim Bisco
1986, 480 pp., $35.00
ISBN 0-89781-198-4
Buffalo: Lake City in Niagara Land
by Richard C. Brown and Bob Watson
1981, 336 pp., $27.95
ISBN 0-89781-036-8
[Hard Cover]
$12.95
ISBN 0-89781-062-7 [Soft Cover]
The Hudson-Mohawk Gateway: An Illustrated History
by Thomas Phelan
1985, 184 pp., $22.95
ISBN 0-89781-118-6
*A Pictorial History of Jamestown and Chautauqua
County*
by B. Dolores Thompson
1984, 128 pp., $19.95
ISBN 0-89781-103-8
*Between Ocean and Empire: An Illustrated History of
Long Island*
by Dr. Robert McKay and Carol Traynor
1985, 320 pp., $24.95
ISBN 0-89781-143-7
*Harbor and Haven: An Illustrated History of the Port
of New York*
by John G. Bunker
1979, 302 pp., $25.00
ISBN 0-89781-002-3
*A Panoramic History of Rochester and Monroe
County, New York*
by Blake McKelvey
1979, 264 pp., $24.95
ISBN 0-89781-003-1
Syracuse: From Salt to Satellite
by Henry W. Schramm and William F. Roseboom
1979, 244 pp., $19.95
ISBN 0-89781-005-8
*The Upper Mohawk Country: An Illustrated History of
Greater Utica*
by David M. Ellis
1982, 224 pp., $22.95
ISBN 0-89781-054-6

NORTH CAROLINA
Asheville: Land of the Sky
by Milton Ready
1986, 136 pp., $22.95
ISBN 0-89781-168-2
Greensboro: A Chosen Center
by Gayle Hicks Fripp
1982, 216 pp., $24.95
ISBN 0-89781-056-2
*Made in North Carolina: An Illustrated History of Tar
Heel Business and Industry*
by David E. Brown
1985, 248 pp., $24.95
ISBN 0-89781-157-7
Raleigh: City of Oaks
by James E. Vickers
1982, 128 pp., $22.95
ISBN 0-89781-050-3
*Cape Fear Adventure: An Illustrated History of
Wilmington*
by Diane Cobb Cashman
1982, 128 pp., $22.95
ISBN 0-89781-057-0

OHIO
Butler County: An Illustrated History
by George C. Crout
1984, 128 pp., $19.95
ISBN 0-89781-123-2
Springfield and Clark County: An Illustrated History
by William A. Kinnison
1985, 152 pp., $22.95
ISBN 0-89781-146-1

OKLAHOMA
Oklahoma: Land of the Fair God
by Odie B. Faulk
1986, 344 pp., $29.95
ISBN 0-8978-173-9
*Heart of the Promised Land: An Illustrated History of
Oklahoma County*
by Bob L. Blackburn
1982, 264 pp., $24.95
ISBN 0-89681-019-8

OREGON
*Lane County: An Illustrated History of the Emerald
Empire*
by Dorothy Velasco
1985, 168 pp., $22.95
ISBN 0-89781-140-2
Portland: Gateway to the Northwest
by Carl Abbott
1985, 264 pp., $24.95
ISBN 0-89781-155-0

PENNSYLVANIA
Allegheny Passage: An Illustrated History of Blair

County
by Robert L. Emerson
1984, 136 pp., $22.95
0-89781-137-2
Erie: Chronicle of a Great Lakes City
by Edward Wellejus
1980, 144 pp., $17.95
ISBN 0-89781-007-4
*Life by the Moving Road: An Illustrated History of
Greater Harrisburg*
by Michael Barton
1983, 224 pp., $24.95
ISBN 0-89781-064-3
The Heritage of Lancaster
by John Ward Willson Loose
1978, 226 pp., $14.95
ISBN 0-89781-001-5 [Hard Cover]
$ 9.95
ISBN 0-89781-022-8 [Soft Cover]
The Lehigh Valley: An Illustrated History
by Karyl Lee Kibler Hall and Peter Dobkin Hall
1982, 224 pp., $24.95
ISBN 0-89781-044-9
Pennsylvania: Keystone to Progress
by E. Willard Miller
1986, 640 pp., $35.00
ISBN 0-89781-171-2
Pittsburgh: Fullfilling Its Destiny
by Vince Gagetta
1986, 624 pp., $35.00
ISBN 0-89781-189-5
Never Before in History: The Story of Scranton
by John Beck
1986, 144 pp., $22.95
0-89781-190-9
Williamsport: Frontier Village to Regional Center
by Robert H. Larson, Richard J. Morris, and John
F. Piper, Jr.
1984, 208 pp., $22.95
ISBN 0-89781-110-0
The Wyoming Valley: An American Portrait
by Edward F. Hanlon
1983, 280 pp., $24.95
ISBN 0-89781-073-2
To the Setting of the Sun: The Story of York
by Georg R. Sheets
1981, 240 pp., $22.95
ISBN 0-89781-023-6

RHODE ISLAND
Rhode Island: The Independent State
by George H. Kellner and J. Stanley Lemons
1982, 208 pp., $24.95
ISBN 0-89781-040-6

SOUTH CAROLINA
Charleston: Crossroads of History
by Isabella G. Leland
1980, 136 pp., $17.95
ISBN 0-89781-008-2
Columbia, South Carolina: History of a City
by John A. Montgomery
1979, 200 pp. $17.95
ISBN 0-89781-006-6
Greenville: Woven from the Past
by Nancy Vance Ashmore
1986, 280 pp., $24.95
ISBN 0-89781-193-3

SOUTH DAKOTA
*Gateway to the Hills: An Illustrated History of Rapid
City*
by David B. Miller
1985, 136 pp., $19.95
ISBN 0-89781-107-0

TENNESSEE
Chattanooga: An Illustrated History
by James Livingood
1981, 206 pp., $19.95
ISBN 0-89781-027-9
*Metropolis of the American Nile: Memphis and
Shelby County*
by John E. Harkins
1982, 224 pp., $24.95
ISBN 0-89781-026-0

TEXAS
Abilene: The Key City
by Juanita Daniel Zachry
1986, 128 pp., $22.95
ISBN 0-89781-150-X
*The Golden Spread: An Illustrated History of Amarillo
& the Panhandle Plains*
by B. Byron Price & Frederick Rathjen
1986, 168 pp., $22.95
ISBN 0-89781-183-61986
Austin: An Illustrated History
by David Humphrey
1985, 376 pp., $27.95
ISBN 0-89781-144-5
Beaumont: A Chronicle of Promise

by Judith W. Linsley and Ellen W. Rienstra
1982, 192 pp., $22.95
ISBN 0-89781-053-8
Corpus Christi: The History of a Texas Seaport
by Bill Walraven
1982, 136 pp., $22.95
ISBN 0-89781-043-0
Dallas: An Illustrated History
by Darwin Payne
1982, 400 pp., $29.95
ISBN 0-89781-034-1
City at the Pass: An Illustrated History of El Paso
by Leon Metz
1980, 126 pp., $19.95
ISBN 0-89781-013-9
*Where the West Begins: Fort Worth and Tarrant
County*
by Janet L. Schmelzer
1985, 152 pp., $22.95
ISBN 0-89781-151-8
*Houston: Chronicle of the Supercity on Buffalo
Bayou*
by Stanley E. Siegel
1983, 296 pp., $29.95
ISBN 0-89781-072-4
In Celebration of Texas
by Archie P. McDonald
1986, 488 pp., $29.95
ISBN 0-89781-165-8
Waco: Texas Crossroads
by Patricia Ward Wallace
1983, 136 pp., $22.95
ISBN 0-89781-068-6

UTAH
Ogden: Junction City
by Richard C. Roberts and Richard W. Sadler
1985, 288 pp., $24.95
ISBN 0-89781-154-2
Salt Lake City: The Gathering Place
by John S. McCormick
1980, 130 pp., $19.95
ISBN 0-89781-018-X

VERMONT
Vermont: An Illustrated History
by John Duffy
1985, 264 pp., $24.95
ISBN 0-89781-159-3

VIRGINIA
*Norfolk's Waters: An Illustrated Maritime History of
Hampton Roads*
by William Tazewell
1982, 224 pp., $22.95
ISBN 0-89781-045-7
RICHMOND: An Illustrated History
by Harry M. Ward
1985, 544 pp., $29.95
ISBN 0-89681-148-8

WASHINGTON
King County And Its Queen City: Seattle
by James R. Warren
1981, 314 pp., $24.95
ISBN 0-89781-038-4
*Where Mountains Meet the Sea: An Illustrated
History of Puget Sound*
by James R. Warren
1986, 288 pp., $24.95
ISBN 0-89781-175-5
A View of the Falls: An Illustrated History of Spokane
by William Stimson
1985, 160 pp., $22.95
ISBN 0-89781-121-6
*South On The Sound: An Illustrated History of
Tacoma and Pierce County*
by Murray and Rosa Morgan
1984, 199 pp., $22.95
ISBN 0-89781-0474-0
Vancouver on the Columbia: An Illustrated History
by Ted Van Arsdol
1986, 200 pp., $22.95
ISBN 0-89781-194-1

WEST VIRGINIA
*Charleston and the Kanawha Valley: An Illustrated
History*
by Otis K. Rice
1981, 136 pp., $19.95
ISBN 0-89781-046-5
Huntington: An Illustrated History
by James E. Casto
1985, 160 pp., $22.95
ISBN 0-89781-101-1
Wheeling: An Illustrated History
by Doug Fethering
1983, 120 pp., $19.95
ISBN 0-89781-071-6

WISCONSIN

*The Fox Heritage: A History of Wisconsin's Fox
Cities*
by Ellen Kort
1984, 256 pp., $22.95
ISBN 0-89781-083-X
Green Bay: Gateway to the Great Waterway
by Betsy Foley
1983, 168 pp., $22.95
ISBN 0-89781-076-7

Canada (Prices in Canadian Dollars)

Brampton: An Illustrated History
by Helga Loverseed
1987
ISBN 0-89781-207-7
Brantford: Grand River Crossing
by Janet Kempster and Gary Muir
1986, 200 pp., $29.95
ISBN 0-89781-184-4
Calgary: Canada's Frontier Metropolis
by Max Foran and Heather MacEwan
Foran
1982, 400 pp., $29.95
ISBN 0-89781-055-4
Edmonton: Gateway to the North
by John F. Gilpin
1984, 320 pp., $29.95
ISBN 0-89781-094-5
Halifax: Cornerstone of Canada
by Joan Payzant
1985, 224 pp., $27.95
ISBN 0-89781-149-6
Hamilton: A City in Symphony
by Sherry Sleightholm
1986, 168 pp., $29.95
ISBN 0-89781-195-X
Hamilton: Chronicle of a City
by T. Melville Bailey
1983, 184 pp., $24.95
ISBN 0-89781-067-8
Kitchener: Yesterday Revisited
by Bill Moyer
1979, 150 pp., $19.95
ISBN 0-89781-004-X
*The Forest City: An Illustrated History of London,
Canada*
by Frederick H. Armstrong
1986, 336 pp., $29.95
ISBN 0-89781-180-1
Mississauga: An Illustrated History
by Roger E. Riendeau
1985, 184 pp., $24.95
ISBN 0-89781-162-3
Oakville, A Place of Some Importance
by Clare & Joseph McKeon
1986, 136 pp., $24.95
ISBN 0-89781-170-4
Where Rivers Meet: An Illustrated History of Ottawa
by Courtney C. J. Bond
1984, 176 pp., $24.95
ISBN 0-89781-111-9
*Regina: From Pile O'Bones to Queen City of the
Plains*
by William A. Riddell
1981, 232 pp., $24.95
ISBN 0-89781-029-5
Saint John: Two Hundred Years Proud
by George W. Schuyler
1984, 200 pp., $27.95
ISBN 0-89781-108-9
Saskatoon: Hub City of the West
by Gail A. McConnell
1983, 128 pp., $27.95
ISBN 0-89781-070-8
The Sudbury Region: An Illustrated History
by Graeme S. Mount
1986, 144 pp., $24.95
ISBN 0-89781-177-1
Toronto: The Place of Meeting
by Frederick H. Armstrong
1983, 304 pp., $29.95
ISBN 0-89781-077-5
Vancouver: An Illustrated Chronology
by Chuck Davis & Shirley Mooney
1986, 288 pp., $29.95,
(USD)$24.95
ISBN 0-89781-176-3
Beyond the Island: An Illustrated History of Victoria
by Peter Barkerville
1986, 144 pp., $27.95,
(USD)$22.95
ISBN 0-89781-192-5
Winnipeg: Where the New West Begins
by Eric Wells
1982, 288 pp., $29.95
ISBN 0-8971-039-2

THIS BOOK WAS SET IN
HELVETICA AND OPTIMA TYPES,
PRINTED ON 70-LB. PRODUCTOLITH GLOSS
AND BOUND BY
WALSWORTH PUBLISHING COMPANY